Michael Eskin, Karen Leeder, Christopher Young (Eds.)
Durs Grünbein

Companions to Contemporary German Culture

Edited by
Michael Eskin · Karen Leeder · Christopher Young

Volume 2

Durs Grünbein

A Companion

Edited by
Michael Eskin · Karen Leeder · Christopher Young

DE GRUYTER

MIX
Papier aus verantwortungsvollen Quellen
FSC® C016439

ISBN 978-3-11-022794-9
e-ISBN 978-3-11-022795-6
ISSN 2193-9659

Library of Congress Cataloging-in-Publication Data
A CIP catalogue record for this book has been applied for at the Library of Congress

Bibliographic information published by the Deutsche Nationalbibliothek
The Deutsche Nationalbibliothek lists this publication in the Deutsche Nationalbibliografie; detailed bibliographic data are available on the internat at http://dnb.dnb.de

Printing and binding: Hubert & Co. GmbH & Co. KG, Göttingen
Printed on acid free paper
Printed in Germany

www.degruyter.com

Table of Contents

Acknowledgements

Above all the editors would like to acknowledge the support of Durs Grünbein, who kindly agreed to be interviewed in Cambridge and who has been generous with his time and energy; and the managers of the Tiarks Fund, University of Cambridge, who sponsored the international event at Pembroke College on which this volume is substantially based. They are also grateful for the assistance of the staff of the Deutsches Literaturarchiv in Marbach am Neckar, the Philologische Bibliothek and the Friedrich Schlegel Graduiertenschule für literaturwissenschaftliche Studien of the Freie Universität Berlin and the Taylor Institution Library in Oxford. Additional research was made possible by the Eugene Ludwig Fund, New College, Oxford, and the Fellows' Research Fund, Pembroke College, Cambridge. We are also especially grateful to Lukas Werner for assembling the Bibliography, to Dr. Alexandra Lloyd for compiling the Index, to Prof. Heiko Hartmann for accepting this volume and founding the series before moving to Akademie Verlag, and to Manuela Gerlof and Christine Henschel from de Gruyter for their patience and careful advice.

Straus and Giroux, 2010), English translation copyright © 2009 by Michael Eskin. Special thanks go to Helen Vendler for permission to reprint 'Europe after the Last Rains. On *Ashes for Breakfast*', first published as 'Oblivion City' in *The New Republic* (5 November 2008, pp. 44–47), copyright © 2008 by Helen Vendler.

Excerpts from Durs Grünbein's *Descartes' Devil: Three Meditations* are reprinted by kind permission of Upper West Side Philosophers, Inc., Copyright © 2010 by Upper West Side Philosophers, Inc., New York.

The editors are also grateful for kind permission to cite the following original poems and texts: Excerpts from 'Rimbaud', copyright © 1938 by W. H. Auden, reprinted by permission of Curtis Brown, Ltd. 'The Whitsun Weddings' taken from *The Whitsun Weddings* © Estate of Philip Larkin and reprinted by permission of Faber & Faber Ltd. 'Solar' taken from *High Windows* © Estate of Philip Larkin and reprinted by permission of Faber & Faber Ltd. Excerpt from 'The Whitsun Weddings' from *Collected Poems* by Philip Larkin. Copyright © 1988, 2003 by the Estate of Philip Larkin. Reprinted by permission of Farrar, Straus and Giroux, LLC. Excerpt from 'Solar' from *High Windows* by Philip Larkin. Copyright © 1974 by Philip Larkin. Reprinted by permission of Farrar, Straus and Giroux, LLC. Excerpts from 'The Whitsun Weddings' and 'Solar' reprinted by permission of The Society of Authors as the Literary Representative of the Estate of Philip Larkin. Excerpts from Marcel Duchamp: *Notes*. Paris, Flammarion, 1999. Excerpts from Durs Grünbein, 'Der Indianer des Geistes. Bagatellen über das Leben des Philosophen Pascal', *Zeitschrift für Ideengeschichte*, 2.1 (2008), C. H. Beck. Excerpts from *Muscheln und Blumen. Literarische Texte zu Werken der Kunst*, ed. by Beat Wismer, Stephan Kunz and Sibylle Omlin. Zürich, Ammann, 2003. Durs Grünbein's translation of Emily Dickinson's 'The Brain – is wider than the sky' from *Gehirn und Denken. Kosmos im Kopf*, ed. by Deutsches Hygiene-Museum, in cooperation with Via Lewandowsky and Durs Grünbein. Ostfildern-Ruit, Hatje Cantz, 2000, © Durs Grünbein.

A Note on Translations

Quotations are generally given only in English, except where a particular linguistic or formal point is being made, or where a reader who has German might particularly benefit from having the original. In the case of quotations from Durs Grünbein himself quotations are given in German and English. Contributors have, where appropriate, cited poems from Durs Grünbein, *Ashes for Breakfast. Selected Poems*, trans. by Michael Hofmann (New York: Farrar, Straus and Giroux, 2005). Translations of prose have generally been cited from the three recent volumes of Grünbein's essays: *Descartes' Devil. Three Meditations*, trans. by Anthea Bell (New York: Upper West Side Philosophers, 2010); *The Bars of Atlantis. Selected Essays*, ed. by Michael Eskin, trans. by John Crutchfield, Michael Hofmann and Andrew Shields (New York: Farrar, Straus and Giroux, 2010); *The Vocation of Poetry*, trans. by Michael Eskin (New York: Upper West Side Philosophers, 2011). These, and any adaptations to them, are all acknowledged in the notes to the individual contributions. Some contributors have provided new translations where none exist, or in order to make a particular linguistic point. These follow the relevant German in square brackets and the primary aim is to provide an accessible working translation. Unless otherwise specified, all other translations are by the author of the chapter.

To avoid unnecessary repetition, however, the titles of Durs Grünbein's main works are given in German only. The titles of individual essays and poems are given both in German and English throughout. For ease of reference a list of translations of these main works is included here, and a fuller Select Bibliography is given at the end of the volume. In Helen Vendler's contribution we maintain the English translations as used in her original article.

Poetry

Grauzone morgens. Gedichte (1988)
[Gray Zone in the Morning. Poems]

Schädelbasislektion. Gedichte (1991)
[Skull Crash Course. Poems]

Von der üblen Seite. Gedichte 1985–1991 (1994)
[From the Bad Side. Poems 1985–1991]

Falten und Fallen. Gedichte (1994)
[Folds and Traps / Folding and Falling. Poems]

Den Teuren Toten. 33 Epitaphe (1994)
[The Dear Departed. 33 Epitaphs]

Nach den Satiren. Gedichte (1999)
[After the Satires. Poems]

Una Storia Vera. Ein Kinderalbum in Versen (2002)
[A True Story. A Children's Album in Verse]

Erklärte Nacht. Gedichte (2002)
[Night Explained. Poems]

Vom Schnee oder Descartes in Deutschland (2003)
[Of Snow, or Descartes in Germany]

An Seneca. Postskriptum. Die Kürze des Lebens (2004)
[To Seneca. Postscript. The Brevity of Life]

Porzellan. Poem vom Untergang meiner Stadt (2005)
[Porcelain. Poem about the Downfall of My City]

Der Misanthrop auf Capri. Historien / Gedichte (2005)
[The Misanthrope of Capri. Histories / Poems]

Gedichte. Bücher I–III (2006)
[Poems. Books I–III]

Strophen für übermorgen. Gedichte (2007)
[Strophes for the Day after Tomorrow. Poems]

Liebesgedichte (2008)
[Love Poems]

Lob des Taifuns. Reisetagebücher in Haikus (2008)
[In Praise of the Typhoon. Diary of a Journey in Haikus]

Germanischer Komplex. Gedichte und Szenen (2009)
[Germanic Complex. Poems and Scenes]

Libellen in Liberia. Gedichte und Berichte (2010)
[Dragonflies in Liberia. Poems and Reports]

Aroma. Ein römisches Zeichenbuch (2010)
[Aroma. A Roman Drawing Book]

Limbische Akte. Gedichte (2011)
[Limbic Acts / Files. Poems]

Koloss im Nebel. Gedichte (2012)
[Colossus in the Fog. Poems]

Prose

Den Körper zerbrechen. Rede zur Entgegennahme des Georg-Büchner-Preises 1995. Mit der Laudatio 'Portrait des Künstlers als junger Grenzhund' von Heiner Müller (1995)
[Breaking the Body. Speech on Receipt of the Georg Büchner Prize 1995. With the Laudatio 'Portrait of the Artist as a Young Border Dog' by Heiner Müller]

Galilei vermißt Dantes Hölle und bleibt an den Maßen hängen. Aufsätze 1989–1995 (1995)
[Galileo Measures Dante's Hell and Gets Stuck on the Measurements. Essays 1989–1995]

Das erste Jahr. Berliner Aufzeichnungen (2001)
[The First Year. Berlin Notebooks]

Warum schriftlos leben? Aufsätze (2003)
[Why Live without Writing? Essays]

Antike Dispositionen. Aufsätze (2005)
[Antique / Antic Dispositions. Essays]

Gedicht und Geheimnis. Aufsätze 1990–2006 (2007)
[The Poem and its Secret. Essays 1990–2006]

Ein kleines blaues Mädchen. Zu Rainer Maria Rilke 'Das Karussell' (2007)
[A Little Blue Girl. On Rainer Maria Rilke's 'The Carousel']

Der cartesische Taucher. Drei Meditationen (2008)
[The Cartesian Diver. Three Meditations]

Die Bars von Atlantis. Eine Erkundung in vierzehn Tauchgängen (2009)
[The Bars of Atlantis. An Exploration in Fourteen Dives]

Vom Stellenwert der Worte. Frankfurter Poetikvorlesung 2009 (2010)
[The Importance of Words. Frankfurt Poetry Lectures 2009]

Dream Index / Aus der Traum (Kartei) (2012)

Michael Eskin

Preface

Since he first broke onto the literary scene with the publication of *Grauzone morgens* in 1988, aged twenty-six, Dresden-born Durs Grünbein has emerged as Germany's most prolific, versatile, successful and internationally renowned contemporary poet and essayist. With upwards of twenty books of poetry and prose that have been translated into many languages (including Russian, Italian, English, Spanish, Swedish and Japanese), dozens of national and international honours and awards (among them, the Georg Büchner Prize, the Friedrich Nietzsche Prize, the Premio Internazionale di Poesia Pier Paolo Pasolini, the Berlin Literature Prize, and the Pour le Mérite for Sciences and Arts), a pocketful of fellowships, visiting positions and reading tours across the globe, recurring TV and radio appearances on matters poetic, cultural and political, and even a double-page spread in a 2007 issue of *Vanity Fair* under his belt, Durs Grünbein is truly, as he himself has recently put it, somewhat of an 'aberration' – a sociological anomaly – when it comes to the poet's overall insignificance and lack of public exposure in the contemporary world. Certainly, no other former GDR poet, or any other German poet of his generation, for that matter, has managed to become a global player on Grünbein's scale.

What is Grünbein's recipe for literary stardom above and beyond sheer luck and the fortuitousness of being in the right place at the right time? What is it about him and his work that has attracted readers, audiences and institutions alike to him, at home and abroad, for the past quarter of a century? While these questions can obviously not be speculated upon – let alone answered – on a personal level within the confines of a book such as this, a close, multi-faceted critical-historical look at his wide-ranging oeuvre may well provide a good, if necessarily incomplete, sense of his trans-cultural import and appeal. And that is precisely what this early volume in De Gruyter's new series, *Companions to Contemporary German Culture*, aims to achieve.

The first-ever anthology of essays in English on the works of Germany's premier contemporary poet – accompanied by an extensive interview – *Durs Grünbein. A Companion* features a range of in-depth readings by an international group of scholars and critics, touching on Grünbein's many artistic themes, motifs and agendas: from growing up and coming of age behind the Iron Curtain to finding his place in a cosmopolitan post-reunification world; from the relationship between science and poetry to the significance of the past (not least antiquity) for our understanding of the present; from the intricacies of the poet's craft to poetry's vital role in the face of mortality; from the question of the poet's responsibility in view of past (and present) political atrocities to the problem of memory, historical understanding and the preservation of tradition, more generally; from the presumed age-old quarrel between philosophy and poetry to the inseverability of the two in the actual life of the (poet's) mind; from the cultural expectation of artistic originality to the artist's inexorable rootedness and participation in a multitudinous concert of voices, styles, traditions and visual images.

What the reader can expect, then, from the present volume is a variegated, yet clearly focused, introduction to the world, life, times and poetic thought of Durs Grünbein – both a 'little man in Germany' as he refers to himself, *and* a seasoned 'cosmopolite' – geared toward both the professional and the general reader interested in aesthetics, literary history or, more broadly, German, European and global cultural matters.

Documenting Grünbein's achievements to date in mid-flight, so to speak, and illuminating them squarely from each contributor's perspective and in light of the particular interests of each (while nonetheless endeavouring to maintain a bird's-eye view on the subject), the present volume is but the first – albeit foundational – effort toward nurturing the emergent body of international Grünbein criticism. As such it will have fully met its own expectations if it succeeds in stirring further interest in Grünbein's and other, related writers' works as well as German culture at large.

Christopher Young

Durs Grünbein and the *Wende*

Durs Grünbein is widely recognized as the most important German poet since reunification. While a citizen of the GDR, he published his first volume of poems (*Grauzone morgens*) with Suhrkamp in 1988, producing at the age of twenty-six a collection that – as Wolfgang Emmerich notes in his extensive, and deceptively titled, *Kleine Literaturgeschichte der DDR* – 'blew away 40 years of East German lyric'.[1] Three volumes and a mere seven years later,[2] Grünbein became the second youngest recipient of Germany's premier literary award, the Georg Büchner Prize (Peter Handke was 31 when he won in 1973, Hans Magnus Enzensberger 34 in 1963); and in 2008, he was inducted as the youngest member of the Ordre Pour le Mérite in Berlin. As the other essays in this volume clearly demonstrate, Grünbein is a poet of world significance. Nonetheless, his rise to fame occurred in Germany and in circumstances that were uniquely German in nature. This chapter sets out to revisit these and to outline the poet's positioning of himself within them.

Grünbein is a stand-out poet – no other German poet of his generation acquired quite such an elevated reputation or followed even remotely his intellectual trajectory over twenty years – but he also exemplifies in some ways the poetry produced by a new cohort of authors since the *Wende*. Periodizations and the step-changes they imply are always subject to analeptic hedging, but there is a certain indisputability about Hermann Korte's observation that the changing of the guard around 1990 was as marked as that of the early 1960s when Hans Magnus Enzensberger, Günter Grass, Günter Kunert and others swept tradition aside to revolutionize the poetic scene.[3] Despite a distinct heterogeneity of styles and ideologies,[4] the outputs of the 1990s cohort, born in the 1950s and 1960s, have several key characteristics in common.[5]

---

1 Wolfgang Emmerich, *Kleine Literaturgeschichte der DDR* (Leipzig: Kiepenheuer, 1996), p. 394.

2 A full list is given in the Bibliography at the end of this volume.

3 Hermann Korte, *Deutschsprachige Lyrik seit 1945*, 2nd edn (Stuttgart: Metzler, 2004), p. 257.

4 Hermann Korte, '"Wenn ein staat ins gras beißt, singen die dichter". DDR-Lyrik der neunziger Jahre', in *DDR-Literatur der neunziger Jahre*, ed. by Heinz Ludwig Arnold (Munich: Text + Kritik, 2000), pp. 122–44 (p. 122).

5 The following paragraphs draw on: Hermann Korte, *Deutschsprachige Lyrik seit 1945*; Hermann Korte, 'Energie der Brüche. Ein diachroner Blick auf die Lyrik des 20. Jahrhunderts und ihre Zäsuren', in *Lyrik des 20. Jahrhunderts*, ed. by Heinz Ludwig Arnold (Munich: Text + Kritik, 1999), pp. 63–106; Hermann Korte, 'Säulenheilige und Portalfiguren? Benn und Celan im Poetik-Dialog mit der jüngeren deutschsprachigen Lyrik seit den 1990er Jahren', in *Schaltstelle. Neue deutsche Lyrik im Dialog*, ed. by Karen Leeder (Amsterdam: Rodopi, 2007), pp. 109–37; Karen Leeder, '"Schreiben am Schnittpunkt". The Place of Contemporary German Poetry', in ibid., pp. 1–30.

First, they share a complex relationship to reality. If the giants of the 1960s kept reality in close range in order to critique and ameliorate contemporary society, their successors in the 1990s held it at a distance:

> For them, the poet's role at the end of the 20th century is bound up in his or her understanding of the process of lyric writing as a practice to which they were *not* called: not as an act of prophesying or the cry of Cassandra, not as a means of salvation, or poetic message in a bottle; nor as some sort of historical-philosophical 'sundial' that in a few lines indicates the 'state' of the era on the eve of the new millennium. Rather, there is a new understanding of writing as a state of permanent, exploratory flux, and not (or no longer) as a medium for messages, expressions of sadness, or sensitivities.[6]

This general agnosticism about poetry's responsibility or ability to produce binding models of broad social applicability goes hand in hand with a marked self-reflexive stance. Language and voice (picking up the thread from poets such as Ernst Jandl and Friederike Mayröcker) and perceptual processes (adding a highly mediatized dimension to the 1970s occupation with the everyday) are constantly stretched, scrutinized and unsettled.

Second, they are fascinated by early European modernism. Baudelaire, Mallarmé, Rilke, Pound, Eliot and Mandelstam roam the imagination of the 1990s, sharpening poetological positions and underscoring a belief in the autonomous nature of poetry at a time of ideological diversity.[7] While the 1990s poets effectively bracket out the Enzensberger generation,[8] two German poets – Benn and Celan – assume great importance.[9] For all their obvious differences, both had connected with European modernism – Benn, most notably, in his seminal essay 'Probleme der Lyrik' and Celan consistently in his poetic practice – and both championed poetry's unique strength as a realm of experience and expression

6 Korte, 'Energie der Brüche', pp. 97–98.

7 A challenging account of this aspect of the period, which uses Grünbein in an innovative way, can be read in Jonathan Monroe, 'Avant-Garde Poetries after the Wall', *Poetics Today*, 21.1 (2000), 95–128.

8 'Bleib steh'n, Wanderer, und lies', Germany, dir: Alexander Kluge, 2007, features death-related poems by Grünbein and Enzensberger and gives an immediate sense of the difference between both poets.

9 For Grünbein, Brecht is much more absent. In a recent interview he stated 'I can rarely remember a Brecht quotation'. Hans-Jürgen Heinrichs and Durs Grünbein, 'Gespräch mit Durs Grünbein. Hinweise auf ein Stück Gedankenmusik', *Sinn und Form*, 60.1 (2008), 47–59 (p. 55). For a rare example of his possible engagement with this particular poet, see Jörg Döning, 'Von den Nachgeborenen. Brechts "Ballade von den Seeräubern" und Durs Grünbeins "O Heimat, zynischer Euphon"', in *Bertolt Brecht (1898–1956)*, ed. by Jörg Döning and Walter Delabar (Berlin: Weidler, 1998), pp. 355–77.

which resists assimilation to the outside world.[10] Their work is used freely and eclectically, Celan revered more as a theoretical muse than as a poet of the Holocaust.[11]

And third, the 1990s cohort follow Benn's admonition that 'the lyric poet can hardly know enough; he cannot work enough; he must be close to everything; he must position himself according to where the world is today, under whatever sign the earth stands this noon'.[12] New poets of the last two decades bring a vast range of reading and learning, primarily from the natural sciences and philosophy, to bear on their poetry. Their work is complex and, more often than not, difficult. Almost certainly as a result, the trend in twentieth-century German poetry to publish poetological reflections has reached a climax over the last twenty years. An abundance of meta-writing, ranging across the issues touched on briefly in these paragraphs, has appeared, and it is a hallmark of the period that without it readers might struggle to grasp the essence of the poems.

Generalizations inevitably level local differences. One need only read Franz Josef Czernin's vitriolic review of Grünbein's *Falten und Fallen* to realize how turbulent these can be.[13] (At stake in this case was nothing less than poetic language itself, Czernin accusing Grünbein of ignoring decades of rupture, scepticism and experimentation.[14]) Nonetheless, most emergent poets of the 1990s could be situated broadly within the contours just outlined. Arguably, however, none falls more squarely within them than Grünbein. *Grauzone morgens* – with its links to classical modernity, the testing of the subject position, its distanced attitude to society and the unsettling play of voice and intertextual reference[15] – displayed many of the above-mentioned characteristics, and others (such as the accretion

10 Korte, 'Säulenheilige und Portalfiguren'.

11 For the main differences between Benn and Grünbein, see Helmut Böttiger and Durs Grünbein, 'Benn schmort in der Hölle. Ein Gespräch über dialogische und monologische Lyrik', *Text + Kritik*, 153.1 (2002), 72–84.

12 Cited in Korte, 'Säulenheilige und Portalfiguren', p. 120.

13 Franz Josef Czernin, 'Falten und Fallen. Zu einem Gedichtband von Durs Grünbein', *Schreibheft. Zeitschrift für Literatur*, 45 (1995), 179–88. Reprinted as 'Falten und Fallen. Zu Durs Grünbeins Gedichtband', in Franz Josef Czernin, *Der Himmel ist blau. Aufsätze zur Dichtung* (Weil am Rhein: Engeler, 2007), pp. 29–56.

14 See Grünbein's reply, 'Feldpost', *Schreibheft. Zeitschrift für Literatur*, 46 (1995), 191–92; Michael Braun's critical stock-taking in the same issue, 'Kleine, verwunderte Fußnote zu einer Polemik von Franz Josef Czernin', pp. 192–95; and Grünbein's debate with Czernin and others in 'Kosmologischer Irrläufer. Fünf Dichter im Gespräch über die Möglichkeit der Poesie', *Frankfurter Allgemeine Zeitung Sonntagsausgabe*, 11 / 12 April 1998, Literatur und Kunst, pp. 49–50.

15 Thomas Irmer, 'Durs Grünbein', in *Deutschsprachige Lyriker der 20. Jahrhunderts*, ed. by Ursula Heukenkamp and Peter Geist (Berlin: Erich Schmidt, 2007), pp. 711–21 (p. 712).

of knowledge and scientific discourse) were in evidence no later than the second published volume, *Schädelbasislektion* (1991). As Grünbein noted variously in this period and in the years directly following: the individual's perception of reality and its linguistic transformation is grounded in the physiological / neurological; the function of the subject in this perceptual process is conditioned and stripped of its individuality by a fullness of voices and stimuli, which ultimately lead to the dissolution of any notion of the self based on wholeness or complete identity; the collapse of the self and neurological conditioning bring radical consequences; and the brain in its materiality of nerves and grey matter assumes the position occupied over the last several centuries by the soul.[16] 'Mein babylonisches Hirn' ['My Babylonish Brain'], as the programmatic essay of the same title suggests, replaces Baudelaire's 'babylonisches Herz' [Babylonian heart].[17]

The intensity with which Grünbein influenced and embodied the poetic criteria of his age has already secured him a central position in future literary histories and anthologies. Indeed, a key characteristic of his complex and fractured voice(s) is precisely the intention to write and speak for the future. Such sentiments might be commonplace in modern writing, but they recur in Grünbein's thinking with particular verve and frequency. In 2002, he wrote:

> Das Dichterwort strebt in die Vertikale wie eine Rakete, sein Betriebsgeheimnis ist die ballistische Kürze. Keiner kann sagen, wo es landen wird. Es strebt fort vom Augenblick und hält ihn gerade deshalb streng fest als eine Art planetarischer Botschaft, die an die Zukunft gerichtet ist oder vielleicht sogar an die Außerirdischen.
>
> [The word of the poet shoots into the air like a missile, its trade secret is its ballistic brevity. No one can say where it will land. Its aim is beyond the present moment, and for precisely that reason it holds the present tight as a sort of planetary message directed at the future, or perhaps even at the extraterrestrial.][18]

And in 2007, he programmatically entitled his new collection *Strophen für übermorgen*. These ambitions certainly captured the imagination of Grünbein's admirers. In his laudatio at the 1995 Büchner Prize ceremony, Heiner Müller noted 'Eine Frau sagte mir, nach der Lektüre eines Gedichts von Durs Grünbein: "Das muß ich in fünfzig Jahren noch einmal lesen"' [A woman said to me after reading

---

16 See in particular, Durs Grünbein, *Den Körper zerbrechen. Rede zur Entgegennahme des Georg-Büchner-Preises 1995. Mit der Laudatio 'Portrait des Künstlers als junger Grenzhund' von Heiner Müller* (Frankfurt a. M.: Suhrkamp, 1995); Durs Grünbein, *Galilei vermißt Dantes Hölle und bleibt an den Maßen hängen. Aufsätze 1989–1995* (Frankfurt a. M.: Suhrkamp, 1996).
17 Durs Grünbein, 'Mein babylonisches Hirn', in *Galilei vermißt Dantes Hölle*, pp. 18–23.
18 Böttiger and Grünbein, 'Benn schmort in der Hölle', p. 72.

a poem by Durs Grünbein: 'I must read that again in fifty years time'].[19] Müller's plaintive 'Ich wollte, ich könnte das' [I wish that was something I could do] has added poignancy since the doyen of East German theatre, already struggling with throat cancer, would be dead before the year was out.

Durs Grünbein is worth reading today, in other words, because he will be read tomorrow. Future editors and scholars, however, will turn to Grünbein not just because of his representative role at the head of a new poetic cohort, nor simply because his desire to speak at some temporal remove might guarantee his work enduring freshness. These are important factors. But Grünbein's future readership is assured, equally, because his rise through the literary establishment captures a significant cultural moment of the first decade after German reunification. From the cusp of unification through the winter of 1993, the German literary establishment smouldered in a series of debates that threw off a plume of political toxin. More vituperative than the 1980s *Historikerstreit* to which it was soon compared – poets, novelists and intellectuals have a way with words when riled – literary polemic expressed deep-seated anxiety, anger and uncertainty about the political responsibilities of culture on both sides of the border since the Second World War. Known as the Christa Wolf debate or the *Literaturstreit*, these arguments form the essential backdrop to Grünbein's phenomenal early success.

Grünbein enjoyed considerable coverage from the moment of his first appearance at the Frankfurt Book Fair in 1988. In 1991, the literary editor of the *Frankfurter Allgemeine Zeitung* (*FAZ*), Frank Schirrmacher, picked him out as the young poet to watch, following up a year later with a positive review of *Schädelbasislektion*.[20] By 1995, Schirrmacher had anointed Grünbein 'the first genuine voice of the new Republic', but not before Gustav Seibt announced in *Die Zeit* that '[n]ot since the early days of Enzensberger, indeed, perhaps not even since Hugo von Hofmannsthal came on the scene has poetry in the German language seen such a favourite of the gods (*Götterliebling*) who spellbinds all attendant'.[21] No poet so extravagantly christened can escape the ire of critics and fellow writers for long, but by the new millennium Grünbein was being hailed as 'the most suitable can-

19 Heiner Müller, 'Portrait des Künstlers als junger Grenzhund', in Durs Grünbein, *Den Körper zerbrechen*, pp. 25–29 (p. 29).

20 Frank Schirrmacher, 'War da irgendein Mythos?', *Frankfurter Allgemeine Zeitung*, 26 March 1992, cited in Sylvia Heudecker, 'Durs Grünbein in der Kritik', in *Schreiben am Schnittpunkt. Poesie und Wissen bei Durs Grünbein*, ed. by Kai Bremer, Fabian Lampart and Jörg Wesche (Freiburg i. Br.: Rombach Litterae, 2007), pp. 37–56 (p. 43).

21 See also, however, Fritz J. Raddatz's sharp and sustained critique of Grünbein's poetry in the same paper: 'Nicht Entwurf der Moderne, sondern Faltenwurf der Mode', *Die Zeit*, 22 September 1995, Feuilleton, pp. 65–66.

a 'potentially utopian space' with a long subliminal hold.[27] (The West German Left, most notably Grass, Walter Jens and Peter Rühmkorf, supported Wolf.) The cultural aftershocks of unification were immense, the discourse corrosive and remarkably undiscerning. While Heiner Müller railed against 'the Stalinism of the West', others reached for the thesaurus of National Socialism, throwing about with wild abandon terms such as 'Vernichtungsfeldzug' [campaign of extermination], 'Liquidierung' [liquidation], 'Pogrom' [pogrom], 'Endlösung' [final solution], the ever popular 'Anschluß der DDR' [annexation of the GDR] and 'Auschwitz in den Seelen' [Auschwitz in their souls] (Jürgen Fuchs).[28] In the eye of the second storm that engulfed her two years later, Wolf, on a trip to California, likened her treatment in the Federal Republic to the hounding of Jews and Communists between 1933 and 1945.

One of the most intriguing aspects of the cultural fall-out from reunification is the turn it took, in certain circles, towards aesthetics. The aestheticization of the debate, however, merely served to politicize it further. Already in his review of Wolf in the spring, Schirrmacher had projected his critique onto the literary culture of the Left in the Federal Republic. As Huyssen recorded: Schirrmacher read *Was bleibt* as 'an apocryphal act of resistance against the Stasi which was then compared to the ethos of a belated resistance to fascism that supposedly prevailed in the post-war culture of the FRG (Grass, Böll, Walser, Weiss et al.)'.[29] There are rights and wrongs to this argument, and none of it was particularly original. But by the eve of reunification in October 1990, Schirrmacher was back with a full-frontal onslaught on the left-literary culture of the post-war period. Joined by Greiner again, and augmented by senior literary critic and scholar Karl Heinz Bohrer, the Right bade farewell to what they saw as the arid literary scene of the 1980s and called for an end to the 'Gesinnungsästhetik' [aesthetics of morals] associated with the Gruppe 47 that had supposedly fostered it over a forty-year period.[30] The literature of the new Republic, hoped the *FAZ*, *Die Zeit* and Bohrer's journal *Merkur*, would decouple literary aesthetics from political and moral utopianism and re-energize a flagging national literature. As Huyssen signed off in 1991, he predicted a wave of *Ostalgie* (well before the term was invented) and noted 'a new *Nullpunktthese* [proclamation of a zero hour] [...] in the making which [could] be expected to play a major role in the foundational myths that

27 Huyssen, 'After the Wall', p. 43.

28 Emmerich, *Kleine Literaturgeschichte der DDR*, p. 465.

29 Huyssen, 'After the Wall', p. 59.

30 More generally on Bohrer, see Jan-Werner Müller, 'Karl Heinz Bohrer on German National Identity. Recovering Romanticism and Aestheticizing the State', *German Studies Review*, 23.2 (2000), 297–316.

[were] bound to spring up around the years 1989 and 1990'. Huyssen was broadly correct on both counts, but – not surprisingly since even the clearest crystal balls cloud over – less accurate on the details of the latter. This *Nullpunktthese*, Huyssen argued, would be 'constructed differently from that of 1945, but it [would] similarly be based on denial of the past and serve to legitimize the new state and the desired and anticipated new culture';[31] and around the third anniversary of unification, Iris Radisch was indeed proclaiming 'Die zweite Stunde Null' [the second zero-hour] in *Die Zeit* with the rejection of 'Gesinnungsästhetik' writ large again: 'In this zero-hour', she noted, 'the younger generation no longer seeks to write epoch-making works, and that is their strength'; a new chapter in literary history was opening 'free from any burden, free from limitation, free from obligation – as free as art has always wanted to be and seldom has been'.[32] And sure enough, in 1995, Grass's *Ein weites Feld* [*Too Far Afield*] was lacerated in the press. But with the benefit of hindsight, it is clear that things were more complicated.

And this brings us back to Durs Grünbein, the 'national poet' in waiting. For the vital fact about Grünbein's rise to prominence is not, as has been claimed, that he was a handy projection figure for a new aesthetic or, by dint of birth-date or ideological innocence, an acceptable personification of German division,[33] but rather that he represented *both* a new, aesthetically orientated poetry *and* a continued engagement with the past. Grünbein's success, after all, was founded on the support of the both the *FAZ* and Heiner Müller. Müller, having encountered Grünbein through the East Berlin theatre scene in the 1980s, secured his literary success in the West (and indeed his first ever publication) with a recommendation to Suhrkamp, and developed a friendship with him that the younger poet would later compare to the relationship of loyalty, trust and mentorship between Joyce and Beckett.[34] Grünbein still describes Müller as the last great 'poet intellectual'.[35] The *FAZ* and Frankfurt publisher Suhrkamp pushed Grünbein's career from 1988 – so much so that detractors denounced the awards of the Darmstadt Academy in 1995 as a stitch-up by the paper, *Die Zeit* launching a particularly embittered and high profile attack. Sharing the honours with Grünbein were *FAZ*

---

31 Huyssen, 'After the Wall', p. 52.

32 Iris Radisch, 'Die zweite Stunde Null', *Die Zeit*, 7 October 1994, cited in Thomas Anz, 'Epochenumbruch und Generationenwechsel? Zur Konjunktur von Generationenkonstrukten seit 1989', in *Schreiben nach der Wende. Ein Jahrzehnt deutscher Literatur 1989–1999*, ed. by Gerhard Fischer and David Roberts (Tübingen: Stauffenberg, 2001), pp. 31–40 (p. 35).

33 See Helmut Böttiger, 'Durs Grünbein. Auf dem Olymp', in Helmut Böttiger, *Nach den Utopien. Eine Geschichte der deutschsprachigen Gegenwartsliteratur* (Vienna: Zsolnay, 2004), pp. 112–25.

34 Heinrichs, 'Gespräch mit Durs Grünbein', p. 55.

35 Interview with Alexandra Kedves, *Neue Züricher Zeitung*, 9 November 2006, p. 38.

staff critic Gustav Seibt, who won the Sigmund-Freud-Preis für wissenschaftliche Prosa, and regular contributor Michael Maar, who took the Johann-Heinrich-Merck-Preis für Kritik und Essay. Müller and the *FAZ* make strange bedfellows, and not surprisingly they read Grünbein differently. But that is the point.

Schirrmacher's interpretation of Grünbein represented a nuanced approach. On the one hand, he valued his direct, non-metaphorical engagement with the GDR and the collapse of socialism.[36] At the same time, he appreciated Grünbein's distanced stance, collapsing two later commonplaces of the poet's self-understanding (the future and archaeology) into a single vector: 'His poems put the transition into words, but in such a way that the reader feels as though he is looking back on it, as if on an archaeological discovery, from the distant future'.[37] Gustav Seibt, however, took a less circuitous route. Grünbein, as he wrote in 1994, represented 'a new era [as] the first poet to overcome the division in German literature', and showed that 'at least part of the public has had enough of literature that is almost solely concerned with wrangling and pique in matters German'.[38] 'Grünbein is the first young author from East Germany', Seibt concluded, 'to whom readers from the West can also listen, not in the spirit of awkward obligation, of embarrassed exchange between the two Germanies, but as one of their own'. The desire of many in the literary media to bury the fabled 'Gesinnungsästhetik' of the old Republic and herald a new beginning could hardly have found clearer expression.

Heiner Müller, when delivering his laudatio on the evening of Grünbein's prize ceremony, was equally unambiguous. In one of the last public appearances before his death, the poet's mentor used the cycle 'Portrait des Künstlers als junger Grenzhund' ['Portrait of the Artist as a Young Border Dog'] from *Schädelbasislektion* to consider the role of the younger generation of poets. Müller's opening serves as an eloquent reminder of the shock effect Grünbein's work induced in the early 1990s: 'Die Texte von Durs Grünbein liegen nicht, nach Goethes Definition von Kunstwerk, wie Kühe auf der Weide. Eher gleichen sie den Tieren, vielleicht sind es Maschinen, die Kafka gegen die Schöpfung gestellt hat' [Contrary to Goethe's definition of the work of art, Durs Grünbein's writings do not rest like cows on a meadow. They are nearer to the animals, or perhaps they are machines, that Kafka set against creation]. Equally important, however, is Müller's elegant and piercingly formulated understanding of Grünbein's poetic mission, or at least of what it ought to be:

---

36 Schirrmacher, 'War da irgendein Mythos?'.

37 Ibid.

38 Gustav Seibt, 'Mit besseren Nerven als jedes Tier', *Frankfurter Allgemeine Zeitung*, 15 March 1994, cited in Heudecker 'Durs Grünbein in der Kritik', p. 45.

> In Grünbeins Gedicht ist eine Generationserfahrung Form geworden, die sich bislang eher als Verweigerung von Form artikuliert hat. Es ist die Generation der Untoten des kalten Krieges, die Geschichte nicht mehr als Sinngebung des Sinnlosen durch Ideologie, sondern nur noch als sinnlos begreifen kann. [...] Die Bilder wechseln, und die Fremdheit bleibt. Diese Generation hat kein Vaterland und keine Muttersprache. Für sie gilt der Brechtsatz: 'Die Situation sind die Mütter der Menschen'. [...] Nach dem Verschwinden der Mütter das Trauma der zweiten Geburt. Der Ichverlust im Spiegel, genauer: der Zerfall des Ich in Spiegelscherben, die es als Mauerkrone verwenden kann oder zur Öffnung von Adern. Die Verszeile 'Und was ich sah war mehr als ich ertrug' formuliert das Trauma. [...] Der Blick ist lidlos. Es ist nicht nur ein Glück, niemandes Schlaf zu sein, unter wieviel Lidern immer. [...] Der Teufel sprach Russisch, nicht, wie Bulgakow noch geglaubt hat, Italienisch mit russischem Akzent, aber wir sind nicht aus dem Auge des Todes, wenn wir die ost-europäische Erfahrung zu den Akten legen, und der Teufel ist sprachbegabt. [...] Das Geheimnis [von Durs Grünbeins] Produktivität ist die Unersättlichkeit seiner Neugier auf die Katastrophen, die das Jahrhundert im Angebot hat, unter den Sternen wie unter dem Mikroskop.
>
> [In Grünbein's poem, the experience of a generation has become form, an experience which until now has expressed itself rather as a refusal of form. It is the generation of the undead of the Cold War, who can no longer understand history by making sense of the senseless through ideology, but can only now understand it as senseless. The images change, but the alienation remains. This generation has no fatherland and no mother tongue. For them Brecht was right when he said: 'Situations are the mothers of people'. [...] After the mothers disappear, comes the trauma of second birth. The loss of the self in the mirror, or rather, the disintegration of the self into shards of mirror that it can use as wall coping, or to slit the wrists. The line 'And what I saw was more than I bore' expresses that trauma. [...] It is a lidless gaze. Being no one's sleep is not all pleasure, no matter how many eyelids one is sleeping under. [...] The devil spoke Russian – not, as Bulgakov thought, Italian with a Russian accent – but by filing away the eastern European experience we have still not escaped the stare of death, and the devil is a gifted linguist. [...] The secret of Durs Grünbein's productivity is his insatiable curiosity about catastrophes, of which this century has plenty to offer, under the stars and under the microscope.][39]

Müller replaces the 'second zero hour' with the 'trauma of second birth'; the cosy arrangement of West German appreciation of an East German poet with the lack of a 'fatherland and mother tongue'; and the 'spirit of awkward obligation, of embarrassed exchange between the two Germanies' with the notion of history as 'senseless'. Müller remained vague about whether the 'generation of the undead of the Cold War' straddled both sides of the old divide: the grain of the text and his own recent experience of a failed cross-German venture at the Brecht Ensemble – by 1995, his front-line collaborators had disappeared back to the West, one of them accusing him of 'fascist tendencies'[40] – suggest rather not. But he left little

39 Müller, 'Portrait des Künstlers als junger Grenzhund', pp. 26–29.
40 Emmerich, *Kleine Literaturgeschichte der DDR*, p. 508.

else to the imagination, his reformed socialist convictions resounding throughout, crowned with a thumping claim of Russian culpability. As these polarized interpretations of the mid-1990s show, Grünbein could be read either as a representative of a new aesthetic, or as a child of the Cold War with the ability and moral duty to dissect the Kafkaesque worlds of totalitarian regimes. Or rather: he could be read *both* as the one *and* as the other.

Similarly distinct positions taken up since in scholarship suggest there was indeed something intrinsically open about the way Grünbein was writing in the 1990s. Although neglecting the literary debates described in this chapter, Fabian Lampart surveys Grünbein's poetry and essays from *Grauzone morgens* to *Nach den Satiren*, with a particular focus on the 'Novembertage' ['November Days'] cycle, which treats the murder of Rosa Luxemburg in 1919, the Hitler Putsch in 1923 and the fall of the Wall in 1989. Describing the mix of biographical background and distanced, observer perspective that many see as a hallmark of Grünbein's poetry, Lampart concludes that the *Wende* had a decisive but delineated effect on the poet:

> The effect of this manifests itself in Grünbein's work more in the way he reflects on the conditions of writing poetry, in an aesthetic, poetological discourse, in which the socio-political factors affecting the writings of an individual are only secondary considerations, as possible variables in the production and exploration of the experience and the writing experience of an individual. [...] If Durs Grünbein has a specific *Wende* experience, then it expresses itself in his poetry not so much as the taking up of a political and social position; rather, the *Wende* provides the backdrop for a new formulation of the fundamental principles of poetics.[41]

Judith Ryan, by contrast, reads the central neurological metaphor of *Schädelbasislektion* as overt political reflection:

> In Grünbein's poetry, the cranial sutures stand in for the 'wall in the head', those traces of the division between former West and East Germany that persist in the psyches of German citizens even after the unification of the two countries in 1991. The brain-stem metaphor [the brainstem being the remnants of the fetal nervous system which is otherwise trans-

41 Fabian Lampart, '"Tropismen an den Rändern alter Formen". Annäherungen an Durs Grünbeins Lyrik aus den Jahren der Wende', in *Engagierte Literatur in Wendezeiten*, ed. by Willi Huntemann and others (Würzburg: Königshausen & Neumann, 2003), pp. 113–47 (pp. 135, 144). Andrea Payk-Heitmann, 'Der 11. September im (fiktionalen) Tagebuch. Überlegungen zu Durs Grünbein und Max Goldt', in *Nine Eleven. Ästhetische Verarbeitungen des 11. September 2001*, ed. by Ingo Irsigler and Christoph Jürgensen (Heidelberg: Winter, 2008), pp. 49–66, argues that Grünbein's responses to the events of 9/11 were, equally, primarily rooted in aesthetics. On Grünbein's wider aesthetics of 9/11, see Volker Mergenthaler, 'Coventry und Dresden, Ninive und Sodom. Durs Grünbeins Koordinaten mythologischer Sinnstiftung nach dem 11. September 2001', in *In the Embrace of the Swan. Anglo-German Mythologies in Literature, the Visual Arts and Cultural Theory*, ed. by Rüdiger Görner and Angus Nicholls (Berlin: de Gruyter, 2010), pp. 168–86.

formed into the adult brain or the spinal cord] represents subconscious attachments to the former East Germany and a more primitive way of life.[42]

Like Heiner Müller, Ryan understands Grünbein's poetry as 'a continual attempt to expose the roots of creativity in trauma, and thus to accord to poetry a privileged role in bearing witness to suffering', suggesting that *Schädelbasislektion* and *Nach den Satiren* (in particular) are a conscious response to the debate about *Was bleibt* – artistically, socially and culturally – across the rupture of the *Wende*.[43] The fact that the 'Novembertage' cycle in *Nach den Satiren* directly follows two poems devoted to the memory of Heiner Müller ('Heiner Müller, auf dann ... Drei Blätter' ['Heiner Müller, Until Then ... Three Sheets'] and 'Brief an den toten Dichter' ['Letter to the Dead Poet') speaks for itself.[44]

The legitimacy of both interpretations is confirmed by what Grünbein later had to say about the poems himself. In 2006, when Suhrkamp re-issued *Grauzone morgens*, *Schädelbasislektion* and *Falten und Fallen* in a single volume, the poet furnished his career-defining middle collection with the afterword it had lacked in 1991.[45] In the space of just several pages, his retrospective gives traction to both readings. Fifteen years after first publication, Grünbein noted that aesthetics had formed a crucial component in the life change introduced by the events of 1989:

> [D]er Übergang von der einen Welt in die andere erzwang nicht nur eine völlig veränderte Lebensweise, sondern auch eine neue Ästhetik. Eine der Folgen war der Wechsel von der Monochromie zu einer plötzlichen Farbigkeit, und damit das Ende der eigenen *Grauen Periode*.
>
> [The transition from one world to the other compelled me not only to a completely different way of life, but also to a new aesthetic. One of the consequences was the shift from the monochrome to a sudden burst of colour, bringing to an end my own *Grey Period*.][46]

---

42 Judith Ryan, 'The Skull beneath the Skin', in *A New History of German Literature*, ed. by David E. Wellbery and others (Cambridge, MA: Harvard University Press, 2004), pp. 959–64 (p. 961).
43 Ibid., p. 963. See also Judith Ryan, 'Das Motiv der Schädelnähte bei Durs Grünbein', in *Schreiben nach der Wende. Ein Jahrzehnt deutscher Literatur 1989–1999*, ed. by Gerhard Fischer and David Roberts (Tübingen: Stauffenburg, 2001), pp. 301–15. In a further essay, Ryan reads the later collection *Vom Schnee* as a reflection of the changed conditions of poetic production since 1989. Judith Ryan, '"Spurlose Frühe". Durs Grünbeins "Vom Schnee" und das Problem der Wende', in *Weiterschreiben. Zur DDR-Literatur nach dem Ende der DDR*, ed. by Holger Helbig and Kristin Felsner (Berlin: Akademie, 2007), pp. 163–81.
44 For a detailed discussion of these poems, see Alexander Müller, *Das Gedicht als Engramm. Memoria und Imaginatio in der Poetik Durs Grünbeins* (Oldenburg: Igel, 2004), pp. 151–216.
45 From the 'Schlußwort zur *Schädelbasislektion*', as written for the publication of Durs Grünbein, *Gedichte. Bücher I–III (Grauzone morgens, Schädelbasislektion, Falten und Fallen)* (Frankfurt a. M.: Suhrkamp, 2006), pp. 385–95.
46 Ibid., p. 388.

Once again, at the end of the statement the move from one pole to another is evident. There is no elaboration on the second, but the first leaves the reader guessing too. If the poem is not just about the 'hündische Seite der Angelegenheit', what does this 'hündische Seite' represent? If the poem gives eloquent witness to 'the rigidity of being fettered in will and placed under surveillance', as Vendler notes elsewhere in this volume,[52] why should a young artist, recently released by the events of history, portray an incarcerated self? And why, at a point of career take-off, does he imagine himself in terms of an animal whose services are no longer required? Obviously, it defies the very nature of poetic language to seek to reduce it to absolute points of reference,[53] and, as the many interpretations of the poem in question demonstrate, its multiple intertexts – from Kafka's *Der Proceß* [*The Trial*] and 'Forschungen eines Hundes' ['Investigations of a Dog'] to Descartes, Goethe and Dylan Thomas – amplify its complexity.[54] As the forty-four-year-old poet writes of his early endeavour, too, the ability adequately to reflect on oneself is precisely the problem *Schädelbasislektion* seeks to address. But it is odd – *very odd* – that in wrestling with such an issue at such an historic moment, Grünbein should project himself into the role of authors who had slipped from fashion and fallen from grace. Echoes of the *Literaturstreit* are unmistakable.[55] Judith Ryan was right in her hunch that *Schädelbasislektion* is shot through with responses to the question *Was bleibt*. What was not immediately apparent, however, when Ryan was writing, was Grünbein's identification, on some unexplained level, with Christa Wolf and others.

This was not, of course, Grünbein's first comment on the literature debate of the early 1990s. Largely overlooked by scholarship is the poet's response to the Wolf Biermann – Sascha Anderson affair in 1991, four years before he would make

52 Vendler, in this volume, p. 205.

53 For a discussion of poetic language with particular reference to Grünbein in comparative perspective, see Meike Adam, '"Das Fremdeste paarend und das nächste treffend". Hofmannsthal, Kafka, Grünbein und der Mehrwert literarischen Sprechens', *KulturPoetik*, 6.1 (2006), 78–95.

54 See, for instance, Peter Hamm, 'Vorerst – oder: Der Dichter als streunender Hund. Lobrede auf Durs Grünbein', *manuskripte*, 33.122 (1993), 103–6; Aris Fioretos and Durs Grünbein, 'Gespräch über die Zone, den Hund und die Knochen', *Akzente*, 43.6 (1996), 486–501 (pp. 491–96); Florian Berg, 'Die Kunst im Zeitalter der Wissenschaft. Über René Descartes bei Durs Grünbein', *Sprache im technischen Zeitalter*, 45.183 (2007), 314–24; Anna Cappellotto, 'Vom pawlowschen Hund zum Grenzhund Durs Grünbeins. Berührungspunkte zwischen sozialen und ästhetischen Experimenten', in *'Ein in der Phantasie durchgeführtes Experiment'. Literatur und Wissenschaft nach Neunzehnhundert*, ed. by Raul Calzoni and Massimo Salgaro (Göttingen: V & R unipress, 2010), pp. 337–57.

55 In fact, Helmut Böttiger selects precisely Grünbein and Wolf as figures of contrast in his entertaining and informative *Rausch im Niemandsland. Es gibt ein Leben nach der DDR* (Berlin: Fannei und Walz, 1994), pp. 76–95.

his own much cited, and less polemical acceptance speech at the Büchner Prize ceremony. In the heat of the Anderson debacle, Grünbein left few in doubt about his feelings, writing in the *FAZ* under the heading 'Im Namen der Füchse: Gibt es eine neue literarische Zensur?' ['On Behalf of the Foxes: Is this a New Literary Censorship?']:

> Mein neuester Albtraum ist eine Bibliothek, von Wolf Biermann zusammengestellt. [...] Natürlich widert mich die Larmoyanz vergeßlicher Kollaborateure genauso an wie den einsamen Rächer. [... Aber d]as verbale Maschinengewehrrattern Wolf Biermanns fährt in die Gesänge wie die Dekrete der einstigen Stalinisten. In beherrschter Raserei sollen, nachdem nun glücklich wieder Boden gewonnen wurde, gewisse Ästhetiken sogleich terminiert werden. Weh denen, die nur die bloßen Hände zu heben haben vor der Übermacht des Begleitgeheuls! Plötzlich, beim Anblick des streunenden Wolfs, versteht man die anthropologische Einsamkeit Hölderlins, die Verlassenheit Mandelstams ('Ich bin ein Chinese'), die Verächtlichkeit Büchners.
>
> [My latest nightmare is a library, compiled by Wolf Biermann. [...] Of course the maudlin complaints of forgetful collaborators repulse me as much as they do that lonely seeker of vengeance. But the clattering of Wolf Biermann's verbal machine gun invades his songs like the decrees of the Stalinists of long ago. Now that we've got firm ground beneath our feet again, certain aesthetics shall be terminated at once, in a sort of composed raging. Woe betide those who can only raise their bare hands before the superpower of the denunciation of accomplices! Suddenly, at the sight of the roaming wolf, one understands the anthropological isolation of Hölderlin, the forlornness of Mandelstam ('I am Chinese'), the contemptibility of Büchner.][56]

Again, the sheer oddity of this constellation – Grünbein speaking out, in the *FAZ* (a paper that had led the way in dishing out opprobrium),[57] against an author of the political stature of Biermann, who had just uncovered a Stasi scandal in the ranks – is striking. Attempting to divine the editorial policy of the *Frankfurter* feuilleton at this time is pointless – in 1993, it even briefly backed Christa Wolf as a strategic manoeuvre against its rival *Die Zeit*. Nor should we forget that Biermann, who used his victory parade through German prize-giving ceremonies in the 1990s to

56 Durs Grünbein, 'Im Namen der Füchse. Gibt es eine neue literarische Zensur?', *Frankfurter Allgemeine Zeitung*, 26 November 1991; reprinted in and cited from *MachtSpiele. Literatur und Staatssicherheit im Fokus Prenzlauer Berg*, ed. by Peter Böthig and Klaus Michael (Leipzig: Reclam, 1993), pp. 325–29 (pp. 325–28).

57 The collection *Verrat an der Kunst? Rückblicke auf die DDR-Literatur*, ed. by Karl Deiritz and Hannes Krauss (Berlin: Aufbau, 1993), which sets itself the goal of rehabilitating GDR literature after the attacks, provocatively cites Frank Schirrmacher's famous sound-bite on its back cover: 'Auch die subversive Literatur der DDR war eine Literatur der Staatsicherheit' [Even the subversive literature of the GDR belonged to the Stasi].

distance himself ever more caustically from all things GDR,[58] was initially criticized for failing to produce the requisite proof (soon supplied by the accused in an attempt to relativize his guilt), or that – for a time at least – not just Anderson but the whole Prenzlauer Berg scene and all it stood for fell under attack. Grünbein's major purpose in writing might have been to attack both the notion of literary censorship ('Was mich stört, ist die Manipulation literarischer Werturteile' [What disturbs me is the manipulation of literary value judgements][59]) and Biermann's desire for a political literature that wears its credentials on its sleeve, but two things are striking. One is his rhetoric – coruscating even by the standards of the time – with its heavy echoes of Müller's 'Stalinism'. The other is the way he anchors himself and his work. 'Wer bin ich, daß ich so spreche?' [Who am I to speak like this?], he asks at the end of the article, repeating verbatim the question he had posed near the beginning, and answering: '1962 in Dresden geboren und von keiner Staatssicherheit in die Eier getreten, bin ich bestenfalls ein ästhetischer Idiot, ein politischer Mutant und ein geographischer Alien' [Born in Dresden in 1962, and never having been kicked in the balls by the Stasi, I am at best an aesthetic idiot, a political mutant and a geographical alien].[60] This is no mere speaking 'aus unterbrochener Langeweile' [from interrupted boredom] or deepest irritation, but a highly conscious act of position-taking in a turbulent literary field. Like many of Grünbein's poetological statements, however, it is both concrete and elusive. The 'aesthetic idiot' – the second word picking up on Aristotle's distinction between two sorts of citizens, the *zoon politikon* (who concerns himself with public life) and the *idiotes* (who concentrates, by contrast, on private affairs)[61] – captures the essence of Grünbein's poetic enterprise as well as the search of the literary establishment of the 1990s for a new beginning beyond the constraints of morals and accusations. The rhetoric of the piece shows equally, however, that literary-political loyalties in that changing world could be surprising and surprisingly charged.

Grünbein's relation to the new aesthetics on the one hand and politics and history on the other is, therefore, complex. He might, at the time, have occasionally offered himself as an easy projection figure, free from the burdens of the German past – as in the interview he gave *Der Spiegel* in 1995 in response to *Die Zeit*'s attack on the award of the Büchner Prize.[62] And he might, now, emphasize the pri-

58 He once accused PDS leader Gregor Gysi of being a 'totalitarian garden gnome'. Roland Berbig, 'Preisgekrönte DDR-Literatur nach 1989/90', in Arnold, *DDR-Literatur der neunziger Jahre*, pp. 198–207 (p. 202).
59 Grünbein, 'Im Namen der Füchse', pp. 325–26.
60 Ibid., p. 329.
61 Ibid., p. 327.
62 This is analyzed in Roland Berbig, 'Preisgekrönte DDR-Literatur nach 1989/90', p. 203.

macy of poetry over politics – as in his remark 'Die Poesie ist nicht das Dessert der Politik, sie ist die Wahrheit, die hinter aller Politik steht' [Poetry is not the dessert that comes after politics, but the truth behind all politics] occasioned by Elizabeth Alexander's poem 'Praise Song for the Day' at the inauguration of US President Barack Obama;[63] or in his comment to Alexander Kluge that his single and sincerest hope is that in a thousand years Mandelstam rather than Stalin will be remembered;[64] or generally in the speech given on his initiation into the Ordre Pour le Mérite in 2008.[65] But it was ultimately this complexity that maintained his support from Left and Right.[66]

It has been important to establish the literary-cultural framework in which Grünbein's early career developed. Much has changed since then – both in terms of his public reception and the field of poetry in general. Hardly surprisingly, Grünbein's work has been subject to greater criticism since his *Götterliebling* days.[67] As Helmut Böttiger recently noted:

> We've almost forgotten already: at the beginning of the nineties, Durs Grünbein was the author of the moment. He embodied what was in the air, and he stirred up the scene with nervous texts that shimmered with a mixture of natural science and theories of perception. The award of the Büchner Prize in 1995 marked the end of this Sturm und Drang phase, and formed a caesura, even, in the work of the then 33 year-old.[68]

---

63 Durs Grünbein, 'Die süße Realität', *Frankfurter Rundschau*, 22 January 2009, p. 35.

64 'Moskauer Menagerie. Poetische Tierschau von Durs Grünbein', Germany, dir: Alexander Kluge, 2007.

65 Durs Grünbein, 'Dieser besondere Kreis. Dankrede zur Aufnahme in den Orden Pour le mérite', *Sinn und Form*, 62.3 (2010), 422–26.

66 See, however, the tone of discontent when Grünbein's name is mentioned by Prenzlauer Berg poet Jan Faktor, 'Warum aus uns nichts geworden ist. Betrachtungen zur Prenzlauer-Berg-Szene zehn Jahre nach dem Mauerfall', in Arnold, *DDR-Literatur der neunziger Jahre*, pp. 92–106.

67 Reviews of *Nach den Satiren*, *Das erste Jahr* and *Strophen für übermorgen*, for instance, were mixed (e.g. Andreas Netwich, 'Der strahlende Eisblock', *Die Zeit*, 8 April 1999, pp. 47–48; Michael Braun, 'Müde dieser alten Welt', *die tageszeitung*, 25 March 1999, p. II; Marius Meller, 'Hauptsache Penis', *Frankfurter Rundschau*, 10 October 2001, Literatur, p. 4; Marius Meller, 'Wenn einem so viel Schönes wird beschert', *Frankfurter Allgemeine Sonntagszeitung*, 7 October 2007, p. 58; Hans-Herbert Räkel, 'Ein Snob in seinem letzten Hemd', *Süddeutsche Zeitung*, 29 November 2007, p. 14; Rolf Spinnler, 'Alles nur Strophen von vorgestern', *Stuttgarter Zeitung*, 15 February 2008, p. 12). Those of *Porzellan* were almost universally poor: Michael Braun, 'Gibt es eine Sprache für das Inferno?', *Neue Züricher Zeitung*, 22 September 2005, Feuilleton, p. 37; Jürgen Verdofsky, 'Trauer mit Goldrand', *Frankfurter Rundschau*, 19 October 2006, Beilage, p. 15; Thomas Steinfeld, 'Bomben, blankpolitert', *Süddeutsche Zeitung*, 6 October 2005, p. 16; Katharina Döbler, 'Forchtbar klassisch', *Die Zeit*, 26 January 2006, p. 56; Dorothea von Törne, 'Grünbein zerdeppert Porzellan', *Die Welt*, 24 December 2005, p. 5.

68 Helmut Böttiger, 'Die Maske wächst in das Gesicht', *Die Zeit*, 6 December 2007, Literatur, pp. 10–11.

Today, Böttiger continued, Grünbein's image is exactly the opposite of what it was then. 'Nowadays Grünbein seems very far from what is "in the air", and he has nothing whatsoever to do with the current waves of lyric.' Young poets of the rhythmic, oral performance scene, for instance, have long viewed him as part of the establishment, while his late rival Thomas Kling, who for many years had been depicted as his mirror image, referred to Grünbein's increasing recourse to classical antiquity as 'Sandalenfilme aus den Grünbein-Studios' [sandal films from the Grünbein studios].

Grünbein himself would hardly dispute the change in perspective (even if public statements such as the speech, entitled 'Unfreiheit' ['Captivity'], delivered in the Frauenkirche in Dresden in 2009, capture the headlines and lead to Grünbein's being painted in literary histories as a poet keen to preserve the memory of the crimes, perpetrators and victims of the GDR).[69] Today he is more likely to talk about the influence of early childhood on his poetry – zoos, post-war ruins, and his crossword-composing grandfather – than the last years of the GDR.[70] In fact, as he stated in the same year as the new postscript to *Schädelbasislektion*:

> Der Beginn meines Schreibens fand auf einem anderen Stern statt. Heute kommen die Texte mir wie ein Archivfilm vor, die Zeilen knistern in Schwarzweiss. Diese Texte vorzulesen, ist mir unmöglich. Ihre Form und Entstehungsgeschichte ist mir fremd geworden: Der Sozialismus war ein Albtraum für mich [...]. Ich wollte irgendwann nur noch weg von dort. Die DDR habe ich nie vermisst und Ostalgie nie verstanden. Ich wollte die Museen der Welt besuchen können, Kirchen, Städte. Alles andere war mir egal.
>
> [My writing at the beginning happened on another star. Today, those texts seem like an archive film to me, the lines crackle in black and white. I find it impossible to read them aloud: their form, the story of their composition, has become alien to me: Socialism was a nightmare for me [...]. At some point, all I wanted was to leave. I have never missed the GDR, never understood *Ostalgie*. I wanted to visit the museums of the world, the churches, the cities. I didn't care about anything else].[71]

As another critic has memorably put it: '[t]he young border dog [...], so recently still pressed into the service of self-repression, hopped out of his image of narrowness: and in mid-flight he saw all the new realities and mutated in one fell swoop into a literary globetrotter'.[72] As the other essays in this volume show, Grünbein's

69 See, for instance, Peter J. Brenner, *Neue deutsche Literaturgeschichte*, 3rd extended edn (Berlin: de Gruyter, 2011), p. 394.

70 See, for instance, Durs Grünbein, 'Meine Jahre im Zoo', *Der Spiegel*, 14 January 2008, pp. 130–31.

71 Interview with Alexandra Kedves, *Neue Züricher Zeitung*, 9 November 2006, p. 38.

72 Eberhard Falcke, 'Ein Clown und Chorknabe, scharf auf die zynischen Witze', *Süddeutsche Zeitung*, 27 March 1999, p. IV.

many collections of poetry and volumes of prose are unmistakably voracious in their cultural and intellectual ambition,[73] and marked by stylistic and formal transformation.[74]

This development and self-enrichment is an important aspect of Grünbein's work, and one that will almost certainly earn him as much credit with future readers as his emergence at the time of the *Wende*. In 1995, Jörg Drews published a collection of post-war German poems under the title *Das bleibt. Deutsche Gedichte 1945–1995* [*This Remains. German Poems 1945–1995*]. Despite the less than oblique reference to the *Literaturstreit* a few years earlier, the volume steers clear of controversy – the editor simply stretching into the new Republic with fifty years' worth of post-war poetry and letting literature speak for itself. Choosing the poems, however, had been difficult, Drews having set himself the challenge of selecting on the basis of quality rather than, necessarily, significance. His commentary on what that arduous assignment revealed is instructive:

> One of the most depressing experiences on re-reading the poems of many authors of the period after 1945 [...] is the garrulous impression not only many of the poems make, but also many of the authors. Once they had found their particular tone, their own way of speaking, countless authors hardly varied or developed it any further. Reading their works with hindsight, it is striking that the 'necessity' of their poetry often amounts to a kind of compulsive repetition: themes are swapped around whilst the language remains the same, and innovation, poetic work, and thus also surprise for the reader, are limited.[75]

Grünbein, of course, made the final cut (with 'Homo sapiens correctus' from *Falten und Fallen* and 'Nicht gut erging es' ['It Didn't Go Well'] from *Den teuren Toten*), despite the fact that in 1995 – according to Bohrer and others – literary standards had 'reached their lowest point since the Second World War'.[76] Had

---

73 Irmer, 'Durs Grünbein'.

74 Lampart, '"Tropismen an den Rändern alter Formen"', p. 136.

75 Jörg Drews, *Das bleibt. Deutsche Gedichte 1945–1995* (Leipzig: Reclam, 1995), p. 252.

76 Karl Heinz Bohrer, 'Erinnerung an Kriterien. Vom Warten auf den deutschen Zeitroman', *Merkur*, 49 (1995); reprinted in *Maulhelden und Königskinder. Zur Debatte über die deutschsprachige Gegenwartsliteratur*, ed. by Andreas Köhler and Rainer Moritz (Leipzig: Reclam, 1998), pp. 137–50 (p. 137). There was a general debate around this time as to whether German literature should orientate itself towards European modernism (Greiner, Schirrmacher, Bohrer) or towards the international norms of entertainment and enjoyment (particularly the influential commissioning editor Uwe Wittstock). As both sides agreed that German literature had reached an all-time nadir, the whole 'Neues Erzählen' movement was exploding and German literature was being read as never before in translation. See Stuart Taberner, 'Introduction', in *German Literature in the Age of Globalisation*, ed. by Stuart Taberner (Birmingham: Birmingham University Press, 2004), pp. 1–24; and Stuart Taberner, *German Literature of the 1990s and Beyond. Normalization and the Berlin Republic* (Rochester, NY: Camden House, 2005), pp. 1–32.

Drews been selecting fifteen years later, Grünbein would have caused him as little headache now as he did then. As the other essays in this volume show, Grünbein still offers readers and scholars much to consider after more than twenty years of publishing. As Emmerich aptly comments in his literary history of the GDR: 'In the early years, Grünbein's subject matter was of course the moribund GDR. That it did not remain his sole preoccupation, and that he was immune to any hint of *Ostalgie*, is testimony to his sovereign intellect, and this is reflected in his aesthetic achievements'.[77] In thirty years' time, when another editor comes to compile an anthology of poetry for the first half century of the Berlin Republic, Grünbein will be well represented, both for quality and significance. Yet his role as a *Wende* poet should not be underestimated, not least because his later writing has never quite shaken it off.[78] In 1991, Andreas Huyssen asked: 'Who, aside from some crazy poet, would ever have thought that one could dance on the Wall?'[79] Perhaps more than any other writer – novelist, dramatist or poet – Grünbein has shown quite how challenging it is to process that moment and its aftermath.[80]

---

77 Emmerich, *Kleine Literaturgeschichte der DDR*, p. 517.

78 See, for instance, Hans-Herbert Räkel, 'Bald bin ich vierzig, Sir', *Süddeutsche Zeitung*, 10 June 2002, p. 14, on the GDR poems in *Erklärte Nacht*; or Grünbein's autobiographical story about how he experienced the fall of the Wall, 'Der Weg nach Bornheim. Wie Rufus Rebhuhn vom Prenzlauer Berg den neunten November 1989 verbrachte. Eine autobiographische Erzählung von Durs Grünbein', *Die Zeit*, 6 November 2008, pp. 59–60. Tellingly, both the poems and the story remain resolutely distanced, the poetic voice never uttering the pronoun 'ich'.

79 Huyssen, 'After the Wall', p. 40.

80 Further on the complexities of history in Grünbein's oeuvre, see Amir Eshel, 'Diverging Memories? Durs Grünbein's Mnemonic Topographies and the Future of the German Past', *German Quarterly*, 74.4 (2001), 407–16; Aniela Knoblich, '"Luftstrom aus alten Städten". Geschichte und Erfahrung des Dichters bei Durs Grünbein', in *Erfahrung und Geschichte. Historische Sinnbildung im Pränarrativen*, ed. by Thiemo Breyer and Daniel Creutz (Berlin: de Gruyter, 2010), pp. 317–31; Hinrich Ahrend, *'Tanz zwischen sämtlichen Stühlen'. Poetik und Dichtung im lyrischen und essayistischen Werk Durs Grünbeins* (Würzburg: Königshausen & Neumann, 2007), pp. 278–320. For a theoretically sophisticated account of how time functions in Grünbein's post-*Wende* poems, see Johann Reißer, '"Langsam kommen die Uhren auf Touren, jede geht anders". Das Auseinanderfallen der Zeitordnungen in Durs Grünbeins Nach-Wende-Lyrik vor dem Hintergrund der Zeitkonzeption Gilles Deleuzes', in *Nach-Wende-Narrationen. Das wiedervereinigte Deutschland im Spiegel von Literatur und Film*, ed. by Gerhard Jens Lüdeker and Dominik Orth (Göttingen: V & R unipress, 2010), pp. 175–90.

Michael Eskin

Durs Grünbein and the European Tradition

Europe's Lover

On numerous occasions, Durs Grünbein has emphasized that he might best be considered a 'Dichter, der auf Deutsch schreibt' [a poet writing in German] rather than a strictly 'deutscher Dichter' [German poet], that his 'Blickwinkel ist immer der der UNESCO' [perspective is always that of UNESCO], and that, *as a poet*, he views himself, in a certain sense, as 'das Gewissen der Menschheit' [the conscience of humanity].[1] Playful-to-facetious-to-presumptuous as these avowals may sound, they do suggest an attempt on Grünbein's part to make a distinction: between the fact that he is undeniably a German poet in terms of birth, citizenship, native language and primary cultural background, *and* the concomitant fact that he is also inescapably emplaced within a world-wide web of historical-cultural relations that undermine and belie any kind of simplistic notion of national-cultural belonging based on such empirical contingencies as place of birth, passport, mother tongue, residence etc. Like Goethe, Heine, Rilke, Kafka and Celan – to name only a handful of his German-writing poetic forebears – Grünbein, it would appear, cannot easily be accommodated within a narrowly conceived framework of national literatures, expressly resisting such labelling. Thus, his characterization by the German media in the wake of the fall of the Berlin Wall as a figure of cultural integration for a reunified Germany in search of a national identity in post-Cold-War Europe is validated by his own, explicitly trans-national, self-presentation.[2]

---

1 For the first two quotations, see Durs Grünbein, *The Bars of Atlantis. Selected Essays*, ed. by Michael Eskin, trans. by John Crutchfield, Michael Hofmann and Andrew Shields (New York: Farrar, Straus and Giroux, 2010), p. x; for the second and third quotations, see '"Cadences in the Gaps of Time". The Poet, the Past, and *Porzellan*. Durs Grünbein in Interview with Michael Eskin and Christopher Young', trans. by Sarah Bowden (included in this volume). Unless otherwise stated, all translations are my own. Durs Grünbein has expressed the notion that he is an author writing in German rather than a strictly German author in multiple private and public conversations with the author and, most recently, at the Autorentage Schwalenberg, Germany (22–24 October 2010).

2 Here, I refer, for instance, to Gustav Seibt's seminal endorsement of Grünbein as 'the first poet to overcome the schism in German literature' and to Frank Schirrmacher's observation that Grünbein 'cannot be viewed as belonging either to the GDR or the FRG, being, rather, the first genuine voice of the new Germany'. See Gustav Seibt, 'Mit besseren Nerven als jedes Tier – Das Neue kommt über Nacht. Durs Grünbein, der naturgeschichtliche Blick und der Berliner Alltag', *Frankfurter Allgemeine Zeitung*, Literaturbeilage, 15 March 1994, p. 1; Frank Schirrmacher, 'Jugend.

Clearly, though, a poet's own avowals as to his cosmopolitanism and global consciousness (or his supporters' clarion calls on his behalf) do not yet mean that they are also borne out in practice. In other words, saying that you are a 'world poet' doesn't yet make you one, as Adam Kirsch has recently suggested in a review of Grünbein's work in English translation, observing that in his verse 'Grünbein often sounds much more sceptical of the cosmopolitan ideal' than his ostensible endorsement of it 'in his essays' would have us believe.[3]

The aim of this chapter, then, is to ask whether Grünbein actually practises what he preaches, and if so, why and in what sense we might indeed want to view him as a poet *writing in German* rather than simply a *German poet*. In pursuing a plausible answer to this question, I limit myself to inquiring into Grünbein's place within the European tradition in particular, leaving it to others to gauge his significance as part of what, since the age of Goethe, has come to be called 'Weltliteratur'.[4] My choice of focus is determined by considerations of pragmatic feasibility and, more importantly, by Grünbein's emphatic self-identification as a European. 'Und doch habe ich mich', he writes in the essay 'Europas Liebhaber' ['Europe's Lovers'],

> immer als Eingeborener dieses Kontinents betrachtet. Ich erwähne das, weil es auch andere gab, weil ich als Teil einer Bevölkerung aufwuchs, die eine Mauer vergessen gemacht hatte, daß sie irgendwann einmal europäisch war. Was sollte man tun, wenn einem das Herz für Europa schlug? Man kompensierte, wohl oder übel, den Verlust und gab sich im Alltag des sozialistischen Lagerlebens zufrieden mit dem, was Nietzsche Fernstenliebe genannt hat. Und so groß war diese Liebe, daß sie mich auch nachher noch weit hinaustrug über den provisorischen Zustand der deutschen Einheit. Reisen bildet, sagt man, manchmal aber kommt es auch einer Wurzelbehandlung gleich. Heute erst fühle ich mich, nach mehreren Amerikabesuchen, wieder als frischgebackener Europäer.

Büchner-Preis für Grünbein', *Frankfurter Allgemeine Zeitung*, 9 May 1995, p. 35; see also Michael Eskin, 'Body Language. Durs Grünbein's Aesthetics', *arcadia*, 37.1 (2002), 42–66 (p. 42).

3 See Adam Kirsch, 'Germany. The Poet After the Fall', *The New York Review of Books*, 57.15, 14 October 2010, pp. 53–57 (p. 56). The works discussed by Kirsch are: *Ashes for Breakfast. Selected Poems*, trans. by Michael Hofmann (New York: Farrar, Straus and Giroux, 2005); *The Bars of Atlantis*; and *Descartes' Devil. Three Meditations*, trans. by Anthea Bell (New York: Upper West Side Philosophers, 2010).

4 Famously, Goethe introduced the concept of 'Weltliteratur' [world literature] in a conversation with Johann Peter Eckermann (dated 31 January 1827): 'National-Literatur will jetzt nicht viel sagen, die Epoche der Weltliteratur ist an der Zeit' [National literature no longer means much, the age of world literature has begun]. Johann Peter Eckermann, *Gespräche mit Goethe in den letzten Jahren seines Lebens*, ed. by H. H. Houben (Leipzig: Brockhaus, 1925), p. 181. For an insightful contemporary treatment of the question of world literature, see David Damrosch, *What is World Literature?* (Princeton, NJ: Princeton University Press, 2003).

[I have always thought of myself as a native of this continent. I mention this because there were others and because I grew up among a people that had forgotten – hemmed in by a wall – that it had once been European. What could I do given that my heart was beating for Europe? I tried to compensate for the loss by resigning myself, amidst the daily grind in the labour camp of socialism, to what Nietzsche called 'love of the most distant'. So strong was my love that it later carried me far beyond the provisional state of German unity. Travelling is educational, they say; sometimes, though, it feels more like a root canal treatment. Not until today, with several extended visits to the US under my belt, do I feel like a new-born European.][5]

Following a brief survey of Grünbein's poetic topography, I go on to discuss what being European actually means for Grünbein, and conclude by homing in on the way his self-perception as a decidedly European poet can be said concretely to inform his poetic practice.

The Poet Adrift

In the recent manifesto poem 'Wenn kein Credo mehr gilt' ['When no Credo is Left'] Grünbein depicts the poet as aimlessly adrift in a sea of ignorance, lacking the navigational beacons of philosophical (and, by extension, scientific) truth as well as the guiding lights of what Jean-François Lyotard has dubbed 'grands récits', i.e. a culture's more or less clearly legible, constitutive 'grand narratives' (palpably captured in the poem's image of the shipwrecked epos):

Auf einem Ozean der Ignoranz
Treibt der Poet, ausgesetzt
Von den Schiffen der Philosophen [...]
In den Wellen verliert er sich,
Findet sich wieder auf hoher See,
Wo das Epos in Trümmer ging [...].

[In an ocean of ignorance / Drifts the poet, cast out / From the philosophers' ships [...] // Losing himself in the waves, / Finding himself on the high seas, / Where the epos shipwrecked [...].][6]

---

5 See Durs Grünbein, 'Europas Liebhaber', in *Antike Dispositionen. Aufsätze* (Frankfurt a. M.: Suhrkamp, 2005), pp. 318–27.

6 See Durs Grünbein, *Libellen in Liberia. Gedichte und Berichte*, ed. by Brigitte Labs-Ehlert (Detmold: Literaturbüro Ostwestfalen-Lippe, 2010), p. 25. On the concept of the 'grand récit', see Jean-François Lyotard, *La condition postmoderne. Rapport sur le savoir* (Paris: Les Éditions de Minuit, 1979), passim.

Taking at face value, for the sake of the present argument, Grünbein's conceit-*cum*-diagnosis of the poet's putative existential predicament (whose historical-cultural validity is not at issue here), we have as good a starting point as any for posing the question: what of the flotsam and jetsam of the presumably ship-wrecked epos (i.e. culture and tradition) might be floating into the purview of Grünbein's drifting poet? Or, put somewhat less metaphorically: what does Grünbein's poet find his bearings by, adrift on the high seas of existence? What are the remnants of his (and our?) culture's presumably once-intact and now-defunct grand narratives that might enable Grünbein, contrary to his poetic avowal, to be or feel *not quite* as lost at sea as he might have us believe? For the logic of Grünbein's conceit suggests that a more or less immediate awareness or memory of what has been lost is the metric that allows him to gauge his deviation from a presumably once-charted course in the first place.

To begin with, the very figure of the poet as sailor (and castaway) suggests that Grünbein's poet, for one, is not simply flailing his limbs, submerged up to his chin and desperately trying to stay afloat. Far from it: from the outset, he has been provided with a raft fully equipped with the 'sails of eloquence' that have already helped Cicero, Ovid, Horace, Virgil, Statius, Spenser and countless others to navigate through 'many a counter winde and tyde'.[7] In other words, in the very act of availing himself of the traditional figure of the poet as navigator, in casting himself as lost *at sea*, Grünbein has already made landfall – 'finding himself', as he puts it – on the shores constituted by those poets and artists that any reader of Grünbein's wide-ranging oeuvre will not fail to recognize as staking out precisely that 'grand narrative' which Grünbein claims has suffered shipwreck: the grand *European* narrative, above all, populated by such favourite personages of Grünbein's as Homer, Herodotus, Simonides, Seneca, Ovid, Horace, Juvenal, Dante, Descartes, Rembrandt, Spinoza, Hals, Averkamp, Shakespeare, Spenser, Goethe, Baudelaire, Rilke, Eliot, Benn, Celan, Mandelstam and Brodsky, as well as many other more or less 'usual suspects' defining the Western cultural canon.

I would like to single out only a few instances of Grünbein's *active*, hands-on engagement with the European tradition by way of 'documenting' that even if he were a non-European native he would *de jure* have to be considered a European

7 For an historical overview of the figuration of poetry in nautical terms, including a plethora of references to primary sources, from Cicero's 'sails of eloquence' (*Tusculanae disputationes*, iv, 5, 9) to Edmund Spenser's poetic ship that must weather 'many a counter winde and tyde' (*Faerie Queene*, vi, 12, 1), see Ernst Robert Curtius, *European Literature and the Latin Middle Ages*, trans. by Willard R. Trask (New York: Bollingen Foundation, 1953), pp. 128–30; see also Michael Eskin, 'Of Poets and Sailors. Celan, Grünbein, and Brodsky', *German Life and Letters*, 60.3 (2007), 315–28 (p. 315).

poet by the sheer force and quantity of canonical European voices resonating throughout his writings.

Let me begin with 'Wenn kein Credo mehr gilt'. If we listen to it closely, we cannot fail to hear the voice of Herodotus in Grünbein's portrayal of the poet as a latter-day Arion – Europe's 'most distinguished singer and musician of that date, and the man who first [...] composed and named the dithyramb', according to the Greek historian.[8] As the story goes, on his voyage from Taenarum back to Corinth, Arion, the 'world's most famous [and wealthy] singer', was forced by a crew of ill-intentioned sailors, who were after his money, 'either to kill himself if he wanted to be buried ashore, or to jump overboard'. After performing one final farewell tune aboard, Arion jumped but, like Grünbein's poet, did not perish. Far from it, in fact, as it was then that, as Herodotus recounts, the most 'extraordinary thing' happened: a dolphin – attracted by Arion's art or summoned by destiny? – 'picked up Arion and carried him back to Taenarum'. (Reading Grünbein's manifesto-poem with Herodotus in mind is particularly called for given that Grünbein has obviously already had recourse to Herodotus in his ruminations on 'Europas Liebhaber', which begins, as the title suggests, from Ovid's Herodotus-based account of the abduction of the Phoenician princess Europa in *Metamorphoses*.[9])

Singing here in four-part harmony with Herodotus and Grünbein we also unmistakeably hear the voices of Homer and Plato. Homer provides the ground bass to Grünbein's lead, which riffs on the *Odyssey*'s seminal meta-poetics of navigation and its perils, while Plato supplies Grünbein with one of the poem's central images: 'Schiffe der Philosophen'.[10] The backup vocals section, finally, is manned

8 For the story of Arion and the dolphin, see Herodotus, *Histories*, trans. by Aubrey de Sélincourt and John Marincola (New York: Penguin Putnam, 1996), pp. 10–11 (book 1, chapters 23–24); for Herodotus's account of the abduction of the Phoenician princess Europa 'probably [by the] Cretans', see *Histories*, p. 4 (book 1, chapter 2).

9 For Ovid's retelling of the story of Europa's kidnapping – this time by Zeus disguised a bull – see *Metamorphoses*, trans. by Frank Justus Miller, 2 vols (Cambridge, MA: Harvard University Press, 1999), I, pp. 118–21 (book 2, ll. 833–75). 'Der erste war Zeus', writes Grünbein in 'Europas Liebhaber', '[e]r trug sie herüber, die schöne Prinzessin, in der typischen Machogestalt eines Stiers' [The first one was Zeus. Shape-shifting into a bull – as befits a macho – he carried her across]. Grünbein, *Antike Dispositionen*, p. 318.

10 By Homer's 'metapoetics of navigation and its perils', I simply mean Homer's continuous reflection on the rhapsode's craft as part of the *Odyssey*'s plot, one of whose central components is precisely Odysseus's shipwreck, survival and multiple retellings of his adventures – at the Phaiakian court, say, or to Penelope upon his return (see especially *Odyssey*, book 6, ll. 240–309; book 7, ll. 264–369; book 18, ll. 124–64; book 22, ll. 330–55; book 23, ll. 310–43). Plato often uses the metaphor of the 'pilot' ('kubernetes') and his ship / sailors to illustrate any given point in Socrates' dialectics – here is one example: 'And what of the pilot – the pilot rightly so called – is he the ruler of the sailors or a sailor? ... We don't ... have to take into account the fact

by the likes of Baudelaire and Brodsky both of whom have extensively availed themselves of the juxtaposition of poetry and navigation, and both of whom Grünbein explicitly singles out as central reference points in his 'poetic trigonometry'.[11] The former's 'voyage' poems and the latter's 'Pis'mo v butylke' ['Letter in a Bottle'] in particular can be said to inform Grünbein's take on the subject of poetry and navigation as it plays out in 'Wenn kein Credo mehr gilt'.[12]

Going through the catalogue of Grünbein's aforementioned favourites more generally, we are presented with a veritable tableau vivant of 'Europe's Best' on Grünbein's poetic stage: Edmund Spenser speaks German in Grünbein's libretto for Henry Purcell's opera *The Faerie Queene*; Simonides, Cicero and Horace are explicitly credited as masters of memorization, rhetoric and poetics; Virgil and Statius are singled out both in their own right and as role models for one of Grünbein's most significant poetic alter egos – Dante, who supplies Grünbein with the master trope of the 'hell' of the modern world, feeding into his engagement with such ancient and modern metropolitan poets as Juvenal, Eliot and Mandelstam; Seneca – one of Grünbein's most memorable masks – helps Grünbein poetically to think through the twofold problem of mortality and transience; Rilke, Benn and Celan are Grünbein's key interlocutors as far as the first half of twentieth-cen-

that he actually sails in a ship'. Plato, *Republic*, trans. by Paul Shorey, 2 vols [Cambridge, MA: Harvard University Press, 2003], I, pp. 58–59 (341c–d). Thus, Grünbein's reference to the 'Schiffe der Philosophen' can be read both literally and figuratively.

11 Grünbein's references to Baudelaire and Brodsky throughout his writings are too numerous to be listed *in toto*; suffice it to mention *Grauzone morgens* (Frankfurt a. M.: Suhrkamp, 1988), p. 26; *Schädelbasislektion* (Frankfurt a. M.: Suhrkamp, 1991), p. 198; *Falten und Fallen* (Frankfurt a. M.: Suhrkamp, 1994), pp. 55–56; *Nach den Satiren* (Frankfurt a. M.: Suhrkamp, 1999), pp. 87–98; *Erklärte Nacht* (Frankfurt a. M.: Suhrkamp, 2002), p. 144. On Grünbein's notion of 'poetic trigonometry', see Grünbein, *Vom Stellenwert der Worte. Frankfurter Poetikvorlesung 2009* (Frankfurt a. M.: Suhrkamp, 2010), p. 31; (English translation) *The Vocation of Poetry*, trans. by Michael Eskin (New York: Upper West Side Philosophers, 2011), p. 31. On the significance of Baudelaire for Grünbein, see also Michael Eskin, 'Stimmengewirr vieler Zeiten. Grünbein's Dialogue with Dante, Baudelaire, and Mandel'shtam', *The Germanic Review*, 77.1 (2002), 34–50; on the significance of Brodsky for Grünbein, see Durs Grünbein and Dorothea von Törne, 'Mir kann die ganze Ostnostalgie gestohlen bleiben', *Wochenpost*, 27 April 1995, pp. 43–46; and Michael Eskin, *Poetic Affairs. Celan, Grünbein, Brodsky* (Stanford, CA: Stanford University Press, 2008), pp. 58–87. I further discuss Grünbein's engagement with Brodsky below. As far as Baudelaire's central role for Grünbein is concerned, it might also be of interest to the reader to know that a daguerreotype of Baudelaire is prominently displayed in Durs Grünbein's Berlin residence.

12 See Charles Baudelaire, 'Un voyage à Cythère' ['Voyage to Cythera'] and 'Le voyage' ['Voyage'], in *Les Fleurs du Mal / Die Blumen des Bösen* [*The Flowers of Evil*], trans. by Friedhelm Kemp (Munich: DTV, 1986), pp. 252, 284; see also Joseph Brodsky, *Novye Stansy k Avguste* [*New Stanzas to Augasta*] (Ann Arbor: Ardis, 1983), pp. 56–64.

tury German-language poetry is concerned – Rilke, above all as a model speech magician and poet of childhood, Benn as Büchner's heir and precursor to Grünbein's own practice of 'poetry as and of science', and Celan as the quintessential German-language poet of memory (and, thus, Simonides' heir); Descartes and his successor Spinoza figure prominently in the companion works *Der cartesische Taucher. Drei Meditationen* and *Vom Schnee, oder Descartes in Deutschland* (Grünbein's verse epic about Descartes's twelve-week sojourn in southern Germany at the beginning of the Thirty Years' War), both of which also make extensive thematic use of the legacy of Dutch painting during the so-called Little Ice Age (especially Rembrandt, Hals and Averkamp); Shakespeare, finally, is revered as the 'Schutzpatron aller Poeten' [patron saint of all poets], and is avowedly as central to Grünbein as to his most important classical German interlocutor, Goethe.[13]

Clearly, however, as a modus operandi or poetic method this kind of cultural appropriation in itself is not at all specific to Grünbein. As Seamus Heaney noted, there is nothing extraordinary about poets turning to the 'great masters of the

13 I beg for the reader's forgiveness for thus galloping through two thousand years of cultural and intellectual history to illustrate my point. I am also fully aware of the fact that Grünbein's dialogues with all of the authors and artists mentioned are far more complex and varied than I make them out to be for heuristic purposes only. Purcell's *The Faerie Queene* with Grünbein's German libretto premiered at the Bayerische Theaterakademie in Munich, on 2 November 2009; for Grünbein's engagement with Simonides, Cicero, Horace, Dante and Mandelstam, see for instance *Galilei vermißt Dantes Hölle und bleibt an den Maßen hängen. Aufsätze* (Frankfurt a. M.: Suhrkamp, 1996), pp. 18–33, 89–104; for Grünbein's recourse to Virgil and Statius, see for instance *Aroma. Ein römsiches Zeichenbuch* (Frankfurt a. M.: Suhrkamp, 2010), p. 95, and *Die Bars von Atlantis. Eine Erkundung in Vierzehn Tauchgängen* (Frankfurt a. M.: Suhrkamp, 2009), p. 42; for Grünbein's engagement with Goethe, Rilke, Benn, Celan, Eliot and Shakespeare, see, for instance, *Antike Dispositionen*, pp. 134–61, *Porzellan. Poem vom Untergang meiner Stadt* (Frankfurt a. M.: Suhrkamp, 2005), passim, and *Gedicht und Geheimnis. Aufsätze 1990–2006* (Frankfurt a. M.: Suhrkamp, 2007), pp. 135–54; for Grünbein's extensive dialogue with Seneca, see, for instance, Seneca, *Thyestes*, Lateinisch und deutsch, aus dem Lateinischen von Durs Grünbein, mit Materialien zur Übersetzung und zu Leben und Werk Senecas, ed. by Bernd Seidensticker (Frankfurt a. M.: Insel, 2002), especially pp. 111–14; for Grünbein's appropriation of the legacy of Dutch painting, see *Vom Schnee, oder Descartes in Deutschland* (Frankfurt a. M.: Suhrkamp, 2003), passim, and *Der cartesische Taucher. Drei Meditationen* (Frankfurt a. M.: Suhrkamp, 2008), pp. 39–144; *Descartes' Devil*, pp. 39–132. See also the following, insightful and informative monographs as a point of entry into Grünbein's complex appropriation of the Western tradition: Hinrich Ahrend, *'Tanz zwischen sämtlichen Stühlen'. Poetik und Dichtung im lyrischen und essayistischen Werk Durs Grünbeins* (Würzburg: Königshausen & Neumann, 2010); Sonja Klein, *'Denn alles, alles ist verlorne Zeit'. Fragment und Erinnerung im Werk von Durs Grünbein* (Bielefeld: Aisthesis, 2008); Michael Eskin, *Poetic Affairs*. Klein in particular devotes ample space to Grünbein's engagement with the visual arts.

past' depending on their 'artistic inclinations' and 'imaginative needs'.[14] In other words, the fact that Grünbein can be said to be a contemporary *poeta doctus*, heavy on the European side, doesn't yet distinguish him from any other of his modern peers who happen to show a high awareness of and engagement with the tradition they happen to have been born into, or been reared and come of age in.[15]

For Grünbein's recourse to the European canon – his 'distant readings' within the European tradition – to be unique in any heuristically interest-bearing sense and more than merely a display of erudition, they would have to evince certain traits or tendencies that could be said to be quintessentially 'Grünbein', specifically endemic to his poetic universe.[16] What are some of these traits and how do they manifest in Grünbein's practice as a poet?

Being European

In order to disclose those features of Grünbein's poetics that would make him an emphatically European poet, we first have to ask what 'European' actually means in the present context. Eschewing a general historical-philosophical discussion of the notions of 'Europe' and 'Europeanism' at this point, I want to focus on what 'being European' can be said to mean for Grünbein.[17]

Two of Grünbein's texts are especially pertinent when it comes to the question of his relation to und understanding of 'Europe': the 2003 essay 'Europas Liebhaber' (from which I have already quoted) and the three poetic-philosophical meditations published as *Der cartesische Taucher* in 2008. Let's take a chronological look at what Europe's self-proclaimed paramour Grünbein singles out about his love-interest. Among the numerous attractive features Grünbein purports to detect in 'Europa' and 'der europäische Mensch' [European man] – includ-

---

14 See Seamus Heaney, 'Envies and Identifications. Dante and the Modern Poet', in *The Poet's Dante. Twentieth-Century Responses*, ed. by Peter S. Hawkins and Rachel Jacoff (New York: Farrar, Straus and Giroux, 2001), p. 240.

15 On the *poeta doctus* in contemporary German poetry, see especially Karen Leeder, 'The "poeta doctus" and the New German Poetry. Raoul Schrott's *Tropen*', *The Germanic Review*, 77.1 (2002), 51–67.

16 On the notion of 'distant reading', see Franco Moretti, 'Conjectures on World Literature', *New Left Review*, 1 (2000), 54–68 (p. 57).

17 For insightful treatments of the twofold question of Europe and Europeanism, see for instance: Hans Magnus Enzensberger, *Ach Europa! Wahrnehmungen aus sieben Ländern* (Frankfurt a. M.: Suhrkamp, 1989); Peter Sloterdijk, *Falls Europa erwacht* (Frankfurt a. M.: Suhrkamp, 1994); Jeremy Rifkin, *The European Dream. How Europe's Vision of the Future is Quietly Eclipsing the American Dream* (New York: Tarcher / Penguin, 2005).

ing 'existentielle Neugier' [existential curiosity], 'geistiges Draufgängertum' [intellectual / spiritual derring-do], 'Charme' and 'Charisma' – one trait unmistakably stands out as the dominant one throughout 'Europas Liebhaber': Grünbein variously describes it as an 'erotischen Hang zur persönlichen Freiheit' [erotic penchant for personal freedom], a 'Verführung zur Freiheit' [seduction into freedom], and a 'Verlangen nach persönlicher Autonomie' [desire for personal autonomy].[18] In *Der cartesische Taucher*, Grünbein picks up the thread of 'Europas Liebhaber' and reiterates his conception of Europe and Europeanism as indelibly bound up with what he refers to as 'raumgreifender Freiheitssinn' [all-encompassing sense of liberty], 'geistige Freiheit' [intellectual / spiritual liberty] and 'Freiheit des Individuums', which I take to mean anything from 'individual freedom' or freedom of the individual, to 'autonomous subjectivity', to 'autonomy of mind'.[19]

Thus, when Grünbein pledges his allegiance to Europe and declares himself an 'europäischer Mensch', he seems to be aligning himself – above and beyond Europe's rich cultural and political history – with what he perceives as Europe's single most-important contribution to human history and culture: the very notion of individual freedom and the autonomy of the subject. In other words, 'Europe' and 'being European' for Grünbein emerge as *ethical* categories; being European means, Grünbein suggests, adopting a certain moral attitude or paradigm predicated on the core values of individual freedom and personal autonomy.[20]

Irrespective of whether this ethical conception of Europe as the seedbed of freedom can be said to make sense historically and politically (after all, even a cursory look at Europe's history, from the Roman Empire to the Third Reich, would seem to relativize the notion that Europe may have had a *de facto* purchase on individual freedom and personal autonomy insofar as both are always also a function of politics), it is precisely this ethical view of what being European is presumably all about that articulates what I take to be Grünbein's idiosyncratic twist on and appropriation of the far-from-homogeneous and linear tradition we call

18 See 'Europas Liebhaber', pp. 320–23.

19 See Durs Grünbein, *Der cartesische Taucher*, pp. 29, 37, 86, 100, 107; *Descartes' Devil*, pp. 30, 37, 83, 96, 102.

20 On 'freedom' as an essentially ethical category, see for instance: F. W. J. Schelling, *Über das Wesen der menschlichen Freiheit*, ed. by Horst Fuhrmans (Stuttgart: Reclam, 1983); Immanuel Kant, *Kritik der praktischen Vernunft / Grundlegung zur Metaphysik der Sitten*, ed. by Martina Thom (Leipzig: Reclam, 1989), e.g. pp. 9–10: 'Der Begriff der Freiheit, sofern dessen Realität durch ein apodiktisches Gesetz der praktischen Vernunft bewiesen ist, macht nun den Schlußstein von dem ganzen Gebäude eines Systems der reinen, selbst der spekulativen, Vernunft aus' [The concept of freedom, insofar as its reality has been proven by an apodictic law of practical reason, is the capstone of the entire edifice of a system of pure, and even speculative, reason].

'European'. In other words, what can be said to make Grünbein an emphatically European author is not so much the fact that he is easily identified as such based on objective external criteria relating to his person as well as objective internal criteria relating to his works, but, rather, the fact that in declaring himself European he also actively shapes the very notion of Europe in 'his own image', so to speak, by idiosyncratically positing it as way of life, an ethics, as opposed merely a geopolitical-cultural-historical space. That is to say, Grünbein does not simply avail himself of the received notion of 'Europe'; rather, he tweaks and recreates in the light of his own self-image as one for whom 'freedom' in its various forms appears to be the preeminent value. Being European, Grünbein suggests, means living and acting European in the specific sense of Europe as the embodiment of a particular ethical code that emphatically valorizes freedom and autonomy. (That Grünbein's very notion of the autonomous individual may itself be derived from such proto-European thinkers as, for instance, Descartes, Kant and Husserl, doesn't in any way diminish the thrust of what I take to be his particular contribution to our thinking about Europe in ethical terms above all.)

An 'Ethics of Europe'

How does all this translate into Grünbein's poetic practice? To what extent is it plausible – given the parameters established by Grünbein himself – to call him a *European* poet in the sense elaborated? I would like to conclude my essay by looking at a handful of works that in my view most overtly articulate Grünbein's 'ethics of Europe' in poetic form, thus poetically instantiating and vindicating his self-conception as a European poet.

Let me start the final section of this chapter by noting that the lodestar of personal freedom and autonomy can be said to have guided Grünbein's poetic project – and this means his *Dichterdasein* as such – since long before he explicitly articulated what I have dubbed his 'ethics of Europe'.[21] It first made its appearance in the guise of what Grünbein refers to as his 'Poetik des Sarkasmus, wie sie mir seit meinen frühesten Schreibversuchen den Ton diktiert' [poetics of sarcasm, which has set the tone for me since my earliest attempts at writing] –

21 For Grünbein's comprehensive, existential notion of 'Dichterdasein', see Olga Olivia Kasaty and Durs Grünbein, 'Ein Gespräch mit Durs Grünbein. Berlin, 26. August 2005', in Olga Olivia Kasaty, *Entgrenzungen. Vierzehn Autorengespräche über Liebe, Leben und Literatur* (Munich: Text + Kritik, 2007), pp. 73–99 (especially pp. 78–79). See also Michael Eskin, 'Wake-Up Call. Durs Grünbein with Rilke, Descartes, and Pushkin', *Poetica*, 41.1–2 (2009), 189–217 (especially pp. 189–91).

a poetics, that is, which is predicated on an uncompromising sense of scepticism, irony and cynicism on the part of the poet, whose task it is, as Grünbein explains in *Das erste Jahr. Berliner Aufzeichnungen* à propos the meaning of the Greek *sarkazein*, 'das Fleisch von den Knochen zu trennen' [to tear the flesh from the bones] and 'mit Zähnen, Händen und Messern, zu Knochen, Gräte und Mark [vorzudringen]' [to penetrate with fangs, hands and knives to the very marrow].[22] Manifest with particular vividness, for instance, in such cycles as 'O Heimat, zynischer Euphon' ['Oh, Homeland, You Cynical, Euphonic Sound'], 'Portrait des Künstlers als junger Grenzhund' ['Portrait of the Artist as a Young Border Dog'], 'Mensch ohne Großhirn' ['Man Without Cerebrum'], *Den teuren Toten*, 'Nach den Satiren' ['After the Satires'], and 'Europa nach dem letzten Regen' ['Europe after the Last Rains'] – it is this *poetics of sarcasm* that, in and through its non-conformist thrust and sense of aesthetic protest, can be said to anticipate Grünbein's 'ethics of Europe'.[23] Picking up on the classical image of the cynic / sceptic as a renegade 'dog' and aligning himself with Osip Mandelstam's and Joseph Brodsky's uncompromising stance as avowedly cosmopolitan poets in a repressive, nationalist environment, Grünbein, too, can be said to have cast himself from the beginning as a Mandelstamian-Brodskyan angry 'poet-*raznochinets*', never granting himself the 'status of the victim'.[24] 'Einer, der mir [...] viel gegeben hat', Grün-

22 See Durs Grünbein, *Vom Stellenwert der Worte*, p. 9; *The Vocation of Poetry*, p. 15; see also *Das erste Jahr. Berliner Aufzeichnungen* (Frankfurt a. M.: Suhrkamp, 2001), p. 63.

23 See Durs Grünbein, *Schädelbasislektion*, pp. 93–107, 109–112; *Falten und Fallen*, pp. 69–80; *Den teuren Toten*, passim; *Nach den Satiren*, pp. 93–114, 143–53.

24 Famously, Osip Mandelstam conceived of himself as a poet-*raznochinets* ('dissenter'), and Joseph Brodsky emphasized the importance 'at all costs [...] to avoid granting yourself the status of the victim'. See Osip Mandelstam, *Sobranie sočinenij*, ed. by Pavel Nerler and others, Mandelstam Society, 4 vols (Moscow: Art-Biznes-Tsentr, 1993–97), III, p. 176; Joseph Brodsky, *On Grief and Reason. Essays* (New York: Farrar, Straus and Giroux, 1995), p. 144. On the classical image of the cynic / sceptic as a dog, see, especially, Diogenes Laertius's lives of Antisthenes, Diogenes and Pyrrho: Diogenes Laertius, *Lives of Eminent Philosophers*, trans. by R. D. Hicks, 2 vols (Cambridge, MA: Harvard University Press, 2000), II, pp. 2–85, 474–518 (especially pp. 5, 13–15, 29, 35, 41, 47–49, 57, 63, 79, 81, 475–77, 481–83, 487). It should be remembered that the 'cynic way of life' used to mean above all a life determined by 'hardihood', 'disregard of feeling' and 'courage' (Diogenes Laertius, pp. 5, 55). Incidentally, the Greek term *kunismos* ('cynicism') derives from *kúon* ('dog'). I should note that in speaking of cynicism and scepticism in the same breath, I do not by any means aim to suggest that the two doctrines are identical, but, rather, that Grünbein's overall 'sarcastic' poetic stance can be broadly characterized as partaking of both the sceptical and the cynical positions. Grünbein's 'Portrait des Künstlers als junger Grenzhund' also alludes to Dylan Thomas's *Portrait of the Artist as a Young Dog* (London: Dent, 1940) – a topic I do not address in this essay. For an in-depth discussion of Grünbein's dialogue with Mandelstam and Brodsky, see Michael Eskin, *Poetic Affairs*, pp. 58–87, 131–47.

bein surmised in a 1995 interview, 'war der russische Dichter Joseph Brodsky – seine Haltung, sich unter keinen Umständen zum Opfer stempeln zu lassen. Das wurde [...] zum Leitmotiv [...] Grund aller meiner [...] Zynismen' [One who meant a lot to me was the Russian poet Joseph Brodsky – his refusal to be cast as a victim under any circumstance became [my] motto [...] the basis for all my [...] cynicisms].[25]

It is in his engagement with the legacy of René Descartes, however, that Grünbein's 'ethics of Europe' most palpably comes to the fore. 'Es gab keinen besseren Europäer als [Descartes]' [There was no better European than Descartes], Grünbein writes in *Der cartesische Taucher* (affirmatively quoting Henri Bergson's assessment of his predecessor); and what makes Descartes the 'best European', according to Grünbein, is his possession, in the highest degree, of precisely that characteristic which Grünbein has adduced as constituting the core of 'European man' – an inveterate desire for 'personal freedom' and 'autonomy':[26] '[...] der Name ["Descartes"]', Grünbein explains, '[ist] ein Inbegriff [...] für das freie Subjekt, den autonom denkenden und handelnden Menschen' [the name 'Descartes' quintessentially signifies [...] the free subject, the autonomously thinking and acting human being].[27]

The fact, then, that in *Vom Schnee, oder Descartes in Deutschland* and *Der cartesische Taucher. Drei Meditationen* Grünbein devotes two entire major works – works moreover which he considers his combined most important achievement to date as a poet – to Descartes can be read as eloquent testimony to the determination with which he appears to be pursuing the 'cause' of 'Europe' and 'European man' on poetic grounds.[28] This is not at all to suggest that Durs Grünbein ought to be considered a kind of propaganda poet along the lines of Virgil under Augustus. It is simply not to lose sight of the important fact that, as Grünbein has emphasized, his poetics is also always an ethics and that the latter, in turn, can be said to be indelibly bound up with the question of 'Europe' – something that is saliently evidenced for instance in Grünbein's idiosyncratic reading of Descartes through the prism of Rilke, as I would like to demonstrate in conclusion.

In a 2007 interview, Grünbein complained that '[d]er Text wird heute als Gegenstand des Konsums begriffen; Texte werden konsumiert wie Speisen und

25 See Grünbein and von Törne, 'Mir kann die ganze Ostnostalgie gestohlen bleiben'.

26 See Durs Grünbein, *Der cartesische Taucher*, p. 33; *Descartes' Devil*, p. 34.

27 See Durs Grünbein, *Der cartesische Taucher*, p. 86; *Descartes' Devil*, p. 84.

28 See Michael Eskin, 'Tauchen mit Descartes. Gespräch mit Durs Grünbein', *Sinn und Form*, 63.3 (2011), 389–402. For an abbreviated version of this conversation, see Michael Eskin and Durs Grünbein, '*Descartes' Devil*. Durs Grünbein im Gespräch mit Michael Eskin', *Trans-Lit2*, 16.1 (2010), 5–9 (p. 5).

Modeartikel, und sie bilden nur für die wenigsten die Aufforderung – ändere dein Leben, du mußt dein Leben ändern' [nowadays, literary texts are treated as objects for consumption; they are being consumed like food or fashion, and only very few readers are attuned to the call they issue: change your life, you must change your life].[29] What is significant in the present context about Grünbein's alignment with Rilke's ethical conception of art as expressed in his sonnet 'Archaischer Torso Apollos' ['Archaic Torso of Apollo'], which famously ends with the injunction 'Du mußt dein Leben ändern' [You must change your life], is that in *Vom Schnee oder Descartes in Deutschland* – Grünbein's poetic exploration of the life and thought of René Descartes against the backdrop of the 'Schrecken des dreißigjährigen Krieges'[30] [ravages of the Thirty Years' War] – it is repeated almost verbatim in the context of a passage that explicitly deals with the question of 'Europas Zukunft' in light of the ravages of war:

> Mag dort der Rabe auf dem Aas Europas Zukunft deuten –
> Du mußt, René, dein Leben ändern. Hier und heute.
>
> [Let the raven there perched on its carrion divine Europe's future –
> You, René, must change your life. Here, today.][31]

In order to appreciate the full significance of these lines in the context of my argument and, more importantly, in the context of Grünbein's ethical poetics, we have to bear in mind that, as I have documented elsewhere, *Vom Schnee* as a whole is premised on a sustained narratological charade, which intentionally blurs the discursive, psychological, ontological and pragmatic boundaries not only between its three main protagonists – Descartes, his valet Gillot and an unspecified narrator – but also between text and context, life and literature, the implied author *and* the real author himself. Both the fictional Descartes and his fictional valet, as I have argued, can plausibly be read as the poet's own master masks or mouthpieces, allowing him to extrovert the process of 'poetic thinking' through a sustained imaginary conversation between two historical, yet also wholly invented, figures.[32]

---

29 See Olga Olivia Kasaty, *Entgrenzungen*, p. 94.
30 See Durs Grünbein, '*Vom Schnee*. Vorrede, Vorstudien, Nachträge', *Sinn und Form* 56.1 (2004), 100–107 (p. 100).
31 See Durs Grünbein, *Vom Schnee*, p. 69. The 'question of Europe' is raised throughout *Vom Schnee* (see, for instance, pp. 65, 67, 94–96).
32 On Grünbein's narrative charades in *Vom Schnee*, see also especially Michael Eskin, 'Descartes of Metaphor. On Durs Grünbein's *Vom Schnee*', in *Schaltstelle. Neue deutsche Lyrik im Dialog*, ed. by Karen Leeder (Amsterdam: Rodopi, 2007), pp. 163–179; and 'Wake-up Call'.

Let me adduce only one – albeit central – passage from *Vom Schnee* by way of illustration of what I mean by Grünbein's narratological charades (following the poet's own designation of the verse epic as a 'Bilderrätsel' [picture puzzle]), before again picking up the thread of Grünbein's juxtaposition of Descartes and Rilke in connection with the question of 'Europas Zukunft'. (While I cannot at this point – due to spatial constraints – take the reader through all the steps necessary fully to grasp Grünbein's intentional blurring of the boundaries between literature and life, text and context, real and implied authorship throughout *Vom Schnee*, I hope to offer at least a smattering of what is going on in the text):[33]

> (1) So wahr ich sitz hier, träumend, wie ich krank darniederlieg ...
> (2) Nein umgekehrt: so wahr ich lieg und träum, ich sitze dort
> (3) Im Winterrock beim Feuer, und die Hand da auf dem Tisch
> (4) Fühlt das Papier ... so weiß ich: Dies ist mein Leib.
> (5) *Hoc corpus meum*. Wo ich bin, wird nie ein andrer sein.
> (6) Auf engstem Raum, gottlob bin ich nicht kleinzukriegen.
> (7) Solang ich denke. 'Vorsicht Freund, wer sagt dir denn,
> (8) Daß dies kein Traum, kein Nachbild ist aus andern Zeiten?
> (9) Vom Schnee verwirrt, wer weiß, bildst du dir ein im Schlaf
> (10) Du sitzt am Tisch'. 'Und lieg im Bett, mein eigner Biograph?'

> [(1) As certain as it is that I am sitting here, dreaming about how I am lying there, sick ... / (2) No, it's the other way around: as certain as it is that I am lying here, dreaming about how I am sitting there / (3) In my winter gown by the fire, and my hand is resting on the table, / (4) feeling the paper ... I know: this is my body. / (5) *Hoc corpus meum*. Where I am, no one else will ever be. / (6) In the tiniest of quarters I am, thank god, not to be defeated, / (7) as long I am thinking. 'Watch out, my friend, who says / (8) That all this isn't but a dream, an after image from a different age? / (9) Confused by the snow, perhaps, you are only imagining in your sleep / (10) That you are sitting at the table'. 'Right, and that I'm lying in bed, my own biographer, as well?']³⁴

Forgoing a discussion of Grünbein's appropriation of Descartes's *Discourse on Method* and *First Meditation* in this passage – palpably bespoken by the poet's emphasis on dreaming, verbatim citations of Descartes's text (e.g. '*Hoc corpus*

33 '*Vom Schnee, oder Descartes in Deutschland*', Grünbein writes, 'ist mancherlei: ein Bilderrätsel, eine philosophische Unterhaltung, eine Hommage an die kälteste Jahreszeit und an die Lehre von der Brechung des Lichts. Ein Bericht von den Schrecken des dreißigjährigen Krieges, das Protokoll von der Geburt des Rationalismus aus dem Geiste des Schnees' [*On Snow, or Descartes in Germany* is many things at once: a picture puzzle, a philosophical conversation, an homage to the coldest season and the doctrine of the refraction of light, a report on the ravages of the Thirty Years' War, the minutes of the birth of rationalism from the spirit of snow]. Grünbein, '*Vom Schnee*. Vorrede, Vorstudien, Nachträge', p. 100.
34 See Durs Grünbein, *Vom Schnee*, p. 140.

meum', '*Solang ich denke*'), and the mention of 'engstem Raum' (a reference to the tiny heated room near the city of Ulm where the philosopher was famously cooped up for twelve weeks in the winter of 1619–20 and where his vocation as a philosopher was revealed to him in a series of dreams) – I would like to direct the reader's attention to what appears to be the virtual impossibility of deciding who is actually speaking in these lines.[35] Is it the implied (or real) author or narrator or the fictional Descartes himself who 'remembers' or 'visualizes' or 'telescopes' himself 'into' his deathbed (l. 1) at Queen Christina's court in Sweden, where the real Descartes died in 1650? And who is the one addressing the speaker as 'friend' (l. 7)? Surely, not his servant, for this would mean overstepping the boundaries of etiquette. Could it be the narrator or implied (or real) author, the one who is the subject of the speaker's – whoever he may be – dream about himself (ll. 1–2)? And is the one asking the final question *within* quotation marks the same personage who speaks *without* quotation marks?[36]

Let me stop my questions here and simply acknowledge the text's own methodological pointer as far as any attempts on the reader's part at solving the riddles it poses might be concerned: aren't they all doomed to failure in light of

35 Descartes's original reads: '[...] ut jam me hîc esse, foco assidere, hyemali togâ esse indutum, chartam istam manibus contrectare, & similia. Manus verò has ipsas, totumque hoc corpus meum esse, quâ ratione posset negari [...] non sim homo qui soleam nocti dormire, & eadem omnia in somnis pati?' [that I am here, sitting by the fire, wearing a winter dressing-gown, holding this piece of paper in my hands and so on. Again how could it be denied that these hands or this whole body are mine? [...] Am I not a human being who sleeps at night and experiences all that in his dreams?]. René Descartes, *Meditationes de prima philosophia / Meditationen über die Erste Philosophie*, trans. by Gerhart Schmidt [Stuttgart: Reclam, 1986], pp. 64–65; *The Philosophical Writings of Descartes*, trans. by John Cottingham and others, 3 vols (Cambridge: Cambridge University Press, 1984–91), II, p. 18). For Descartes's depiction of the 'poêle' [heated room] in which he was staying while in Germany in the winter of 1619–20, see *Discours de la méthode suivi d'extraits de la Dioptrique, des Météores, de la Vie de Descartes par Baillet, du Monde, de l'Homme et des Lettres*, ed. by Geneviève Rodis-Lewis (Paris: Garnier-Flammarion, 1992) p. 33. It is well known that while Descartes did have a valet named Gillot in the 1630s, in the winter of 1619–20 he was, on his own testimony, sojourning in Germany by himself. The historical Gillot was born in 1614 and was, as Descartes wrote to Constantijn Huygens on 9 March 1638 and to Marin Mersenne on 31 March 1638, respectively, 'le premier et presque le seul disciple que j'ai jamais eu [et] presque celui du monde qui sait le plus de ma Méthode' [the first and only real student I've ever had [and] virtually the only person in the world who knows as much about my method as I do]. René Descartes, *Correspondances*, ed. by Charles Adam and Guy Milhaud, 8 vols (Paris: Gallimard, 1936–63), II, pp. 169, 218.

36 Interestingly, addressing another as 'friend' is not only a rhetorical staple throughout Grünbein's poetry, but also an idiosyncrasy in real life (for instance, in his correspondence with the author). See especially Michael Eskin, *Poetic Affairs*, pp. 71–87.

the confusion caused by the snow – 'Vom Schnee verwirrt' (l. 9)? Even so, however, one thing has become clear, namely, that whenever Grünbein has Descartes speak, it is not at all clear if it isn't Grünbein himself who 'fühl[t] das Papier' while writing about the philosopher, whom he explicitly refers to as his 'Doppelgänger' elsewhere in *Vom Schnee*.[37]

And so – to return to Grünbein's triangulation of Descartes and Rilke ('Mag dort der Rabe auf dem Aas Europas Zukunft deuten – / Du mußt, René, dein Leben ändern. Hier und heute') – it could be argued, in view of *Vom Schnee*'s narrative convolutions, that: (1) in having the fictional René Descartes address himself (read also: in addressing himself through the mask of Descartes) in Rilke's words, which have come to epitomize the ethical thrust of poetry and art in general, Grünbein poetically stages (and thus highlights) precisely that thrust. The fact that Descartes and Rilke share the same first name – Rainer Maria Rilke having been born René – adds an onomastic twist to Grünbein's juxtaposition of the poet and the philosopher. (2) In doing so in the immediate vicinity of raising the question of 'Europe's future', Grünbein links the ethics of poetry to the latter, thereby underscoring that his very own *Dichterdasein* ought to be viewed as inseparable from the question of Europe and being European.

Thus, if Grünbein can be said to be a European poet above and beyond the contingencies of birth, language, culture and residence, it is because he has made the question of Europe, understood as a mode of being and a way of life, an integral part of his poetic practice. In choosing *poetically* to impersonate the man whom he considers the 'best European', Grünbein suggests that his *very being as a poet* ought to be taken as European through and through.

The question of 'Grünbein and the European Tradition' has revealed itself as far more intricate than its historical-genealogical orientation might have suggested. That Grünbein is part and parcel of the European tradition understood as a diachronic cultural-political system characterized by certain political, religious, and socio-cultural traits is a given. What can be said to make him a truly (if idiosyncratically) *European* poet, though, is his adoption of an 'ethics of Europe' as a core constituent of his poetics. And it is on the basis of such an approach to Grünbein as a *European* poet that he may indeed justly be considered both a German poet and a poet who merely happens to be writing in German.

---

37 See Durs Grünbein, *Vom Schnee*, p. 32. I should note that engaging in an in-depth discussion of the question of the continuity between the real author and his textual manifestations (as an implied author, narrator, character, etc.) would take me beyond the confines of my present argument. I have addressed this and related questions (with recourse to theorists such as Wayne C. Booth and Boris Tomashevsky, among many others) in 'Descartes of Metaphor'; 'Wake-up Call'; and *Poetic Affairs*.

Ian Cooper

Grünbein and Anglo-American Poetry. Dickinson, Pound, Larkin

Poetry written in English has an undeniably important place in Durs Grünbein's work. Indeed the list of poets in English to whom Grünbein in some way refers, or whose presence has been noted in his writing, far exceeds the scope of any approach to his poetry aiming to do more than enumerate: it includes Shakespeare, poets of the nineteenth century (Dickinson, Hopkins), many of the twentieth (Eliot, Pound, Auden, Carlos Williams, Stevens, Larkin, Brodsky) as well as various contemporary figures (Ashbery, Heaney, Paterson).[1] To take the role of these writers seriously means understanding their relation to each other in order to grasp their significance for a reading of Grünbein and the characteristic themes of his work – poetry and the body, poetry as 'address' and 'conversation', the place of history.

This essay examines Grünbein's treatment of these themes with primary reference to three poets, two American and one English, who bear with special pertinence on his concerns: Emily Dickinson, Ezra Pound and Philip Larkin. The grouping has a historical coherence of its own, revealing a trajectory in the relation of poetry and presence, or in the understanding of poetry as what the modern German tradition calls world-disclosure: from the fraught religious meditations of Dickinson, through the aesthetic Modernism of Pound, to the evasions and absences of Larkin's English elegiac sublime. Grünbein engages with these poets variously through allusion, translation and critical appreciation, and discussing their role allows us to reflect on Grünbein's connections to other poets in English, too, as well as on patterns and ideas which take us far beyond exclusive concern with their own work, and into the deeper context of affinities and assumptions underlying Grünbein's poetry. For this constellation intersects with the German background on which Grünbein draws: the figure linking most clearly Dickinson's lyric subjectivity – powerfully and conflictingly spiritual, haunted by death and finitude – to the Modernist universe of quasi-redemptive artistry, is

---

1 For a selection of critical accounts discussing Grünbein's relation to individual figures mentioned here, see Florian Berg, *Das Gedicht und das Nichts. Über Anthropologie und Geschichte im Werk Durs Grünbeins* (Würzburg: Königshausen & Neumann, 2007), p. 29; Michael Eskin, *Poetic Affairs. Celan, Grünbein, Brodsky* (Stanford: Stanford University Press, 2008); Sonja Klein, *'Denn alles, alles ist verlorne Zeit'. Fragment und Erinnerung im Werk von Durs Grünbein* (Bielefeld: Aisthesis, 2008), p. 146; Alexander Müller, *Das Gedicht als Engramm. Memoria und Imaginatio in der Poetik Durs Grünbeins* (Oldenburg: Igel, 2004), pp. 35–36.

Nietzsche. And Nietzsche is himself heir to a Romantic sensibility of which one much later, culturally specific expression in poetry is Larkin.

The German intellectual background involving Nietzsche is also a German poetic background involving, for instance, Hölderlin, Rilke and – pre-eminently for Grünbein – Paul Celan. What is the nature of the relation between the various English-speaking figures and Celan, from whom Grünbein derives much of his own conception of poetry? Though Grünbein traces this conception ultimately to Mandelstam, it is in Celan that central terms such as 'presence' and 'voice' are given fullest explication; and it is Celan, as a poet writing in German, who is most immediately taken up, by reception and cultural osmosis, into Grünbein's work. We may wonder, however, whether Grünbein's professions of poetic allegiance, simultaneously to Celan and to a figure such as Pound, can represent a straightforward position, and we may ask, therefore, what lies behind the characteristic claim of Grünbein's work to 'polyphonic' multiplicity, drawing such figures together in moments of poetic 'presence'.[2] By examining Grünbein's relation to Anglo-American poetry in the context of the modern German lyric as represented by Celan, it is possible to understand better, and more critically, Grünbein's own presuppositions.

Syllable and Sound

In a collaborative book project published in 2000, which expresses Grünbein's abiding interest in bodily science (particularly neurology), he provides a translation of a poem by Emily Dickinson. As well as explicitly treating the subject of the brain, Dickinson's poem has a characteristic movement of expansion and narrowing, drawing together identity and otherness. Grünbein's translation follows it closely:

The Brain is – wider than the Sky – For – put them side by side – The one the other will include With ease – and You – beside –	Weiter als Himmel – ist das Hirn – Denn – leg sie Seit an Seit – Nimmt dieses jenen leicht noch auf Und Dich – wie nebenbei –
The brain is deeper than the sea – For – hold them – Blue to Blue – The one the other will absorb – As Sponges – Buckets – do –	Das Hirn ist tiefer als das Meer – Denn – halt sie Blau an Blau – Wie Schwämme – Eimer – absorbieren Saugt eins das andre auf –

2 See Durs Grünbein, 'Mir kann die ganze Ostnostalgie gestohlen bleiben', in *Wochenpost*, 27 April 2005, pp. 43–46 (p. 44).

The Brain is just the weight of God –	Das Hirn wiegt grad soviel wie Gott –
For – Heft them – Pound for Pound –	Denn – stemm sie – Gramm für Gramm –
And they will differ – if they do –	Das kontrastiert – wenn überhaupt –
As Syllable from Sound –	Wie Silbe hier und Klang –[3]

In Dickinson the brain is an opening to great width and depth, and at the same time brings these back to the physical locus of consciousness which grasps and so in a sense exceeds them. There is an ambivalence in Dickinson's lines, though, which in Grünbein is flattened. Where Dickinson's 'just the weight of God' can be construed as suggesting both that God and the brain are exactly ('just') identical in weight, and that the brain is simply ('just') God's pressing in on the physical world through consciousness, Grünbein sounds only the first possibility: 'Das Hirn wiegt grad soviel wie Gott'. In his version of the line there is no (even ambiguous) breaking open of nature; presence is coterminous with the brain's physical – weighty – extent. But Grünbein is attentive to the formal tautness of Dickinson's poem, and to the typically deceptive simplicity which it produces (to which Celan, in his own translations of Dickinson, richly responded). Those qualities associated with Dickinson can also be felt in some of Grünbein's pared-down verses in *Schädelbasislektion*, his own most sustained poetic reflection on the physical determinations of subjectivity, and especially on the brain:

Der Tag davor, die Nacht, der Tag danach,
So absolut getrennt durch Exegese,
Dem Ende aller Trends im Großen Trema,
Sind sie den Hemisphären gleich
Erstarrt, objektlos, unumkehrbar zwei
Wie nach dem Schnitt die Nervenbahnen,
Ins Blaue tastend wie das Wort *Läsion*.
Die beiden Apfelhälften, stummer Kern.

[The day before, the night, the day after / – Separated so absolutely by exegesis – / The end of all movement in the Great Diaeresis, / They are like the hemispheres / Rigidified, without object, irreversibly two / Like nerve tracts after the incision, / Feeling their way to blue like the word *lesion*. / The two halves of the apple, mute core.][4]

3 *The Complete Poems of Emily Dickinson*, ed. by Thomas H. Johnson (Boston: Little, Brown, 1960), no. 632 (references to Dickinson's poems follow this edition and give Johnson's numbering). Grünbein's translation appears in *Gehirn und Denken. Kosmos im Kopf*, ed. by Deutsches Hygiene-Museum, in cooperation with Via Lewandowsky and Durs Grünbein (Ostfildern-Ruit: Hatje Cantz, 2000), p. 17.

4 Durs Grünbein, 'Die Leeren Zeichen', in *Schädelbasislektion* (Frankfurt a. M.: Suhrkamp, 1991), p. 72 (ll. 4–8).

Grünbein's poem of halving, in which a line such as 'Sind sie den Hemisphären gleich' is Dickinsonian both in its rhythm and in the simultaneity of sameness and distinction which its emphases suggest, produces a variation on Dickinson's own themes of space and mental physiology in 'The Brain is wider than the Sky' – the association of Grünbein's 'hemispheres' is at once geographic and neural. And the presence of Dickinson may extend beyond that; Grünbein's 'Hemisphären [...] unumkehrbar' have a recognizable precursor in a poem in which Dickinson says: 'The Earth reversed her Hemispheres – / I touched the Universe'.[5] Where Dickinson's turning hemispheres reveal to her the absoluteness of terrestrial finitude ('and I alone – / A Speck upon a Ball'),[6] Grünbein's halves are irreversible in their relentless disclosing of a bodily, nervous substratum underlying the perception of time ('der Tag [...] die Nacht'). The sense of nervous exposure, apparently derived in part from Dickinson (though scarcely with regard to the dominant theological concerns of Dickinson's poems), is one basis for the understanding of history which occupies Grünbein's later work, and which he sought to theorize in his speech on receiving the Georg Büchner Prize.[7] The body laid bare as a complex of nerves is one of Grünbein's earliest poetic themes, and it is arguably the cause, in his work, of a lasting ambivalence in the relationship between the dissected object and the role of the (poet as) dissector. (That ambivalence is ultimately Nietzschean in origin – issuing, in the form Grünbein receives it, from Nietzsche's own account of language and metaphor as nerve reflexes.[8]) Dickinson's explorations of finitude are for Grünbein part (with Büchner and Nietzsche) of a nineteenth-century nexus in which the claims of material existence achieve descriptive power. She provides colouring for what he thinks of as historical consciousness founded in its own physical constitution, and that colour is blue: in Dickinson the shade of the brain which holds the immensities of the sea ('Blue to Blue') – in Grünbein of both the incised nervous system and the metallic word ('lesion') with which the poem probes it.

There are other respects in which *Schädelbasislektion* reveals a connection with Dickinson, though this must be seen also in a wider context. Grünbein's interest in the body further expresses itself in a scattered sequence of contemporary

---

5 Dickinson, *Complete Poems,* no. 378 (ll. 4–5).

6 Ibid., ll. 5–6.

7 See Durs Grünbein, *Den Körper zerbrechen. Rede zur Entgegennahme des Georg-Büchner-Preises 1995. Mit der Laudatio 'Portrait des Künstlers als junger Grenzhund' von Heiner Müller* (Frankfurt a. M.: Suhrkamp, 1995), p. 13.

8 Friedrich Nietzsche, *Werke. Kritische Gesamtausgabe*, ed. by Giorgio Colli and Mazzino Montinari, 8 vols (Berlin: de Gruyter, 1988), III.2, p. 373. On Grünbein and Nietzsche, see Eskin, *Poetic Affairs*, pp. 69–70, 117–18.

variations on the epitaph lyric (subsequently expanded to form the collection *Den teuren Toten. 33 Epitaphe*), each of which describes, with emotional detachment, a dead body and its attendant scene. Thus: '*Berlin.* Ein Toter saß an dreizehn Wochen / Aufrecht vorm Fernseher' [*Berlin*: a dead man sat for about thirteen weeks / Upright in front of his television], or: 'In einer U-Bahn, früh am Morgen, lag ein Toter / Erwürgt mit einem Draht' [In an underground railway, early in the morning, a dead man / Lay strangled with a wire].[9] These descriptions do not obviously suggest the genre of the epitaph lyric. The oblique relation to a poetic tradition is quite self-conscious, being (literally) underlined by horizontal bars at the top and bottom of each text (removed once the poems were included in a collection with the explanatory term 'epitaph' in its subtitle), presumably intended to create a lapidary and inscriptive appearance which the poems themselves do not necessarily convey. Nor do they contain any injunction to the reader, which the classical tradition of epitaph poetry tends to involve – not even an injunction *not* to read, producing interruption and caesura, the genre convention taken up by Celan in 'Engführung' ['Straitening']: 'Lies nicht mehr – Schau! / Schau nicht mehr – geh!' [Read no longer – look! / Look no longer – go!].[10] Their main point of convergence with the tradition is with the Romantic (specifically, the Wordsworthian) understanding of epitaphs as marking 'a place where nature and the human overlap', and 'both start speaking the same language'.[11] (These are the terms of Wordsworth's *Essays upon Epitaphs*.[12]) Though Grünbein's poems are in all obvious respects devoid of Romantic nature, they are clearly indebted to this principle:

> Sein kahler Schädel
> Hing über die zerstochne Sitzbank wo mit Filzstift
> In Kinderschrift geschrieben stand 'Du Arschloch!'
>
> [His bald skull / Hung over the slashed seat where with felt pen / Was written in a child's writing 'You arsehole!'][13]

9 Grünbein, *Schädelbasislektion*, p. 38 (ll. 1–2) and p. 46 (ll. 1–2).

10 Paul Celan, 'Engführung', in *Gesammelte Werke*, ed. by Beda Allemann and Stefan Reichert, 5 vols, 2nd edn (Frankfurt a. M.: Suhrkamp 1992), I, p. 197 (ll. 6–7). See the discussion of epitaph verse in John Bayley, *Housman's Poems* (Oxford: Clarendon, 1992), pp. 7–12.

11 Alexander Regier, *Fracture and Fragmentation in British Romanticism* (Cambridge: Cambridge University Press, 2010), p. 45. On the written dimension of that language, see for example Hartmut Böhme, 'Die Ästhetik der Ruinen', in *Der Schein des Schönen*, ed. by Dieter Kamper and Christian Wulf (Göttingen: Steidl, 1989), pp. 287–304 (p. 287).

12 William Wordsworth, *Essays upon Epitaphs*, in *The Prose Works of William Wordsworth*, ed. by W. J. B. Owen and Jane Worthington Smyser, 3 vols (Oxford: Clarendon, 1974), II, pp. 49–96.

13 *Schädelbasislektion*, p. 46 (ll. 4–6).

The Romantic epitaph stands for the dissolution of the human into nature (and nature's reception of the human); Grünbein's scenes of modern death show bodies becoming part of an urban landscape which – likewise – produces inscribed monuments to the merging of a life with its insentient surroundings. Where the epitaphs of *Schädelbasislektion* are concerned with human decay (cf. 'Verwesung', p. 38, l. 4), the implicit other half of Wordsworth's equation (or 'overlap') is developed by Grünbein in a later series of poems in *Nach den Satiren* entitled 'In der Provinz' ['In the Provinces']. Here animal corpses fester on roads, farm tracks and railway embankments:

> Eingefallen am Bahndamm,
> Liegt ein Hundekadaver quer im Gebiß
> Kreideweiß numerierter Schwellen, erstarrt.
>
> [Shrivelled on the railway embankment, / A dog's carcass lies across the mouth / Of chalk-white numbered sleepers, rigid.][14]

The language of epitaphs, Wordsworth might be taken to mean and Grünbein explicitly suggests, is also the language of nature's exposure to the human – now the inscriptions (chalked numbers) are signs of a natural environment being encroached on by the rhythms of technology. But the borders between the three elements (the human, the natural and the technological) are highly fluid. Grünbein's implicit identification of human being with numeration and faceless technological activity here should, perhaps, be seen as his own contemporary expression of that ultimate dissolution, immanent in the Romantic project 'to dissolve all distinctions in culture' (specifically by uncovering the organic language of nature), namely the effacement of its own founding distinction 'between humans and machines'.[15] When that distinction is (inevitably) blurred, the organic constitution of consciousness becomes also material, mechanistic and technical. While for poets working within the Romantic scheme technology haunts nature and language as a spectre, for Grünbein its ubiquity is a given: hence the metropolitan transport networks and electronic media which bring forth and frame dead bodies in *Schädelbasislektion*, and the tracks which all but remove the human from the scenes of 'In der Provinz' (except, possibly, as reduced to a natural – animal – remnant). The epitaph is central to Grünbein's poetry because it is writing (inscription) in the condition of ambiguity produced by the Romantic effacement: between the human and the natural, conscious language and material

14 Durs Grünbein, 'In der Provinz', in *Nach den Satiren. Gedichte* (Frankfurt a. M.: Suhrkamp, 1999), p. 9, I (ll. 1–3).
15 Michael Minden, *Modern German Literature* (Cambridge: Polity, 2011), p. 55.

bodies (Dickinson's 'syllable' and 'sound'), mind and machine. Epitaphs are the characteristic markers of what Grünbein, in the title of his earliest collection (*Grauzone morgens*), names the 'grey zone' in which his poetry is written.

This is both his closeness to Emily Dickinson and the source of their difference. In making the epitaph an organizing principle of *Schädelbasislektion* and 'In der Provinz', Grünbein may be said to offer a contemporary variation on Dickinson's own practice: 'Dickinson wrote many poems about the centrality of the graveyard in her small world. The burial ground penetrated deeply into her work'.[16] Dickinson's 'small world', like Grünbein's much larger world of cityscapes and cosmopolitan trajectories, circles around the grave. But where in Dickinson the grave is the focal point of a defined, determinate existence – a network of lives (including the life which gives rise to the poems) limited firstly by their relations to each other and ultimately by death – in Grünbein it has the character, however sober and contemporary the governing tone, of an artistic conceit, a figure of writing. That is, perhaps, the essence of his relationship to Romantic poetry. Like Wordsworth but unlike Dickinson, Grünbein recurs not so much to the grave itself, as standing for the saturation of life by death, but to the epitaph as the moment in which life becomes text (Wordsworth 'links the act of dying to that of writing').[17] As such his epitaph poems may be said to deflect the force of mortality, by channelling it into an aesthetic correlate. Dickinson, for her part, hints in a well known poem at the difficulties of an association with graves which would make them adjuncts of an imaginative impulse:

> We do not play on Graves –
> Because there isn't Room –
> Besides – it isn't even – it slants
> And People come –
>
> And put a Flower on it –[18]

Here the grave does not yield to any purpose other than announcing the sheer presence of death. This is firstly because of its angularity ('it slants'), which closes down any attempt to 'play' over its surface (which might, for instance, involve tracing a finger round its inscriptions), and secondly because such activity is at odds with the symbolic place of graves in communal life – being constantly

16 Karen Mills Campbell, 'Poetry as Epitaph', *Journal of Popular Culture*, 14 (1981), 657–68 (p. 660).
17 Dewey W. Hall, 'Signs of the Dead. Epitaphs, Inscriptions, and the Discourse of the Self', *English Literary History*, 68.3 (2001), 655–77 (p. 658).
18 Dickinson, *Complete Poems*, no. 467 (ll. 1–5).

interrupted when 'People come'. That interplay, in Dickinson, between death and a social world, is as alien to Grünbein as it is to Wordsworth, both of whom rather align death with the processes of writing, and neither of whom experiences mortality – as does Dickinson when faced with gravestones – as a force impinging on them, crowding in on their attempts to speak of it. Whatever fractures their poetry may suggest or take as its theme, death itself remains, for them, eminently legible. This is different both from Dickinson, for whom the slant of the grave's surface makes it inaccessible to 'play', and from Celan, for whom it is its own negation, defying decipherment and opening instead to pure movement ('Lies nicht mehr [...] geh!' [Read no longer [...] go!]). In Dickinson and Celan that movement is death bearing on subjectivity as the pressure of narrowing (Dickinson's 'Because there isn't Room' is analogous to what Celan understands as 'straitening' ['Engführung']). The angle marked out by the grave inflects our whole being as something we cannot grasp. We are narrowed to a point – in the intersection of horizontal plane (Celan in 'Engführung' speaks of movement through grass) and vertically imposing stone – where there is no space left for reading. Their poems close so absolutely into death that the vantage point of poets like Wordsworth and Grünbein, observing the textual play of epitaphs, is surpassed.

Dickinson's 'slant' has a direct counterpart in Celan, which then appears – modified – in Grünbein, too. In his 'Der Meridian' ['The Meridian'] (his own Büchner Prize speech, of 1960), Celan refers to poems (and poets) as themselves having a slant – what he calls an angle of inclination. A fully 'aktualisierte Sprache' [actualized poetic language], he says,

> kann ja wohl nur in dem Gedicht dessen zu finden sein, der nicht vergißt, daß er unter dem Neigungswinkel seines Daseins, dem Neigungswinkel seiner Kreatürlichkeit spricht.
>
> [can no doubt only be found in the poem of one who does not forget that he speaks under the angle of inclination of his existence, the angle of inclination of his creatureliness.][19]

All poems capable of such language, for Celan, are slanted or inclined; they bear a 'creaturely' aspect which is the poet's own. The creaturely poem lays itself bare in its determinate bodily (or, as Celan says elsewhere, its worldly, 'terrestrial') horizon, and in so doing opens itself properly to exposure and receptiveness, to a certain ethical being towards others which, the 'Meridian' speech goes on to argue, has as an ultimate point of reference something the poem cannot ever adequately refer to at all, namely a 'utopian' horizon.[20] That point is always, for terrestrial

---

19 Celan, *Gesammelte Werke*, III, p. 197.

20 Celan, 'Utopie', in *Gesammelte Werke*, III, p. 199. For Celan's definition of poetry as 'ein terrestrisches, ein kreatürliches Phänomen' [a terrestrial, a creaturely phenomenon], see 'Die

language, strictly unnameable, but the poem can approach it through its encounter with a world of others, and feel it – against the ever-present pull of negativity which (for example in Celan's poem 'Tenebrae') threatens to warp creaturely existence into animal subjection – as the condition of its own possibility. Dickinson's slanting graves likewise narrow the poem to a barely decidable co-existence of negation and fullness, in which only the abyssal realization of finitude as the grounding of social being discloses the terrestrial horizon in its limit ('I touched the Universe'). Grünbein takes up Celan's Dickinsonian angle of inclination. It is present in his account of Büchner's interest in dissected bodies: 'daß er hier Aufschluß suchte, gerade hier, über etwas, das der ganzen kreatürlichen Existenz ihre Richtung gab' [that here – especially here – he sought information about something that gave the whole of creaturely existence its direction].[21] The creaturely angle in Grünbein is marked out by the anatomy of nerves, the body laid bare as sensory material, and then by the lettering of epitaphs in which the human and the natural merge. This is certainly in keeping with Celan's view that what Büchner asserts against the claims of idealizing art ('ach, die Kunst' [alas – art][22]) is the body: 'das Natürliche und Kreatürliche' [the natural and the creaturely].[23] It is not, however, convergent with Celan's (and, implicitly, Dickinson's) conviction that poetry's challenge to the notion of sovereign art lies in reflecting an embodied historical and ethical life which is conscious of its limitation by mortal finitude. Because Grünbein takes only the continuum of material being, whether in the form of opened cadavers or neural mechanisms, as the foundation of his understanding of the 'creaturely', and because that material preoccupation is itself a product of the Romantic dissolution of boundaries between man, nature and (ultimately) machine, his poems on the subject of death end up suggesting precisely the Romantic pendant to mechanization and technology – namely the sovereign invulnerability (autonomy) of art. This means a certain kind of poetry which is always to some extent – Celan says – forgetful of its own finitude and determinacy. Thus *Schädelbasislektion* and 'In der Provinz' turn, complementarily, to an equation (or dissolution) of the human and the natural whose actual origin – as a conceit of art, or a reflex of aesthetic distance on the part of the poet giving voice to it – the poetry only obliquely discloses. The first presents lyric epitaphs through which the poet accommodates the caesura of death to the claims of writ-

---

Dichtung Osip Mandestams', in Paul Celan, *Der Meridian. Endfassung, Vorstufen, Materialien*, ed. by Bernhard Böschenstein and Heino Schmull (Frankfurt a. M.: Suhrkamp, 1999), pp. 215–21 (p. 215).

21 Grünbein, *Den Körper zerbrechen*, p. 12.

22 Celan, *Gesammelte Werke*, III, p. 191.

23 Ibid. See also Sonja Klein's chapter in this volume.

ing, the second various scenes of creaturely decomposition in which the tropes of 'displacement' might most pertinently be read as delineating, in marked distinction from the practice of Dickinson and Celan, the poet's own absence, as a mortal creature, from his poems.

This particular tendency runs throughout Grünbein's work, and produces perhaps its most abidingly interesting tensions. In the later collection *Strophen für übermorgen*, the opening poem ('Spruchtäfelchen' ['Votive tablet'])[24] deploys the epitaphic convention with a deeper tenderness than either *Schädelbasislektion* or *Nach den Satiren* – in a tone of address it speaks of birth as the onset of the body's return to darkness, its implied progressive detachment from the datum of consciousness called 'you':

> Draußen die Nacht – im Innern ihr Hall.
> So von Geburt an, so wird es sein
>
> In all den Jahren, der Zeit, die dir bleibt.
> [...]
> Blutiger Irrtum – der Körper. Er treibt
> Verrat gegen dich, ein Komplize der Nacht.
>
> [Outside the night – inside its echo. / It will be like this from birth onward, / Through all those years, the time you'll have left. [...] // Bloody mistake – the body. It commits / Treachery against you, complicit with the night.][25]

These later poems turn the epitaph into a figure of voice and speaking – as the title of another piece in the collection ('Vocis Imago') explicitly suggests. They rely on a multiple synaesthesia. The 'image of voice', the poem says, is the sound of rain ('Regenlaut', l. 1) – it conjures the setting of original language, that is, of human articulation barely separable from primeval noise: 'Bild der Stimme bist du, frisches Echo / Erster Sprachen aus dem Wälderrauschen' [You are the image of voice, the fresh echo / Of first tongues from forest noise].[26] (Dickinson's account of the relation between 'syllable' and 'sound' is clearly still significant for Grünbein in this poem.) 'Vocis Imago' is an epitaph poem because – again in Wordsworthian fashion – it speaks (or pictures, as the dripping moisture of primitive forest[27]) the decomposition of the human and the natural. We can sense be-

---

24 The title refers to a small, decorative wooden plaque ('Spruchtafel') inscribed with a saying or quotation (often a biblical verse), and given on such occasions as births and baptisms. See also Sonja Klein's chapter in this volume.
25 Durs Grünbein, *Strophen für übermorgen* (Frankfurt a. M.: Suhrkamp, 2007), p. 9 (ll. 1–7).
26 Durs Grünbein, 'Vocis Imago', in *Strophen für übermorgen*, p. 35 (ll. 5–6).
27 Ibid., l. 8.

hind this poem, as we sensed behind the Büchner speech and *Schädelbasislektion*, Nietzsche's view of language as an accrual of 'anthropomorphic' projections ('Anthropomorphismen') on to primal natural processes.[28] And anthropomorphism has, unsurprisingly, been found by a dominant strand of Nietzschean literary criticism to be central to Romantic lyric: 'anthropomorphism seems to be the illusionary resuscitation of the natural breath of language, frozen into stone by the semantic power of the trope'.[29] The resuscitation of natural breath, which Grünbein practises and knows to be illusionary, is frozen into the stone of epitaph, into an inanimate emblem endowed both with 'anthropomorphic' – speaking – qualities and with the force of natural decay. In a further poem, Grünbein's use of the device becomes fully self-conscious; he names it in the terms of Romantic critical rhetoric. The title of the brief sequence, 'Drei Vokalisen aus der Krisenzeit' ['Three Vocalizes from the Time of Crisis'], again suggests voice, but voice is itself a figure of writing: 'Die Hand zuckt beim Schreiben von *prosopopoiia*' [The hand quivers writing *prosopopoeia*].[30] Stones – through epitaphs – speak by virtue of the poet who 'freezes' his own living breath into text from which no life can re-emerge, except as something factitious and stylized, encased in the emblematic language of conceit and trope. That is what de Man calls 'the deadly negative power invested in the figure' of anthropomorphism.[31] Grünbein recognizes that process but does not challenge it. His hand, writing out *prosopopoeia*, shadows the hand of the critic who does likewise. In both, the commitment to a Nietzschean version of Wordsworthian Romantic hermeneutics sets itself against, for example, Celan's use of the same image (of frozen breath):

> Tief
> in der Zeitenschrunde,
> beim
> Wabeneis
> wartet, ein Atemkristall,
> dein unumstößliches
> Zeugnis. ('Weggebeizt')[32]
>
> [Deep / in the fissure between times, / at / the ice-comb / waits, a breath crystal, / your unassailable / testimony. ('Corroded Away')]

---

28 Nietzsche, *Werke*, III.2, p. 374.

29 Paul de Man, *The Rhetoric of Romanticism* (New York: Columbia University Press, 1984), p. 247.

30 Durs Grünbein, 'Drei Vokalisen aus der Krisenzeit', in *Strophen für übermorgen*, pp. 111–13 (p. 111, I, l. 8).

31 De Man, *The Rhetoric of Romanticism*, p. 247.

32 Paul Celan, 'Weggebeizt', in *Gesammelte Werke*, II, p. 31 (ll. 15–21).

Celan's 'breath crystal', the fragile and fleeting natural remnant of address, discloses not any transgression or merging of the human, but the singularity of a speaking other who witnesses – relates to – the world in a certain way. This 'simple act of being addressed by another and thus of being called into the world and universe that is established by a shared use of language', is for Celan unassailable.[33] The testifying address is present neither as any referential content, nor as a trope of language, since in either case the poem would co-opt it and rob it of its singular force. It penetrates writing but writing cannot define it. Not the least significant aspect of Grünbein's work is the ambivalence it evinces in both taking Celan's notion of address as a model for poetry and drawing on poetic traditions which run counter to it.

Presence and Persona

The question of voice, with its roots in Grünbein's conception of poetry in terms of the body, is a pressing one throughout his work.[34] It recurs, often in the form of a tension, in his various treatments of encounter and address. This is especially apparent in both *Nach den Satiren* and *Erklärte Nacht*. These reveal an expansion of voice and its possibilities: various examples of the 'Rollengedicht', in which a specific persona, historical or otherwise, is adopted as the perspective of the poem, are prominent in these works. Grünbein's poetry in this mode attends to what he calls 'das Stimmengewirr vieler Zeiten' [the tangle of voices of many times],[35] bringing together different voices in individual lyrics and the relations within sequences of poems. Here, one figure in Anglo-American poetry emerges as an inescapable point of reference. Grünbein has remarked that:

> Mit siebzehn lieh mir ein Freund ein zerfleddertes Taschenbuch der *Cantos* von Ezra Pound [...] Seither schreibe ich in einer Erwartung, die gleichzeitig rückwärts- und vorwärtsgewandt ist, und dieser unmögliche Zustand, einige Atemlängen zwischen Antike und X, läßt sich nur aushalten, indem ich mich langsam und zeilenweise meiner Stimme vergewissere, dieses Körpers und dessen, was sich im Innenohr fing.

33 Ulrich Baer, *Remnants of Song. Trauma and the Experience of Modernity in Charles Baudelaire and Paul Celan* (Stanford: Stanford University Press, 2000), p. 203.

34 See also Ruth J. Owen's article in this volume.

35 Durs Grünbein, 'Mein babylonisches Hirn', in *Galilei vermißt Dantes Hölle und bleibt an den Maßen hängen. Aufsätze 1989–1995* (Frankfurt a. M.: Suhrkamp, 1996), pp. 18–33 (p. 21); 'My Babylonish Brain', in *The Bars of Atlantis. Selected Essays*, ed. by Michael Eskin, trans. by John Crutchfield, Michael Hofmann and Andrew Shields (New York: Farrar, Straus and Giroux, 2010), pp. 59–71 (p. 61).

> [When I was seventeen a friend lent me a tattered paperback copy of Ezra Pound's *Cantos* [...] Since then I have been writing in a state of expectation which is directed simultaneously backward and forward, and this impossible condition, some breath lengths between the ancient world and X, can only be endured by ascertaining – slowly, line by line – what my voice is, what this body is, and what it is that got caught in my inner ear.][36]

Voice, the double movement of poetry through time (forward and back) and the precarious co-presence of ancient and modern, are linked to the example of Pound. That example clearly lies behind Grünbein's practice of the 'Rollengedicht' and his adoption of historical personae (especially of poets) more generally. Indeed the whole idea of poetic personae in the modern sense is traceable to Pound, who fashioned it into a term of art, using it as the title both of an early book of poems (1909) and of a subsequent edition of collected works (1926). Writing just after the outbreak of the First World War about the movement known as 'Vorticism', which he co-founded, Pound produced an account of his practice from which Grünbein's concerns are not distant: 'I began this search for the real in a book called *Personae*, casting off, as it were, complete masks of the self in each poem. I continued in a long series of translations, which were but more elaborate masks'.[37] Pound's technique of constructing 'masks of the self' is continued in Grünbein's own strategy of *assemblage*, finding 'alter egos' through which to create 'poetic patchworks that emphatically advertise their fabrication from materials spanning Western culture, from Homer to the present'.[38] Indeed of Pound it has been said that 'in assembling personae he gives a shape and significance to the literary tradition whose techniques he is learning'.[39] Grünbein, too, in referring to Pound, alludes to a process of learning – of the need constantly to ascertain the nature of his voice in attending to the voices he has heard ('mich meiner Stimme vergewissere [...] und dessen, was sich im Innenohr fing'; see above). And Pound's 'literary tradition', alongside the relation of 'tradition' to the 'individual talent' discussed by his contemporary Eliot, finds expression in the process

---

36 'Kurzer Bericht an eine Akademie', in *Antike Dispositionen. Aufsätze* (Frankfurt a. M.: Suhrkamp, 2005), pp. 11–14 (pp. 12–13). Grünbein discusses Pound at greater length in Aris Fioretos and Durs Grünbein, 'Gespräch über die Zone, den Hund und die Knochen', *Akzente*, 43.6 (1996), 486–501 (pp. 487–89).

37 Ezra Pound, 'Vorticism', *The Fortnightly Review*, 96.573 (1 September 1914), 461–71 (pp. 463–64).

38 Michael Eskin, 'Stimmengewirr vieler Zeiten. Grünbein's Dialogue with Dante, Baudelaire, and Mandel'shtam', *The Germanic Review*, 77.1 (2002), 34–50 (p. 34).

39 K. K. Ruthven, *A Guide to Ezra Pound's* Personae *(1926)* (Berkeley: University of California Press, 1969), p. 9.

of transmission which Grünbein identifies as necessary for the apprehension, across time, of a 'physical presence' in the voice of his interlocutors:

> seine [the poem's] Magie [ist] die physische Präsenz eines Sprechers, der immer woanders oder lange schon tot ist. In den verschiedenen Rhythmen, den verdichteten Bildern wird die Vorstellung des einzelnen synchronisiert mit der Wahrnehmung aller – solange es Überlieferung gibt.
>
> [its [the poem's] magical secret is the physical presence of a speaker ever on the move, or long dead. In the variety of rhythms in the shuffle of images, the imagination of one individual is synchronized with the perception of all – as long as such things are handed on.][40]

From his earliest work, 'Pound identified his poetry with the revival of dead voices'.[41] That achievement of presence, in Grünbein's descriptions, has a whirling quality ('Stimmengewirr') and a gathering spiral trajectory ('Spiralbahn') which invite comparison with Pound's definition of the 'vortex' as 'a radiant node or cluster [...] from which, and through which, and into which, ideas are constantly rushing'.[42]

The most obvious respect in which Pound can be seen as a force in Grünbein's poetry is not in fact any specific affinity with the *Cantos*, but the development by Grünbein of themes and personae bearing on ancient Rome.[43] Pound more than any other modernist poet drew on Roman themes in order to address his contemporary situation, and Grünbein has made a point of seeing Imperial Rome as the 'prototype' of that in modern experience which has been defined by empires, the waning of empires and the cities at the centre of the 'vortices' they produced.[44] The device of adopting a Roman poet as mouthpiece for reflections on modern experience was not invented by Pound – an important ear-

40 Grünbein, 'Mein babylonisches Hirn', p. 22; 'My Babylonish Brain', p. 62.

41 Sanford Schwartz, *The Matrix of Modernism. Pound, Eliot, and Early Twentieth-Century Thought* (Princeton: Princeton University Press, 1985), p. 137.

42 See Grünbein's poem 'In Tunneln der U-Bahn' ['In Tunnels of the Underground Railway'], *Schädelbasislektion*, pp. 31–35 (ll. 137–38): 'Unterwegs auf der Spiralbahn / toter Jahrhundertstimmen' [Travelling on the spiral track / Of the dead voices of centuries]); Pound, 'Vorticism', p. 469. Both connect the image of the underground railway to poetic activity. See 'Vorticism', p. 465, and Pound's poem 'In a Station of the Metro', in *Personae. Collected Shorter Poems of Ezra Pound* (London: Faber and Faber, 1952), p. 119. The title of Grünbein's poem corresponds closely to that of Pound's.

43 See also Ruth J. Owen's article in this volume.

44 For example, in the essay 'Schlaflos in Rom. Versuch über den Satirendichter Juvenal' ('Sleepless in Rome. Essay on the Satirical Poet Juvenal'), in *Antike Dispositionen*, pp. 328–68 (p. 339).

lier example in English poetry is Samuel Johnson's *The Vanity of Human Wishes* (1749), an 'imitation' of Juvenal's Tenth Satire which influenced Robert Lowell and belongs to the wider context of Grünbein's own Roman writing.[45] But Pound's *Homage to Sextus Propertius* (1919), in which the elegies of Propertius are creatively rendered into English and arranged in a complex edifice 'that both interprets the historical original and expresses the preoccupations of the modern translator', is the decisive instance in the twentieth century (and Propertius 'the last major single *persona* in Pound's work').[46] If Pound adopted Propertius because the Latin poet's disillusion with the Augustan Empire struck him as being in refracted continuity with his own attitude to the British,[47] then Grünbein's use of Roman personae in relation to present imperial, or post-imperial, experience effectively draws not only on Latin writers themselves but also on those who have sought, before Grünbein, to speak through them.

Both *Nach den Satiren* and *Erklärte Nacht* contain several Roman poems, notably in the sequences 'Historien' ['Histories'] and 'Neue Historien' ['New Histories'] – the titles of which may afford reminiscences of Lowell's collection *History* (1973), where Juvenal is a significant source – and in the series of 'counterparts' to Juvenal's Third Satire (in the title sequence 'Nach den Satiren').[48] Repeatedly in these poems, the adoptive persona is used to approach the themes of exile and estrangement. Thus in 'Klage eines Legionärs aus dem Feldzug des Germanicus an die Elbe' ['Elegy of a Legionary from the Elbe Campaign of Germanicus'],[49] the legionary returns home to find himself displaced in his native region (a variation on Grünbein's defining concern with the experience of inner exile ensuing on German reunification). The turns of displacement are given more complex treatment in various pieces impersonating, or describing the fate of, Seneca in exile. The poem 'Julia Livilla', for example, includes among its effects an overlaying of the contemporary situation (the trope of *Wende*) with a reiteration of Celan's 'turn of breath' ('Atemwende'[50]) as the recurrent respiratory dis-

45 See Theodore Ziolkowski, 'Two Juvenal Delinquents. Robert Lowell and Durs Grünbein', *Classical and Modern Literature*, 26.1 (2006), 12–32 (on Johnson, p. 15).

46 Hugh Witemeyer, 'Early Poetry 1908–1920', in *The Cambridge Companion to Ezra Pound*, ed. by Ira B. Nadel (Cambridge: Cambridge University Press, 1999), pp. 43–58 (p. 51). The standard work on the *Homage* is J. P. Sullivan, *Ezra Pound and Sextus Propertius. A Study in Creative Translation* (Austin: University of Texas Press, 1964).

47 See Witemeyer, 'Early Poetry', p. 52.

48 Ziolkowski, 'Juvenal Delinquents', p. 26 (and on Lowell's 'compressed translations of passages from the Tenth Satire' in *History*, see p. 21).

49 *Nach den Satiren*, pp. 14–15.

50 Celan, *Gesammelte Werke*, III, p. 195.

turbance suffered by the historical Seneca ('wenn der Husten / Spätnachts zurückkehrt' [when the cough / Comes back late at night].[51] The cough splutters as a bodily expression of the poem's various tensions.[52] And the elegiac topos of the distant friend, used by Grünbein in this poem and others in his Roman mode, is frequently reflected in a spatial sensibility which emphasizes simultaneous separation and connection – the distant places of exile oriented towards the unreachable homeland by the nexus of the *imperium*.

That spatial sense, marked out by lines of travel and conquest, is implicitly present in a poem in English to which Grünbein has made reference, and which – though no 'persona' is adopted – is one poet's imaginative response to the life of another.[53] W. H. Auden begins his sonnet 'Rimbaud' thus: 'The nights, the railway arches, the bad sky [...] the cold had made a poet'.[54] By the end of the poem Auden's railway arches, casting the shadow of Roman viaducts, give way to desert plains (and one colonial adventure has been replaced by another): 'Now, galloping through Africa, he dreamed / Of a new self'.[55] 'Rimbaud' is about ceasing to be a poet ('from the lyre [...] estranged'[56]) – the possibility of adopting a 'new self' comes about when the old (poetic) self is shed, and Auden finishes by suggesting that any such new self will be an accommodation, haunted by inauthenticity: Rimbaud's dream is of making 'His truth acceptable to lying men'.[57] Grünbein's Roman poems might be said to push against Auden here, while clearly drawing on his poem's underlying colonial topography. They are about becoming poetic when estrangement (understood in terms of exile: the sense of separation in connection) makes it necessary both to capture and to disturb the patterns of historical experience in a moment of what Grünbein calls 'presence' and Pound calls 'the real', speaking with and through others who enter the poems as shifting conjunctions of lyric personae. Yet the problem with Pound's view is attendant also on Grünbein's. For Pound these personae can 'coexist because they are contemporaries in the mind of the poet, for whom they have a significance that transcends the claims of historical time' – this is the essence of Pound's 'real time'.[58] Grünbein's understanding is not essentially different from this, and his persona poems can tend,

51 Durs Grünbein, *Erklärte Nacht. Gedichte* (Frankfurt a. M.: 2002), p. 70 (ll. 24–25).
52 See Eskin, *Poetic Affairs*, pp. 79–80.
53 See Durs Grünbein, *Vom Stellenwert der Worte* (Frankfurt a. M.: Suhrkamp, 2010), p. 20.
54 W. H. Auden, 'Rimbaud', in *The English Auden. Poems, Essays and Dramatic Writings 1927–1939*, ed. by Edward Mendelson (London and Boston: Faber and Faber, 1977), pp. 237–38 (ll. 1–4).
55 Ibid., ll. 12–13.
56 Ibid., l. 8.
57 Ibid., l. 14.
58 Ruthven, *Pound's* Personae, p. 9.

like Pound's, to suggest an invulnerability or detachment on the part of the poet assembling these constellations which – far from revealing a properly historical consciousness, as we might expect from the title 'Historien' – reduces historical experience to the aesthetic analogues he is capable of finding for it. The difficulty is not the multiplicity of voices speaking in a poem ('aus wie vielen Stimmen sich die eigene Stimme zusammensetzte' [how many voices one's own voice comprised]),[59] but that the poems give little scope for taking the source of this multiplicity to be anything other than a unitary selecting subject which, however, scarcely lets itself be glimpsed behind the insistence that it is polyphonic and multiple. The strong Nietzschean element which Grünbein shares with Pound – and the suggestion of inscrutable aesthetic sovereignty which it produces – tells against any attempt at receptive diversity here, as elsewhere it tells against a treatment of death which would be other than a device of art.[60] If the experience of history involves exposure to events which exceed and challenge the idea of an enclosed, isolable subjectivity, then the organizing consciousness of these history poems is not itself historical. Its instinct, like Pound's, is to 'transcend' historical time (to occupy the place which, Celan says, poems seek but which they cannot know). This means any response to historical circumstance it seeks to offer, in the form of encounters and conjunctures of 'presence', can seem indeterminate and adventitious – as if 'the real', the centre of the vortex, were nothing but the poet's inviolate self.

Grünbein's treatment of Roman models, however, also reveals a subtler historical sensibility, which does not require such concealments. Curiously the distance between Grünbein and Pound opens when they appear to come closest together – through Pound's Propertius and Grünbein's Juvenal. In Pound's *Homage* 'Propertius was made a twentieth-century literary figure'.[61] Grünbein's third poem in 'Nach den Satiren' (entitled 'Der lange Schlaf' ['The Long Sleep']) arguably does the same for Juvenal by using his own Third Satire to articulate 'a vision of Berlin during and since World War Two'.[62] But where Pound's poem develops the conceit behind *Personae* into the sophisticated adoption of one particular figure (Propertius) as unitary speaker, Grünbein derives from his source an ironic counterpoint which allows him to explore historical themes without Pound's masks. The poem has certain (possibly inevitable) affinities with Samuel John-

59 Grünbein, *Vom Stellenwert der Worte*, p. 37.
60 On Pound and Nietzsche, see for example Schwartz, *Matrix of Modernism*, pp. 85–86.
61 Sullivan, *Pound and Sextus Propertius*, p. 36.
62 Ziolkowski, 'Juvenal Delinquents', p. 28.

son's 'London: A Poem in Imitation of the Third Satire of Juvenal' (1738).[63] In Johnson's poem Juvenal's critique of metropolitan life serves as the basis for the speaker's account of his desire to leave London. In Grünbein's poem it frames the impossibility of leaving Berlin, except perhaps for another metropolis which would be simply a further avatar of Juvenal's Rome.[64] It is not, though, Grünbein's (perhaps fanciful) vision of Rome as archetype which gives the poem its power. This comes rather from his distilling Juvenal's view of Rome as a city of noise and sleeplessness (*insomnia*) into fluid, dreamlike impressions of Berlin as a city built on historical experience that can only partly be excavated (on 'Die Knochen einer Zeit, als die Familien sich in Lager teilten' [The bones of a time when families divided into camps][65]) – having at its core great forgetting and an absence of history ('Wieviel Schweigen geht / Verschüttet in den Ballungsräumen' [How much silence is / Spilt in the high-density areas].[66] The final lines of this poem might be said to rise naturally to a historical sense at which Pound in *Homage to Sextus Propertius* can arrive only obscurely,[67] and which Grünbein's own meditations on history by means of various poetic alter egos are, for want of determinacy, not fully able to realize. The noise of Berlin penetrates the rhythms of sleep, and the resulting condition of perpetual disturbance – between waking and forgetting – is plausibly stated as the experience not of a constructed persona, but of connected lives on which the poem's images bear: 'Berlin ... durch Haut und Wände drang / in ihren Schlaf, in deinen Schlaf, in meinen Schlaf' [Berlin ... entered through skin and walls / Into their sleep, into your sleep, into my sleep].[68]

On the End of an Event

Grünbein's most ambitious historical reflection is the sequence *Porzellan. Poem vom Untergang meiner Stadt* (2005), comprising forty-nine poems of ten lines each, and treating the historical impact of the Allied bombing of Dresden (his

63 Samuel Johnson, 'London: A Poem in Imitation of the Third Satire of Juvenal', in *The Yale Edition of the Works of Samuel Johnson*, 15 vols (New Haven and London: Yale University Press, 1958–1985), VI, pp. 47–61.
64 See Ziolkowski, 'Juvenal Delinquents', p. 27: 'In the eternal analogy of Rome / Berlin or Rome / New York the metropolis is doomed over and over again throughout history'.
65 'Die Dritte (Der lange Schlaf)', in *Nach den Satiren*, pp. 103–8 (p. 105, l. 56).
66 Ibid., p. 108 (ll. 149–50).
67 See Sullivan, *Pound and Sextus Propertius*, p. 34: 'In the *Homage* Pound is forced, despite himself, to adopt an historical view'.
68 'Die Dritte (Der lange Schlaf)', p. 108 (ll. 151–52).

native city). Impact has, throughout the sequence, a symbolic analogue in the image of Dresden porcelain, both evocative of a particular place and characterized by fragility. The tension of *Porzellan* lies in the simultaneous connection and separation between Grünbein – and it is his voice, rather than that of a Poundian constructed speaker, which we hear – and the events to which the poem refers. This is the source of many subtle patterns of identification and distance in the sequence.[69] It also makes *Porzellan* a central text in the poetics of detachment which we have traced in Grünbein – specifically because it invites consideration with an English poet whose work also revolves around such processes.

In the thirtieth poem of *Porzellan*, the Dresden crockery which gives the sequence its title is shattered in nuptial celebration: 'Polterabend. Unvergeßlich, Topf und Tassen fliegen / An den Bordstein, von Erwachsenenhand geschleudert' [Eve-of-the-wedding-party. Unforgettable: pot and cup crash / On the pavement, flung by a grown-up's hand].[70] Unforgettable because of the spectacle of *adults* behaving with such abandon, the scene begins by insinuating a child's perspective, which however becomes only part of a general external standpoint rendered finally as the suggestion that we, or the poetic speaker, are looking at a photograph.[71] The poem moves between the thoughts of various parties present to produce the tone of an amused, ironic or (increasingly) wistful onlooker, perhaps reacting not to the scene itself but to its subsequent presence as an image:

> Dann der Kuß, wenn Braut an Bräutigam sich schmiegt –
> Eine Ewigkeit, und die beginnt ab heute.
> Dieser Augenblick ... nie mehr zurückzuholen,
> Weiß die Tante, und der Onkel denkt sich seinen Teil.
> Schade nur um Urgroßmutters Kasserolle,
> Was kann sie dafür? Noch sind die Turteltäubchen geil,
> Sprich verliebt, denkt sich der Photograph und mahnt:
> 'Bitte lächeln.'

> [Then the kiss, when bride cuddles up to groom – / An eternity, and it begins from today. / This moment ... never to be regained, / The auntie knows, and the uncle looks knowingly on. / Just a pity about great-grandmother's casserole dish, / What can she do about it? The lovebirds are still randy, / That is, in love, the photographer thinks and reminds them / To 'smile please'.][72]

---

69 See Anne Fuchs, 'The Bombing of Dresden and the Idea of Cultural Impact', in *Cultural Impact in the German Context. Studies in Transmission, Reception, and Influence*, ed. by Rebecca Braun and Lyn Marven (New York: Camden House, 2010), pp. 41–59 (pp. 49–53).
70 Durs Grünbein, *Porzellan. Poem vom Untergang meiner Stadt* (Frankfurt a. M.: Suhrkamp, 2005), poem 30 (ll. 1–2).
71 Ibid., poem 30 (l. 9).
72 Ibid., poem 30 (ll. 3–10).

At the centre of the shifts in perspective is a moment which, the poem says, can never be regained – that insight is granted to a figure in the poem, but only as it were as an afterthought ('Weiß die Tante'), having been stated with a reflective certainty that stretches beyond the narrated scene and would seem to be shared by the lyric voice. The celebratory vignette ('Polterabend', in which porcelain is broken in anticipation of a marriage) reproduces the same structure (or lacuna) of memory which determines the historical story of *Porzellan*: the moment of change cannot be recaptured or experienced again (certainly not, the poem may suggest, by one who looks years later upon a photograph, or writes a poem), though it defines everything that comes after it.

Grünbein's evocation has a clear precursor (and explicit point of reference) in another nuptial poem, 'probably the best modern example of a poem using a detached observer as speaker'.[73] In 'The Whitsun Weddings' (1964), Philip Larkin describes a Saturday train journey (from northern England to London) during which, periodically, newly married couples come aboard. The centre of the poem is a farewell gathering on a station platform, witnessed by the speaker from his carriage:

> Struck, I leant
> More promptly out next time, more curiously,
> And saw it all again in different terms:
> The fathers with broad belts under their suits
> And seamy foreheads; mothers proud and fat;
> An uncle shouting smut.[74]

Grünbein's celebration restages Larkin's scene: the 'uncle shouting smut' becomes a more reticent figure in *Porzellan*, but is unmistakeably present ('und der Onkel denkt sich seinen Teil'). Unlike in *Porzellan*, where the narrating speaker is part of a complex relation of separation and belonging with regard to the evoked scene, Larkin's poem is spoken from an entirely detached point of view; but Larkin's 'speaker, who never leaves the train [yet] seems to know what everyone on the platform thinks',[75] presages Grünbein's own, attributing to people insights and opinions at a distance of memory. And Larkin's traveller is as much the poet himself as the narrating voice of *Porzellan* is that of Grünbein. Moreover in 'The Whitsun Weddings' too, there is the intimation of a powerful moment pressing

---

73 Neil Covey, 'Larkin, Distance, and Observation', *Modern Language Studies*, 23.3 (1993), 11–25 (p. 20).
74 Philip Larkin, 'The Whitsun Weddings', in *The Whitsun Weddings* (London: Faber and Faber, 1964), p. 22 (ll. 33–38).
75 Covey, 'Larkin, Distance, and Observation', p. 20.

within the details of everyday life: the eternity, which, in Grünbein, begins in the joyous breaking of china ('Eine Ewigkeit, und die beginnt ab heute'), is that which Larkin senses in his train or 'this frail / Travelling coincidence'[76] of existences thrown fleetingly together (Larkin's apprehension of fragility is transposed by Grünbein into the unifying and fragmentary motif of porcelain).

Each Whitsun wedding leads Larkin's solitary spectator to reflect on the transformation that has just been wrought in those he sees, 'or how their lives would all contain this hour' (l. 68). The moment of change, in Grünbein's terms, is both irrecoverable and omnipresent, as in a different register is the rupture which lies behind *Porzellan*, the destruction of Dresden in a furnace of aerial fire which overlays both the image of the city's porcelain kilns and the happy breakages of the 'Polterabend'. Larkin's farewell gatherings on English railway platforms are both deeply strange to Grünbein's historical theme and, in the language he uses to capture their momentary appearance and passing, fully apposite to it:

> All posed irresolutely, watching us go,
> As if out on the end of an event
> Waving goodbye
> To something that survived it.[77]

Here too, the receding group crystallizes into the quality of photograph, impressing the contours of an image in the speaker's memory. And Larkin's 'event', punctually coming about in the stopping of a train but continuing in the lives of 'survivors' borne away from it, is structurally the same as that moment which has been seen as central to Grünbein's understanding of poetry, and to which Grünbein himself has made manifold reference. For an event thus conceived is 'a private or public occurrence, matter, happening, or encounter' which 'somehow or other exceeds and transgresses the ordinary', and which is intensely bound up with 'the perceiving subject *for whom* it is and, as such, constitutes itself as an event in the first place'.[78] This is what Grünbein calls the 'Ereignis' or event. Insofar as it aims to be what Grünbein calls 'dialogic' (marked by an essential receptiveness), poetry is always both response to an event and, therefore, itself imbued with the character of an event ('Ereignischarakter') – as an act of utterance it becomes a happening in which some encounter or transgression or realignment takes place. Of poetry we can say 'dass die Stimme oder das Sprechen selbst zum

76 Larkin 'Whitsun Weddings', p. 23 (ll. 74–75).
77 Ibid., pp. 21–22 (ll. 30–33).
78 Eskin, *Poetic Affairs*, p. 19.

Ereignis wird' [that voice or speaking itself becomes an event].[79] The field of language and subjectivity which an event defines, and which a poem exemplarily expresses, belong to the event's unfolding. 'The Whitsun Weddings' and *Porzellan* respond to an event which flickers in a change of light. In the former it is the interruption, in spots of shade amid glare and movement, of what Seamus Heaney calls 'Larkin's sunstruck distances', flashing 'randomly and pointlessly'.[80] In Grünbein's poem it is that lighting of the night sky which brought ruin ('Untergang'). Both register those moments not as separate from the subjectivity of the lyric voice which speaks of them, but as having the character of event only by virtue of relation to that 'perceiving subject' – hence perhaps the excessive note in Larkin's annexation of thoughts and feelings, and certainly the sense, in Grünbein, that it is precisely the distance between the speaker in *Porzellan* and the event of destruction which draws him into the sphere of meaning which it determines.

The relation between 'The Whitsun Weddings' and Grünbein's approach in *Porzellan* is, however, complex. Larkin's poem is marked by a 'fracture' between the 'vivid impression it creates of a known community', and the sense in which 'the speaker's relationship with the newly married couples climbing aboard the train suggests that this community is not *entirely* known'.[81] That disparity contributes to the elegiac feel of the poem, and is intensified (not overcome) by the poem's end, which is in a subtle solitude. Intensity is curiously allied here to indeterminacy. As the train approaches its terminus, there is a feeling of restriction,[82] followed in a quintessential Larkin end-cadence by one of sinking physical (not to mention male sexual) release:

> And as the tightened brakes took hold, there swelled
> A sense of falling, like an arrow-shower
> Sent out of sight, somewhere becoming rain.[83]

All the gathered potential of Larkin's event ('what it held / Stood ready to be loosed with all the power / That being changed can give'[84]) is channelled into

---

79 Helmut Böttiger and Durs Grünbein, 'Benn schmort in der Hölle. Ein Gespräch über dialogische und monologische Lyrik', *Text + Kritik*, 153.1 (2002), 72–84 (p. 78). See also *Vom Stellenwert der Worte*, p. 52: 'Poesie ist Subjektmagie als Sprachereignis' [poetry is subjective magic as an event of language].

80 Seamus Heaney, 'Joy or Night. Last Things in the Poetry of W. B. Yeats and Philip Larkin', in *The Redress of Poetry* (New York: Farrar, Straus and Giroux, 1995), pp. 146–63 (p. 152).

81 Stephen Regan, *Philip Larkin* (Basingstoke: Palgrave, 1997), p. 17.

82 Larkin, 'Whitsun Weddings', p. 23 (ll. 72–73).

83 Ibid., p. 23 (ll. 77–79).

84 Ibid., p. 23 (ll. 75–76).

an ending whose subtlety and culminating rhythmical power are matched by the completeness with which it dissipates, in a flight of simile and the fineness of rain, any connection between lyric speaker and perceived world. There is no suggestion that Larkin's speaking consciousness is 'changed' by the transformation it recognizes, or the people it encounters. Forces of interruption or encounter opening in the poem are in the end defused, because the subjectivity by which they are registered and expressed consciously disengages itself from the possibility that it shares a common horizon of experience with the lives it observes. This is the 'seeming capacity of Larkin to escape from his poems', and has been seen as part of his Romantic inheritance.[85] It is analogous to the way Grünbein's various conceptions of poetic language, as for example epitaph and polyphony, often serve to deflect his own finite subjectivity into an indeterminate aesthetic distance.

Larkin's poems can be seen as 'breaking open into pleasure, and a kind of easing, at the moment where [...] recognition [is] most pungent'.[86] The easing can be relief and extrication (directly proportionate to the pleasure his last lines invariably give). Here we can find, perhaps surprisingly, the source of Larkin's oblique relevance to the German context, for the 'opposite principle' of this movement is that of Celan, whose 'poems deliberately drive himself and his reader into a narrow place where the horror [...] can be seen most intently, felt most intensely'.[87] The obvious parallel and contrast to 'The Whitsun Weddings' in this regard is 'Todesfuge' ['Death Fugue'], which 'in Celan's rhythmical lines with their compelled, hypnotic recurrences' also produces the movement of a train.[88] From that train, however, no-one alights unchanged, and its destination is a fate from which there is no extricating: where smoke, vapour (Larkin's 'gouts of steam'[89]) and the upward and downward patterns of swelling and falling – of cadence – draw together ('ein Grab in der Luft' [a grave in the air][90]) in an annihilation that is not reflected on by means of any formal mastery of the poem (as it is, for example, in Larkin's 'Aubade'[91]), but determines it completely.

It is Celan's sense of a shared historical rupture which underlies Grünbein's idea of the poem as event – the fissures which spread through *Porzellan* are off-

---

85 John Bayley, 'The Last Romantic. Philip Larkin', in *Selected Essays* (Cambridge: Cambridge University Press, 1984), pp. 93–102 (p. 94).

86 Bayley, *Housman's Poems*, p. 181.

87 Ibid.

88 Ibid., p. 67.

89 Larkin, 'Whitsun Weddings', p. 22 (l. 58).

90 Celan, *Gesammelte Werke*, III, p. 63 (l. 35).

91 Philip Larkin, 'Aubade', in Larkin, *Collected Poems*, ed. with an introduction by Anthony Thwaite (London: The Marvell Press and Faber and Faber, 1988), pp. 208–9.

shoots of the 'meridian' on which, for Celan, poems occur as moments of encounter ('Begegnung'[92]) on the vast plane of dispersal and separation. Grünbein takes Larkin's thought of an event and 'something that survived it' (see above), and turns it to the particular circumstances of a historical happening and its aftermath. In doing so he employs in many of his vignettes (such as the 'Polterabend') an elegiac tone which fixes on the remembered detail of lost objects and locales. Sometimes this is done (as it often is in Larkin) in order to contrast them with the greyness of what came after – in the first poem of *Porzellan* he evokes that superficial closing of wounds effected by the post-war (East German) settlement: 'Ein strenges Einheitsgrau / Schloß die Wunden, und von Zauber blieb – Verwaltung' [An austere standard grey / Closed the wounds, and what remained of the spell was – administration].[93] But the elegiac mode is itself ambivalent: 'Elegie, das kehrt wie Schluckauf wieder' [Elegy, that returns like hiccups].[94] It is 'a recurring hiccup and thus a mild bodily dysfunction',[95] a self-conscious or even embarrassing version of that 'turn of breath' in which Celan says the poem receives the address of an 'other' and is constituted as a moment of encounter. In Grünbein's elegy there flashes the world – of Dresden – that was lost, but only as the realization firstly that the poet does not belong to it (that it is 'nie mehr zurückzuholen'), and secondly that in evoking it he subsumes it to his own late-born subjectivity. Thus near the end of the sequence, the lyric voice splits against itself in summoning survivors' aggression towards 'Diese Brut, die Krieg nur aus den Kinosesseln kennt' [This brood which knows war only from the cinema seats].[96] In the refractory snapshots making up *Porzellan*, the lyric stance does not encounter a historical world that is its own, but nor does it meet anything that is properly other than itself (since the experience of others instantly becomes a function of its own belatedness).

The 'hiccup' of elegy – the vocal expression of this mismatch in the poem's subjectivity – marks both the presence, in *Porzellan*, of Celan and his insistence on the ethical structure of poems as conversations ('Gespräch'[97]), and the haunting absence in Grünbein's own voice of that which makes such a structure possible. For Celan the poem has to have a fundamental generosity, such that it 'läßt [...] das ihm, dem Anderen, Eigenste mitsprechen: dessen Zeit' [allows [...] that which is most his, the other's, own to speak too: the other's time].[98] To hear

92 Celan, 'Der Meridian', *Gesammelte Werke*, III, p. 198.
93 *Porzellan*, poem 1 (ll. 6–7).
94 Ibid., poem 1 (l. 10).
95 Fuchs, 'Bombing of Dresden', p. 49.
96 *Porzellan*, poem 42 (l. 8).
97 Celan, 'Der Meridian', *Gesammelte Werke*, III, p. 198.
98 Ibid.

the time of the other is the necessary aim of all poems; to such time, the 'event' of Grünbein's poem itself generously opens, catching the presence of lives from which it is irrevocably separate but which determine it. Yet that time can never, in fact, be heard as other – it can only be styled into meaningful vignettes by a poetic consciousness which, in making a theme of fragmentation, imposes itself as a force of unity. *Porzellan* can produce no voice, however ostensibly critical of the narrating speaker, which would not serve to foreground another aspect of that speaker's situation; Grünbein's poem knows nothing of those radical movements of self-alienation, within the time of poetic utterance, which characterize Celan.[99] That is because Grünbein's poetics has a lesser doctrine of otherness, and so ultimately of encounter, than Celan's – it has no regard to that truly Other of which other people ('jeder Mensch' [every person]) are 'figures' ('eine Gestalt dieses Anderen' [a figure of this Other]), and by virtue of which are met both in their human distinctness and in the common horizon defined by that place, or non-place ('Utopie'), which poems – figurative language – cannot name but to which for Celan they are always directed ('Das Gedicht sucht, glaube ich, auch diesen Ort' [The poem seeks, I believe, this place too]).[100] Following Celan's image of a poetic meridian, we can say that 'one cannot ever see the utopian light except as reflected *from* the things it illuminates in this world'.[101] Grünbein's poetry, though it stages many encounters, never yields to that stranger horizon. Larkin sometimes knows the light which illumines Celan's latitudes – and knows it, as in the poem 'Solar', like Celan as the gift of the Other – but only through a soaring lift into endless space, not as reflected in the world of encounter: 'Simplified by distance / Into an origin [...] Coined there among / Lonely horizontals [...] You give for ever'.[102]

Larkin and Grünbein are often one another's converse. Where a poem such as 'The Whitsun Weddings' effects disengagement through appropriation, *Porzellan* derives its evocative sympathy from a premise of distance. And the poem feels the difficulty of this keenly (in it lies perhaps the full meaning of its title motif) – that Grünbein's authentic response to the caesura from which his poem emerges, and whose association is with rupture and disparateness, can only take the form of

---

99 Identified, for example, by Werner Hamacher in 'Die Sekunde der Inversion. Bewegungen einer Figur durch Celans Gedichte', in *Paul Celan*, ed. by Werner Hamacher and Winfried Menninghaus (Frankfurt a. M.: Suhrkamp, 1988), pp. 88–126.

100 Celan, 'Der Meridian', in *Gesammelte Werke*, III, p. 198, first two quotations; ibid., p. 199 (second quotation).

101 Raymond Geuss, 'Celan's Meridian', *boundary 2*, 33 (2006), 201–26 (p. 215).

102 Philip Larkin, 'Solar', in Larkin, *High Windows* (London: Faber and Faber, 1999 [1974]), p. 27 (ll. 9–21).

smooth epic sequence and formal calculation, whose effect is sovereign and unitary. Accordingly the 'hiccup' does not occur as any real disturbance in the lyric voice of *Porzellan*, but rather as a cumulative self-awareness spoken of several times as 'shame' ('flößt [...] die Stadt mir Scham ein, nichts als Scham' [the town instils shame in me, nothing but shame]; 'das alte Schamgefühl erwacht' [the old feeling of shame awakens]; 'Treibt seine Faxen / Mit der Scham, der Schande' [Fools around / With shame, with disgrace]).[103] Larkin, to whose work any such feeling is alien,[104] characteristically rounds a poem into (meticulously achieved) ease; Grünbein likewise produces a poem of crafted colloquial facility, in which however the – Larkinesque – stance of ironic observation and lyric adeptness is a cause of underlying self-recrimination. We might say that shame pertains not simply to any one rupture (the instances of it in *Porzellan* vary in their specific points of reference), but to a wider sense of 'historical excess that can never be adequately grasped'.[105] Because, unlike in Celan, the poem has no way of receiving that excess – whether by showing itself to be vulnerable in its exposure to history or susceptible to transformation by any Other – it is thrown back on to its own inner processes and subjective constitution. In the terms of a philosophical analysis of the matter, 'what appears in shame' is 'the fact of being riveted to oneself'.[106] The poetic consciousness behind *Porzellan* is exposed to itself as its own excessive lack of exposure – the ethical reflex can only be internalized, as a feeling of shame: something like an indefinite change of tincture from within, blushing the white surfaces of Dresden china. But in this, *Porzellan* comes closer than any other of Grünbein's works to disturbing that Nietzschean, or Poundian, understanding of presence which is, in the end, only the 'illusionary resuscitation' of lived experience through the self-masking operations of aesthetic refraction and stylization. That is demonstrated by shame itself, the poem's spreading sense of an ethical involvement which is neither definable in terms of cultural codes – unlike guilt – nor able to be channelled (and so averted) by aesthetic reflexes. If it is correct to say that Grünbein's shame appears as a blush on the pale glazed textures of porcelain, then in it rises to the surface of the poem a bodily presence which is quite different from the cultivated tropes of epitaph or the sovereign organization of personae, in which the determinacy and affectability of the poetic consciousness are held at arm's length. In *Porzellan* that distance is closed, and consciousness is rather 'riveted' to itself – which is to say, to the

103 *Porzellan*, poem 8 (ll. 5–6), poem 11 (l. 2), poem 42 (l. 4).
104 See Bayley, *Housman's Poems*, p. 52.
105 Fuchs, 'Bombing of Dresden', p. 40.
106 Emmanuel Levinas, *On Escape*, trans. by Bettina Bergo, introduced and annotated by Jacques Rolland (Stanford: Stanford University Press, 2003), p. 64.

symbol (fragile china) which it finds for its experience – in the shameful acknowledgement of an excess. Though Grünbein cannot do justice to what is felt as excess, his shame at not being able to do so hints at an insight into what that excess is: 'the question of shame speaks [...] of the human subject as implicated in, but not reducible to, the collective existence of a given society, as well as of society as the universal condition of the human'.[107] In *Porzellan* the inner experience of shame is the poem's oblique opening to an outside, which is and can only ever be the sphere of historically embedded relation between singular human beings, whom poems can never name but to whom they are always responding. Celan saw this as the characteristic exteriority of the poem in its search for the (non-)place which defines it: 'wir sind weit draußen' [we are far outside].[108] Its formulation in terms directly applicable to *Porzellan*, though, comes from Emily Dickinson:

> Shame is the shawl of Pink
> In which we wrap the Soul
> To keep it from infesting eyes –
> The elemental Veil
> Which helpless Nature drops
> When pushed upon a scene
> Repugnant to her probity –
> Shame is the tint divine.[109]

Shame is an ethical response in the particular body which links it to all other bodies – to 'Nature' – and so to the origin, beyond bodies, of bodily existence itself: to the divine.[110] Some version of this is present in Celan's account of the 'utopian' horizon. Grünbein, like Larkin, shares neither Dickinson's theology nor Celan's equivalent questing for the place from which poems, ultimately, speak. In *Porzellan*, however, he achieves a poetic subtlety and – sometimes in tension with his inclination to detachment – moments of openness to the subjective experience of historical complexity which draw him near to both.

107 Michael Minden, 'Even the Flowering of Art isn't Pure. Günter Grass's Figures of Shame', in *Changing the Nation. Günter Grass in International Perspective*, ed. by Rebecca Braun and Frank Brunssen (Würzburg: Königshausen & Neumann, 2008), pp. 23–35 (p. 25).

108 Celan, 'Der Meridian', *Gesammelte Werke*, III, p. 199.

109 Dickinson, *Complete Poems*, no. 1412.

110 On Dickinson's poem see also Minden, 'Flowering of Art', pp. 24–25.

Karen Leeder

Durs Grünbein and the Poetry of Science

It has often been pointed out that the late 1980s and 1990s saw a paradigm shift in German poetry. This chimed with the coming to prominence of a new cohort of poets, those born in the late 1950s and 1960s, and ushered in a new understanding of the poetic enterprise. In his authoritative overview of the period, Hermann Korte draws attention to the 'generational shift' and the increased reflexivity of the new poetry.[1] Other critics have pointed out the level of abstraction and difficulty inherent in it.[2] While drawing out the overriding preoccupations and tendencies, however, Korte also rightly insists on the tension between the sheer waywardness of groupings and impulses characterizing this most various and vigorous of poetic moments.[3] In retrospect one of the most significant of these can be seen to be what Peter Geist calls the 'paradigm shift from a historical interrogation of reality to one drawing on the natural sciences'.[4] Korte, too, sees the rapprochement between the two spheres of knowledge (poetry and science) as one of the key developments of the 1990s, and others have identified what has been termed a 'scientific turn', a 'cognitive turn' or the rise of the *poeta doctus* as the defining characteristic of these years.[5] This chapter seeks to read Grünbein's intense engagement with the natural sciences up to c. 1995 against the backdrop

1 Hermann Korte, 'Energie der Brüche. Ein diachroner Blick auf die Lyrik des 20. Jahrhunderts und ihre Zäsuren', in *Lyrik des 20. Jahrhunderts*, ed. by Heinz Ludwig Arnold (Munich: Text + Kritik, 1999), pp. 63–106 (pp. 95–96).

2 Karen Leeder, '"Schreiben am Schnittpunkt". The Place of Contemporary German Poetry', in *Schaltstelle. Neue deutsche Lyrik im Dialog*, ed. by Karen Leeder (Amsterdam: Rodopi, 2007), pp. 1–30.

3 He sets out the different groupings in *Deutschsprachige Lyrik seit 1945*, 2nd rev. edn (Stuttgart: Metzler, 2004), pp. 245–93; Klaus-Michael Bogdal, 'Klimawechsel. Eine kleine Meteorologie der Gegenwartsliteratur', in *Baustelle Gegenwartsliteratur. Die neunziger Jahre*, ed. by Andreas Erb (Opladen: Westdeutscher Verlag, 1998), pp. 9–31.

4 Peter Geist, '"die ganz großen themen fühlen sich gut an". Die Wiederkehr des Politischen in der jüngeren Lyrik', in *Junge Lyrik*, ed. by Heinz Ludwig Arnold (Munich: Text + Kritik, 2006), pp. 98–117 (p. 102).

5 Korte, *Deutschsprachige Lyrik seit 1945*, p. 280; the term 'scientific turn' comes from Swantje Lichtenstein (herself a young poet of note), *Das lyrische Projekt. Rhetorik, Räumlichkeit und Wissenschaft* (Munich, Iudicium, 2004), p. 15; 'the cognitive turn' based on 'a poetics of understanding' is explored by Friedrich W. Block, '"Erfahrung als Experiment". Poetik im Zeitalter naturwissenschaftlicher Erkenntnistheorien', in Arnold, *Lyrik des 20. Jahrhunderts*, pp. 248–64; Karen Leeder, 'The "poeta doctus" and the new German literature', *Germanic Review*, 77.1 (2002), 51–67.

of its historical moment and the particular trajectory of the poet himself. It cannot hope to provide a full account of this engagement; something that has anyway been the subject of numerous critical approaches over the past decade and notably the pioneering monograph by Anna Alissa Ertel, which appeared while this volume was in preparation.[6] It explores rather how this phase functioned within the poet's development and how it has determined his later work. In line with many critics I argue that science provides a vehicle for Grünbein to distance himself from his origins in the GDR and to find a foothold in the united Germany. It also, however, allows him to explore affinities with literary forbears (especially Büchner, Benn and Goethe) and to develop a poetics of the body and a new diction that attempt to answer that historical moment more broadly. In this he shares affinities with a number of other poets of the same generation whose origins lie not in the GDR but in West Germany and Austria. However, this phase will also prove vital in developing a larger poetological framework and allowing Grünbein to define poetry itself as a liminal, dialogic, even utopian, enterprise; an understanding which will outlast his explicit engagement with the natural sciences and which runs contrary to his much-trumpeted cynicism.

Along with significant interventions by older writers (chief among them Hans Magnus Enzensberger) works of the 1990s (and in some cases beyond) by many of the most significant younger poets have placed science at the heart of their poetic project: Thomas Kling, Franz Josef Czernin, Albert Ostermeier, Marcel Beyer, Raoul Schrott, Brigitte Oleschinksi, Ulrike Draesner, Barbara Köhler and of course Durs Grünbein himself. However, if poetry has entered the 'laboratory of the twentieth century'[7] in an unprecedented way over the last two decades or so, it has done so in pursuit of very particular areas of knowledge (though the lines drawn here are by no means absolute). Quantum physics, for example, has been a dominant interest for poets like Enzensberger and Schrott;[8] Draesner has made a notable poetic study of the effects of gene manipulation in her 'radical translations' of Shakespeare's sonnets, 'Twin Spin'; and Barbara Köhler has explored computers, complex mathematics, artificial intelligence, genetics and quantum

6 I address the body of critical work on this subject below. Anna Alissa Ertel, *Körper, Gehirne, Gene. Lyrik und Naturwissenschaft bei Ulrike Draesner und Durs Grünbein* (Berlin: de Gruyter, 2011).

7 Karen Leeder, 'The Poetry of Science and the Science of Poetry. German Poetry in the Laboratory of the Twentieth Century', *German Life and Letters*, 60.3 (2007), 412–29, upon which I draw for this chapter.

8 Raoul Schrott, *Tropen: Über das Erhabene* (Munich: Hanser, 1998). On Schrott compare Iain Galbraith, 'The Poet and the Pendulum: Composition and Metaphor in the Poetics of Raoul Schrott', in Leeder, *Schaltstelle*, pp. 213–30.

uncertainty in her *Niemands Frau* (2007).[9] Numerous poets (including some of these mentioned above and Grünbein himself) have shown a particular interest in the biological or life sciences; especially elements of anthropology, neurology, genetics and molecular biology, which represent key advances in science of the late twentieth and early twenty-first century and which have impacted on society as central interpretative paradigms. This has led to a highly-charged interest in the body in recent poetry: a subject which has been widely commented upon.[10] It should be noted, however, that the poetry of the 1990s has not simply focussed on a scientific, anatomical examination of the body *per se*, but has also used this as a stepping stone to generate a poetic programme of sorts. The commentator Erk Grimm observed in 1995:

> Contemporary poetry extends deep into the inner regions of the body, it reflects the inside of the pharynx, larynx, trachea, cerebrum and all the grammatical insides. [...] Projected into the realm of the anatomical, it turns on simulated representations of wholeness, like the body, brain and the illusion of an 'I', instances of wholeness that only become apparent by dint of incisions, tears and ruptures.[11]

Durs Grünbein has been one of the key proponents of this new poetry. Indeed by many he is seen as its representative figure – for better and for worse.[12] His rise to prominence in the early 1990s was conditioned by his adoption of the themes and

9 Ulrike Draesner, 'Twin Spin: Sonette von Shakespeare – Radikalübersetzungen', and the essay 'Dolly and Will', in Peter Waterhouse, Ulrike Draesner and Barbara Köhler, *:to change the subject* (Göttingen: Wallstein, 2000), pp. 11–33. A first account is given in Karen Leeder, '"Übungen der Zugewandtheit". Ulrike Draesner's Poetics of Correspondence', in Leeder, *Schaltstelle*, pp. 231–62; On Köhler see Margaret Littler, 'Strange Loops and Quantum Turns in Barbara Köhler's *Niemands Frau*', in *An Odyssey for Our Time. Barbara Köhler's 'Niemands Frau'*, ed. by Georgina Paul (Amsterdam: Rodopi, 2013), *forthcoming*.

10 Jörg Magenau, 'Der Körper als Schnittfläche. Bemerkungen zur Literatur der neuesten Neuen Innerlichkeit', in Erb, *Baustelle Gegenwartsliteratur*, pp. 107–21; Anne-Rose Meyer, 'Physiologie und Poesie. Zu Körperdarstellungen in der Lyrik von Ulrike Draesner, Durs Grünbein und Thomas Kling', *Gegenwartsliteratur. A German Studies Yearbook*, 1 (2002), 107–33; Michael Eskin, 'Body Language. Durs Grünbein's Aesthetics', *arcadia*, 37.1 (2002), 42–66; Ruth Owen, 'Bodies in Contemporary German Poetry', in Leeder, *Schaltstelle*, pp. 269–91.

11 Erk Grimm, 'Das Gedicht nach dem Gedicht. Über die Lesbarkeit der jüngsten Lyrik', in *Deutschsprachige Gegenwartsliteratur. Wider ihre Verächter*, ed. by Christian Döring (Frankfurt a. M.: Suhrkamp, 1995), pp. 287–311 (p. 293).

12 Fabian Lampart rightly demonstrates the problems inherent in trying to treat Grünbein as representative in any sense in '"Der junge Dichter als Sphinx". Durs Grünbein und die deutsche Lyrik nach 1989', in *Schreiben am Schnittpunkt. Poesie und Wissen bei Durs Grünbein*, ed. by Kai Bremer, Fabian Lampart and Jörg Wesche (Freiburg i. Br.: Rombach, 2007), pp. 19–36, though he does not treat the group of poets of science.

modes of modern science and also fed back into the proliferation of this kind of poetry. He exploited a widespread domestication of popular science that gave his work an immediately contemporary relevance (though I shall argue below that his choice of subject matter also had further important grounds). It brought him immediate attention from newspaper writers and a literary industry, arguably keen to seek legitimacy through an association with the hard sciences. Indeed, eclipsing his treatment of GDR themes or the city, Grünbein's engagement with science determined his early reception to an overwhelming degree.[13] But it also brought him detractors. Judith Ryan pointed out in 2001 that even critics favourable to Grünbein's project often felt the need to defend him against charges of abstruse intellectualism, on the one hand, or the suspicion of simply raiding scientific fields rich in exotic technical jargon, on the other.[14] And in 1995, in a caustic polemic aimed at the collection *Falten und Fallen*, the poet Franz Josef Czernin charged him with showy displays of learning and esoteric terminology that were meant, he claimed, to demonstrate his urbanity: 'chasing down big feelings or humanistic ideas with synthetic concepts culled from neurology, chemistry, computer science or communications technology'. Moreover, he interpreted the overwhelmingly positive reception of this strand of poetry as a sign of a critical bias against a politically engaged Brechtian legacy and in favour of Gottfried Benn, indicative of a restorative age retreating into an abstract high modernism.[15] For all that Czernin's critique is, perhaps, unduly pointed, many of his keen observations go a long way to diagnosing the conflicted state of German poetry at this historical juncture (and I shall return to Benn below). Indeed Grünbein is not the

13 Compare Iso Camartin, 'Die Anatomie und das Lebensgefühl', in *Peter-Huchel-Preis 1995. Durs Grünbein, Texte, Dokumente, Materialien*, ed. by Wolfgang Heidenreich (Baden-Baden, Zurich: Elster, Rio, 1998), pp. 25–32; Ruth Owen, 'Science in Contemporary Poetry. A Point of Comparison between Raoul Schrott and Durs Grünbein', *German Life and Letters*, 54.1 (2001), 82–96; Ron Winkler, *Dichtung zwischen Großstadt und Großhirn. Annäherungen an das lyrische Werk Durs Grünbeins* (Hamburg: Kovač, 2000); Alexander Müller, *Das Gedicht als Engramm. Memoria und Imagination in der Poetik Durs Grünbeins* (Oldenburg: Igel, 2004); Bremer, Lampart and Wesche, *Schreiben am Schnittpunkt. Poesie und Wissen bei Durs Grünbein*, as above. A useful survey is contained in the *Text + Kritik* volume on Grünbein and also in Sylvia Heudecker, 'Durs Grünbein in der Kritik', in Bremer, Lampart and Wesche, *Schreiben am Schnittpunkt*, pp. 37–56.

14 Judith Ryan, 'Das Motiv der Schädelnähte bei Durs Grünbein', in *Schreiben nach der Wende. Ein Jahrzehnt deutscher Literatur 1989–1999*, ed. by Gerhard Fischer and David Roberts (Tübingen: Stauffenburg, 2001), pp. 301–15 (p. 301).

15 Franz Josef Czernin, 'Falten und Fallen. Zu einem Gedichtband von Durs Grünbein', *Schreibheft. Zeitschrift für Literatur*, 45 (1995), 179–88 (p. 179). Reprinted as 'Falten und Fallen. Zu Durs Grünbeins Gedichtband', in Franz Josef Czernin, *Der Himmel ist blau. Aufsätze zur Dichtung* (Weil am Rhein: Engeler, 2007), pp. 29–56.

only poet to suffer such attacks.[16] But before analyzing the role of the natural sciences in his work, it is worth setting out the context.

Poetry and Science

Poetry and science were long thought of as allied spheres of learning: Lucretius's *De rerum natura* was written in poetic form, for example; for Dante the two realms were indivisible. Nevertheless, the fundamental split came in the seventeenth century. As a result, in the modern age poetry and science have more often been thought of as irreconcilable opposites – an opposition the philosopher Mary Midgley has recently argued we can ill afford.[17] But if the professional specialization of knowledge was separating poetry and science – the 'cave of making' from 'the laboratory' – in popular culture, they were united within an ongoing debate at least. This split is attested to by C. P. Snow's definition of the 'two cultures' and the debates that have ensued.[18] Responding in 1968 to Aldous Huxley's 1963 treatise 'Science and Literature', Jürgen Habermas famously argued that, in the modern world, science affects ordinary people only through its application in technology and the social consequences:

> Taken for itself, knowledge of atomic physics remains without consequence for the interpretation of our life-world, and to this extent the gulf between the two cultures is inevitable. Only when with the aid of physical theories we can carry out nuclear fission, only when information is exploited for the development of productive or destructive forces, can its revolutionary *practical results* penetrate the literary consciousness of the life-world: poems arise from consideration of Hiroshima and not from the elaboration of hypotheses about the transformation of mass into energy.[19]

16 The very similar charges levelled at Schrott are documented in Leeder, 'The "poeta doctus"', as above.

17 Mary Midgley, *Science and Poetry* (London: Routledge, 2000).

18 Ertel summarizes the issues in *Körper, Gehirne, Gene*, pp. 12–23. Useful contributions to the debate include *The Third Culture: Literature and Science*, ed. by Elinor Schaffer (Berlin: de Gruyter, 1998) and Robert Cordle, *Postmodern Postures: Literature, Science and the Two Cultures Debate* (Aldershot: Ashgate, 1999).

19 Jürgen Habermas, 'Technischer Fortschritt und soziale Lebenswelt', in *Technik und Wissenschaft als Ideologie* (Frankfurt a. M.: Suhrkamp, 1968), pp. 104–19 (p. 107); Jürgen Habermas, 'Technical Progress and the Social Life-World', in Habermas, *Toward a Rational Society*, trans. by Jeremy J. Shapiro (Cambridge: Polity Press, 1987), pp. 50–61.

However, in recent decades the well-policed boundaries between the two disciplines have been broken down; both by scientists and by writers, many of whom have begun to work together, but also by academics examining the links between them. Together they have explored not only the effects of science on literature, but also the traffic in the opposite direction and, what is more, the similarities between their processes.

There are several reasons for this. On one level it is a symptom of a widespread domestication of technology: it is almost inevitable that with the popularization of science over the last decades, it should become a more integrated part of cultural expression.[20] Gottfried Benn, the German poet who first led writers into what he called the 'laboratory of words', suggested it was the duty of the poet to be engaged fully in the fabric of the present day: 'Der Lyriker kann gar nicht genug wissen, er kann gar nicht genug arbeiten, er muß an allem nahe sein, er muß sich orientieren, wo die Welt heute hält, welche Stunde an diesem Mittag über der Erde steht' [The lyric poet can hardly know enough; he cannot work enough; he must be close to everything; he must position himself according to where the world is today, under whatever sign the earth stands this noon].[21] Writing about science can thus be interpreted as a necessary part of being involved in contemporary reality. And one might wonder whether Grünbein's vocabulary, for example, is really as esoteric or obscurely technical as Czernin claims, given the extensive availability of such information on the web.

But there has also been an important shift in the kind of science that has been drawn on by writers. For those addressing physics the subject matter of choice is emphatically that of Goodall's Third Science – ushered in by the Copenhagen statements of 1927 – that is where the apparent hierarchies and certainties of classical science have dissolved into the esoteric uncertainties of quantum mechanics and relativity. But these are also the governing principles of the work addressing biology and genetics for example. Chance and indeterminacy are the fundamental characteristics of describable reality. Identity is increasingly seen as the result of chemical processes, or governable genetic sequences. More important, however, the observer is not merely involved in, but also creates, the world he perceives. To cite Werner Heisenberg's famous statement on quantum uncertainty: 'Even in science the object of the search is no longer nature itself, but man's investigation of nature'.[22] This brings perception – rather than, say, ob-

20 Christian Gruber, *Literatur, Kultur, Quanten. Der Kampf um die Deutungshoheit und das naturwissenschaftliche Modell* (Würzburg: Königshausen & Neumann, 2003).
21 Gottfried Benn, 'Probleme der Lyrik', in Benn, *Sämtliche Werke*, ed. by Gerhard Schuster and Holger Hof (Stuttgart: Akademie 1986–2003), 7 vols, vol. VI (2001), pp. 9–44 (p. 36).
22 This is quoted in Raoul Schrott, *Tropen: Über das Erhabene* (Munich: Hanser, 1998), p. 161.

jective truth – to the fore, in a way that draws the two disciplines closer in a new way.

Finally there has been a shift in the status and understanding of science in recent years, led by writers such as Thomas S. Kuhn and Karl Popper. The so-called 'linguistic turn' has highlighted an approach that might lead to a more differentiated understanding of the two cultures. Richard Rorty's pragmatist view, outlined in *Contingency, Irony, and Solidarity*, has served to highlight the primacy of language in our experience of the world.

> If we could ever become reconciled to the idea that most of reality is indifferent to our descriptions of it, and that the *human self is created by the use of vocabulary* rather than being adequately or inadequately expressed *in a vocabulary*, then we should at last have assimilated what was true in the romantic idea that truth is made rather than found. What is true about this claim is just that languages are made rather than found, and that truth is a property of linguistic entities, of sentences.[23]

Of course the notion that the scientific view of the world is one among many possible realities is challenging to a culture based on Enlightenment notions of scientific progress – though not perhaps quite as challenging as it was even a few years ago. As Michael Luntley has argued in debate with Rorty in 1995, 'the end of modernity signals the end of the idea that the language of physics is the language of the world'.[24] This approach locates science as a linguistically and culturally contingent discourse within a spectrum of vocabularies with which we describe our experience of being in the world.

The implications for a traditional understanding of the relationship between science and literature are profound. According to Rorty scientific revolutions are thus merely 'metaphoric re-descriptions of nature' rather than 'insights into the intrinsic nature of nature'.[25] There is no space here to set out these debates in detail.[26] For the moment it is important to hold on to the fact that they combine to contribute to a plural, multivalent understanding of reality, but also that they contribute to a view of science as embedded in a cultural context and embodying culture in its beliefs and assumptions about the world. Moreover, it makes of

---

23 Richard Rorty, *Contingency, Irony, and Solidarity* (Cambridge: Cambridge University Press, 1989), pp. 7.

24 Michael Luntley, *Reason, Truth and Self: The Postmodern Reconditioned* (London: Routledge, 1995), p. 143.

25 Rorty, *Contingency*, pp. 16–17.

26 For a very useful survey I am indebted to Peter D. Smith, *Metaphor and Materiality: German Literature and the World View of Science 1780–1955* (Oxford: Legenda, 2000).

science simply a language used to describe the world, and in highlighting metaphor, it comes close to the basic premise of poetry.

A poetry of science such as developed in the early 1990s can be seen to partake of all these developments. All of them also impact upon traditional understandings of the relationship between poet and reader and the communicative gesture of the poem. The Nobel Laureate and immunologist Miroslav Holub, posits a 'profound complementarity' between the disciplines in an essay on the poetry of science.[27] On the surface at least this might seem counterintuitive. Science has traditionally tried to strip language down to a single, logical, localized meaning; poetry, on the contrary, exploits as many possible meanings and interactions between words and thoughts as it can. Scientific papers set out to make statements that do not represent an end in themselves, but seek outside verification from experiment; the truth of poetic statements is verifiable only from within the framework of the mood, style and reference of the poem. As Holub comments:

> The aim of scientific communication is to convey unequivocal information about one facet of a particular aspect of reality to the reader, and to the collective, anonymous thesaurus of scientific data. The aim of poetic communication is to introduce a related feeling or grasp of the one aspect of the human condition to the reader, or to the collective mind of cultural consciousness.[28]

However, closer examination reveals that if poetry and science appear to move in opposite directions, they do not necessarily move towards opposite extremes. They share an economy based on perception and articulation, whether in the form of conceit or hypothesis, metaphor or proof. Moreover, science needs poetic language. Indeed, it borrows regularly from metaphorical language. Poetry can be used to express scientific ideas in a manner that takes them beyond the narrow realm of scientific discourse and anchors them within the broader cultural and historical context.[29] The best of the poems written in recent years do not simply sample scientific vocabulary; they incorporate scientific principles into the fabric of the poetry – raising questions about the position of the observer, the nature of metaphor, and the possibilities of all language to describe the world.

---

27 Miroslav Holub, 'Poetry and Science. The Poetry of Science / The Science of Poetry', in Miroslav Holub, *The Dimension of the Present Moment and Other Essays* (London: Faber, 1990), pp. 122–46.
28 Ibid., p. 135.
29 Lavinia Greenlaw, 'Unstable Regions. Poetry and Science', in *Cultural Babbage. Technology, Time and Invention*, ed. by Francis Spufford and Jenny Uglow (London: Faber and Faber, 1996), pp. 215–26 (p. 217).

Grünbein and Science

The natural sciences are one of the thematic centres of gravity in Grünbein's early collections – especially *Grauzone morgens* (1988), *Schädelbasislektion* (1991), *Falten und Fallen* (1994) and those essays written between 1989–1995 and for the most part gathered in *Galilei vermißt Dantes Hölle und bleibt an den Maßen hängen* (1996). Critical accounts of Grünbein's development have concurred in identifying a caesura, which coincides with the award of the Büchner Prize in 1995. Though *Falten und Fallen* already includes poems which indicate the way ahead, as does the epigraph form of *Den teuren Toten* (1994), the publication of *Nach den Satiren* (1999), containing poems written between 1994 and 1999, heralds a definitive move from modern science towards the ancient past, and the encounter with the classical heritage.[30] Polemically the critic Michael Braun spoke of 'Grünbein's voluntary emigration into Classicism', and this shift signalled a mixed reception, to say the least, though it is anything but closed to the world at large.[31] However, before focusing in the rest of this chapter on the importance of the theme to Grünbein's early thinking and writing, it is worth noting that the natural sciences continue to remain important after this point.

This can be seen especially in the poet's largely anatomical view of the human body and strong interest in death, but the concentration of technical vocabulary and the exploration of poetic models associated with biological science largely give way to new interests. This is not to delineate any absolute divisions, however. Critics have continued to recognize the relevance of such themes in his later work: Walter Erhart, for example, has traced the importance of physics in *Vom Schnee oder Descartes in Deutschland* (2003).[32] One might also argue that in his return to Goethe in *Aroma* (2010), Grünbein is in some ways revisiting some of his previous concerns in a new light. Moreover, it has anyway been argued by Florian Berg, for example, that the supposed caesura in fact disguises a much more

---

30 This caesura has been the subject of frequent critical observation – if varying aesthetic weighting; Thomas Irmer, 'Durs Grünbein', in *Deutschsprachige Lyriker des 20. Jahrhunderts*, ed. by Ursula Heukenkamp and Peter Geist (Berlin: Erich Schmidt, 2007), pp. 711–21 (p. 712); Hermann Korte, 'Habemus poetam. Zum Konnex von Poesie und Wissen in Durs Grünbeins Gedichtsammlung "Nach den Satiren"', *Text + Kritik*, 153.1 (2002), 19–33; Helmut Böttiger, 'Die Maske wächst in das Gesicht', *Die Zeit*, 6 December 2007, Literatur, pp. 10–11.

31 Michael Braun, 'Die vernetzte Zunge des Propheten. Eine kleine Strömungslehre zur Lyrik des 21. Jahrhunderts', in Arnold, *Junge Lyrik*, pp. 37–57 (p. 38).

32 Walter Erhart, 'Literaturwissenschaft und Physik. Aus Anlass von Durs Grünbeins "Vom Schnee oder Descartes in Deutschland" (2003)', in *Literaturwissenschaft – interdisziplinär*, ed. by Lothar van Laak and Katja Malsch (Heidelberg: Synchron, 2010), pp. 115–26.

sustained engagement with history and anthropology.[33] Nevertheless, this area of thought has demonstrably had an impact on Grünbein's oeuvre and his development as a whole.

Certainly Grünbein was vocal during the early 1990s on the relationship between the two disciplines in interviews, essays and poetological statements. He also enjoyed a notable presence as a commentator on poetry and science and, a few years later, was also often in dialogue with scientists in a public context.[34] Echoing Benn's demand that the poet be at the height of his time Grünbein observes, 'Dem Denken dort zuzuhören, wo es gerade, und immer wieder sich neu formiert, gehört zu den verdammten Hausaufgaben des Dichters' [Listening to thought in those places where it is in the process of and is constantly forming itself anew, belongs to the blasted homework of the poet].[35] Elsewhere, again echoing Benn, he pinpoints the contemporaneity of the poet as residing essentially in a 'naturwissenschaftliche Zeitgenossenschaft' [contemporaneity in / through the natural sciences].[36]

This move is made explicit retrospectively in Grünbein's own 'Schlußwort zur *Schädelbasilektion*' ['Epigraph to *Schädelbasislektion*'], written for the edition of his first three volumes of poetry in 2006. Here, looking back over the intervening fifteen years, the interest in the sciences is identified closely with the unification of Germany and the call for a new world view and a new diction to accompany it.

> Dieses Buch ist das Protokoll einer Flugbahn. Es beschreibt den Absprung aus der einen, die unsanfte Landung in einer ganz anderen, wenn auch benachbarten Welt. [...] Es galt von einem Tag auf den anderen sich radikal auszunüchtern.

33 Florian Berg, *Das Gedicht und das Nichts. Über Anthropologie und Geschichte im Werk Durs Grünbeins* (Würzburg: Königshausen & Neumann, 2007).

34 Ernst Peter Fischer and Durs Grünbein, 'Vermessen. Wissenschaft zwischen Ratio und Spiritualität', http://www.gartenheim.de/aktuelles-neu/veranstaltungsarchiv/vermessen.html; Ernst Pöppel and Durs Grünbein, 'Schauder des Schaffens. Durs Grünbein im Gespräch mit dem Neurowissenschaftler Ernst Pöppel', *Der Spiegel*, 51 (2003), 214–20; 'Sehnsucht zerebral: Der Dichter Grünbein und der Hirnforscher [Wolf] Singer', *Süddeutsche Zeitung*, 17 October 2001, p. 20.

35 Durs Grümbein, *Galilei vermißt Dantes Hölle und bleibt an den Maßen hängen. Aufsätze 1989–1995* (Frankfurt a. M.: Suhrkamp, 1996), p. 13. Ertel offers a detailed discussion of this essay, 'Ameisenhafte Größe' ['Ant-like Size'], which she regards as central, *Körper, Gehirne, Gene*, pp. 24–31.

36 Anke Bienderra, Sabine Wilke and Durs Grünbein, '"Wie kann man zwei auseinanderbrechende Jahrhunderte verbinden?" Interview mit Durs Grünbein', in Sabine Wilke, *Ist alles so geblieben, wie es früher war? Essays zu Literatur und Frauenpolitik im vereinten Deutschland* (Würzburg: Königshausen & Neumann, 2000), pp. 113–21 (p. 115).

> [This book is the protocol of a certain trajectory. It charts taking off from one world and the uneven landing in a quite different, if adjacent, one. [...] It was a question of a radical sobering up from one day to the next.][37]

For Grünbein this involved bidding farewell to one ideology, 'Die strenge und einseitige Logik von Geschichte und Geschichtstheologie' [the strict and one-sided logic of history and a theology of history], in favour of another: 'eine neue, noch unbestimmte Grammatik der Naturwissenschaften, [...] den Geist von Fakten und Statistik. [...] Eine andere Sachlichkeit mußte her' [a new and still uncertain grammar born of the natural sciences, the spirit of facts and statistics. [...] A new sobriety was called for].[38] Interesting here is the way that ideological, historical and linguistic dimensions are conflated. It is after all the 'grammar' of the natural sciences which he seeks, underlining the extent to which this shift to a new (political) reality also denotes the search for a new language adequate to it. Michael Braun homes in on this aspect: signalling Grünbein's embrace of scientific terminology as the way out of an experience of a 'linguistic crisis' common to many from the former GDR after 1990.[39]

This ideological interpretation, along with its linguistic ramifications, is of vital significance then; but it is perhaps not the only one. At one level, it is quite understandable that the release from the all-encompassing ideologically-determined dogma of life in the GDR would necessarily demand the search for a kind of alternative framework and diction. Helmut Böttiger, for example, argues that science functions as a kind of 'stabilization' for Grünbein.[40] But, of course, many poets did not seek such a radical shift of mode; preferring, for example, to critique precisely those perversions of the past from within the same frame of reference. Equally, at the same time, many poets in Germany as a whole, and beyond, made the same move without the backdrop of the GDR past. And the linguistic crisis faced by those emerging from the shadow of dictatorship might perhaps simply be regarded as a more acute form of larger currents experienced by writers across a wide spectrum. This suggests that there are other factors in play, which are not as accessible to Grünbein in his retrospective interpretation.

---

37 Durs Grünbein, *Gedichte. Bücher I–III (Grauzone morgens, Schädelbasislektion, Falten und Fallen)* (Frankfurt a. M.: Suhrkamp, 2006), pp. 385–95 (p. 385).

38 Ibid., p. 386.

39 Michael Braun, 'In aufgerissenen Sprachräumen. Eine Begegnung mit Gedichten der neunziger Jahre', in Döring, *Deutschsprachige Gegenwartsliteratur*, pp. 271–85 (p. 277).

40 Helmut Böttiger, 'Durs Grünbein. Die sibirischen Abenteuerspielplätze', in Helmut Böttiger, *Rausch im Niemandsland. Es gibt ein Leben nach der DDR* (Berlin: Fannei und Walz, 1994), pp. 86–95 (p. 90).

Heiner Müller's insightful speech on the occasion of the award to Grünbein of the 1995 Büchner Prize, hints at a similar overall interpretation when he speaks of Grünbein's poems as emphatically giving form to the 'experience of a generation'. Moreover, he identifies that generation in terms which have now come to define the intellectual agony of the final years of the GDR: 'Es ist die Generation der Untoten des kalten Kriegs, die Geschichte nicht mehr als Sinngebung des Sinnlosen durch Ideologie, sondern nur noch als sinnlos begreifen kann' [It is the generation of the undead of the Cold War, who can no longer understand history by making sense of the senseless through ideology, but can only now understand it as senseless].[41] Müller's speech is remarkable in many ways, which have yet to be adequately assessed; however, significant here is that, while pinpointing Grünbein's poetry as rooted in the experience of the collapse of the GDR, he suggests that the resonance might extend much further. It is, for example, the catastrophes of the twentieth century as a whole, 'unter den Sternen wie unter dem Mikroskop' [under the stars and under the microscope], which Müller sees taking shape in Grünbein's verse (p. 29); his is the poetry of 'Endzeit' [an end time] (p. 28), which might well be the end of the GDR but could certainly be interpreted more broadly – especially given the rhetoric of death, the undead and vampirism, with which the poems are described. Moreover, Grünbein's poetry, he claims, stands in the shadow of Poe and Kafka, answers that of Lord Chandos and Rilke;[42] thereby indicating an explicitly modernist lineage; and comes equipped, moreover, with the 'kalte[r] Blick' [cold gaze] (p. 28), the 'Ichverlust' [loss of self] (p. 28), the 'X-ray vision' (p. 29), the quality of a 'Maschine' [machine] (p. 26) or of poetry 'under the microscope' (p. 29), which are characteristic of a much broader modernist impulse. Going further, Müller makes Grünbein's poems representative of a radically disenfranchised lyric subjectivity – one without 'Vaterland' or 'Muttersprache' [fatherland, mother tongue] – which of necessity extends beyond the immediate political frame of reference (p. 27). Müller's account culminates in a

---

41 Heiner Müller, 'Portrait des Künstlers als junger Grenzhund', in Durs Grünbein, *Den Körper zerbrechen. Rede zur Entgegennahme des Georg-Büchner-Preises* (Frankfurt a. M.: Suhrkamp, 1995), pp. 25–29 (p. 26). The chapter by Chris Young in this volume also discusses this speech. Müller's words have been taken to represent the dilemma of this generation and of the last years of the GDR more generally by, for example, Wolfgang Emmerich, in his 'The GDR and its Literature An Overview', in *Re-reading East Germany: The Literature and Film of the GDR 1949–2009*, ed. by Karen Leeder (Cambridge: Cambridge University Press, 2013), *forthcoming*.

42 Compare Durs Grünbein, 'An Lord Chandos. Ein Fax aus der Zukunft', in Durs Grünbein, *Gedicht und Geheimnis. Aufsätze 1990–2006* (Frankfurt a. M.: Suhrkamp, 2007), pp. 75–76; 'To Lord Chandos: A Fax from the Future', trans. by Andrew Shields, in Durs Grünbein, *The Bars of Atlantis. Selected Essays*, ed. by Michael Eskin, trans. by John Crutchfield, Michael Hofmann and Andrew Shields (New York: Farrar, Straus and Giroux, 2010), pp. 72–76.

striking description of Grünbein's poetry; as one which finds its muse in the computer and its images in the very material of the present: 'Seine Bilder sind Röntgenbilder, seine Gedichte Schatten von Gedichten, aufs Papier geworfen wie vom Atomblitz' [His images are X-rays, his poems are shadows of poems, projected onto the paper as if by an atomic flash] (p. 29). If I have dwelled on this laudatio, it is because, while seeming to hail Grünbein as a product of a particular GDR experience, it implies that his poetry recalls and answers a particular kind of modernism and is simultaneously that of a contemporary condition that extends far beyond the experience of the socialist state.

Grünbein and Tradition

I have argued elsewhere that Grünbein's poetry taps into currents far broader than the immediate political ones, which he himself highlights and which tend to take centre stage. Müller's laudatio allows us a way in to defining what they might be. Firstly: the coldness identified by Müller – both in the 'kalter Blick' [cold gaze] noted above, and in a sound emerging 'aus der Kälte [...] der transsibirische Sound des entblößten Herzens' [coming from the cold [...] the Trans-Siberian sound of the heart laid bare] – is a key trope.[43] This might be read as part of a broader 'aesthetic of coldness', addressed by Helmut Lethen in his important volume *Verhaltenslehren der Kälte* (1994), which attempted to characterize the sobriety of the German interwar period. Indeed, Grünbein himself makes the connection in an interview with Helmut Böttiger, and the link has been noted by a number of distinguished commentators.[44] Grünbein even dubs poetry one of the 'kalte Medien' [cold media] – in a phrase taken from one of his 'MonoLogische Gedichte' ['MonoLogic Poems'], themselves a tribute to the poet Gottfried Benn.[45] It is a moot point whether Lethen is really important to Grünbein per se. Coldness is certainly a significant term, and returns in various formulations throughout his aesthetic essays, though it could certainly be argued that Grünbein's poetry itself is anything but cold.[46] Of greater interest is the fact that Grünbein makes the link with Lethen via

43 Müller, 'Portrait des Künstlers als junger Grenzhund', p. 386.
44 Helmut Böttiger and Durs Grünbein, 'Benn schmort in der Hölle: Ein Gespräch über dialogische und monologische Lyrik', *Text + Kritik*, 153 (2002), 72–84 (p. 79 and 80); Helmut Lethen, *Verhaltenslehre der Kälte* (Frankfurt a. M.: Suhrkamp, 1994). For example, Erk Grimm, 'Mediamania? Contemporary German poetry in the age of new media information technologies. Thomas Kling and Durs Grünbein', *Studies in Twentieth-Century Literature*, 21 (1997), 275–301.
45 Durs Grünbein, *Grauzone morgens* (Frankfurt a. M.: Suhrkamp, 1988), p. 81.
46 Compare, for example, Sonja Klein's essay in this volume.

the poet Gottfried Benn, who does not feature in Lethen's book (nor indeed in Müller's account), but represents a figure of fascination for the younger poet.[47]

Benn is not the only literary forbear whose legacy Grünbein explores through the medium of science; and before focusing on this poet it is worth mentioning at least some of the important figures. In his recourse to the discourse of the natural sciences it is clear that Grünbein is also placing himself self-consciously within the tradition of European literature. Indeed, the title of one essay in his *Galilei vermißt Dantes Hölle und bleibt an den Maßen hängen* takes up Baudelaire's metaphor of the Babylonian heart, but changes it to 'Mein Babylonisches Hirn' ['My Babylonish Brain'] to indicate 'der neue Schauplatz, leidenschaftsloser, und in der kälteren Lust' [a new place of chillier pleasures].[48] This place is one freighted by the murderous protocols of modern history, but might also be one where 'ein anderer Ton, der den Fragmenten (der Überlieferung) wie den Fraktalen (des eben Wahrgenommenen) zu einem konfabulierenden Sprechen verhilft' [a new tonality that places fragments (tradition) and fractals (the recently absorbed) in a new conversation].[49] This in order to create a new chemistry and, one might say, a new literature.

His celebrated Büchner Prize speech of 1995, 'Den Körper zerbrechen' ['Breaking the Body'] sheds light on Büchner the young scientist and begins with a quotation which is almost programmatic: 'Was haben die Schädelnerven der Wirbeltiere mit Dichtung zu tun? [...] Welcher Weg führt von der Kiemenhöhle der Fische zur menschlichen Komödie, von rhythmisierter Prosa zur Ausstülpung des Gehirns in den Gesichtsnerv?' [What do the cranial nerves of vertebrates have to do with poetry? What path leads from the gill chambers of fish to the human comedy, from rythmicized prose to the brain's outpouring into the facial nerve?].[50] His speech takes up the earlier playwright's own interest in the brain and sees Büchner as acutely relevant to the present day, precisely for having managed to bring the scientific and creative discourses together: 'Was ihm gelang, war nichts Geringeres als eine vollständige Transformation: Physiologie aufgegangen in Dichtung.' [What he managed to achieve was nothing less than a complete trans-

---

47 Here I disagree with Ruth Owen, who sees the links to Benn as 'tenuous': Owen, 'Bodies in Contemporary German Poetry', p. 270. Compare Peter Geist, 'Gegenglück und Ausdruckskrisen – Das schwierige Decouvrieren Bennscher Lyrik in der DDR', *Jahrbuch der Gottfried-Benn-Gesellschaft*, ed. by Joachim Dyck, Hermann Korte and Nadine Jessica Schmidt, vol. 3 (2012), *forthcoming*.
48 Durs Grünbein, 'Mein babylonisches Hirn', in *Galilei vermißt Dantes Hölle*, pp. 18–33 (p. 30); 'My Babylonish Brain', trans. by Michael Hofmann, in *The Bars of Atlantis*, pp. 59–71 (p. 69).
49 'Mein babylonisches Hirn', p. 31; 'My Babylonish Brain', p. 69.
50 Durs Grünbein, 'Den Körper zerbrechen', in *Galilei vermißt Dantes Hölle*, pp. 75–86 (p. 75); 'Breaking the Body', trans. by Andrew Shields, in *The Bars of Atlantis*, pp. 12–21 (p. 12).

formation: physiology absorbed into literature].[51] Once again 'eine härtere Grammatik, ein kälterer Ton' [a harder grammar, a colder tone] is noted in the writing which will emerge.[52] But it is important to note the same multilayered approach as identified above in Grünbein's poetry.

Grünbein makes no secret of his affinities with Büchner's literary programme of anthropological realism, pitched in Büchner's day against the dominant Classical idealism which Büchner so despised. Indeed, he reads Büchner's lecture on cranial nerves explicitly as a literary manifesto.[53] But Grünbein extends this examination to make what Michael Eskin terms 'the signal unprecedented point that a truly humane ethics and politics cannot but be based on the recognition that "the nerve [must be put] in first place" and "the body declared the highest authority"'.[54] That this also involves a political impulse is clear. In insisting that life is sufficient to itself, he extrapolates a principled objection to 'jeder Art von Gesellschaftsvertrag, sozialer Reform, Revolution oder Utopie' [every kind of social contract, social reform, revolution or utopia], noting that the price for seeking utopias of the soul is played out 'auf den Knochen zerschundener Körper, bezahlt mit den Biographien derer, die mitgeschleift werden ins jeweils nächste häßliche Paradies' [on the bones of mangled bodies paid for with the biographies of those who are dragged along into each successive ugly paradise].[55] The vehemence of this statement indicates that Michael Eskin is right to associate it with Grünbein's own acute first-hand experience of the costs of utopian thinking: 'with a totalitarian ethics and politics predicated on the Pavlovian principle of a "collective reflexology", whereby each member of the body politic had to be disciplined into conformity, physiologically subdued to act and react in response to the stimuli of the "higher goals" of totalitarian dogma'.[56]

But Grünbein's thinking surely goes further than that. He pinpoints the barbaric episodes inherent in *any* constitution, the mounds of dismembered bodies left by the wayside in *any* democracy. Tellingly he cites an exchange between Mercier and Danton from Büchner's play *Dantons Tod* [*Danton's Death*]: 'Man arbeitet heut zu Tag Alles im Menschenfleisch. Das ist der Fluch unserer Zeit. Mein Leib wird auch jetzt verbraucht' [these days, everything is fashioned out of human flesh. It's the curse of the age. And now my body is to be used as

51 'Den Körper zerbrechen', p. 76; 'Breaking the Body', p. 13.

52 Ibid., p. 76; ibid., p. 13.

53 Ibid., p. 78; ibid., p. 15.

54 Michael Eskin, '"The Diving Bell and the Bristlemouth". The Art of Grünbein's Prose', in *The Bars of Atlantis*, pp. vii–xx (p. xvi). Eskin is quoting from the essay itself: 'Den Körper zerbrechen', p. 79; 'Breaking the Body', p. 16.

55 'Den Körper zerbrechen', pp. 79, 83; 'Breaking the Body', pp. 16, 19.

56 Eskin, '"The Diving Bell and the Bristlemouth"', p. xvii.

well].[57] It is difficult not to see in this a reference both to Büchner's own day, but also to contemporary capitalism. The fact that this same phrase is used by the poet Volker Braun in his own excoriating critique of an age 'after the massacre of illusions' simply underlines it.[58] But it is also worth noting that, here as in the other essays, there may be a projected coolness of observation which does not necessarily involve coldness or cynicism. What Grünbein seeks through his exploration of Büchner is a biochemical basis for literature: alive to the existential, biological, political and linguistic constructions of the self in the present.

Grünbein's debt to the writers discussed here has been treated extensively by various commentators, so the comments here are of necessity brief.[59] Much less has been written about his relationship with Goethe in this regard, though this will surely change since the publication of his *Aroma: ein römisches Zeichenbuch* in 2010. Here it is perhaps worth mentioning the fruitful approach taken by Judith Ryan. While reading the central neurological metaphor of *Schädelbasislektion* as an overt political reflection (the brain-stem metaphor representing 'subconscious attachments to the former East Germany' and the cranial sutures standing for an almost Kafkaesque literalization of 'the wall in the head'), she nevertheless points up a persuasive connection between Goethe and Grünbein, which has largely gone uncommented upon.[60] For Ryan Grünbein's fascination with this forbear is driven by an inevitable rivalry, but she also sees Grünbein's reflections on the human cranium as a continuation of Goethe's anatomical studies, his poetic and osteological obsession with Schiller's skull and Goethe's own poetry: for example 'Im ernsten Beinhaus' ['In the Solemn Burial Vault'] of 1826.[61] This is doubtless a productive line of reflection.

57 'Den Körper zerbrechen', p. 83; 'Breaking the Body', p. 19.

58 Partly quoted in the poem 'Nach dem Massaker der Illusionen' ['After The Massacre of Illusions'] in Volker Braun, *Tumulus* (Frankfurt a. M.: Suhrkamp, 1999), p. 28 and further in the note to the poem (p. 41). Also in the poem 'Lagerfeld', p. 44. I discuss this in detail in Leeder, '"After the Massacre of Illusions": Specters of the GDR in the work of Volker Braun', in *Transformations of German Cultural Identity 1989–2009*, ed. by Anne Fuchs and Kathleen James Chakraborty, special edition of *New German Critique*, 116 (Spring 2012), 103–18.

59 See for instance, Olav Krämer, 'Bildliches Denken als Erkenntnismodus zwischen Poesie und Wissenschaft. Grünbein über Dante, Darwin, Hopkins und Goethe', in Bremer, Lampart and Wesche, *Schreiben am Schnittpunkt*, pp. 241–57; Michael Eskin, '"Stimmengewirr vieler Zeiten". Grünbein's Dialogue with Dante, Baudelaire, and Mandel'shtam', *Germanic Review*, 77.1 (2002), 34–50; Alexa Hennemann, *Die Zerbrechlichkeit der Körper. Zu den Georg-Büchner-Preisreden von Heiner Müller und Durs Grünbein* (Bern: Lang, 2000).

60 Judith Ryan, 'The Skull beneath the Skin', in *A New History of German Literature*, ed. by David E. Wellbery and others (Cambridge, MA: Harvard University Press, 2004), pp. 959–64 (p. 961).

61 Ibid., pp. 960, 963 and 964.

I would like, however, to turn finally to Gottfried Benn. Benn was both a scientist and poet (famously pictured at his desk, looking down a microscope), who championed a monologic form of poetry (pitched explicitly against the dialogic impulse of a politically committed poetry identified with Brecht). The cool, cerebral, ironically detached view of the observing outsider that characterized Gottfried Benn's own diction (especially for Grünbein, his late *Statische Gedichte* [*Static Poems*]) can certainly be glimpsed in Grünbein. However, in interviews he interestingly champions the Russian poet Osip Mandelstam over Benn, precisely on the basis of a human tone pitched against the 'cosmic chill' of the universe, along with the prospect of dialogue and utopia.[62] Interestingly, Grünbein understands Benn's poetry as the result of two things, which he dubs 'Temperatur und Temperament' [temperature and temperament].[63] On the one hand, then, he sees Benn's as an appropriate response, in that it mimics the cynicism and coldness of his own age; but, on the other hand, it betokens a particular attitude; that is an insight into the continuing nightmare of history and the vision of a future without any prospect of justice, equality or fraternity.[64]

The provocative move on Grünbein's part is to link the attitudes that governed while Benn was writing (here the 1940s and early 1950s) to those that inspired contemporary capitalism (as he does in his discussion of Büchner). But his conclusion is the opposite of Benn's: instead of mimicking the temperature of the age, poetry for Grünbein must work against it: 'Je härter die Verhältnisse, je trostloser und kälter, umso mehr Rauschgift wird gebraucht, um den permanenten Druck auszuhalten. So wird der Lyriker zum Rauschgiftdealer' [The harder the conditions, the bleaker and colder, the more drugs are needed to bear the permanent pressure. The poet becomes a drug dealer].[65]

So at one level Grünbein is also working through his relationship with a vital and controversial literary forbear and, moreover, one who indicates a certain approach to the role of poetry and political engagement. This relationship will continue to haunt Grünbein beyond his immediate interest in science; and his recent essays for reissued volumes of Benn's poetry represent a further more critical reckoning with the poet.[66] But, again, Grünbein is not the only poet to be inter-

62 'Mein babylonisches Hirn', p. 28, 'My Babylonish Brain', p. 67. On Grünbein's debt to this poet see Eskin, '"Stimmengewirr vieler Zeiten"', as above.

63 Böttiger and Grünbein, 'Benn schmort in der Hölle', p. 80.

64 Ibid.

65 Ibid., p. 82.

66 Durs Grünbein, 'Palette für Mohn. Nachwort', in Gottfried Benn and Thomas Florschuetz, *Blumen* (Berlin: Insel, 2011), pp. 79–90; Durs Grünbein, 'Elegien für einen Irrtum. Vorwort', in Gottfried Benn, *Statische Gedichte (Gedichte 1937–1947)* (Berlin: Insel, 2011), pp. 7–34.

ested in Benn at this juncture.[67] In their emphasis on clinical observation and coolness of tone, many writers reveal a marked debt to the poet – one of the key but unrecognized influences, as Hermann Korte has argued, of recent decades of poetry: for example, Ulrike Draesner, Norbert Hummelt, Peter Waterhouse.[68] Benn's influence extends not only to the use of medical imagery and anatomical vocabulary common to many of these poets, however, but also to an understanding of the place of the poet at work. And these poets, like Grünbein, start, too, from the modern subject of their own age, and the work at language.

Grünbein and a Poetology of Science

The discussion of literary forbears leads directly to (and overlaps in part with) the question of how Grünbein uses the discourse of science, and biology in particular, to develop and refine his own poetological programme; one adumbrated in Müller's observations. In an interview of 1996, Grünbein referred to the lyric possibilities of writing 'als könnte ich jenseits von Glück und Unglück sein. Zum Beispiel, indem ich einfach nur biologische Prozesse beobachte und beschreibe oder auch anthropologische Gegebenheiten, die auch in längeren Zeitabständen immer verkehren' [as if I could be beyond happiness or unhappiness. For example, in simply observing biological processes and describing them, or anthropological conditions, which always occur at extended intervals].[69] In many ways his poetological essays and poems are a direct working out of that project. For example, in the poem 'Inside out, outside in', one of the cycle of 'Niemands Land Stimmen' ['No Man's Land Voices'] in *Schädelbasislektion*, the journey of life is, as Ruth Owen points out, stripped of any potential *Bildungs*-narrative and becomes condensed instead into a simple biological course: 'Von der Zygote im Reagenzglas zur Autopsie' [From the zygote in the test tube to autopsy].[70] The lyric subject (here, interestingly, standing with Büchner in his back-pack amidst the markedly increasing cold) is determined to strip life to its

---

67 A good indication can be found in *Ich bin nicht innerlich: Annäherungen an Gottfried Benn*, ed. by Jan Bürger (Stuttgart: Klett Cotta, 2003).

68 Hermann Korte, 'Säulenheilige und Portalfiguren? Benn und Celan im Poetik-Dialog mit der jüngeren deutschsprachigen Lyrik seit den 1990er Jahren', in Leeder, *Schaltstelle*, pp. 109–37.

69 Annette Pfeiffer, 'Streunen auf beiden Seiten: Ein Gespräch mit Büchner-Preisträger Durs Grünbein', *Süddeutsche Zeitung*, 13 March 1996, p. 25.

70 Durs Grünbein, *Schädelbasislektion. Gedichte* (Frankfurt a. M.: Suhrkamp, 1991), pp. 39–45 (p. 42); Owen, 'Bodies in Contemporary Poetry', p. 274.

essence: 'War da irgendein Mythos?' [Was there any myth?].[71] It is beyond the scope of this essay to attempt to establish and describe an overall and consistent poetology to be gleaned from Grünbein's essays and poetry (even if such a thing were thought to exist). However, his scientific essays do outline an 'aesthetic credo' of sorts which is the more stimulating for the gradual evolution of ideas in new directions, as well as its contradictory impulses.[72] Here I will simply point to some of the factors which might relativize what has gone before, and which will become important for Grünbein's later development. There are two main aspects to this. Firstly, Grünbein's elaboration of the place of poetry (which picks up Müller's observation about a placeless poetry); and, secondly, a perhaps surprising reaction to the ethos of 'coldness' and anti-utopianism which has been highlighted thus far.

Anna Alissa Ertel does an excellent job in tracing a shift in Grünbein's overall understanding and evaluation of the place of poetry in the course of his essays. The key shift for her is from an insistence on a neurological poetics founded on 'Erkenntnis' (knowledge).[73] This is based on the inalienable 'sezierende[r] Blick' [dissecting gaze] of the poet: one which strips away the flesh and truly sees. Grünbein himself has drawn attention to the link between the 'dissecting gaze' and the 'X-ray' vision which both serve to strip the flesh from the bones. Moreover, as he explains, this process can be linked to an 'aesthetic of sarcasm' which has at its etymological root the separation of bones and flesh.[74]

For Grünbein this kind of vision offers a way out of a paradoxical stalemate between artistic autonomy and political engagement, but also frees him from an experience of 'Spätgeborensein' [being born too late] that is lacking the knowledge which would ally him to other curious spirits and his own time.[75] But where is this freedom, the release to be found? Ertel is absolutely right when she points to the accumulation of non-places which mark Grünbein's work at this stage: from the 'Schreiben am Schnittpunkt' [writing at the intersection], which has stimulated so much discussion of Grünbein's scientific interest, to the many 'intermediate

---

71 *Schädelbasislektion*, p. 45.

72 Michael Eskin's term: '"The Diving Bell and the Bristlemouth"', p. xiii.

73 See Ertel, *Körper, Gehirne, Gene*, pp. 24–36, though, as is apparent here, I disagree about the degree and type of the change in Grünbein's approach. This is something dealt with especially by Tilmann Köppe, 'Grünbeins Idee von der Erkenntnis des Dichters', in Bremer, Lampart and Wesche, *Schreiben am Schnittpunkt*, pp. 259–70.

74 Grünbein, *Galilei vermißt Dantes Hölle*, p. 43. Aris Fioretos and Durs Grünbein, 'Gespräch über die Zone, den Hund und die Knochen', *Akzente*, 43.6 (1996), 486–501 (p. 500).

75 Grünbein, 'Ameisenhafte Größe', pp. 13, 15.

spaces, marginal or liminal zones' to be found in essays and poems alike.[76] In these 'no-man's lands', one can hope to find a precarious but miraculous potential; 'eine Art rührender Alchemie' [a kind of moving alchemy]; 'Zeichenschau, Zauberei, inspiriertes Spiel' [a show of signs, magic, inspired play], that is poetry.[77]

In his later, programmatic essay 'Warum schriftlos leben' ['Why Live Without Writing'] (1999), Grünbein goes further, however, insisting on the importance of the eccentric, dilettante position of the poet to see what even the specialists cannot. His 'arielgleiche Beweglichkeit' [Ariel-like agility], within the realm of the natural sciences gives him a unique and privileged place and the vision that goes with it.

> Er spricht von dem Privileg, das sich im Schreiben verbirgt, dank der Beobachtungsgabe und des poetischen Kalküls unmittelbare Aussagen zum Menschsein zu treffen, die erscheinende Welt in Notaten zu binden und sie gleichzeitig zu übersetzen in Metaphysik.
>
> [He [the poet] goes on to talk about the privilege conferred by writing – the privilege of using his gift of observation and his verbal finesse to make explicit statements on being human, to make notes on the real world and translate it at one and the same time, into metaphysics.][78]

It is worth noting the shift of emphasis from poetry of 'Erkenntnis' to what Ertel terms a 'self-confident postulate of a privileged access to truth on the part of poetry'.[79] Noteworthy, too, is that it does not shy from a metaphysics. And this is explicitly based on observation, but also on verbal finesse; and it finds its place in the no-place of poetry.

From this vantage point much is to be seen that is not amenable to 'Erkenntnis' alone and that moves beyond a clinical realism or an indifferent observation. It is implied, for example, in the focus on perception in Grünbein's essay on 'Darwin's Eyes'.[80] Moreover, it allows one to see the things that have been left behind: for example, the monstrous deep-sea fish stranded by evolution, or the lives abandoned by progress in the cycle 'In der Provinz' ['In the Provinces'].[81] But this is not

---

76 Grünbein, 'Drei Briefe' ['Three Letters'], in *Galilei vermißt Dantes Hölle*, pp. 40–54 (p. 46). Ertel's poetological chapter takes this title, as does the volume edited by Bremer, Lampart and Wesche. The quotation comes from Ertel, p. 28.

77 Grünbein, 'Ameisenhafte Größe', pp. 13–14.

78 Durs Grünbein, *Warum schriftlos leben. Aufsätze* (Frankfurt a. M.: Suhrkamp, 2003), pp. 39–40; 'Why live Without Writing', trans. by Michael Hofmann, *The Bars of Atlantis*, pp. 92–115 (pp. 96–97).

79 Ertel, p. 33.

80 Durs Grünbein, 'Darwins Augen', in *Gedicht und Geheimnis*, pp. 65–74; 'Darwin's Eyes', trans. by Andrew Shields, *The Bars of Atlantis*, pp. 47–55 (p. 53).

81 Durs Grünbein, 'Zeit der Tiefseefische', *Galilei vermißt Dantes Hölle*, pp. 237–46; 'The Age of Deep-Sea Fish', trans. by Andrew Shields, in *The Bars of Atlantis*, pp. 39–46. 'In der Provinz',

a neutral gaze, nor indeed the cold gaze of an X-ray vision. Recalling the mounds of dismembered bodies left by the wayside of history of the Büchner Prize speech, it is a gaze which sees also with passion, with despair (albeit in a 'moderate tone') and with pity.[82] And this makes of poetry also a political vision. A case in point would be the marvellous poems where Grünbein explicitly addresses a 'Röntgenblick' [X-ray vision], which hold together sobriety, humanity and melancholy in an exquisite balance.[83] It is this, I would argue, that underscores a (productive) tension in much of Grünbein's early work and which is product of his engagement with the sciences.

Grünbein and the Science of Poetry

I shall now conclude with a closer examination of how 'Beobachtungsgabe' and 'poetisches Kalkül' come together in Grünbein's work itself. He makes no secret of the anatomical basis of interest in poetry: 'Mich beschäftigt etwa die Frage, ob man das, was seit drei- oder vierhundert Jahren mit dem Begriff Seele verbunden wird, jetzt durch Erkenntnisse der Genetik oder Physiologie erweitern soll' [For example, I am concerned with the question of whether the thing that has been linked with the idea of the soul for the last three or four hundert years can now be extended on account of the discoveries of genetics or physiology].[84] His is a reversal of the Cartesian body / soul dichotomy, with pre-eminence given now to the body. His second collection, *Schädelbasislektion*, begins with a laconic image of the human being as the sum of its anatomy.

> Was du bist steht am Rand
> Anatomischer Tafeln
> Dem Skelett an der Wand
> Was von Seele zu schwafeln
> Liegt gerad so verquer
> Wie im Rachen der Zeit
> (Kleinhirn hin, Stammhirn her)
> Diese Scheiß Sterblichkeit.

in Durs Grünbein, *Nach den Satiren. Gedichte* (Frankfurt a. M.: Suhrkamp, 1999), pp. 9–13; compare also 'Im Museum der Mißbildungen' ('In the Museum of Deformities'), *Galilei vermißt Dantes Hölle*, pp. 221–28.

82 'Verzweiflung in moderatem Ton', in Durs Grünbein, *Strophen für übermorgen. Gedichte* (Frankfurt a. M.: Suhrkamp, 2007), pp. 124–25.

83 Durs Grünbein, *Falten und Fallen* (Frankfurt a. M.: Suhrkamp, 1994), p. 28; *Nach den Satiren*, pp. 197–99.

84 Durs Grünbein, 'Tausendfacher Tod im Hirn', *Der Spiegel*, 9 October 1995, pp. 221–30 (p. 230).

> [What you are is defined on the margins / Of anatomical plates / The skeleton on the wall / Blathering something about soul / is simply too absurd / As in the jaws of time / (Cerebellum willy brain-stem nilly) / This bloody mortality.][85]

Any metaphysical claim to significance is apparently dismissed, in order to insist on the rudest of physiological realities; something common to many of the poems in the volume. Such dissection is a repeated feature, and the iteration of Latinate body parts (usefully catalogued by Ertel) enacts a kind of fragmentation of the body, not unlike a hyper-modern echo of a Renaissance *vanitas* poem, but in any case disintegrating any idea of a stable human identity.[86] However, there is more at stake here than might first appear; and the poem also sets the tone for much of Grünbein's writing both in its tricksiness, the apparent throwaway cynicism and the diction, which has reminded commentators of Benn. It is clear that Grünbein's answer to the question posed by this poem points beyond the anatomical plates and the words 'Homo sapiens' customarily printed on them. Man is the sum of anatomy and language. But, more than that, this apparently bleakest of little poems is rhymed; and it is not for nothing that the rhyme scheme yokes together 'Zeit' and 'Sterblichkeit': the very axis of the Renaissance *memento mori*.

The poem 'Biologischer Walzer' ['Biological Waltz'] from *Falten und Fallen* gives a more elaborate display of what is at stake, but this time not looking inside the body but viewing humankind from without. It is the first in a central cycle in the collection 'Mensch ohne Großhirn' ['Man without Cerebrum'].[87] It is a prominent poem, frequently appearing in national newspapers and almanachs at the time of publication, and has been often analyzed, but it sets out some of the points very clearly.

> Biologischer Walzer
>
> Zwischen Kapstadt und Grönland liegt dieser Wald
> Aus Begierden, Begierden die niemand kennt.
> Wenn es stimmt, daß wir schwierige Tiere sind
> Sind wir schwierige Tiere weil nichts mehr stimmt.
>
> Steter Tropfen im Mund war das Wort der Beginn
> Des Verzichts, einer langen Flucht in die Zeit.
> Nichts erklärt, wie ein trockener Gaumen Vokale,
> Wie ein Leck in der Kehle Konsonanten erbricht.

85 Grünbein, *Schädelbasislektion*, p. 11.
86 Ertel, *Körper, Gehirne, Gene*, p. 64.
87 Grünbein, 'Biologischer Walzer', in *Falten und Fallen*, p. 71.

Offen bleibt, was ein Ohr im Laborglas sucht,
Eine fleischliche Brosche, gelb in Formaldehyd.
Wann es oben schwimmt, wann es untergeht,
Wie in toten Nerven das Gleichgewicht klingt.

Fraglich auch, ob die tausend Drähtchen im Pelz
Des gelehrigen Affen den Heißhunger stillen.
Was es heißt, wenn sich Trauer im Hirnstrom zeigt.
Jeden flüchtigen Blick ein Phantomschmerz lenkt.

Zwischen Kapstadt und Grönland liegt dieser Wald
... Ironie, die den Körper ins Dickicht schickt.
Wenn es stimmt, daß wir schwierige Tiere sind
Sind wir schwierige Tiere weil nichts mehr stimmt.

[Between Cape Town and Greenland there is this forest / Of desires, desires that nobody knows. / If it is true that we're difficult creatures/ We're difficult creatures because there's nothing that's true. // Steady drops in the mouth, the word was the start / Of renunciation, a long flight into time. // Nothing explains how a palate that's dry can vomit / Vowels, a leak in the trachea consonants. / It remains to be seen why this ear is in the specimen glass / A fleshy broach, yellow in formaldehyde. / When it floats to the top, or when it sinks, / Or what balance sounds like in nerves that have died. // Doubtful too whether the thousand little wires in its fur / Can sate the ravenous ape who's so eager to learn. / Or whether sorrow's revealed in cerebral currents, / A phantom pain steers every fleeting gaze // Between Cape Town and Greenland there is this forest / ... Irony, sending the body into the thick of it. / If it is true that we're difficult creatures / We're difficult creatures because there's nothing that's true.]

The title is the first thing that provokes questions. The poem uses an anapaestic waltz rhythm (a syncopated Viennese Waltz, not the dactylic rhythm one might normally associate with it) to trace the development of humankind. The poem is circular like the waltz, a kind of rondo form (the end is in the beginning, as it were), and is structured by a single recurring theme. But to point forward for a moment, the title also signals the intricate physiological processes of the human body: likened to a biological waltz surely not because they are graceful rather than disastrous, but because of the underlying patterns of the dance. That fragility is also there in the poem: both in the tension between the subject matter and the jaunty rhythm, and in what might be called a fundamental 'Unstimmigkeit' [dissonance] about the poem: 'nichts mehr stimmt' (l. 4, l. 20). It seems to want to set out a hypothesis quoted from elsewhere: 'Wenn es stimmt' (l. 1), but moves from an apparently cautious proposition – 'wenn es stimmt' – to a more fierce determination: 'nichts mehr stimmt' (l. 4). The tone is distanced and aphoristic, and suggests in its rhetorical structure – that of a chiasmus – that it hopes to persuade us of a case. But the chiastic structures serve first and foremost to draw attention to the central component – here the sly turn on 'sind wir / wir sind' [are we / we are] which goes to the core of Grünbein's anthropological project: 'Wenn es stimmt, daß wir schwierige Tiere sind / Sind wir schwierige Tiere weil nichts mehr stimmt.'

Like the earlier poem from *Schädelbasislektion*, it asks what makes a human being. Here, though, it focuses on a significant turning point between models – this time in a temporal mode and within an anthropological framework. It addresses the moment that separates man and beast (also pointed up in Grünbein's Büchner essay).[88] At this point, the poem implies, man lost the instinctual unity with the world that belonged to his animal being, with the result that 'nichts mehr stimmt' (l. 4). The 'schwieriges Tier' can, of course, make his way in the world, assert himself 'zwischen Kapstadt und Grönland' (l. 1), can make the world his own. Yet something stands in the way: the 'Wald / aus Begierden, Begierden die niemand kennt' (ll. 1–2). On closer reading, the ironic scientific experiment to fix man as an uncomfortable anomaly within a zoological framework is set against a much more traditionally romantic notion of a primitive and unknown part of humankind that eludes scientific analysis. The forest becomes a (Freudian) symbol of the wildness / wilderness belonging to the primitive and ancient regions of the human brain – those resistant to the logical order and Cartesian clarity of the conscious mind. This is linked – via the idea of the 'sylvan' – of course with poetry. At this point a third aspect is introduced: that of the origins of language (ll. 4–8).

If this poem reiterates the advance of humankind towards civilisation, then it is presented here above all as a linguistic advance. And language is presented as the origin of meaning. What our human culture has done for the development of the human is judged sceptically in the third and fourth strophe: the attempts to master nature make of man an ape. Grünbein seems on the point here of offering physiology as a kind of fundamental ontology of poetry (something also taken up in his essays), but looked at closely, the poem itself actually insists on the questionable nature of the natural sciences, as Ruth Owen has pointed out: 'Nichts erklärt' (l. 7), 'Offen bleibt' (l. 9), 'Fraglich auch' (l. 13).[89] This is underlined by the uncertainty of tone created by the use of anapaests. And if, as Alexander von Bormann has argued, we take the anapaests seriously they lend a searching tone to the poem.[90] The medical experiments here cannot offer a final answer, mourning

88 'Den Körper zerbrechen', p. 77; 'Breaking the Body', p. 14.

89 Ruth Owen, 'Science in Contemporary Poetry', p. 93.

90 Alexander von Bormann, 'Im Dickicht des Nicht-Ich. Durs Grünbeins Anapäste', in *Signaturen einer Gegenwartsliteratur. Festschrift für Walter Hinderer*, ed. by Dieter Borchmeyer (Würzburg: Königshausen & Neumann, 1999), pp. 171–84 (p. 181).

is not measurable as an electronic impulse in the brain, and man has become a recalcitrant and unforthcoming laboratory ape; what remains intact is the mystery of the origin of language.

It is also interesting that the understanding of the development of language presented here (and in Grünbein's essays) as a thoroughly physical and physiological process is linked with a much more wilfully intangible interpretation of the same as something inaccessible to such enquiry. Out of that tension comes the force of the last strophe: ' ... Ironie, die den Körper ins Dickicht schickt' (l. 18).

The form of the poem also deserves comment. The slightly whimsical rhythm of the waltz breaks down in the final strophe, revealing the self-consciously constructed irony of the piece: it reflects after all on the nature of humankind, but does so in language, which is implicated precisely in the problem that the poem is trying to address. But it is not just any language: rather, acutely self-conscious poetic language. Von Bormann has pointed out that it has pretty much the form of an alchaic ode. But this ode is not simply an ode for a lost world, it turns the 'Trauer' [mourning] that fails to be registered in the brain into an ironic resistance: a Socratic recognition of how little humans know. In this the poem finishes on a note of mystery and uncertainty. Behind the forest of desire hides language, and with it a dark unknowing that marks the limit of the world of science, but one might argue the beginning of the possibilities of poetry.

Conclusion

Grünbein's poem, ambitiously enough, seeks to link the 'civilization' of humanity, the metaphor of humankind caught uncomfortably between discourses of science and theology, and the origins of language. It does this in a language that is conscious of its own implicated nature and has at its heart a powerful sense of scepticism, irony and, most importantly, *uncertainty*. Grünbein harnesses the investigative power of science – whether anthropology, anatomy or neurology – as a way of explaining the world, but his real interest lies precisely at the point where science fails, in the uncertainty of human experience and its translation into poetic metaphor – and it is there that poetry can begin.

That could stand as a conclusion to this essay. But I want to step back again and locate Grünbein's poetry as part of the larger argument about science and poetry that I sketched in at the start. Gillian Beer points out that the relationship between literature and science is not one of straightforward derivation or reflection: 'post-modernism is collateral with plate tectonics, not dependent on it'. The relationship between these diverse human activities is instead 'deeper than that and more mobile. Both draw on, are to some degree controlled by, and in their turn help to form, the common anxieties of the time'.[91]

Certainly Grünbein's poems offer powerful expressions of the anxieties of his time, of our time. It is no chance that the poems inhabit the world of biological science at a time where this discipline has most revolutionized our understanding of ourselves and our perception of the world. Grünbein does not content himself, however, with documenting the 'effects' of science – as Habermas had claimed literature might be limited to doing – but takes a scientific understanding of the world as a starting point for his poem. In his book on science and literature since Goethe, Peter D. Smith argues that science and literature are best understood as 'dialectically interconnected' which seems to me a useful starting point for thinking about their relation.[92] Poetry becomes an instrument of investigation, but not one that seeks to eliminate ambiguities, rather one that comes into its own where those ambiguities begin, and can offer a different and perhaps greater truth. Whilst this chimes with the science of our day, the poems are not exhausted in that gesture, they offer a complex aesthetic response to the world they encounter, one founded on the power of poetry, but aware of its own processes.

And, in this, Grünbein's work might be said to be akin to work by a number of writers, those I set out at the beginning of the essay, especially Schrott, Draesner, Köhler and Kling. The interest in scientific discourse can be seen as part of a reaction to our times (including but not limited to the experience of the *Wende*). Moreover, it can be seen as a way to engage with literary forbears with a pressing interest for the present day. But it also speaks to the cultivation of tradition in modern European poetry and of a contemporary renaissance in the ancient trope of the *poeta doctus* or 'learned poet' (that is the embodiment of the conjoining of the two discourses). This is certainly not a peculiarly German, let alone post-GDR, phenomenon – as witnessed by the significant amount of similarly distinguished poetry in English, for example.[93]

---

91 Gillian Beer, 'Discourses of the Island', in *Literature and Science as Modes of Expression*, ed. by Frederick Amrine (Dordrecht: Kluwer Academic Publishers, 1989), pp. 1–27 (p. 18).

92 Smith, *Metaphor and Materiality*, p. 21.

93 Wilfried Barner, 'Poeta Doctus. Über die Renaissance eines Dichterideals in der deutschen Literatur des 20. Jahrhunderts', in *Literaturwissenschaft und Geistesgeschichte. Festschrift für Richard Brinkmann*, ed. by Jürgen Brummack and others (Tübingen: Niemeyer, 1981), pp. 725–52. The interest in the UK, for example, is evidenced in a wealth of publications: the anthology *A Quark for Mister Mark: 101 Poems about Science*, ed. by Maurice Riordan and Jon Turney (London: Faber, 2000) provides an overview and *Contemporary Poetry and Contemporary Science*, ed. by Robert Crawford (Oxford: Oxford University Press, 2006) gives an excellent

It might well be that kind of large-scale aesthetic enterprise represented by Grünbein's early work has already had its day. What Erk Grimm dubs the 'encyclopaedic drive toward expansion' of an 'epistemological turn', seems to have made way, in poets even a little younger, for a poetry more modest and local.[94] But, as was noted at the start of this essay, Grünbein, too, has moved away from such a concentrated engagement with sciences, citing frustration at the insistence of the critics that he keep repeating the success of *Schädelbasislektion*, but also feeling that that there would be no further breakthrough in that area in his lifetime, and that like a scientist he would simply move on.[95] The fact is, however, that he took the poetics forged in the encounter with science with him. The shift of emphasis to the classical world and its authors refines that poetics further and extends it, especially through a further dimension, that of memory. But that gesture in Grünbein and the other poets I have mentioned towards what might be termed a 'metaphysics of contingency' which underpins and determines our contemporary lives, remains.[96] And that is a gesture that seeks to bring 'cold comfort', but comfort, nevertheless.[97]

---

account. Note Miroslav Holub's more sceptical essay on the possibilities of poetry included here, pp. 47–68. Most recently *Science in Modern Poetry. New Directions*, ed. by John Holmes (Liverpool: Liverpool University Press, 2012) extends the debate.

94 Erk Grimm, 'Die Neue Schlichtheit in "Lyrik von Jetzt". Poetische Diskursverschiebungen in der deutschsprachigen Gegenwartsdichtung nach 2000', in Leeder, *Schaltstelle*, pp. 479–504 (p. 493).

95 Wolfgang Frühwald and Durs Grünbein, 'Die Lust, sich im Universum zu bewegen. Ein Gespräch mit dem Dichter Durs Grünbein über Poesie, Neurobiologie und die Bilder vom Menschen', in *Das Design des Menschen. Vom Wandel des Menschenbildes unter dem Einfluss der modernen Naturwissenschaften*, ed. by Wolfgang Frühwald (Cologne: DuMont, 2004), pp. 294–309 (p. 303); Arno Widmann, 'Jeder Zeitungsleser ist Schillerianer: Ein Gespräch mit Durs Grünbein', *Berliner Zeitung*, 25 September 2004, magazine, p. M04: http://www.berliner-zeitung.de/archiv/ein-gespraech-mit-dem-dichter-durs-gruenbein-jeder-zeitungsleser-ist-schillerianer,10810590,10216382.html.

96 I borrow the phrase from Peter Thompson: http://ernstbloch.wordpress.com/2012/03/29/my-metaphysics-of-contingency/.

97 Durs Grünbein, 'Schwacher Trost' ('Cold Comfort'), in Durs Grünbein, *Erklärte Nacht. Gedichte* (Frankfurt a. M.: Suhrkamp, 2002), p. 67.

Alexander Regier

Philosophy and Poetry in Durs Grünbein's Prose

Durs Grünbein ends his prose collection *Gedicht und Geheimnis* with a famous quotation from Ludwig Wittgenstein: 'Philosophie dürfte man eigentlich nur *dichten*' [Philosophy ought really to be written only as a form of *poetry*].[1] This is a suggestive and emphatic closure to a volume that confirms Grünbein's deep investment in poetical theory and his serious commitment to the connection of poetry and philosophy. As a number of people have pointed out, in this volume and elsewhere, Grünbein's writing evidences, from the very start of his career, a deep interest in philosophy – including its long history and its relationship to poetry. This interest manifests itself in various ways, some more open than others. Wittgenstein makes another framing appearance, for instance, providing the epigraph to the earlier *Falten und Fallen*: '"Seltsamer Zufall, daß alle die Menschen, deren Schädel man geöffnet hat, ein Gehirn hatten"' [Strange coincidence, that every man whose skull has been opened had a brain!].[2] Seneca acts as another obvious and important philosophical reference for Grünbein. *An Seneca* not only provides us with Gerhard Fink's translation of Seneca's *De Brevitate Vitae*, but also with an essay on the thinker by Grünbein as well as a poem ('An Seneca') that functions as a commentary on the treatise, endorsing the Senecan idea that: 'Mach auf Sein und Zeit / Dir deinen eignen Reim im Stillen' [Of being and time make / Sense on your own in quiet].[3]

---

1 Grünbein does not reference the quotation, which is taken from *Vermischte Bemerkungen*. See Ludwig Wittgenstein, *Vermischte Bemerkungen / Culture and Value*, ed. by G. H. von Wright, in collaboration with Heikki Nyman, trans. by Peter Winch (Oxford: Blackwell, 1980), p. 24. Neither does he put "dichten" in italics as it appears in the original edition. Winch's translation of the sentence reads: 'philosophy ought really to be written only as *poetic composition*' (p. 24e). I have adopted the translation that Marjorie Perloff provides as an epigraph for her book *Wittgenstein's Ladder*, which includes a relevant commentary on the difficulty of translating this phrase. See Marjorie Perloff, *Wittgenstein's Ladder. Poetic Language and the Strangeness of the Ordinary* (Chicago: University of Chicago Press, 1996), p. ix.

2 Durs Grünbein, *Gedichte. Bücher I–III (Grauzone morgens, Schädelbasislektion, Falten und Fallen)* (Frankfurt a. M.: Suhrkamp, 2006), p. 249. See also # 207 in Ludwig Wittgenstein, *Über Gewissheit / On Certainty*, ed. by G. E. M. Anscombe and G. H. von Wright, trans. by Denis Paul and G. E. M. Anscombe (Oxford: Blackwell, 1969), pp. 28, 28e.

3 Durs Grünbein and Lucius Annaeus Seneca, *An Seneca. Postskriptum. Die Kürze des Lebens* (Frankfurt a. M.: Suhrkamp, 2004), p. 10. On Grünbein and Seneca see also Hinrich Ahrend, *'Tanz zwischen sämtlichen Stühlen'. Poetik und Dichtung im lyrischen und essayistischen Werk Durs Grünbeins* (Würzburg: Königshausen & Neumann, 2010), especially pp. 354–68.

Grünbein's use of the phrase 'sich einen Reim machen' [literally: to make a rhyme for oneself] playfully invokes and illustrates how the philosopher Seneca becomes a figure through which the poet Grünbein explores ideas of history as well as the process of poetic production itself. As Michael Eskin has shown, classical philosophy and poetry in the widest sense (from Chrysippus to Horace) are highly relevant for Grünbein's thinking about poetic form and subject matter throughout his writing process, and find their way into a great many of his poems.[4]

While Ancient and classical thinkers remain fundamental touchstones for Grünbein, his work also engages directly with some of the central figures of modern philosophy. For instance, he addresses the lives and thought of René Descartes and Blaise Pascal in immediate and unique ways. His 2008 piece 'Der Indianer des Geistes. Bagatellen über das Leben des Philosophen Pascal' ['The Indian of the Spirit. Bagatelles on the Life of the Philosopher Pascal'] presents Grünbein's speculations in a tone that elicits very private, biographical, almost intimate, dimensions of the seventeenth-century thinker. He imagines a situation in which:

> Es ging ihm [Pascal] gut, er hatte soeben ein Vorurteil unterdrückt. Lässig schlenderte er über ein paar Bohlenbretter, die den Rand einer Baugrube bedeckten und unter seinen Schritten leicht federten, hinüber zum Eingangsportal der Sorbonne.
>
> [He [Pascal] was doing well, he had just suppressed a prejudice. Casually, he sauntered over a couple of planks that covered the edge of a building pit and were feathering slightly under his steps, over to the front gate of the Sorbonne.][5]

Grünbein's engagement here does not, however, remain solely on the anecdotal level. He also presents Pascal as an important thinker who pushes thought – a central category for Grünbein – to its limit: 'Pascals Methode war es [...] das Denkbare über alles Denkbare hinaus offenzuhalten' [It was Pascal's method

4 Two further aspects of Grünbein's constant interest in classical literature and arts are his translations of Aeschylus and Seneca as well as his work with classical and classicist visual art. See Seneca, *Thyestes*, lateinisch und deutsch, aus dem Lateinischen von Durs Grünbein, mit Materialien zur Übersetzung und zu Leben und Werk Senecas, ed. by Bernd Seidensticker (Frankfurt a. M.: Insel, 2002); Aischylos, *Sieben gegen Theben*, aus dem Griechischen von Durs Grünbein (Frankfurt a. M.: Suhrkamp, 2003); Aischylos, *Die Perser. Stück und Materialien*, aus dem Griechischen von Durs Grünbein (Frankfurt a. M., 2001). For a particularly intriguing example relating to the visual arts, see Grünbein's literary contextualizations of Peter Cornelius's oeuvre in an exhibition catalogue accompanying Cornelius's work: Peter Cornelius and Durs Grünbein, *Die Götter Griechenlands*, ed. by León Krempel and Peter-Klaus Schuster (Berlin: DuMont, 2004).
5 Durs Grünbein, 'Der Indianer des Geistes. Bagatellen über das Leben des Philosophen Pascal', *Zeitschrift für Ideengeschichte*, 2.1 (2008), 69–84, (p. 69). Unless otherwise indicated, translations from the German are mine.

[...] to hold open the thinkable beyond everything thinkable].[6] Grünbein shows repeatedly how the Jansenist is also in active conversation with Descartes, another founding figure of modern philosophy. Tellingly, he repeatedly returns to the discussions of the relation of language and the conception of modern subjectivity:

> Pascal war einer von den seltenen Menschen, denen es als Anmaßung erscheint, wenn sie ich sagen. [...] [Es] mußte ein Denken geben, das von allem *Ich denke* frei war. [...] Descartes, murmelte er, überflüssig und unschlüssig. Wer das Sein im Denken verankerte und dazu ein Ich als Halteseil brauchte, dem war nicht zu helfen.
>
> [Pascal was one of these rare people to whom it seems presumptuous to say 'I'. [...] There had to be, a thinking that was free of all the *I think*. [...] 'Descartes', he murmured, 'superfluous and incoherent'. You cannot help one who anchors being in thinking and needs an 'I' as a guy rope for that.][7]

Descartes is a cornerstone of, and in many ways the most obvious example for, Grünbein's engagement with philosophy. Despite this implicit acknowledgement of Pascal's criticisms, a number of questions traditionally associated with Cartesian philosophy are constant themes in Grünbein's work. For instance, from the early *Schädelbasislektion* onward, Grünbein's writing is deeply invested in examining the epistemological and ethical dimensions of the supposed dualism of body and mind, in particular in relationship to science.[8]

The presence of Descartes in Grünbein's work has become even more evident in his writing since *Schädelbasislektion*. One of Grünbein's most ambitious and important books to date – *Vom Schnee oder Descartes in Deutschland* – elevates Descartes to a titular figure in and for Grünbein's poetry. Importantly, according to Grünbein this volume is his 'Hauptwerk' [main work], the book that is 'closest to [his] heart' and where he 'went out on a limb as a poet more than in any of [his] other writings'.[9] In many ways, *Vom Schnee* deals with how poetic form responds to the demands of philosophical thought. It does so in a characteristically multilayered way. For instance, the canto 'Drei Philosophen bei Tisch' ['Three Philosophers at Table'] imagines a – very visceral – meal during which Descartes,

---

6 Ibid., p. 78.

7 Ibid., pp. 69, 70 and 71.

8 See, for instance, Grünbein's statements on poetry and ethics in *Entgrenzungen. Vierzehn Autorengespräche über Liebe, Leben und Literatur*, ed. by Olga Olivia Kasaty (Munich: Text + Kritik, 2007), p. 73.

9 Ibid., p. 83. For the two latter quotations, see: '*Descartes' Devil* – Durs Grünbein in Conversation with Michael Eskin'. (http://westside-philosophers.com/publishing2/book_pages/ddevil.php).

Hobbes and Gassendi ('drei der Größten' [three of the greatest]) heatedly exchange views on a number of philosophical topics, including the status of poetry: '"Die Poesie – nichts hab ich so wie sie geliebt", / Schrieb im *Discours* der Mann [...]' ['Poetry – I loved nothing like her' / Wrote the man in the *Discours*].[10] Descartes, stereotypically figured as focussed solely on rationality and intellect, is here imagined as a lover of poetry, already invoking a theme of emotional attachment and poetry that will concern us in more detail later. Throughout *Vom Schnee*, Grünbein develops and takes up themes that pervade the Cartesian corpus in a similar way. The poems reveal that Grünbein is invested in a representation of Descartes that goes beyond a common image of him as a Rationalist philosopher whose main, and questionable, contribution to philosophy is the formulation of modern mind-body dualism. In fact, Grünbein deems this received image to be a result of insufficient attention to how important the categories of the imagination and, ultimately, the poetical, are for Descartes. It is worth mentioning that this repositioning is very much in conversation with the portrayal of Descartes that has emerged in certain philosophical circles over the last few decades, including attention to the ethical dimensions of the Cartesian project.[11] So, while his intervention does not follow orthodox philosophical discourse or traditional representations of Descartes, Grünbein's treatment of the French thinker certainly betrays an awareness of the reception history surrounding him.

Grünbein's investment in a differentiated view of Descartes's reception becomes particularly evident in his companion piece to *Vom Schnee*, namely *Der cartesische Taucher. Drei Meditationen*.[12] Here, Grünbein offers us a reading of Descartes as a 'Wegbereiter einer anthropologisch fundierten Poetik' [paving the way for an anthropologically based poetics].[13] It is not surprising that the 'poetics' Grünbein discovers are immediately relevant to the production of his own lyri-

10 Durs Grünbein, *Vom Schnee oder Descartes in Deutschland* (Frankfurt a. M.: 2003), p. 132.

11 For instance, E. M. Curley, *Descartes against the Skeptics* (Cambridge, MA: Harvard University Press, 1978); Katherine J. Morris, *Descartes' Dualism* (London: Routledge, 1996); Justin Skirry, *Descartes and the Metaphysics of Human Nature* (London: Continuum, 2005). While Grünbein alludes to his interest in Descartes studies in his interview with Eskin (he mentions reading scholars such as Stanley Cavell, Peter Machamer and J. E. McGuire), *Descartes' Devil* does not deal with scholarship in any academic form – it is simply a different project.

12 Grünbein himself uses the term 'companion' and calls them 'two sides of a coin'. See 'Durs Grünbein in Conversation with Michael Eskin'.

13 Durs Grünbein, *Der cartesische Taucher. Drei Meditationen* (Frankfurt a. M.: Suhrkamp, 2008), p. 12; *Descartes' Devil. Three Meditations*, trans. by Anthea Bell (New York: Upper West Side Philosophers Press, 2010), p. 15. On the role of anthropology in relation to questions of philosophy and poetry see Florian Berg, *Das Gedicht und das Nichts. Über Anthropologie und Geschichte im Werk Durs Grünbeins* (Würzburg: Königshausen & Neumann, 2007).

cal work. Grünbein calls his own Cartesian *Meditations* 'lockere Meditationen' [loosely connected meditations].[14] The informal dimension that this description invokes ('locker' is also 'relaxed') only relates to their form. A page into the third meditation, Grünbein is not shy to provide the reader with a 'lockere' autobiographical anecdote that illustrates his affinity:

> einer der schönsten Momente meiner wiedergewonnenen Freiheit war, irgendwann im Frühjahr 1990, der Tag, als ich in Paris an einer Kreuzung stand und das blaue Straßenschild las: *Rue Descartes*. In diesem Augenblick hüpfte mir vor Freude das Herz unterm T-Shirt.
>
> [one of the most beautiful moments of my regained freedom was a day in the spring of 1990, when I stood at an intersection in Paris and read the blue street sign: *Rue Descartes*. At that moment my heart leapt with joy under my T-shirt.][15]

For all the informality of style (down to the T-shirt) and the supposedly anecdotal tone, it is important to see that they do not in any way suggest a lack of ambition or depth for the remainder of the work (after all, this is about having regained freedom too, and finding a *Rue* that leads to *Vom Schnee*). The 'lockere Meditationen' are, from the very beginning, more than a passing philosophical commentary on Descartes. They give Grünbein an opportunity to articulate how certain aspects of Descartes's thought relate to the category of the poetical, including Grünbein's own understanding of it. Descartes becomes the figure through whom Grünbein reflects his own relationship to poetry and history. In many ways, Grünbein's self-understanding as a poet results directly from an engagement with Descartes's writings and thought.

Grünbein's meditations are, however, more than a supplemental or explanatory account of his poetical practice. *Descartes' Devil* is a significant piece of critical and poetical writing in its own right. It forms part of a larger set of Grünbein's writings – his works in prose – that are often overlooked in the reception of the aspects of his work that deal with philosophy. While, for instance, Eskin and Sonja Klein have provided significant commentaries on the importance of philosophy to Grünbein's poetry, these insightful contributions most often deal with his lyrical work.[16] Though they both remark just how prolific Grünbein is as an author of prose texts, be they essayistic or autobiographical, these prose writings are sel-

14 Grünbein, *Der cartesische Taucher*, p. 11; Grünbein, *Descartes' Devil*, p. 15.
15 Grünbein, ibid. (German), p. 86; ibid. (English), p. 83.
16 See especially Michael Eskin, *Poetic Affairs. Celan, Grünbein, Brodsky* (Stanford: Stanford University Press, 2008), pp. 58–87; Sonja Klein, *'Denn alles, alles ist verlorne Zeit'. Fragment und Erinnerung im Werk von Durs Grünbein* (Bielefeld: Aisthesis, 2008).

dom the subject of sustained analysis. This is not for a lack of material.[17] Grünbein's constant output in prose has been gathered in collections such as *Galilei vermißt Dantes Hölle und bleibt an den Maßen hängen*, *Warum schriftlos leben*, *Antike Dispositionen*, *Gedicht und Geheimnis*, or stands on its own, such as in *Das erste Jahr*, *Bars von Atlantis* and the already mentioned *Der cartesische Taucher*.[18] Many of these prose writings expand the reflections on poetry's relationship to philosophy that are so evident in Grünbein's poems. Given his widely known interest in philosophical works, the lack of scholarship on Grünbein's prose with a philosophical dimension is rather remarkable. Hinrich Ahrend's work is an exception, bringing together the analysis of prose and poetry.[19] His extensive analysis is especially strong in uncovering the particularly *essayistic* dimensions of Grünbein's prose and how it relates to the production of his lyrical work. Building on, but departing from, Ahrend's commentary regarding this relation, in this essay I want to concentrate on how Grünbein's theoretical prose as a whole negotiates specifically the tension between philosophy and poetry. Thus, while it is hardly news that Grünbein is interested in philosophy, this piece wants to address a scholarly gap by focussing on Grünbein's theoretical writing, and to pay special attention to how his prose reflects on the relationship between poetry and philosophy, both openly and covertly. Implicitly, I also want to draw attention to Grünbein as a significant prose writer, who produces theoretical prose writings whose subtlety and conceptual ambition often rival some of his strongest poems.

In the cases that scholars do cite Grünbein's writings in prose, they overwhelmingly understand them as vehicles to approach his poetry.[20] As with many other

---

17 See Eskin's introduction to Durs Grünbein, *The Bars of Atlantis. Selected Essays*, trans. by John Crutchfield, Michael Hofmann and Andrew Shields (New York: Farrar, Straus and Giroux, 2010).

18 In 2010, an English translation of a selection of Grünbein's essays (*The Bars of Atlantis*), as well as *Descartes' Devil. Three Meditations* appeared. The publication of *The Vocation of Poetry*, trans. by Michael Eskin (New York: Upper West Side Philosophers, 2011), a year later continues this very welcome development, which will undoubtedly contribute to the appreciation of Grünbein's standing as an important contemporary European voice.

19 See Ahrend, *'Tanz zwischen sämtlichen Stühlen'*.

20 For a representative sample of this practice, see: Amir Eshel, 'Durs Grünbein's Mnemonic Topographies and the Future of the German Past', *The German Quarterly*, 74.4 (2001), 407–16; Mario Zanucchi, 'Das Diorama und der sarkastische Blick. Kritische Betrachtungen zur Poetik Durs Grünbeins', *Weimarer Beiträge. Zeitschrift für Literaturwissenschaft, Ästhetik und Kulturwissenschaften*, 51.2 (2005), 219–35; Theodore Ziolkowski, 'Two Juvenal Delinquents. Robert Lowell and Durs Grünbein', *Classical and Modern Literature*, 26.1 (2006), 12–32; Ian Cooper, 'Direction, Disruption, Voice. Durs Grünbein's "Historien" and "Neue Historien"', *The Germanic Review*, 84.2 (2009), 99–121.

authors, essayistic writing is used to explicate and read poetical work. I hope to show that this is only part of the story. Thus, while I believe it is helpful to use the prose to illuminate the poetry, and I want to pay attention to this dimension, it is also important to focus on the internal poetical and rhetorical dimensions of Grünbein's theoretical prose. Grünbein himself encourages a reading along both of these lines, highlighting his ambivalent relationship regarding the precise status of his own prose vis-à-vis his poetry. On the one hand, he claims, that he started to write essays 'um mir selbst Klarheit zu verschaffen' [gain clarity for [him]self] and 'um transparenter zu sein für meine Zeitgenossen' [be more transparent for [his] contemporaries].[21] He also admits that he does not intend to engage with other genres of prose such as the novel: 'Ich habe bis heute meine Scheu vor der reinen Prosa' [Even today I still have a certain fear of pure prose].[22] On the other hand, Grünbein asserts that 'wenn man jetzt bei mir die Frage nach meinen Essays stellt, dann stellt man bei mir gleichzeitig die Frage nach meinen Gedichten' [if one now asks the question about my essays, then one is simultaneously asking the question about my poems].[23] Significantly for our concerns here, the question regarding the relationship between poetical writing and the theoretical essay is also figured through the question of philosophy and its connection to poetry.

Grünbein's essays present a complex overlap between genres, styles and thinking that makes theoretical claims about both poetry and philosophy. He states, for instance that 'Auch glaube ich nicht wirklich an die Trennung von Philosophie und Poesie, vielmehr – ich wehre mich gegen sie' [Also, I do not really believe in a separation between philosophy and poetry, rather – I resist it].[24] As this essay will show, this resistance takes several significant forms. Specifically, I will stress two major aspects of Grünbein's theoretical positioning – or the 'resistance' – in his prose, and discuss why they are relevant. First, I will focus on Grünbein's insistence on the common origin of philosophy and poetry, and how, he claims, that symbiotic relationship is destroyed. Here, it will be of particular importance to understand that while philosophy 'betrays' poetry in various forms, the two remain inextricably tied to one another. The discussion will specifically call attention to the nostalgic elements of Grünbein's conjectural history of poetry. Secondly, the essay will turn to Grünbein's own contribution to this imagined genealogy of poetics, namely his idea of 'poetical thinking'. I will explore

21 Kasaty, *Entgrenzungen*, p. 77.
22 Ibid., p. 77.
23 Silvia Ruzzenenti and Durs Grünbein, 'Poetik und Essay. Ein Interview mit Durs Grünbein', *Euphorion*, 102.4 (2008), 503–13 (p. 505).
24 Ibid., p. 509.

what aspects of 'poetical thinking' are crucial to understand Grünbein's oeuvre better and how it challenges us as readers. My discussion will include a short reading of a poem by Grünbein to illustrate how these aspects of 'poetical thinking' map onto Grünbein's lyrical praxis.

Origins

In the titular essay of *Gedicht und Geheimnis*, Grünbein addresses the issue of philosophy through one of his favourite themes, namely the importance of historical analysis. Given Grünbein's intense investment in the role of history for poetry, it is not all that surprising that he turns to aetiology to clarify the relationship between poetry and philosophy. This move itself has, of course, a long and venerable tradition. Discussions about the origin of poetry are a common feature in Western poetics. For Grünbein, poetry and philosophy spring from the same source, they have a common origin. The geographical location in the Western context for this narrative is Ancient Greece.[25] Despite their common heritage, poetry claims to be older and more venerable than philosophy, Grünbein stating that in the time just after the great works of Homer or Hesiod were produced everybody knew 'daß Philosophie anfangs nur ein Abfallprodukt war' [that philosophy was originally a mere waste product] of the great narratives.[26] Both spheres seem to exist side by side, philosophy growing into a discipline of 'kluge Textauslegung und -deutung' [clever textual analysis and interpretation].[27] However, at one point there is a deep rupture between the two spheres. Grünbein locates the moment of this break in pre-Socratic times, with Plato's work consolidating the fissure.[28] Subsequently, the rupture becomes established through '[j]ahrtausendelange Gewöhnung' [thousands of years of habituation].[29]

What causes the rupture between philosophy and poetry? Several of Grünbein's essays deal with this question. In one of these, entitled 'Zur Frage des Stils' ['On the Question of Style'], his answer provides one of the keys for appreciating his understanding of the relationship between philosophy and poetry. In short,

25 At one point, however, Grünbein goes back even further by invoking the poetry of ancient Egypt. See Durs Grünbein, *Gedicht und Geheimnis. Aufsätze 1990–2006* (Frankfurt a. M.: Suhrkamp, 2007), p. 23; *Bars of Atlantis*, p. 62.
26 Ibid. (German), p. 86; ibid. (English), p. 84.
27 Ibid. (German), p. 86; ibid. (English), p. 84.
28 Grünbein is curiously specific on this point. The break happens between Parmenides and Heraclitus. See Grünbein, *Gedicht und Geheimnis*, p. 86; Grünbein, *Bars of Atlantis*, p. 84.
29 Ibid. (German), p. 80; ibid. (English), p. 81.

philosophy 'betrays' poetry. The main betrayal consists in philosophy's move – against poetry – to claim language as the purveyor of truth. Philosophy claims, 'widerrechtlich' [unlawfully], the 'Inbesitznahme von Sprache zum Zwecke des Wahrheitsvorteils' [taking possession of language for the purposes of prioritizing truth].[30] Grünbein's description intimates how the negative consequences of such usurpation expand over a number of levels. Philosophy claims language 'zum Zwecke', as a means, nothing more. Unsurprisingly, the poet rejects such a view of the realm of language as not only unlawful but also limiting. The violence of the unlawfulness results in a seeming advantage of a particular version of truth ('Wahrheitsvorteil'). It is paralleled by the brutality of 'Inbesitznahme' [taking possession of] which reduces language's many dimensions to its function as a property (to be used purely functionally). Philosophy demeans language by reducing it to a means. It is an 'Anmaßung' [arrogance] and ends in 'Tyrannei' [tyranny]. Simultaneously, this 'Inbesitznahme' also disfigures truth because after its successful claim on language '[erscheinen] Stil und Gedanke mittlerweile als Getrenntes' [style and thought seem completely distinct today].[31] Once this distinction becomes accepted it is not only philosophers who come to believe of thinking: 'Ganz so, als sei das Ästhetische hierbei nur sekundär, die Ausdrucksform der Erkenntnis, die als primär vorausgesetzt wird, sklavisch verpflichtet' [As if the aesthetic were merely of secondary importance here, as if the form of expression were slavishly beholden to the supreme role of cognition].[32] Such an understanding of thinking, and of philosophy as the system that monitors that understanding, keeps poetry and philosophical thought apart. It conceives of philosophy and poetry not only as distinct but even as competing, possibly opposing, expressions. It is no surprise that Grünbein invokes Plato's fantasy of poetry's banishment from the Republic here.

Readers of 'Zur Frage des Stils' will be quick to point out that Grünbein's essay also maintains that the alleged 'Inbesitznahme' of poetry was not completely successful. In fact, he states that precisely because of the initial betrayal, poetry and philosophy are 'bis heute aneinandergekettet' [chained to each other to this day].[33] We will turn to the important conceptual implications of this connection – this chain – shortly. It is instructive, however, to reiterate that 'Zur Frage des Stils' is not the only place where Grünbein worries and writes about the 'betrayal' of poetry by philosophy. He repeats this concern in a variety of ways

30 Ibid. (German), pp. 81–82; ibid. (English), p. 80.
31 Ibid. (German), p. 82; ibid. (English), p. 80.
32 Ibid. (German), p. 82; ibid. (English), p. 80.
33 Ibid. (German), p. 82; ibid. (English), p. 80.

throughout his oeuvre. Depending on the occasion, the scene of the rupture is figured in terms of interpersonal relationships, religious or political trespasses, the vocabulary of the Enlightenment, or discussed in relation to the law.

In 'Das Gedicht und sein Geheimnis' ['The Poem and its Secret'], Grünbein repeats the description of the break as a 'Usurpation' [usurpation] by philosophy.[34] In the process, poetry suffers from an 'Enteignung' [dispossession], thus leaving it as the older but poorer part of the relationship. Philosophy has given itself the authority to dispose – in fact disseize? – poetry in that manner, and it creates the criteria by which this new relationship is maintained.[35] This process ends in a 'totale [...] Entmündigung' [complete disenfranchisement] of poetry, a description that does not only have filial connotations and reminds us of the link of language and authority (it is the Vor*mund* that speaks in lieu), but also resonates with the Kantian *Unmündigkeit* which we can only escape if we think philosophically (not poetically).[36] Philosophy seizes its own responsibility unilaterally, and subsequently establishes the rules by which thought is judged. Such a transgression cannot be denounced easily from within any system of thought. Thus it is understandable that Grünbein varies the vocabulary of law and disenfranchisement with the rhetoric of religion and sin. For him, the division of poetry and philosophy, their rupture, not only breaks the law, but also transgresses a moral or spiritual code. Their 'Entzweiung' [falling out] is an 'Ursünde' [primordial sin], thus tainting everything that comes in its aftermath.[37] This is, then, not only a political 'Machtübernahme' [coup], but also a morally conditioning factor that predetermines the relationship between philosophy and poetry as marred.[38]

---

34 Ibid. (German), p. 86; ibid. (English), p. 84.
35 Ibid. (German), p. 86; ibid. (English), p. 84.
36 Ibid. (German), p. 86; ibid. (English), p. 84. Famously, Kant's answer to the question 'Was ist Aufklärung?' [What is Enlightenment?] is: 'Aufklärung ist der Ausgang des Menschen aus seiner selbstverschuldeten Unmündigkeit' [Enlightenment is mankind's exit from its self-incurred immaturity]. See Immanuel Kant, *Was ist Aufklärung? Ausgewählte kleine Schriften* (Hamburg: Meiner, 1999), p. 20; Immanuel Kant, 'An Answer to the Question. What is Enlightenment?' in *What is Enlightenment? Eighteenth-Century Answers and Twentieth-Century Questions*, ed. by James Schmidt (Berkeley: University of California Press, 1996), pp. 58–64, (p. 58). The phrasing of this foundational text in philosophy resonates through Grünbein's text: whoever is 'unmündig' cannot speak for himself, he needs a 'Vor*mund*' [a legal guardian] whose signature, voice (and mouth) will stand in for him. Grünbein's text unmistakably invokes the way in which the establishment of such a 'Vormund' can also be '*ent*mündigend' [legally – and philosophically – incapacitating]. The question remains whether the Kantian identification of 'Unmündigkeit' is itself 'entmündigend'.
37 Grünbein, *Gedicht und Geheimnis*, p. 82; Grünbein, *Bars of Atlantis*, p. 80.
38 Ibid. (German), p. 81; ibid. (English), p. 80.

The multiplicity of ways in which Grünbein speaks about the division between the poetical and the philosophical is instructive. He seems to be attempting to find a vocabulary in which to couch the event, to identify adequate terms through which to conceptualize and narrativize it. This variety of framing discourses is not a sign of confusion. Rather, it is a way of acknowledging the multidimensional results that the break between poetry and philosophy entails. This rupture affects not only our understanding of two particular genres of writing. The implications go beyond such an isolated concern. Why? Because poetry and philosophy ultimately configure – through language – how we construct and understand the very category of truth that regulates the law, human interaction or even religion. The prioritization of a particular version of truth ('Wahrheitsvorteil') that philosophy seeks, results from understanding the significance of establishing what counts for truth, and how we make it count. It is not after but *through* the rift that philosophy establishes philosophical truth as a norm, and as a norm that is distinct (in fact, defines itself through its distinction) from poetry. Grünbein ventriloquizes a common attitude that embraces the results of such a process as follows:

> Trotz aller Höhenflüge der Poesie, keiner, der sich für zurechnungsfähig hält, würde je zweifeln an der Überlegenheit der Philosophie, ihrem Privileg auf das höhere und höchste Prinzip.
>
> [Despite all the lofty flights of poetry, no one who considers himself of sound mind would dream of questioning the superiority of philosophy, nor its privileged access to the higher and highest principle.][39]

Again, we shall see shortly why the story is not as bleak as this knowingly hyperbolic statement makes it sound. Nevertheless, it is worth emphasizing that the fictional genealogy that Grünbein sketches here is so powerful that it is absolute ('keiner') and forms what we might liken to the determination of simple intuitions (is to consider oneself to be 'zurechnungsfähig' [of sound mind] also ideological?).

Grünbein offers an even more powerful frame for narrativizing and illustrating the story of the rift between philosophy and poetry: love and betrayal. In his essay 'Die Stimme des Denkers' ['The Thinker's Voice'] that deals with Nietzsche – a figure who lies between philosophy and poetry – Grünbein, once more, narrates the history of philosophical thought and poetry: 'Philosophie und Dichtung, im Grunde ist es die Geschichte einer unglücklichen Liebe' [Philosophy and poetry,

39 Durs Grünbein, *Antike Dispositionen* (Frankfurt a. M.: Suhrkamp, 2005), p. 191; Grünbein, *Bars of Atlantis*, p. 239.

in essence the story of an unhappy love affair].[40] The history of poetry and philosophy is, at its heart, one of two star-crossed lovers. The love seems to be 'unglücklich' [unhappy]; if only the circumstances had been different, poetry and philosophy would remain harmoniously united. However, Grünbein soon corrects any such idealizing misunderstanding:

> Philosophie und Dichtung – es war ein Euphemismus zu sagen: die Geschichte einer unglückliche [sic] Liebe. In Wirklichkeit war es die eines Verrats, eines Liebesverrats. Seine lange, verworrene Chronik handelt von der Inbesitznahme der Sprache zum Zwecke des Wahrheitsvorteils, und fällt zusammen mit jener der Ideengeschichte selbst.
>
> [Philosophy and poetry – it was a euphemism to call it the story of an unhappy love. In reality, it was the story of a betrayal, a betrayal in love. Its long, muddled chronicle tells of the seizure and occupation of language for the purpose of privileging truth, and it coincides with the history of ideas.][41]

Not only does philosophy betray poetry, but it is the worst kind of betrayal, one of a beloved. The discipline that supposedly lives from its love of wisdom comes into being by betraying and subsequently denying its love for poetry. The nature of this betrayal is important for the subsequent history of the two disciplines. The betrayal of love is committed in order to gain control over language's way of constructing and evaluating truth. And, while the betrayal is absolute, it cannot be hidden. Philosophy's moment of cheating is exposed throughout the history of poetry and philosophy. It is significant that Grünbein chooses the figure of 'Liebesverrat' [betrayal in love]. Even more than other forms of betrayal, betrayal in love does not end with the moment of initial transgression. This wound does not heal and, in fact, connects the two former lovers forever. As we already noted, through the betrayal poetry and philosophy are 'aneinandergekettet' [chained together].[42] The division is a constant reminder of the transgression, a rupture that

---

40 Ibid. (German), p. 186; ibid. (English), pp. 233–34. The translation of 'Liebe' as a casual 'love affair' rather than as 'love' is a little unfortunate here, especially since philosophy ends up betraying poetry. In any case, it should be noted that, once more, Grünbein's vocabulary has wider philosophical references and connotations. This time he invokes yet another philosopher who theorizes the dividing line between philosophy and poetry, namely Heidegger. Grünbein's 'Im Grunde' [in essence] suggests more than that he wants simply to get to the bottom of the story. It references an origin and prime motive ['Grund'] which will also uncover the reasons behind the history that unfolds from that origin. Given the context, the Heideggerian undertones seem undeniable, specifically in relation to Heidegger's *Der Satz vom Grund* (Pfullingen: Neske, 1958).

41 Grünbein, *Antike Dispositionen*, pp. 188–89; Grünbein, *Bars of Atlantis*, p. 236.

42 Ibid. (German), p. 190; ibid. (English), p. 238.

simultaneously binds the two parties without ever letting them forgive each other. The break and the tensions that come with it form, almost involuntarily, the context in which any conceptualization of the relationship between poetry and philosophy will take place. The betrayal marks and determines the relationship and its history.

The story of the split between philosophy and poetry is not a new one. The account of the break itself has a history. And certain elements of Grünbein's portrayal of the original difference fit into a particular tradition. For instance, the location of the split between these two forms of writing and thinking in pre-Socratic times is a feature of many conjectural histories of language and poetry.[43] That does not mean that Grünbein's conceptualization is not original; it does, however, mean that he places himself – knowingly, no doubt – in a longer genealogy of poetics. His is, to a certain degree, a poetics of nostalgia. The unspoken assumption behind Grünbein's various descriptions of 'usurpation', 'sin' or 'betrayal' is that things were better before the rupture. The break marks a loss which is being mourned. The idealized memory of the period of wholeness that preceded it can be read as an attempted compensation. It is nostalgia for harmony, but also for power: before philosophy claimed language as a way of privileging a certain type of truth, poetry was the main verbal authority. This authority, this power, is irrevocably lost for poetry. Each time this break returns – whether wilfully or not – we are reminded that poetry has lost this authority, but, also, will never give up its claim on philosophy. One thing should be clear, however: Grünbein's nostalgia does not include a desire to form, or follow, a utopian vision of a return to the state before the initial rupture. While it emphasizes the loss and harm that poetry suffered, poetry also gains strength from that history. Grünbein's alternative vision encompasses a repositioning of poetry and philosophy without wanting to return to a time before the 'betrayal'. He suggests that a 'Wiedergutmachung' [atonement] for the sin philosophy has committed would mean 'eine Poetik der Philosophie zu schreiben' [writing a poetics of philosophy].[44] As the remainder of this essay will show, examining Grünbein's vision of such a poetics allows us to understand further how poetry and philosophy are crucial categories in, and for, his work.

---

43 On the topic of poetry and philosophy in pre- and post-Socratic times see Marcel Detienne, *The Masters of Truth in Archaic Greece*, trans. by Janet Lloyd (New York: Zone Books, 1996); Ramona A. Naddaff, *Exiling the Poets. The Production of Censorship in Plato's 'Republic'* (Chicago: University of Chicago Press, 2002). For its continued relevance for a contemporary poetics see Simon Jarvis, *Wordsworth's Philosophic Song* (Cambridge: Cambridge University Press, 2007), pp. 1–32.

44 Grünbein, *Antike Dispositionen*, p. 192; Grünbein, *Bars of Atlantis*, p. 240.

Poetic Thinking

As we have seen, poetry and philosophy are, despite their troubled history, chained to one another. While this chain also is a reminder of a rupture, Grünbein simultaneously attempts to re-imagine the connection more positively. He offers an account in his prose that imagines the relationship in a way that has immediate relevance for our understanding of his poetic production. For Grünbein, poetry is always connected to thought. In fact, poetry is deeply conceptual. That is, thought is not only the topic of poetry but also has a direct bearing on poetic form and its generation. As one of the interlocutors in *Descartes' Devil* states: 'Die Poesie beschäftigt sich, wie ihre jüngere Schwester, die Philosophie, mit Ideen' [Poetry, like its younger sister, philosophy, deals in ideas].[45] Poetry's subject and focus of attention is, thus, with concepts. In fact, Grünbein contends, poetry is more conceptual and intellectual than most artistic forms. In an only slightly coded reference to Horace's *ut pictura poesis* and Lessing's *Laokoon* he states that 'Überhaupt zeigt Lyrik deutlicher als andere Formen die zerebrale Seite der Kunst' [It is true in general that poetry is one of the most cerebral of the arts].[46] Ultimately, poetry illustrates better than other aesthetic forms that art has a cerebral side, a reflective and reflexive dimension. It exemplifies an important aspect of the aesthetic, a conceptual side. Poetry is closer to this cerebral, intellectual and, ultimately, philosophical aspect of art than other forms of writing, painting, music or the plastic arts. Again, this relationship has a dual aspect to it and exhibits a certain dynamic of involuntary interdependence. Just as poetry has a philosophical and abstract dimension, philosophy has converse debts to poetry: 'Solange das philosophische Denken nicht umhin kann, auf Metaphern, Gleichnisse, Sinnbilder zurückzugreifen, bleibt es, wie lose auch immer, an Poesie gebunden und dieser verpflichtet' [As long as philosophical thought cannot avoid falling back on metaphors, similes, and symbols, it remains, however loosely, bound up with poetry, and indebted to it].[47] It is relevant that Grünbein speaks about thinking itself here: 'philosophical thinking' and not only its verbal expression – if we could separate the two – is beholden to poetry. Most importantly, Grünbein insists that this relationship is not simply circular.

To appreciate fully how we might explore and describe the way in which these two spheres interact and relate, we need to consider what *kind* of thinking is possible for Grünbein, what kind of thinking occurs in and through the poetical.

45 Grünbein, *Der cartesische Taucher*, pp. 118–19; Grünbein, *Descartes' Devil*, p. 111.
46 Grünbein, *Gedicht und Geheimnis*, p. 32; Grünbein, *Bars of Atlantis*, p. 70.
47 Grünbein *Der cartesische Taucher*, p. 119; Grünbein, *Descartes' Devil*, p. 112.

In order to explore this in some detail, I will now turn to Grünbein's central idea of 'poetical thinking'. In *Das erste Jahr*, he asks us to imagine, and embrace, a conjectural link between thinking, language and poetry:

> Man stelle sich vor, es gäbe ein Denken, das an bestimmte, sonst nur schwer zugängliche Stellen kommt, wie Zahnseide zwischen die hinteren Backenzähne oder ein Endoskop in den Magen. Gewisse Stellen wird es überhaupt zum erstenmal anschaulich machen, einzelne Nebengänge des unüberschaubaren seelischen Höhlensystems, das sich durch den Körper aller Menschen zieht und nur durch findige, kühn in die noch ungesicherten Stollen vorstoßende Phantasie entdeckt werden kann. Dieses Denken ist das poetische Denken, und es ist keine Domäne der Dichter und Literaten, vielmehr die Methode vieler kleiner Suchtrupps, die aus verschiedenen Richtungen aufgebrochen sind, ohne voneinander zu wissen, ein Heer von Phänomenologen, das daran arbeitet, die gemeinsame Vorstellungswelt zu erweitern.
>
> [Imagine a thinking that could penetrate into certain otherwise hard-to-reach places, like dental floss between the wisdom teeth or an endoscope going into the stomach. It will make certain places visible for the very first time – individual branches of the otherwise intractable psychic cave system that runs through the bodies of all humans and can be discovered only by a resourceful imagination audaciously pushing forward into still unsecured galleries. This thinking is poetic thinking, and it is not the exclusive domain of poets and literati; rather, it is a method used by many small search parties that have started out from several directions unbeknownst to one another, an army of phenomenologists working on expanding the confines of our shared imaginaries.][48]

Grünbein uses a curious and intriguing thought experiment to introduce us to his idea of poetical thinking, an idea that turns out to be crucial to his poetic theory. Significantly, his example reappears, in precisely the same form (though Grünbein does not indicate this self quotation), as a central paragraph in the essay 'Das Gedicht und sein Geheimnis' discussed above. Grünbein advances the possibility of 'poetic thinking' as the category that will allow us to describe and articulate the type of conceptual interdependence that links poetry and philosophy in a productive way. It is thus important not only that there is an interdependence (Grünbein has already established this) but also what form that relationship takes, if it is not to relapse into a simple (and simplistic) opposition.[49]

---

48 Durs Grünbein, *Das erste Jahr. Berliner Aufzeichnungen* (Frankfurt a. M.: Suhrkamp, 2001), p. 82; Grünbein, *Bars of Atlantis*, pp. 90–91.

49 It should be said that, evidently, the idea of poetic thinking is not new. Just as with the location of the rupture between poetry and philosophy in pre-Socratic times, Grünbein follows a genealogy and positions himself within it. The links to romantic poetics are especially strong, but there is also a noteworthy parallel with contemporary work in the area of the history of philosophy. While this contextualization is relevant for Grünbein's larger reception, I want to maintain the focus on his prose writing.

For Grünbein, poetical thinking allows us to uncover, explore and discover certain areas of our mind that cannot be reached otherwise. It is a technique that makes things that are otherwise unseen 'anschaulich' [visible], it allows them to be seen and understood. The hidden spaces Grünbein speaks about are all internal to the human body and psyche; he likens the process of poetical thinking to an endoscopy or reaching the cavities between the teeth that are furthest away from the mouth's opening. This thinking is a process that is clinical and diagnostic, partly hygienic but potentially painful. Grünbein's imagery invokes his long-standing fascination with science and the physical body. There is nothing mechanical about this clinical poetical thinking, though, as some might suspect. In fact, the most significant component of exploring these new areas of thought is the imagination. Grünbein limits and specifies that it is only through a 'findige, kühn [...] vorstoßende Phantasie' [only by a resourceful imagination audaciously pushing forward] that we enter into the 'unüberschaubare [...] seelische [...] Höhlensystem [...], das sich durch den Körper aller Menschen zieht' [the otherwise intractable psychic cave system that runs through the bodies of all humans].[50] The body and the imagination here do not inhabit two different spheres. Indeed, poetical thought combines and intersects the spheres of the imagination and the physical human body. Grünbein's imagery is only partly grotesque; thought here is visceral, it connects to the body. In fact, the way poetical thinking allows us to think outside the juxtaposition of thought and body is indicative of how it will help to overcome the dualism between philosophy and poetry. Such an approach also allows us to reconsider the ways many of us have previously, and maybe hastily, adopted certain figures as paradigmatic examples which construct and defend this dualism. Grünbein's main example here is Descartes whom, as we saw in the introduction, he casts not as the founder of dualism and a philosopher in the orthodox sense (one that would rely on the betrayal of poetry), but rather as a figure who has a deep and perceptive sense for the power of poetical thought. In *Descartes' Devil*, he imagines and subtly teases out the importance of a shared imaginary for the dimensions of Descartes's thinking. At one point he imagines Descartes as 'eher Dichter als Philosoph' [more of a poet than a philosopher]; at that point, Grünbein intimates, we need to ask 'Was [...] hat die große Entdeckung des Franzosen, sein Ego cogito, das der Philosophie auf die Sprünge half, mit poetischer Intelligenz zu tun?' [What does Descartes's great discovery, his *Cogito*, his *I think*, which jump-started modern philosophy, have to do with poetic intelligence?].[51] One answer Grünbein gives is that the philosophical subject and the

50 Grünbein, *Das erste Jahr*, p. 82; Grünbein, *Bars of Atlantis*, pp. 90–91.

51 Grünbein, *Der cartesische Taucher*, p. 88; Grünbein, *Descartes' Devil*, pp. 85–86.

poetical subject are much more closely related than we often assume. And poetic intelligence (roughly similar to 'poetic thinking') might be a key to understanding the link between the 'kognitive[s] Ich' [cognitive 'I'] and the 'lyrisches Ich' [poetic 'I'], both of which construct themselves through language.[52] Grünbein is clear on this point: he thinks it is crucial to comprehend that many of Descartes's philosophical problems and difficulties are best understood as linguistic problems. Descartes's *Ego* is a 'Sprachproblem' [linguistic problem], but not in a positivistic sense. Rather, it leads us to uncovering the 'lyrisches Ich' [poetic 'I']. Thus, ultimately, the ego's 'Element, wenn irgend etwas, ist Sprache' [element, if anything, is language].[53]

What seems to be crucial about poetic thinking is that it uncovers and makes us understand dimensions of our own language and thinking to which we do not normally have access; and that these new insights reconfigure the way we look at certain disciplines (such as poetry and philosophy) as well as the activities that are connected with them (such as thinking itself and its linguistic dimensions and representation). Grünbein is attempting to reconfigure the way we perceive, classify and judge thinking itself. He is thus asking us to imagine a different type of thought, a more productive and agile way of thinking. Poetic thinking is not just to think about something in poetic terms. Poetic thinking is to think poetically about thinking. Grünbein imagines this thinking to cut across the conceptual orthodoxies that we normally use to delimit areas of inquiry. This thinking is not only 'vorstoßend', it also allows us to reconfigure our horizons: 'die gemeinsame Vorstellungswelt zu erweitern'. The expansion of these confines involves reconfiguring our conceptual framework when it comes to forms and conventions of thought. These might include what we can call 'scientific' thinking, a certain poetical genre, or, most crucially, what we call philosophical thought. Poetical thinking is reconceptualizing these boundaries by attempting to imagine a form of thinking that is not restricted to the conceptual limitations that a philosophical way of thinking has established (post poetry).

Historically, we have restricted our definition of what makes for thought, partly as a result of the 'usurpation' and 'betrayal' of poetry by philosophy that Grünbein describes. Furthermore, we have seen how the understanding of it along philosophical lines reproduces the assumptions that the rupture puts in place. Hence 'poetical thinking' needs to be imagined, it is not bound by the same rules as non-poetical thinking. Similarly, it does not accord to the stereotypes of what we understand as poetry, if we juxtapose it against philosophy. Poetical

52 Ibid. (German), p. 90; ibid. (English), p. 87.

53 Ibid. (German), p. 89; ibid. (Engish), pp. 86–87

thinking pushes the 'shared imaginaries' in such a way that we can reconceptualize poetry itself. That is why this way of thinking is 'keine Domäne der Dichter und Literaten'. It goes beyond our familiar categories of philosophy and poetry, and invites us to 'expand' the way we think. And that includes the way we think about thinking itself. We can thus form part of one of these curious 'Suchtrupps', doing reconnaissance work as part of a 'Heer von Phänomenologen'. Grünbein's oddly militaristic tone here might seem to contradict what otherwise would seem a rather unconventional and anti-foundational proposal. But the crucial thing is that these search parties are neither centrally organized nor are they fighting under the particular banner of an 'exclusive domain' (we might think of them as non-centralized cells). Thus, poetical thought is neither a centralizing impulse nor inclusive in a colonizing fashion. Rather, it is a way of remodelling and reconfiguring the forms of our understanding – our 'shared imaginaries' – that emphasize the peculiar power of the poetical; and we always have to keep in mind that here the poetical is restricted to its orthodox definition through poetry, a poetry that itself is positioned in contrast to philosophy. Poetical thinking occurs both inside and outside of what we normally understand poetry and philosophy to be.

Thoughtful Thinking

It becomes increasingly clear why it is significant that Grünbein insists that poetical thought is not only restricted to the 'poets and literati'. Part of his impulse here is to disassociate poetical thought from the orthodox understanding of poetry that results from its betrayal by philosophy. However, while Grünbein is at pains to stress that poetical thought is not restricted to what we normally think of as poetry or literature, he does not exclude these spheres. In fact, Grünbein faces the challenge of how he can imagine in his own lyric practice a poetical thinking, how he can present us with a thinking 'das daran arbeitet, die gemeinsame Vorstellungswelt zu erweitern', a thinking that cuts across the normal classifications of poetry and philosophy.[54] Thus, while poetical thinking might happen elsewhere, and may take on many different and unpredictable forms, the question we ask as Grünbein's readers is immediately: what does 'poetical thinking' mean for his own poetic practice? Surely, it is desirable that poetry should be part of the extension of the 'gemeinsame Vorstellungswelt'. That is, poetical thinking must happen in the lyric, too. It is important to understand what form this takes, and what consequences it might have for our understanding of poetry, Grünbein's in

---

54 Grünbein, *Das erste Jahr*, p. 82; Grünbein, *Bars of Atlantis*, p. 91.

particular. Significantly, Grünbein himself introduces these issues directly when he imagines a possible ideal of lyric poetry:

> Ein Ideal lyrischer Dichtung könnte so aussehen: viele kleine Sensationen auf einer einzigen Buchseite, aufgereiht auf den schwarzen Fernleitungsdrähten der Zeilen, und hin und wieder lassen sich ein paar Gedanken darauf nieder und lauschen dem Singen der Drähte. Unter Poesie, murmelte einmal ein Romancier, der in Wahrheit ein verkleideter Dichter war, unter Poesie verstehe ich die Mysterien des Irrationalen, wahrgenommen durch rationale Worte.
>
> [Ideally, lyric poetry could look something like this: many small sensations on a single page arranged along the black long-distance wires of its lines, and now and then a few ideas settle on them and listen to the singing in the wires. 'By poetry', a novelist who was really a poet in disguise once said, 'I understand the mysteries of the irrational perceived through rational words'.][55]

The ideal of lyric poetry that is imagined here consists of sensations united on a single sheet of paper, which nonetheless remain mobile. The lines of the poem turn into the vehicles for communication, a conductor. The lines and sensations themselves hang suspended, and the thoughts that land on them – like birds on a wire – listen to the sound that their swinging movement makes. They do not move on the page, but their oscillation helps to form the sound that these conductors produce, their 'singing'. This is a description of the musicality of language and, typically for Grünbein, the poetic and conceptual song can be produced by a wire, not necessarily by an organic human voice. But this tool of communication, this conductor of thought and music, also transmits a song that is often discarded as white noise. Poetry concerns the 'Mysterien des Irrationalen', which are transmitted through the conductor on the page, namely the words that are printed.[56] The words themselves are not irrational, and this is not a vision of poetry as mysticism. However, Grünbein's comment does point towards a fundamental aspect of that most intellectual of arts, poetry: it is conceptual, but its conceptual power and intellectual force cannot be classified as commonly philosophical or rational. Nevertheless, poetry has the ambition to account for a way in which we can think. In fact, it has the ambition to account for a way of thinking that is more accurate

55 Grünbein, *Der cartesische Taucher*, p. 119; Grünbein, *Descartes' Devil*, p. 112. Immediately before this passage, Grünbein once again cites Wittgenstein's dictum with which this essay opened.

56 Grünbein's text here directly invokes Vladimir Nabokov's work on Nikolai Gogol. After claiming that 'Gogol's play [*The Government Inspector*] is poetry in action', Nabokov explains what he 'means' by poetry: precisely the 'mysteries of the irrational as perceived through rational words'. Vladimir Nabokov, *Nikolai Gogol* (New York: New Directions, 1944), p. 55.

if less rigid than the way that we normally choose. This leaves us wondering how the thoughts that land on the poetical line, which functions as a conductor, can be transmitted. And, furthermore, what they would transmit that prevents us from classifying it in an established way. According to Grünbein, one of the things that these thoughts transmit is the observation of our surroundings, both affectively and intellectually.

For Grünbein, an active engagement with our context shows that our sensibilities cut across the theoretical or systematic accounts that compartmentalize them in a one-dimensional manner. Poetry is the result of our active and complex engagement with the world, and in that sense observation on its own can already be poeticizing:

> Der Dichtung ebenso wie jeder wirksamen Heilsbehandlung zugrunde liegt eine Fülle von Einzelbeobachtungen, Schocks oder Glücksmomenten, die jedes Mal anders erzählte Geschichte des Erlebens von Sterblichkeit, Vernunft und Passion. Hier wie dort führt erst die Versuchsanordnung zu neuen Ergebnissen, der freie Fall durch die Netze der Tradition hindurch auf den Boden persönlicher Wahrnehmung und Existenz. Empirisch handeln heißt, dem alten griechischen Wortsinn nach: im Wagnis stehen, mit dem Scheitern auf du und du.
>
> [Poetry like every curative treatment is based on an abundance of individual observations, shocks, or moments of happiness, on the story – each time told differently – of the experience of mortality, reason, and passion. Here as well as there, it is only the test arrangement that leads to new results, the free fall through the nets of tradition to the floor of individual perception and existence. In the sense of the ancient Greek word, to act empirically means: be in the middle of the risk, be close to failure.][57]

The individual observations form the basis for what then becomes poetic thinking. Grünbein's poetic thinking, then, is grounded in the particularity of experience. Experience seems to provide the link between 'cerebral' poetry and the immediate and singular event on which it is based. What type of individual observations ('Einzelbeobachtungen') does Grünbein have in mind? We find one example of these recorded in his poem 'Villen am Comer See' ['Villas on Lake Como'].[58] Broadly speaking, the poem concerns an observation about the natural world and about how certain natural phenomena can seem reflections of a wider poetical question, namely the question of form and content. Taking its cue from a singular observation, Grünbein's poem helps us to account for a way of understanding how poetic thinking could be 'at work' regarding these categories. That

57 Grünbein, *Das erste Jahr*, p. 279.

58 Durs Grünbein, *Strophen für übermorgen. Gedichte* (Frankfurt a. M.: Suhrkamp, 2007), pp. 118–19.

is, the poem is an instance of how poetical thinking helps Grünbein to construct a set of 'conductors' on the page, to live up to the ideal of lyrical poetry; at least, that is part of what the poem attempts, I believe. In its first strophe we read:

> Was war zuerst, die Form des Ufers, Sinusform,
> Der sich das Wasser fügt bei allem Widerstand?
> Oder das Wasser, das sich selbst die Fassung gab,
> Ein Schleifstein, flüssig, für das Felsenbecken,
> Der Buchten formt, Halbinseln, grüne Zungen. (ll. 3–7)
>
> [What came first, the form of the shore, sinus form, / To which the water complies against resistance? / Or the water, that gave itself its own frame, / A grindstone, liquid, for the rock basin, / That forms bays, peninsulas, green tongues.]

In these lines, the question as to how the binding form of the shore relates to the water, and which one claims priority, is also a question about poetic form and content. Grünbein reflects here, poetically, on a question that, in the terms of orthodox thought, is impossible to answer. Water that gives itself its own frame, its own limits, is beyond our normal imagination. And Grünbein's invocation of a 'fluid grindstone' insists and intensifies these images of conceptual tension and contradiction. This, then, is also a question about philosophy and poetry.

The reason for the conceptual tension and division between linguistic form and content is that philosophy claimed to ignore the conceptual import of form, aesthetics. Grünbein, we remember, complains that this is to make a crucial mistake: 'Ganz so, als sei das Ästhetische hierbei nur sekundär, die Ausdrucksform der Erkenntnis, die als primär vorausgesetzt wird, sklavisch verpflichtet' [As if the aesthetic were merely of secondary importance here, as if the form of expression were slavishly beholden to the supreme role of cognition].[59] We know this is a grave mistake because 'Denken und Ausdrucksfindung kommen aus ein und derselben Quelle' [Thinking and articulation come from one and the same source].[60] Grünbein's poem attempts to think a way out of this dichotomy. Its lines try to act as conductors for our thought, and ask us to reconsider the way we understand the boundary between form and content. As he asks, in a similar vein, elsewhere:

> Macht der Gedanke den Stil, oder ist es umgekehrt der Stil, der den Gedanken für sich antreten läßt [...]? Die Frage ist weniger leicht in den bekannten Schematismus von Form und Inhalt, Inhalt und Form zu übertragen, als es den Anschein hat.

---

59 Grünbein, *Gedicht und Geheimnis*, p. 82; Grünbein, *Bars of Atlantis*, p. 80.
60 Ibid. (German), p. 81; ibid. (English), p. 79.

> [Does thought make style, or is it actually style that has thought line up for it [...]? It's not as easy as it may seem to translate this problem into the familiar schematism of form and content, content and form.][61]

This reconsideration is not only about the form and content of poetry. It is also about the form and content of thinking itself. As an instance of poetic thinking, this expands our 'shared imaginaries' in such a way that we reconsider what we take to be the boundaries of our thought. Poetry presents one opportunity to explore the possibilities that such a reconsideration opens up. Thus 'Villen am Comer See' is not only about the process and the shape of thought, and how that thought is expressed. The ultimate challenge of this poem is to reconsider the activity of thinking itself, and how thinking is tied to the forms of its expression, its linguistic representation.

Language is at the intersection between the two spheres that Grünbein designates as 'water' and 'shore': 'Leicht verschiebt, / Ein bloßer Laut, sich hier das Grau ins Blau' [Easily shifts, / A simple sound, itself here the grey to blue, ll. 11–12]. The grey of the stone becomes the blue of the sea by the mere shifting of a simple and exposed ['bloßer'] sound: 'Grau' becomes 'Blau'. Language is fluid and hard at the same time. It allows us to formulate the question of how to cut across – conceptually and linguistically – the boundaries that we assume to be given naturally (the shore, the water), but that turn out to be constructed entities, malleable by the shifting of two consonants. This is not so much about the arbitrariness of language; rather, it is about how brittle the borders of our thinking are, and how both poetry and philosophy need to remember that. The last stanza of the poem varies its initial question thus: 'Was war zuerst? Natur als Sprache – oder Stil?' [What came first? Nature as language – or style?, ll. 43–44]. Since style is intimately connected to thinking via language, the poem's question 'Was war zuerst?' is not only chronological or ontological. It is also a question about logic. It thereby combines two of the most orthodox moves of philosophical thinking: the search for origin and conceptual priority. That the poem does not contain a reply is significant. It refuses to answer a question whose terms already predetermine the answer. There is, on a very deep level, no difference between style and language. And in this sense, it is relevant that the 'origin' that is sought here, at least superficially, is the moment where philosophy and poetry divide. But this division, which seems so natural and intuitive now, is wrongheaded. If we want to use our 'findige Phantasie' [resourceful imagination] to be 'kühn' [audacious] in pushing forward into parts of our imagination, then we will have to give up on

61 Ibid. (German), p. 81; ibid. (English), p. 79.

the idea that we can verbalize or understand our insights and experiences in a way that accords to divisions such as philosophy and poetry. These separations are the result of, and perpetuate, an inaccurate and simplistic account of the world that surrounds us. That might mean that we have to give up on the way we commonly account for the means that we use to understand the world. Poetical thinking, in poetry and elsewhere, allows us to think through this challenge, and ultimately to reconsider what thinking is. It also challenges us to consider the consequences of that thinking. That is, poetical thinking forces us to reconsider what we believe to be the very basic structures of the way we account for our surroundings. This puts up a whole host of categories for scrutiny: the idea of nature, the human subject or, in this particular case, the division between thought and language.[62] What 'poetic thinking' ultimately challenges us to do is to re-think the very category of thought. If this is so, we can fully appreciate the serious implications of the claim that poetry is cerebral and conceptual. Poetry, then, is conceptual in that it animates and responds to a complete overhaul of our cognitive assumptions and apparatus. Simultaneously, the secure place of poetry, as the counterfoil to philosophy, disappears. That means there is no fixed or secure place for poetry anymore either. Poetic thinking really is not limited to the spheres of the *literati*, and that includes literary critics.

I want to close these brief readings of some of Grünbein's texts with two final suggestions. First, it seems clear that Grünbein's essays are deeply concerned with the relationship between poetry and philosophy in a variety of ways, and that this is a fertile area of study. The description of the rift between poetry and philosophy places Grünbein in a particular place within a wider picture of literary history and poetic theory. His account reveals a certain nostalgia, but also a willingness to radically re-think the fundamental assumptions of poetic production. It is from the latter that the second and more significant suggestion arises: Grünbein uses his essays, and his discussion of philosophy and poetry, to advance a radical way of re-conceptualizing thought itself. Via the category of 'poetical thinking', a way of thinking that pushes the imagination and disrupts orthodox classification, he invites us to reconsider what we think makes for thought, and why poetry must be linked to it. If we take Grünbein's proposals seriously, we accept that poetry is not only conceptual, but that poetical thinking – more than poetry or philosophy – will be the most productive way to extend our imaginative horizons.

62 There is a body of scholarship that deals with similar approaches, although their immediate subject matter is quite separate. See, for instance, Cary Wolfe, *What is Posthumanism?* (Minneapolis: University of Minnesota Press, 2010); Timothy Morton, *The Ecological Thought* (Cambridge, MA: Harvard University Press, 2010).

Noël Reumkens

Concept(ion) versus Ekphrasis. Durs Grünbein's Approach to the Pictorial Arts

Durs Grünbein may well be considered one of Germany's most eminent contemporary poets, but we should not forget that he began his career in performance art. No publication on his work would be complete without a discussion of his preoccupation with the pictorial arts, not least because he has worked with important visual artists on several occasions. Via Lewandowsky, for instance, picked up lines by Grünbein in his 1998 project *Traumführer Berlin* [*Dream Guide Berlin*] as well as in *Ei der Demokratie* [*Egg of Democracy*], a sculpture on the Augustusplatz in Leipzig commemorating the demonstrations that were held every Monday in the run-up to the fall of the Iron Curtain.[1] And Markus Lüpertz's book *Daphne. Metamorphosen einer Figur* [*Daphne. Metamorphosis of a Figure*] contains three poems written by Grünbein on Lüpertz's own work.[2] Moreover, Grünbein himself has repeatedly referred to the fundamental similarities between literature and the pictorial arts, most explicitly in his extensive conversation with Heinz Norbert Jocks.[3]

This aspect of Grünbein's endeavour has yet to be researched extensively, although it has sometimes been treated in other contexts. In *Das Gedicht und das Nichts*, Florian Berg, for example, devotes part of a chapter to the poem 'Inframince' that draws upon Marcel Duchamp's concept of the *infra-mince*.[4] Sonja Klein's *'Denn alles, alles ist verlorne Zeit'. Fragment und Erinnerung im Werk von Durs Grünbein* also dedicates a chapter to the role of images in the process of memory.[5] Nonetheless, much still remains to be explored and most of the texts discussed in the present chapter have not yet been examined by scholarship from this perspective.

I cordially thank Levin Chin and the editors for their revisions of this chapter.

1 Via Lewandowsky, 'Via Lewandowsky', online catalogue, 7 Dec 2011 (http://www.vialewandowsky.de).

2 Markus Lüpertz and Durs Grünbein, *Daphne – Metamorphose einer Figur* (Cologne: Wienand, 2006).

3 Heinz-Norbert Jochs and Durs Grünbein, *Durs Grünbein im Gespräch mit Heinz-Norbert Jocks* (Cologne: DuMont, 2001).

4 Florian Berg, *Das Gedicht und das Nichts. Über Anthropologie und Geschichte im Werk Durs Grünbeins* (Würzburg: Königshausen & Neumann, 2007), pp. 134–36.

5 Sonja Klein, *'Denn alles, alles ist verlorne Zeit'. Fragment und Erinnerung im Werk von Durs Grünbein* (Bielefeld: Aisthesis, 2008), pp. 71–82.

Like Dresden, the city of his youth, Grünbein's poetry is characterized by 'fragmentariness'. As he explains himself:

> wir werden immer nur inmitten von Bruchstücken leben, zwischen den Resten abgebrochener Projekte. Der Horizont ist verstellt von lauter *abandoned works.*
>
> [we will always live amid fragments, among the remnants of aborted projects. The horizon is completely obstructed by *abandoned works.*][6]

For Grünbein, pictorial works of art, like everything else in the world around him, can be looked upon as fragmentary, 'abandoned works' in a state of decay. Although these are integrated into his own work and new life is breathed into them, Grünbein does not merely describe them, along the lines of a conventional appropriation of pictorial works of art for literature, but explores different ways of approaching them intermedially.

One of the most traditional ways of crossing intermedial thresholds is undoubtedly *ekphrasis*, i.e. the verbal or literary representation of a visual work of art.[7] In traditional ekphrastic poetry, the subject matter of the poetic description is a clearly defined, concrete work of art – for example a painting, a sculpture or an etching. Over the last century, a strong interest in the conceptual has brought about a profound change in the way audiences receive the pictorial arts. In twentieth-century art, cognitive images have become central, and these require a very different approach on the part of intermedial literature. When art ceases to be pictorial and becomes conceptual, the question is how or if it can be represented ekphrastically at all.

Conceptual art is, evidently, about the framing verbal propositions that used to be secondary to the actual, tangible work of art.[8] In conceptual art, the work of art itself becomes obsolete, disappears and is replaced by ideas: in other words, by texts. The increased interest in conceptuality in the twentieth century can be subsumed under what American art critic Craig Owens designated as the movement away from the material work of art to its theoretical and conceptual frame.[9] Intermedial literature referring to the pictorial arts today often draws on this con-

6 *Durs Grünbein im Gespräch mit Heinz-Norbert Jocks*, p. 19.
7 James Heffernan, *Museum of Words. The Poetics of Ekphrasis from Homer to Ashbery* (Chicago: University of Chicago Press, 1993), p. 26.
8 Sabeth Buchmann, 'Conceptual Art', in *Dumonts Begriffslexikon zur zeitgenössischen Kunst*, ed. by Hubertus Butin (Cologne: DuMont, 2006), pp. 49–53 (p. 49).
9 Craig Owens, 'From Work to Frame, or, is there Life after "The Death of the Author"?', in Craig Owens, *Beyond Recognition. Representation, Power, and Culture*, ed. by Scott Bryson and others (Berkeley: University of California Press, 1992), pp. 122–39 (p. 122).

ceptual frame rather than on tangible, concrete works of art, as is the case in traditional ekphrasis. As we shall see, many of Grünbein's poems bear evidence of this movement from work to frame.

In his extended 2001 interview with Heinz-Norbert Jocks, Grünbein explicitly denounces the notion of a purely ekphrastic approach when it comes to his own reception of works of art:

> Es gibt in der Literatur das Genre der Bildbeschreibung, den Versuch mit Worten malerische Effekte zu erzielen, im Grunde also eine Transposition. Das Ganze ist aber völlig unklar, denn am Ende ergeben sich immer nur Gedankenbilder anstelle der visuellen Reize, wie sie das Bild auslöst.
>
> [In literature there is the genre of picture description, the attempt to produce painterly effects by using words, which is, in essence, nothing but transposition. The whole thing, however, is totally unclear, because in the end this only ever brings about mental images instead of the visual stimuli the picture generates.][10]

For Grünbein, essentially, ekphrasis is impossible because ultimately poems cannot evoke visual effects, but instead produce mental images or concepts. Grünbein's intermedially orientated poetry is very much indebted to developments in twentieth-century artistic production and thinking. As we shall see, it never follows the visual programme prescribed by a particular pictorial work of art, but instead reflects upon the work's paramedial frame, which consists of every instance of framing, regardless of what media are used and whether these are auto- or allographic, i.e. produced by the artist him- or herself or by others. The paramedial frame is the porous but marked transitional zone between a work, or oeuvre, and the (social) world surrounding it. The term 'paramedial' bears analogies not only to Gérard Genette's 'paratext', but also to Jacques Derrida's 'parergon' and to Urs Meyer's notion of the 'paramedium'.[11] It is employed here to indicate any element outside the work (loosely following Genette) that might be medially distinct from the work itself, yet 'belongs' to it as a 'parergon' by virtue of a relation of relative contiguity. A title, for instance, can be viewed as a paramedial (micro-)text belonging to a non-textual work of art; and the same is true for conceptual and theoretical frameworks produced in texts and / or spoken language by visual artists.

---

10 *Durs Grünbein im Gespräch mit Heinz-Norbert Jocks*, p. 35.

11 Jacques Derrida, 'Parergon', in *Die Wahrheit in der Malerei* (Vienna: Passagen, 1992) pp. 31–144; Gérard Genette, *Paratexte. Das Buch vom Beiwerk des Buches* (Frankfurt a. M.: Suhrkamp, 2001); Urs Meyer, 'Transmedialität (Intermedialität, Paramedialität, Metamedialität, Hypermedialität, Archimedialität). Das Beispiel der Werbung', in *Transmedialität. Zur Ästhetik paraliterarischer Verfahren*, ed. by Urs Meyer and others (Göttingen: Wallstein, 2006), pp. 110–30.

This chapter will explore Grünbein's approach to the visual arts by discussing several poems in depth. The first two, 'Grauer Sebastian' ['Grey Sebastian'] and '[Disiecta membra]', focus on artistic practice, i.e. the process of conceiving and conceptualizing the work of art in question. 'Wärmeplastik nach Beuys' ['Warmth Sculpture After Beuys'] and the three poems from the cycle 'Posthume Innenstimmen' ['Posthumous Inner Voices'], by contrast, draw upon two conceptual frameworks produced by artists working in the field of the pictorial arts.

'Grauer Sebastian'

Instances of traditional ekphrasis are the exception in Grünbein's oeuvre. However, the first poem I wish to discuss here – 'Grauer Sebastian', published in *Nach den Satiren* (1999) – contains a meticulous ekphrastic description of a painting of Saint Sebastian by Andrea Mantegna (ill. 1), displayed at the Ca' d'Oro in Venice:

Grauer Sebastian

Fünfzehn Pfeile trägt er im Leib bei Mantegna,
Zwei in den Lenden, zwei um den Nabel, einen im Bauch,
Sieben im Schienbein und Schenkel und Knie.
'Nichts außer Gott ist von Dauer: der Rest ist Rauch.'
Sagt ein Spruchband rechts unten, geschlungen
Um eine Kerze, die eben verlischt. Fünfzehn Pfeile, –
Zwischen den Rippen steckt einer, über der Brust, unterm Hals,
Keiner im Herzen. Doch welcher war tödlich?
Nichts verrät der geöffnete Mund, die Zunge, schon trocken,
Entfärbt die Gesichtshaut, der Blick des Gefolterten, – Gott,
Warum so viele Schmerzen auf einmal?
Seine Peiniger haben sich schlafen gelegt. Er allein
steigt aus den Himmeln, die bald schon herrenlos sind.

So hat ihn der Meister gesehn, selbst friedlos im Alter,
Wie nach durchwachter Nacht. So gehört er den Schatten,
Frierend auf schwarzem Grund und im kalten Licht.
Den Körper zum Vorwurf gekrümmt, im Rücken
Gefesselt die Hände, Märtyrer –
Betet er etwa nicht?

Venedig
Ca' d'Oro

[Grey Sebastian // In Mantegna's depiction, he has fifteen arrows in his body, / Two in his loins, two around the navel, one in his abdomen, / Seven in his shin and thigh and knee. / 'Nothing is eternal, except God: the rest is smoke', / It says on a ribbon on the bottom right, looped / Around a candle that is just going out. Fifteen arrows, – / Between the ribs there is one, above the chest, below the neck, / None in the heart. But which one was lethal? / The open mouth discloses nothing, the tongue, already dry, / The skin on his face colourless, the look of the tortured one, – God, / Why so much pain at once? / His torturers have lain down to sleep. He alone / is descending from the heavens that soon will be lordless. // This is how the master saw him, himself restless with age. / Like after a night of vigil. Thus he belongs to the shadows, / Freezing on a black floor in cold light. / His body writhing in reproach, on his back / His hands are tied, martyr – / Does he not pray? // Venice / Ca' d'Oro][12]

ill. 1: Andrea Mantegna: *Saint Sebastian,* 1490, Ca' d'Oro, Venice, Italy

12 Durs Grünbein, *Nach den Satiren* (Frankfurt a. M.: Suhrkamp, 1999), p. 196.

The first part of the poem, before the strophe break, provides a detailed account of the exact position of the arrows protruding from the martyr Sebastian's body, and is only interrupted by the quotation of the text written on the ribbon that is twisted around a candle in the bottom right corner: 'Nihil nisi divinum stabile est. Caetera fumus' [Nothing is stable if not divine. The rest is smoke]. This text introduces a shift from the actual, hagiographic subject of the painting to its transmedial theme of *vanitas*.

The act of pinpointing the exact position of the arrows is, in itself, an explicitly ekphrastic one: the poem thus seems to show the restrictions imposed on it by its subject, the painting. Rather than freeing itself from the limitations of Mantegna's naturalistic painting, it subjects itself to it by providing an exact iconic inventory of what is on display in the painting.

However, the descriptive inventory provided is contrasted with verbalized questions. The first of these concerns the actual moment of death, as the lyrical 'I' asks which of the visible arrows was the lethal one ('Doch welcher war tödlich?'). It is a rhetorical question, as it is immediately followed by the assertion that the martyr's open mouth can no longer give an answer ('Nichts verrät der geöffnete Mund'). Because the saint is no longer able to reply, the next question is addressed to God: 'Warum so viele Schmerzen auf einmal?' But, once again, there is no answer. The final question 'Betet er etwa nicht?' – asked after the strophe break in the last line of the poem – refers to the saint's hands, which are tied behind his back ('im Rücken / Gefesselt die Hände') and therefore not visible in the painting.

After the break, the atmosphere is completely different from that of the first part of the poem. The lyrical subject's gaze seems to have been diverted from the illusionary, mimetic painting to what is or *was*, in fact, *behind* the painting, i.e. to the creative process, the work in the studio. The first line of the second strophe makes a decisive break from the hagiographic account of Saint Sebastian's life and death – the conventional iconographic register in which to interpret Mantegna's painting – by introducing the notion of the master, in this case the master painter Andrea Mantegna himself. The shift from God to the (human) master is indicative of the shift in interpretation of all religious art in general. After the *grand récit* of Christianity has been discarded as being just that – a story – sacred works of Christian art are no longer primarily judged for *what* they depict, but rather for *how* they depict it, i.e. for their artistic value.

In the second part of the poem, the featured scene is stripped of its mythical, Christian dimension and focuses on the depiction of the model in Mantegna's studio: 'So hat ihn der Meister gesehen'. The model is freezing on a black floor, or against a black background, which alludes to a nocturnal setting in cool light. He is squirming, though not as a result of the pain inflicted by the arrows protruding from his body, but rather as a reproach to the painter after a whole night of posing. In the end, the Saint's martyrdom is reintroduced into the poem, but – as we have seen – God has now descended from heaven and become an artist. The martyr is not a martyr for Christianity but a martyr for the sake of art.

What becomes obvious in this poem is Grünbein's interest in what lies beyond the fringes of the physical, tangible work of art, which in itself is nothing more than a residue, the fragmentary remainder of a process, or an 'abandoned work', as he describes it. A work of art is never finished, but is instead infinite in its explorative possibilities. The questions asked in the poem illustrate these possibilities and, in this manner, show the reader that there is more to comprehending a painting than just 'collecting' its apparent content. This content is, in fact, merely a fragment waiting to be completed (though only seemingly) by a recipient-cum-producer. The unanswered questions expose the gaps in which the work of art is actually completed and thus co-produced by its recipients. This chimes with the notion of *Leerstellen* [gaps] as introduced by Wolfgang Iser in Reception Theory, which itself was based on Roman Ingarden's concept of *Unbestimmtheitsstellen* [spots of indeterminacy]. Every work of art entails gaps that need to be filled by its recipients in order for an interpretation to take place. It is for this reason that 'Grauer Sebastian' ends with a question mark, signalling the painting's – and the poem's – openness. This openness allows the work of art to be connected not only to the world of the recipients, but also to other works of art, as illustrated in another poem, '[Disiecta membra]'.

'[Disiecta membra]'

As already indicated in the introduction to this chapter, fragmentariness fulfils a fundamental role in the constellation of Grünbein's lyric oeuvre. It is akin to another central concept in Grünbein's poetic universe, that of 'Zwischenräume' [interspaces]. According to Grünbein, the search for such interspaces can be viewed as the common denominator between literature and the visual arts. In Grünbein's poetry, the exploration of such interspaces is activated by the inclusion of particular elements: fragments, derived from an original entity that comprised fragments or was never more than a fragment itself.[13] By inserting these el-

13 As Michael Braun postulates in the context of Grünbein's fragmentariness: 'No "loss of the centre" (Sedlmayr) is thus to be lamented. The fragmentary is a profit, for – as a consumable and communicable product of art – it too has become capable of a self-referential staging'. Michael Braun, '"Vom Rand her verlöschen die Bilder". Zu Durs Grünbeins Lyrik und Poetik des Fragments', in *Text + Kritik*, 153.1 (2002), pp. 4–18 (p. 16).

ements, the poem opens up interspaces that need to be crossed and explored in what Grünbein describes as 'Wanderungen durchs kollektive Gedächtnis' [strolls through collective memory].[14]

In 2003, the Aargauer Kunsthaus in Switzerland published the anthology *Muscheln und Blumen* [*Mussels and Flowers*]. The anthology's title was loosely based on that of Jean Arp's and Sophie Taeuber-Arp's multimedia collaboration *Muscheln und Schirme* [*Mussels and Umbrellas*], in which the former's poems are combined with the latter's drawings. For the anthology, authors were asked to write a text based on one or more of the works of art in the museum's collection. Grünbein was one of many poets to contribute, choosing Kurt Seligmann's *La deuxième main de Nosferatu* [*The Superfluous Hand*] of 1938 (ill. 2) as the point of departure for a poem that exemplifies a wandering through collective memory.

> [Disiecta membra]
>
> Und schwindeln macht der Anblick all der Hände
> Auf Instrumenten, Theken, Klinken, Manualen.
> Grazile, derbe, krumme dort am Lenkrad, an Geländern.
> Sie leisten Schwerarbeit, die Arbeit am Normalen:
>
> Und erst die Einsicht dann ins Wirbeln vieler Glieder:
> Das bin ja ich in all den Andern, dieses Und-und-und ...
> Mit jeder Schwiele, jedem Finger kehrt der Ekel wieder.
> Und bitterer Speichel sammelt sich im Mund.
>
> Aus dem Schlamassel Ordnung, nichts hält dich heraus.
> Sie alle tun nur, was sie können – handeln, richten.
> Die Füße, wie von selber fliehn sie Bett und Haus.
> Am Körper zerren Kräfte, unsichtbar-uralt, Gewichte.
>
> [And dizzying the sight of all these hands / On instruments, counters, handles, manuals. / Delicate, rough, crooked on steering wheels, on banisters / They perform heavy work, work on normal things // And only then the insight into the whirl of many limbs / For that is me in all the others, this and-and-and ... / With every welt, every finger the disgust returns / And bitter saliva gathers in the mouth. // From the mess of order, nothing keeps you out. / They're all only doing what they can – act, build. / Feet, as if automatically, flee from bed and home. / Forces pull the body down, invisible-ancient, weights.][15]

---

14 Durs Grünbein, 'Mein babylonisches Hirn', in *Gedicht und Geheimnis. Aufsätze 1990–2006* (Frankfurt a. M.: Suhrkamp, 2006), pp. 19–33 (p. 31).

15 *Muscheln und Blumen. Literarische Texte zu Werken der Kunst*, ed. by Beat Wismer, Stephan Kunz and Sibylle Omlin (Zurich: Ammann, 2003), p. 143.

ill. 2: Kurt Seligmann: *The deuxième main de Nosferatu* [The Second Hand of Nosferatu], 1938, Aargauer Kunsthaus, Aarau, Switzerland

Paramedially – i.e. in its title – Seligmann's painting refers to the film *Nosferatu* which, in turn, is a cinematic treatment of Bram Stoker's *Dracula*. Thus Grünbein inscribes his poem in what can be regarded as an intermedial chain of citation, in which temporally and physically distinct *membra* are connected. The 'second hand of Nosferatu', which one could believe to be visible in the lower left corner of Seligmann's painting, is literally a *disiectum membrum*. It is, as it were, cut out of (the film) *Nosferatu* and placed in the composition of the painting.

Grünbein's choice of this specific painting from the vast collection of the Aargauer Kunsthaus is paradigmatic, for it illustrates what he considers to be the essence of his own poetry and of art in general: the bridging of interspaces through the poetic combination of otherwise separate entities, 'von Ereignisinsel zu Ereignisinsel' [from one incident isle to another]. It is in this light that the poem's second strophe must be interpreted. There, the lyric subject recognizes itself in *others* ('Das bin ja ich in all den Andern'), which can be interpreted as an allusion to the intertextual and intermedial affiliation between works of art. Moreover, there is mention of 'dieses Und-und-und' [this and-and-and] that refers to the artistic act of combining otherwise distinct, insular elements. In art, such elements are connected and the otherwise hidden linkages between them are laid bare.

Even though the first strophe could be interpreted as a listing of elements visible in Seligmann's painting, Grünbein's poem can hardly be considered a description of it. Although this poem contains fewer ekphrastic elements than 'Grauer Sebastian', there is a certain similarity between the two that goes beyond the fact they both spin off from a 'traditional' work of art. Both poems are not ekphrases in the traditional sense, but rather describe the creative and artistic forces at work *behind* them. Both take an existing work of art as a point of departure for poetic reflections on the process of conceiving a work of art in general. Central to both is the metonymic, syntagmatic shift from the tangible work to its paramedial frame, to the conditions under which the works – standing in for works of art in general – were conceived.

In the next poem I shall discuss, 'Wärmeplastik nach Beuys', Grünbein's interest in the work of art as an open work (Umberto Eco) becomes apparent in a similar, but reversed way. In this case, the poem proceeds not from a tangible, physical work of art, but rather from the conceptual framework created by a visual artist.

'Wärmeplastik nach Beuys'

The poem 'Wärmeplastik nach Beuys' was first published in *Grauzone morgens*.[16] Before German reunification, Grünbein had only been able to appreciate Beuys's influence on contemporary art through articles and reproductions.[17] The poem he wrote on the latter's oeuvre exemplifies the extent to which the Düsseldorf artist and self-proclaimed shaman influenced other young artists and writers, as even Grünbein, who was – according to his own words – leading a more or less secluded life in the GDR, far away from the Fluxus-art-driven North-Rhine-Westphalian cities, was inspired to write about the West German's work.

Wärmeplastik nach Beuys

Erst als der geile Fliegenschwarm
aufstob in äußerster Panik
um seine Beute tanzte wie

eine Wolke von Elektronen mit
hohem Spin, sah man die beiden
Jungvögel nackt.

16 See Noël Reumkens, 'From Work to Frame in Intermedial References. Joseph Beuys in Three Contemporary German Poems', *Trans – Revue de littérature générale et comparée*, 8 (July 2009), 1–14 (http://trans.univ-paris3.fr/spip.php?article365).

17 *Durs Grünbein im Gespräch mit Heinz-Norbert Jocks*, p. 41.

Es war Zwölf Uhr mittags und dieser
böse Zufall nichts
als eine Gleichgewichtsformel

für zwei gedunsene Madennester
wie Spiegeleier
leicht angebraten im Straßentiegel
aus Teer und Asphalt.

[Only after the horny swarm of flies / ascended in utmost panic / danced around its prey like // an electron cloud with / high spin, could one see those two / naked fledglings. // It was noon and this evil / coincidence nothing / but an equilibrium formula // for two bloated maggot nests / like fried eggs / slightly roasted in a street pot / of tar and asphalt.][18]

In keeping with the subtitle of the third part of the collection *Grauzone Morgens* in which it appears – 'Glimpses and Glances' –, this poem can be summarized as a 'glimpse' of two birds' corpses being digested by a swarm of flies spinning around them like an electron cloud ('wie eine Wolke von Elektronen mit hohem Spin'). The small corpses are lying on the street in what is described as a 'Straßentiegel', a crucible or pot made out of tar and asphalt. The only explicit reference to Joseph Beuys is to be found in the poem's title.

In this poem, a relatively trivial scene is elevated to the status of a work of art, in a sort of 'natural performance'. The poem uses Beuys's name and the term 'Wärmeplastik' in order to isolate the scene from its surrounding reality and present it as a work of art. In doing so, Grünbein copies the strategic use of the artist's signature, as introduced by Marcel Duchamp in his ready-mades. (Duchamp would use his signature to grant a found object – i.e. a ready-made – the status of a work of art.) The natural (semi-)still-life is 'pre-fabricated' by nature. It is the superscription with Beuys's name and the term belonging so clearly to the conceptual framework of his artistic work that 'installs' the ready-made natural scene as a work of art.

The 'Wärmeplastik' mentioned in the title of the poem is not an actual, existing work of art but, on the contrary, a highly elusive term used to describe the totality of phenomena or energies that can be subsumed under the heading of Beuys's 'extended art concept'.[19] It contains the element 'Wärme', considered the energy source behind everything, which holds a central position in Beuys's the-

18 Durs Grünbein, *Gedichte. Bücher I–III (Grauzone morgens, Schädelbasislektion, Falten und Fallen)* (Frankfurt a. M.: Suhrkamp 2006), p. 56.

19 On the extended art concept, see, for instance, Barbara Lange, 'Soziale Plastik', in *Dumonts Begriffslexikon zur zeitgenössischen Kunst*, p. 276.

oretical framework. 'Warmth' should, in the context of Beuys's work, not only be interpreted in the physical sense, but also in the sense of human warmth, e.g. of love. The other element, 'Plastik', in the Beuysian sense of the word, refers both to the 'plastic' art of sculpture, as well as to the totality of energetic potential that is present in the world and in human society. Beuys believed in an evolutionary 'warmth' warehoused in everything around us, an idea he expressed in his work through the application of thermoplastic materials, i.e. materials that change their physical consistency under the influence of temperature changes (such as the tar and asphalt that are mentioned in this poem). This evolutionary warmth is present in the whole 'Wärmeplastik', which is, in fact, a ready-made 'Gesamtkunstwerk', an enormous, all-encompassing performance. The dead birds devoured by a swarm of flies, as described in the poem, are a symbol of this evolutionary warmth, a detail taken from the whole of the 'Plastik'.

The ready-made natural scene depicted in Grünbein's poem is therefore denoted by Joseph Beuys's theoretical framework, the 'extended art concept', into which it is inscribed by the use of the term 'Wärmeplastik' and the name Beuys. A very similar, though more complicated, technique is employed in the poetic cycle 'Posthume Innenstimmen' which is undoubtedly one of the most prominent references to an artistic conceptual framework in the whole of Grünbein's oeuvre.

'Posthume Innenstimmen'

The title of this cycle signals what is at the semantic core of the five poems, namely voices – or, to use another word – language. Four of the five are constructed from *disiecta membra* taken from the extensive plurimedial oeuvre of the French artist and *bête noire* of Dada, Marcel Duchamp. Typical of the work of Duchamp is the way its impact – like that of Beuys[20] – is largely based on the textual apparatus that accompanies the more conventionally designated 'works of art'. Duchamp was one of the first proponents of Western art to integrate texts – verbal reflections on his art – into his oeuvre. It is hardly surprising, therefore, that Grünbein chose to focus in 'Posthume Innenstimmen' on the conceptual, textual apparatus that surrounds the 'works' paramedially.

The poems, published in Grünbein's first book after the *Wende*, are significantly more complex than 'Wärmeplastik nach Beuys'. 'Posthume Innenstimmen'

---

20 See Thierry De Duve, '"Man can never expect to start from scratch; he must start from Ready-made things like even his own mother and father". Marcel Duchamp im Interview with Katherine Kuhs', in *The Artist's Voice. Talks with Seventeen Artists* (New York: Harper and Row, 1962), p. 90.

illustrates a free, associative processing of impulses originating from Duchamp's extensive artistic oeuvre, combined with other elements: the remnants of inner voices and quotations used in a way similar to that of Duchamp's *objets trouvés*. It would be impossible to discuss all five of these highly sophisticated poems in detail within the confines of this chapter, so I will focus on passages in three of them that unambiguously engage in dialogue with Duchamp's work: 'Inframince', 'Après l'amour' and 'French Kiss'.[21]

The first of three poems from the cycle 'Posthume Innenstimmen' that I will discuss here, 'Inframince', is one of the most interesting, as it refers specifically to a part of Marcel Duchamp's conceptual framework, albeit to one that is less 'notorious' than his ready-mades:

Inframince

Unverwandt streunend, der Traum eine Lichtung im Ich
Nimmst du die Sprache der Dinge mit unter die Haut.
Jeder in seiner Welt ... unerkannt ... soviele Welten.
Was sich hier zeigt bleibt versteckt, was sich erinnert
Vergeht an der Drehung des Strickes an dem du hängst.
'Hab mich verirrt.'/
            'Name?'/
                  'Auf Wiedersehn.'/
                        'Komm zurück.'
Die Sache wird inhaltsleer wenn du denkst, kein Vergleich
Mit diesem Hirn, schwimmend im Liquor, ein grauer Schwamm.
Sprache zerfällt, unverdaut, die verwest wie Pupillen,
Ur-Zeit verramscht wie die Meeresschildkröten auf Bali.
Archimedes' Punkt, unter uns gesagt, ist kein Ort.
Das Übel liegt an der Wurzel der Sätze, am Grund
Der Idiome und Stile, die man irgendwann sattkriegt.
Über der Zeit das Vergessen spricht fließend Latein.

[Unrelated, wandering, the dream is a clearing in the Self / You take the language of things under your skin. / Everyone in his own world ... unrecognized ... that many worlds. / What shows itself here remains hidden, what recalls itself / Passes in the twist in the rope by which you are hanging. / 'I've got lost'/ / 'Name?'/ / 'Goodbye'/ / 'Come back.' / The thing becomes meaningless when you think, nothing compared / To this brain, floating in liquor, a grey sponge. / Language disintegrates, undigested, it decomposes like pupils, / Prehis-

21 Of the other two poems in 'Posthume Innenstimmen', 'Dieu trompe-l'œuil', contains explicit references to the philosopher René Descartes (whose life and work is of great importance to Grünbein). Although clearly linked to the other poems semantically, the last poem in the cycle, 'Fisch im Medium' ['Fish in Medium'], is devoid of any overt references to either Duchamp or Descartes.

> tory remaindered like the sea turtles of Bali. / The Archimedean point, entre nous, is not a place. / The problem lies at the root of sentences, at the base / Of idioms and styles that one eventually gets tired of. / Over time forgetting speaks fluent Latin.[22]

Due to its enigmatic character, the concept of *infra-mince* (written as two words by Duchamp himself) never became part of the art-historical discourse on the Dada artist, let alone of twentieth-century art history in general. The term is composed of the French adjective *mince*, meaning lean or thin, and the Latin prefix *infra-*, meaning 'below'. In analogy to the familiar term 'infrared', one could infer that *infra-mince* denotes something that is 'below thin', so thin that it can barely be perceived. Duchamp coined the neologism in his notes but never actually defined it, claiming the concept could only be illustrated, not defined. Duchamp's own illustrations of *infra-mince*, moreover, are superbly vague:

> 1. Le possible est un infra mince.
>
> [The possible is an infra-mince.]
>
> [...] Le possible impliquant le devenir – le passage de l'un à l'autre a lieu dans l'infra mince.
>
> [The possible, which implies becoming – the passage from one entity into the other – takes place in the infra-mince.]
>
> 9v. Pantalons de velours – leur sifflottement (dans la marche) par frottement des 2 jambes est une séparation infra mince signalée par le son (ce n'est pas? un son infra mince)
>
> [Velvet trousers – the sound (whilst walking) as a result of the chafing of the legs is an infra-mince separation, which is indicated by the sound (isn't it, an infra-mince sound).]
>
> 11v. Quand la fumée de tabac sent aussi de la bouche qui l'exhale, les 2 odeurs s'épousent par infra mince (infra mince olfactif).
>
> [When tobacco smoke also smells of the mouth that exhales it, the two odours are wed by infra-mince (olfactory infra-mince).]
>
> 15. Peinture sur verre vue du côté non peint donne un infra mince.[23]
>
> [A painting on glass, viewed from the unpainted side, creates infra-mince.]

---

22 Durs Grünbein, *Gedichte. Bücher I–III*, p. 106.

23 Marcel Duchamp, *Notes* (Paris: Flammarion, 1999), pp. 21–22.

These definitions – if one can even see them as such – merely add to the enigma. Nonetheless, there are some semantic properties that appear in more than one of Duchamp's illustrations of the term. For instance, most explanations explicitly refer to some sort of duality (the passage from one entity into the other, the chafing of two legs, the smell of smoke and breath combined). Another typical feature of *infra-mince* can be found in its subtleness, illustrated inter alia by the minimal sound that velvet trousers make whilst walking or the olfactory nuance caused by the smell of breath mingling with exhaled tobacco smoke. The combination of this duality and subtleness in part produces a third characteristic feature, that is, moreover, common to each of Duchamp's illustrations: in-betweenness.[24] *Infra-mince* is present in a duality between two entities (in Duchamp's illustrations: between one thing and another, between legs, between smells, between the painted and unpainted side of glass), but indiscernibly, or at least unnoticed in everyday life or experience of it.

In light of the spectrum of meanings carried by *infra-mince* – a conspicuous aspect of Grünbein's poem is that it seems to have no direct relation to the Duchampian concept. This, in Grünbein's own words, has been grafted onto it by means of its title:

> In dem fünfteiligen Zyklus 'Posthume Innenstimmen', der als solcher schon eine Erklärung in Sachen Poetik enthält (er spielt auf einen Seelenfundus an, in dem die eigenen Ahnen noch immer lebendig sind), ist den Gedichten der Titel regelrecht aufgesetzt. Bis auf eines zitieren sie alle Marcel Duchamp. Sie gehen zurück auf ein Paar überraschend anmutige Radierungen und erotische Wortspielereien aus dem Spätwerk dieses Meisters der avantgardistischen Sinnverweigerung und -neustiftung. Es handelt sich um eine Art der Übertragung, in diesem Fall von einer Kunstform auf die andere, von der Zeichnung auf das Gedicht, mit allen Fehlerteufeln, die ein solches Verfahren herbeiruft.
>
> [In the five-part cycle 'Posthumous Inner Voices' – itself already a poetological commentary of sorts (alluding as it does to a psychic reservoir in which one's ancestors are still alive) – the title has literally been grafted onto the poems. Except for one, they all quote Marcel Duchamp. They all hark back to a handful of surprisingly graceful etchings and instances of erotic wordplay in the late works of this avant-garde master of the subversion and innovation of meaning. It is a kind of transposition, in this case from one art form to another, from drawing to poetry, with all the pitfalls that such a procedure entails.][25]

---

24 Florian Berg refers to another illustration Duchamp gives of his *infra-mince*, namely that of the hollow space in the paper, between the front and back of a thin sheet. Thus, *infra-mince* is about the attempt to leave the two-dimensional surface of the sheet and to extend into a third dimension. Applied to language this would imply a transformation from the letter, the word, to actual things. Florian Berg, *Das Gedicht und das Nichts*, pp. 135–36.

25 Durs Grünbein, *Gedichte. Bücher I–III*, pp. 387–88.

As in 'Wärmeplastik nach Beuys', Grünbein copies Marcel Duchamp's use of the artist's signature introduced in his ready-mades. The quoting of puns and concepts derived from Duchamp's late work in their titles 'installs' Grünbein's elusive poems as works of art that are in-between his own and the French master's oeuvre. An interpretation of the poem 'Inframince' can therefore proceed from the eponymous term's semantic property of in-betweenness, as described above, and isolating a number of significant passages that – influenced by the quotations – bear traces of this property.

The first four lines of the poem are semantically interwoven with the cycle's title. Grünbein himself considers the poetic text as a 'Protokoll innerer Blicke' – a 'record of inner views or glances'. The first four lines of this text introduce the notion of isolation, especially in line three, which – with a reference to Ludwig Wittgenstein's dictum 'the limits of my language are the limits of my world' – points to the solitariness of every human being: 'Jeder in seiner Welt [...] unerkannt [...] soviele Welten'. Everyone is confined to his or her own world, distanced from the others.

Poetry, however, is a place where inner voices, wandering around in a (seemingly) unrelated way, can pause and even tarry, as Grünbein puts it:

> Gedichte sind Pausen im Sterben, zumindest auf dem Papier. Über den Satzspiegel hinaus verschieben sie das Einzelleben ihres Verfassers ins Grenzenlose. Sie versetzen ihn in eine Art Gegen-Zeit, in der jeder zum Zeitgenossen wird, wenn er nur teilnimmt an dieser aufwendigen Praxis, ob als Liebhaber, Leser oder als schreibender Gesprächspartner selbst.
>
> [Poems are pauses in dying, at least on paper. Transcending the layout on the page, they displace their author's individual life beyond bounds. They transport you into a kind of antitime, in which you become everybody's contemporary no sooner than you engage in this unconventional practice – be that as aficionardo, a reader or poetic interlocutor.][26]

Poetry allows the voices of those long since dead to become present, creating a conceptual conversation, a dialogue between the writer and his predecessors, who thus become contemporaries. In 'Inframince' this is indicated by the freely aligned dialogue featured in lines six to ten. Interestingly though, this dialogue seems to fail. After the first voice states that it has lost its way, the second – ignoring what the first has said – asks for its name. However, there is no expectation of an answer, but rather a farewell, which is then reciprocated with the wish to re-

26 Durs Grünbein, 'Betonte Zeit', in *Gedicht und Geheimnis* (Frankfurt a. M.: Suhrkamp, 2007), pp. 95–112 (p. 106); 'Accented Time', in *The Bars of Atlantis*, ed. Michael Eskin, trans. by John Crutchfield, Michael Hofmann and Andrew Shields (New York: Farrar, Straus and Giroux, 2010), pp. 116–31 (p. 126).

turn. The collapse of dialogue is used here as an illustration of the isolation that comes with our everyday use of language, which can only be overcome within the constructed, authored world of the poem.

In 'Z wie Zitat' ['Q for Quotation'] Grünbein postulates: 'Nirgendwo zeigt sich der Zwischenraum, der Ort, an dem die Identitäten im Zwiegespräch zirkulieren, so klar wie im Zitat' [Nowhere is the interspace, the place where the identities circulate in dialogue, as clear as in quotation].[27] The 'Zwischenraum' or interspace between the writer and his predecessors becomes perceptible in quotations that exist in-between two inner voices. As in '[Disiecta membra]' this in-betweenness, the line between alterity and identity, is deconstructed. In '[Disiecta membra]' the lyrical subject recognizes itself in the others: 'Das bin ja ich in all den Andern'. In 'Inframince', a reversed situation of recognition is at work: the presence of others in oneself, in one's own language, is recognized, even if it is difficult to pin down. What the poem is trying to show is that quotations, or 'psychic reservoirs' as Grünbein calls them, are *infra-mince*: that they are, as it were, immersed in our language and impossible to grasp by simple naming. If, however, one does not recognize their presence or does not see the comparison between one's own consciousness and that of others, then language becomes empty – as is suggested in the poem itself: 'Die Sache wird inhaltsleer wenn du denkst, kein Vergleich / Mit diesem Hirn'. Grünbein uses Duchamp's notion of the *infra-mince* to criticize everyday language: 'Das Übel liegt an der Wurzel der Sätze, am Grund / Der Idiome und Stile, die man irgendwann sattkriegt'. Even when one has had enough of language, of idioms and styles, it is poetic language that makes visible – or rather audible – what remains hidden in everyday language. In poetry, the seemingly unrelated, or distinct, becomes related again in an *infra-mince* fashion. The poem 'Inframince' itself serves as a perfect example of this since it illustrates Duchamp's *infra-mince* without trying to 'capture' it and – considering the title as part of the frame of the poem rather than the poem itself – without even mentioning it or its creator. Duchamp's voice and ideas are thus illustrated in the poem in the same way he illustrated his own concepts. *Infra-mince* is not defined, nor is it discussed in the poem, rather it is exemplified by the poetic use of language, in the bridging of interstices.

Whereas 'Inframince' does not contain any references to Duchamp's actual physical works of art, two of the other poems in 'Posthume Innenstimmen' – 'Après l'amour' and 'French Kiss' – explicitly refer to two of the French artist's etchings, which form part of a themed series entitled *The*

27 Durs Grünbein, 'Z wie Zitat', in *Gedicht und Geheimnis*, pp. 77–80 (p. 80).

ill. 3: Marcel Duchamp: *Après l'amour* [After Loving], 1968, etching from Arturo Schwarz's *The Large Glass and Related Works,* Vol II

Lovers.[28] Besides the explicit reference to the homonymous etching (ill. 3), 'Après l'amour' contains several references to other equally erotic works by Duchamp, such as *Paysage Fautif* [*Wayward Landscape*] and his last great work *étant donnés* [*Given*]:

> Après l'amour
>
> Gleich nach dem Vögeln ist Liebe der bessere Stil.
> Die Tierhaut entspannt sich, das Herz fängt sich ein.
> Flacher Atem bläst Schweiß aus den Schlüsselbeinmulden.
> Auf der Zunge zergangen, löschen Spermien den Durst
> Auf den Nachwuchs. Die Achselhöhlen, den müden Bauch,
> Alles holt sich der Schlaf. Wie nach zuviel Theologie
> Kehren die Laken sich um. Altes Dunkel am Rand,
> Neue Ränder im Dunkel. Die Kniekehlen zwitschern
> Zweistimmig stimmlos ihr Post-Coital, ein Rondeau.

---

28 This series was added to Arturo Schwarz's book *Large Glass and Related Works* (1967) to illustrate Duchamp's *Large Glass. The Large Glass* [*Le Grand Verre*] is another title of *La Mariée Mise à Nu par ses Célibataires, même.* See Arturo Schwarz, *The Large Glass and Related Works* (Milan: Schwarz Gallery, 1967).

Eben noch naß, richten die Härchen wie Fühler sich auf.
Betäubt, *summa summarum* gestillt, hört dieser Schmerz
Des Lebendigseins bis zur Erschöpfung auf wehzutun.
Zurück in der Zeit, sind die Körper an keinem Ziel.
Gleich nach der Liebe ist Vögeln der bessere Stil.

[Right after fucking, love is the better style. / The animal skin relaxes, the heart gets a hold of itself. / Shallow breath blows sweat out of the clavicle hollows. / Dissolved on the tongue, sperm slakes the thirst / For offspring. The armpits, the tired abdomen, / Everything falls prey to sleep. Like after too much theology / The sheets reverse. Familiar darkness at the edges, / New edges in the darkness. The backs of knees chirp / In two-part harmony voiceless their post-coital, a round. / Still just wet, the little hairs raised like feelers. / Dazed, *summa summarum* satisfied, this pain / Of being alive stops hurting to the point of exhaustion. / Back in time, the bodies are at no destination. / Right after love fucking is the better style.][29]

In this poem, the subject matter of the etching – 'after love' or 'after sexual intercourse' – and of the series of etchings as a whole remains present. The opening lines mention love and 'vögeln', a colloquial expression for sexual intercourse, and line nine refers to 'Post-Coital', which is directly related to the poem's title. Moreover, the rest of the poem is characterized by a high degree of physicality, expressed in semantic entities such as 'animal skin', 'clavicle hollows', 'sperm', 'armpits', 'abdomen', 'backs of knees', 'little hairs', 'bodies'.

When comparing this poem with the etching to which it refers, it is immediately apparent that the text radically distances itself from its visual pre-text, thus avoiding an ekphrastically induced congruence. There are no actual 'Kniekehlen' visible in Duchamp's etching. The image shows only the upper bodies of a man and a woman embracing each other. Together with the verb 'zwitschern', the word 'Kniekehlen' reminds us instead of another work by Duchamp, namely *étant donnés*, an installation that features a woman lying naked on her back in a briar in a more or less naturalistically depicted landscape (ill. 4). Although the installation gives off no audible sound, by way of semantic contiguity the idyllic landscape alludes to birds singing. Moreover, the passage 'Altes Dunkel am Rand, / Neue Ränder im Dunkel' can be viewed as an implicit nod to the dark edges of *étant donnés*'. The woman in the briar is visible through a hole in a door, behind which there is another hole in a wall, causing a double framing.

It goes without saying that this naked, prone woman can be related to the notion of *après l'amour*. The same is true of another artwork to which the poem alludes, the notorious *Paysage fautif* (ill. 5). At first sight, this work seems nothing

29 Durs Grünbein, *Gedichte. Bücher I–III*, p. 107.

ill. 4: Marcel Duchamp: *Étant donnés: 1. La chute d'eau, 2. Le gaz d'éclairage* [Given: 1. The Waterfall, 2. The Illuminating Gas], 1946–1966, Philadelphia Museum of Art, Philadelphia, USA

but an abstract, organic form on a dark background. However, the story behind it caused a stir long after Duchamp's death, when it appeared the artist had used his sperm to create it. The passage 'Auf der Zunge zergangen, löschen Spermien den Durst / auf Nachwuchs' in combination with the 'Post-Coital' can be read as implicit references to *Paysage fautif*. Grünbein is certainly aware of the work's status as a rather titillating footnote to art history, since he refers to it in his epic poem *Vom Schnee*, where we read: '"Wo die *peinture* entsteht, gerührt aus Malerschweiß." / "*Trompe-l'œuil*, du weißt, ist eine Schwarzkunst. – Wetten, / Daß da ein Meister ist, der malt mit seinem ... Samen?"' [Where *peinture* is born, stirred by painter sweat. / *Trompe-l'œuil*, you know, is black magic. – Want to make a bet, / That there is a master, who paints with his ... semen?][30]

The link between the genesis of *Paysage fautif* and the theme of the poem is quite obvious: like the prone woman in *étant donnés*, the painting containing a

30 Durs Grünbein, *Vom Schnee oder Descartes in Deutschland* (Frankfurt a. M.: Suhrkamp, 2003), p. 41.

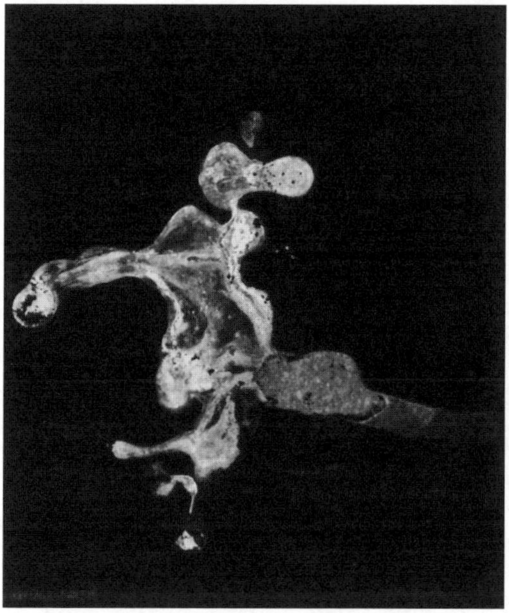

ill. 5: Marcel Duchamp: *Paysage fautif* [Faulty Landscape], 1946, Museum of Modern Art, Toyama, Japan

man's semen holds an indexical relation to the act of love-making (or the simulation thereof) and is thus to be viewed as *post-coital*. Moreover, there is a strong correlation with the cycle's title 'Posthume Innenstimmen', since both of the works discussed here, *étant donnés* and *Paysage fautif*, were not presented to an audience until after Duchamp's death.

The poem, in many ways, is the result of a very intimate contact between Grünbein as its writer and Duchamp as its voice, albeit in an *infra-mince* sort of fashion. This in-betweenness is in harmony with the erotic undertone in some of the works in Duchamp's oeuvre. Grünbein, not surprisingly, identifies the quoting writer (in this case himself) with a lover and the act of quoting with sexual intercourse: 'Wer zitiert, liefert sich aus. Im unendlichen Sprachspiel nimmt er den Part der Geliebten ein, die dem Geliebten sich hingibt zur Penetration' [Whoever quotes exposes himself. In the never-ending language game he/she assumes the part of the beloved, who opens him/herself to penetration by the lover.][31] The

31 Grünbein, 'Z wie Zitat', p. 77.

infra-mince contact established in the poem, compared by Grünbein himself to the act of love-making, is in perfect harmony with Duchamp's highly erotic oeuvre. This intimacy is not only apparent in the highly physical and – again, in accordance with Marcel Duchamp's oeuvre – even erotic 'Après l'amour', but also in the next poem featured in the cycle, 'French Kiss'.

French Kiss

Aus meinem Zwischendrinsein kein Hehl, mach ich zuletzt
Was draus zu machen mir einfällt, nicht viel, ein Gedicht.
Plötzlich wird Pfeifen im Wald zur besten Methode.
Streichhölzer, Tische, Nachtbars sind hier nur Holz.
Die Stimme bleibt weg in den einzelnen Pausen.
Unterm Moos, unerwartet gibt eine Liebe Laut –
Zungenschlag wie das Quietschen von Gummistiefeln.
Ohne Anfang und Ende ist er jederzeit da, dieser
Ablauf der Mythen und Fakten tauscht und maskiert
Wie im Schachspiel die Hirne. Und was heißt schon
Eine-stehende-Welle-verlassener-Zeit? Etwa Rauch?
Was am Tauchen zum Bleiben reizt ist der Übergang.
Die Gefahr, daß im Innehalten die Frage stirbt.
Einsam auf weiter Flur steht ein gelangweiltes Und.

[About my being in-between no secret, I eventually make / What springs to mind of it, not much, a poem. / Suddenly, whistling in the woods becomes the best method. / Here, matches, tables, night clubs are merely wood. / The voice stays away pending individual rests. / Under the moss, unexpectedly a love gives off sounds – / Speech like the squishing of rubber boots. / Without beginning or end it is always there, this / Run-down of myths and facts changes and masks / The brains as if in a game of chess. Anyway, what is / A-standing-wave-of-abandoned-time? Smoke perhaps? / What it is about diving that makes you want to stay is the transition. / The danger that in pausing the question dies. / Completely alone stands a lonely, bored And.][32]

This poem refers to Marcel Duchamp's etching *Morceaux choisis d'après Rodin* [*Pieces Chosen after Rodin*] (ill. 6), a work that at first sight is itself a two-dimensional drawing of Auguste Rodin's famous statue *The Kiss*. The poem is therefore comparable to '[Disiecta membra]' which also presents its readers with an intermedial chain consisting of two affiliated visual pre-texts and the poem itself. Despite the discernable inter-iconic relation between the two works, there is – the obvious medial distinction notwithstanding – one conspicuous difference between Rodin's statue and Duchamp's etching. Whereas the man in Rodin's *Kiss* has his

32 Durs Grünbein, *Gedichte. Bücher I–III*, p. 108.

ill. 6: Marcel Duchamp: *Morceaux choisis d'après Rodin* [*Pieces Chosen after Rodin*], 1968, etching from Arturo Schwarz' *The Large Glass and Related Works,* Vol. II

hand on the outside of the woman's thigh, Duchamp's etching has it lying between the woman's legs. This difference is very much in keeping with the erotic tendencies in Duchamp's oeuvre as a whole, illustrated not only by the aforementioned *étant donnés* and *Paysage fautif*, but also by his famous alter ego of *Rose Sélavy*, a pseudonym and pun on the phrase *éros, c'est la vie*, i.e. 'Eros, that's life'.[33]

Similarly to 'Inframince', 'French Kiss' draws upon a scepticism about language to celebrate the poem as the place where the deficiencies of everyday speech can be overcome. Like 'Après l'amour', where the poem is the result of love-making between inner voices, 'French Kiss' stages poetry in terms of highly intimate contact. The title 'French Kiss' can be interpreted as a metaphor for this contact between two entities. Moreover, there is a contiguity between the tongue and the speech it produces, whilst the adjective 'French' reflects the nationality of the artists of the poem's two visual pre-texts.

In poetry, the voice of everyday speech is absent because it is brought to a pause. A pausing voice, however, would imply silence, but in this poem it is re-

33 See Arturo Schwarz, *The Complete Works of Marcel Duchamp* (New York: Delano Greenidge, 2000), p. 875.

placed by something subdued in an invisibly thin interface between two tongues. The tongues as *partes pro toto* still refer to language, but to another sort of language than the one that is always ('jederzeit') present, namely the poetic one. The fact that this language is *infra-mince* is indicated by the use of an illustration similar to those Duchamp himself produced to clarify the concept of *infra-mince*. The comparison of 'Zungenschlag' with the squelching of rubber boots (l. 7) appears as an appropriation of Duchamp's own illustration of the concept, or even as a pastiche of his notes. The in-betweenness that – as we have seen above – is such an evident semantic feature of all things *infra-mince* is mirrored in Grünbein's poem very much in the way that Duchamp appropriates Rodin's *Kiss* for his own (eroticizing) purposes.

The three poems of the 'Posthume Innenstimmen' cycle discussed here provide examples of Grünbein's rather conceptual approach to the pictorial arts. The first poem 'Inframince' is in keeping with his modus operandi in 'Wärmeplastik nach Beuys'. The element taken from Duchamp's theoretical frame (i.e. his notes) is superimposed onto the text which thus becomes a highly complex and allusive illustration of the concept. This technique, in turn, is analogous to Duchamp's own ways of illustrating it. While two poems, 'Après l'amour' and 'French Kiss', both have visual pre-texts, explicit references to these remain limited. In 'Après l'amour', they are virtually replaced by allusions to two other Duchampian works through which an inadequate inter-iconic relation is revealed or presented in the poem. The relation is inadequate, because the analogy between the visual works of art has less to do with visually discernable characteristics than with the concepts from which they actually originate. The same is true for 'French Kiss', in which it is the kiss itself, rather than the work of art, that takes on the metaphorical form, illustrating – again – *infra-mince* or, to paraphrase Grünbein himself, the 'Und-und-und' typical of all works of art. Moreover, in all three poems the 'Innenstimmen', or quotations, as a highly intimate contact, are metaphorically linked to erotic tendencies in Duchamp's work. With 'Posthume Innenstimmen', Grünbein has thus created an intricate masterpiece of intermedial referencing that, on a meta level, relates that which is referred to the act of referring itself.

Conclusion

In many ways, Grünbein's intermedial poetry is not intermedial. In fact, as we have seen, Grünbein explicitly denounces the possibility that a visual work of art can be successfully transposed into a literary text, arguing that the literary text can only produce 'mental images instead of the visual stimuli caused by the picture'.[34] Even though the first two poems discussed in this chapter are still clearly marked as proceeding from existing works of art, it is obvious that most of Grünbein's poetry on visual works of art focuses not so much on paintings, etchings and installations themselves as on the way they were conceived by their respective creators.

The same is true for the last four poems discussed in this chapter, which all explicitly allude to their status as a post-product referring to and appropriating 'abandoned works' created by others. The principal difference and added artistic achievement, though, is that the Beuys and Duchamp poems not only draw upon their intermedially inspired conception, but also actively employ concepts borrowed from the paramedial frames of the artists concerned, without in any way losing their relative autonomy. Instead, they illustrate the way Grünbein's poetry avoids ekphrasis and the 'servile' role of description. Thus, not only medial, but also oeuvre boundaries are rendered porous: the poems are evidently written by Grünbein, but they are also clearly inscribed into a framework that belongs to a different field of artistic production. This goes beyond simple inspiration, the poems discussed in this chapter subtly bridging the interspace between literature and the pictorial arts.

In this respect, Grünbein's modus operandi is very similar to the way other contemporary poets and prose writers approach the visual arts. Authors such as Friederike Mayröcker, Thomas Kling and Ulrike Draesner all shift attention away from actual works of art to the contexts in which they are embedded and which have been traditionally given less importance. In Mayröcker's poem 'La Clairière nach Giacometti' ['La Clairière after Giacometti'],[35] for example, we find references to the conceptual, textual framework of the work mentioned in the poem's title. And Kling and Draesner – like Grünbein in the poem 'Wärmeplastik nach Beuys' – both refer to Joseph Beuys's extended concept of art and theory of evolutionary warmth in their poems 'porträt JB. fuchspelz, humboldtstrom, tomatn' ['portrait JB. fox fur, humboldt current, tomatoes'] and 'Beuystafel' ['Beuys Tablet'].[36]

Elements such as the creative process, the interaction between the spectator and the work, the artist's biography and – last but not least – the discursive, conceptual framework surrounding an oeuvre have replaced the physical work of art as the primary point of attention for these authors. In Grünbein's poetry the works of art themselves are not superfluous, but they are looked upon as fragments, as

---

34 *Durs Grünbein im Gespräch mit Heinz-Norbert Jocks*, p. 35.

35 Friederike Mayröcker, *Gesammelte Gedichte* (Frankfurt a. M.: Suhrkamp, 2004), pp. 241–42.

36 Thomas Kling, *brennstabm* (Frankfurt a. M.: Suhrkamp, 1991), p. 60; Ulrike Draesner, *gedächtnisschleifen* (Munich: Luchterhand, 2008 [Frankfurt a. M.: Suhrkamp, 1995]), pp. 19–20.

metonymical pars-pro-toto elements that refer or bear witness to a *bigger picture*. This bigger picture consists of the work itself and its surrounding framework, its *parergon*. However, such frameworks are not necessarily medial. Rather, they consist of mental images, of impressions that are in fact open to a transposition in language. In Grünbein's poetry, works of art are themselves never – or rarely – directly transformed into words, as is traditionally the case with ekphrasis. Instead the linguistic, verbally captured part of the extended work of art – the concepts surrounding the visual – is incorporated to bridge interstices the poet deems impossible to bridge via ekphrasis.

Andrew Webber

Wunderblock. Durs Grünbein and the Urban Arts of Memory

Durs Grünbein's writing is insistently concerned with memorative processes. It enacts what might be called, on a suitable model for this classically inclined writer, the arts of memory – *artes memoriae*.[1] This memory work is carried out in particular through the spatial dimension, and this in particular through the treatment of urban spaces, ancient and modern. Grünbein's work turns on configurations of time, both personal and cultural, and space, both personal and cultural; and the city enjoys a special status as a complex location for these configurations. The intention in this chapter is to consider how memory work is conducted in texts of Grünbein's devoted to modern urban conditions and their binding to the past. Urban representations are seen as having an exemplary status for the writing project of this key poet of late modernity and its fundamental concerns with relations between the dimensions of time and space, history and topography, memory and orientation.

In discussing Grünbein's representations of cities of memory, this essay is guided by the preeminent analyst of urban *Zeiträume* or time-spaces, Walter Benjamin. Grünbein follows Benjamin in exploring the temporal dimension through its imbrication in the spatial, fascinated by the interactions and tensions that are at work between the two.[2] If Grünbein's work can be understood, in his own formulation, as registering forms of *Chronogramm*, of the writing of time,[3] it also produces what we might, by extension, call chrono-topograms. That is, it records the sort of intimate but dialectically complicated conjunction of the dimensions of time and space that Benjamin explores through the *Zeitraum* configuration. As set out in model fashion in *Das Passagen-Werk* [*The Arcades Project*], Benjamin's study of urban modernity and its representational systems in nineteenth-century Paris, and redeployed through the more personal forms of his Berlin texts, this configuration is above all concerned with the ambiguous relationships between

---

1 For a classic account of the *artes memoriae*, see Frances Yates, *The Art of Memory* (London: Routledge and Kegan Paul, 1966).

2 By way of example, in *Das erste Jahr*, the day is described as stretching for a length of time ('eine Zeitlang') as the voices of the birds of Berlin draw the subject into depths of space ('Raumtiefen'). Durs Grünbein, *Das erste Jahr. Berliner Aufzeichnungen* (Frankfurt a. M.: Suhrkamp, 2001), p. 29.

3 Durs Grünbein, 'Kurzer Bericht an eine Akademie', in *Antike Dispositionen. Aufsätze* (Frankfurt a. M.: Suhrkamp, 2005), pp. 11–14 (p. 12).

processes of temporal and spatial passage.[4] In the explorations of nineteenth-century Paris and of early twentieth-century Berlin, both historical and topographical motions are constitutionally subject to stand-still, reversal and displacement. The motions, halts and turnings of the two dimensions are bound up with each other in complex ways, and it is this sort of chrono-topographical complexity that we can see operating in the work of Grünbein.

If Benjamin is adopted here as a critical guide, it is because he has a particular affinity with Grünbein's urban representations and their attachment to the cultural disposition of modernism. He occupies a special place in the intertextual network around Grünbein's writings on urban spaces and experience, a network which also includes such classic poetic constructions of the city as the Paris of Charles Baudelaire, the London of T. S. Eliot and the Berlin of Gottfried Benn and Bertolt Brecht. In particular, Benjamin's theorizations of urban systems of representation serve to relate the intertextual element to the intermedial, the constellations of text with forms of visual mediation that is also a pervasive feature of Grünbein's work. The model for this intermedial constellation is allegory, as discussed by Benjamin in its classic early modern form in *Ursprung des deutschen Trauerspiels* [*The Origin of German Tragic Drama*] and in its adapted modern forms, not least through the urban writings of Baudelaire, in the *Passagen-Werk*. Allegory, whether in the isolated form of Dürer's *Melancholia* or the both crowded and isolated text-images of Baudelaire's *Les Fleurs du mal* [*The Flowers of Evil*], is particularly concerned with the representation of states of being and of affective conditions. Melancholy remains the distinctive affective keynote of allegorical representation in its modern urban form, attuned to the dialectical forms of passage caught in standstill. And in the postmodern conditions of Grünbein's urban text-imaging, with its self-conscious reference to the allegorical image-thinking of Benjamin, that affective constellation finds new forms.[5]

Through this Benjaminian perspective, Grünbein is understood as constructing forms of psycho-topography, representations of urban space that are freighted with particular psychical investments, at once retrospective and prospective, positive and negative, nostalgic and melancholic. Dresden and Berlin are the cities (home and adopted) that are subject to special attention in what follows.

4 When Grünbein describes his own interest in urban space as deriving less from the 'Passagenwerk' of the old European cities than from their reconstructed form after destruction, he nonetheless references the Benjaminian passage-work as the unconscious of the modern city. Durs Grünbein, 'Der verschwundene Platz', in *Antike Dispositionen*, pp. 279–91 (p. 284).

5 For a discussion of Benjamin's allegorical 'Denkbild' [thought image] in the context of Grünbein's own relationship to thought-images, see Heinz-Norbert Jocks and Durs Grünbein, *Durs Grünbein im Gespräch mit Heinz-Norbert Jocks* (Cologne: DuMont, 2001), pp. 37–38.

These are cities that are distinct in their dimensions, styles and cultural historical status; yet they also occupy common ground in the processes of destruction and reconstruction that have shaped their modern histories. The representation of the two cities – in both lyric and prose texts – is seen to turn upon an unresolved dialectic between the witnessing of historical evidence (the abiding presence of the past, that is, in the spatial dimension) and its elusiveness, even to the point of oblivion. Here, another of Grünbein's intertextual correspondents, Freud, serves to illuminate the traces, the resistances and the losses that are recorded in the work of the urban psycho-topographer. Like Benjamin, a key figure in Grünbein's construction of modernity, Freud has a particular claim to a role here. The ironically knowing intertextual dialogue that Grünbein sustains with Freud will be explored through the latter's allegorical modelling of a particular device for the understanding of the workings of memory: the *Wunderblock.*

This essay takes its cue from the end of my book, *Berlin in the Twentieth Century. A Cultural Topography*, where Grünbein figured as a millennial counterpart to Benjamin, undertaking critical work of *allegoresis* on the psycho-topographical disposition of Berlin around 2000, as Benjamin had done on the city of his childhood around 1900.[6] Following Benjamin, my work on the cultural topography – in particular the psycho-topography – of twentieth-century Berlin focused especially on the figurative logic of allegory. I understood this trope precisely as fashioning a particular conjunction of space and time: allegory as a *mise-en-scène* of the historical in altered spatial form. It is historical experience placed and spoken otherwise, following the etymology of allegory as an other (*allos*) place of speaking (*agora*), or a place for speaking in other forms. This conjunction of space and alterity was the guiding principle for understanding the cultural topography of the city in its historical development, with the models for this allegorical understanding drawn from Freud and more especially from Benjamin.

From Freud the project drew such allegorical constructions as the description of the city of Rome, projected in *Das Unbehagen in der Kultur* [*Civilization and its Discontents*] as a model for the human psyche. Freud's dilemma is how to represent the paradoxical simultaneity of non-simultaneous experience that characterizes the elaborate temporal structures of the psyche. He tries to make the psyche and its economy of memory understandable through the exemplary structure of cultural memory that is the eternal city of Rome, with its archaeological accretions and superimpositions. It is an allegorical project that Freud sees as

6 Andrew J. Webber, *Berlin in the Twentieth Century. A Cultural Topography* (Cambridge: Cambridge University Press, 2008), p. 299.

necessarily failing, but one to which he nonetheless devotes substantial time and space. He clearly wants this psycho-topographical projection to carry on working on the reader's memory as a mnemonic device, even as he passes on to other attempts at modelling the peculiar, indeed arguably inconceivable, spatio-temporal continuum of the unconscious. By what Freud calls its 'eindrucksvolle Kontrastwirkung' [impressive effect of contrast],[7] the failed allegory gains a certain dialectical, contrastive purchase upon what he famously calls – in another, more abstract allegorical figure – the other scene or place of spectacle of the unconscious, a 'Schauplatz' that is defined above all by its condition of alterity.[8]

As a counterpart to the city of Rome, there is another, more compact and everyday allegory that gives substance to the other scene or *Schauplatz*, one that casts a relationship between the workings of the psyche and graphic representation: the *Wunderblock*. This ephemeral apparatus from the world of childhood around 1900 is a more proximate form of speaking otherwise of the other place of the unconscious. What English calls the 'mystic writing pad' is a device of writing or picturing, or combinations of the two, made up of a wax block, a sheet of waxed paper above it and a transparent celluloid sheet above that. It maintains imprints of everything that is inscribed upon it in the wax block underneath, even as the double-sheet is lifted to clear what has been represented and make space for new inscriptions. This is the sort of non-simultaneous simultaneity of information that Freud understands the psyche to have. But the naïve technology of the child's toy also has its limits. While it might have the magical appearance of a total memory machine, a palimpsest where the layers of inscription are co-present in the wax block of the unconscious, these are also subject to distortion, etched with loss, by each new inscription.

The *Wunderblock* is a wonderful apparatus, like the marvellous 'memory machine' of the psyche in Grünbein's essay 'Mein babylonisches Hirn' ['My Babylonish Brain'].[9] But it is also one that cannot fully work: the prosthetic machine meant to overcome memory blocks in turn suffers blocks in its mnemotechnical wonders. As Freud's allegorical work moves between an image of the city and an apparatus of recording, so Grünbein conceives of the psyche as an urban machinery. As one who lives 'post-Freud' and after the 'Einbruch' [incursion] of neurology,[10] he shades the post-Freudian psychoanalytic view (which extends,

---

7 Sigmund Freud, *Das Unbehagen in der Kultur*, in *Gesammelte Werke*, ed. by Anna Freud and others, 18 vols (Frankfurt a. M.: Fischer, 1999), XIV, p. 429.
8 Sigmund Freud, *Die Traumdeutung*, in *Gesammelte Werke*, II.3, p. 51.
9 Durs Grünbein, 'Mein babylonisches Hirn', in *Galilei vermißt Dantes Hölle und bleibt an den Maßen hängen. Aufsätze 1989–1995* (Frankfurt a. M.: Suhrkamp, 1996), pp. 18–33 (p. 19).
10 Durs Grünbein, *Das erste Jahr*, p. 32.

for instance, to a 'media unconscious')[11] into a neuro-scientific one, when he projects an allegory of the brain as a nocturnal 'neuronal metropolis', overloaded by information. The brain as city is seen to be in a constant state of exception or emergency, an 'Ausnahmezustand',[12] and as such analogous to the historical and present condition of Berlin, where the 'Wunder', or miracle, is that nocturnal curfews are not in operation to enable the ongoing 'Ausnahmezustand' of the city's process of reconstruction.[13] In Grünbein's conception, Berlin as paradigmatic city of modernity and the psyche of the city-writer as paradigmatic inhabitant share in the condition that Giorgio Agamben has seen as setting the paradigm for modern political culture.[14] City and psyche are thus cast together in the exceptional state of the Babylonian brain.

The move from the idealized cultural space of the eternal city of Rome, idealised even in its status as an amalgamation of archaeological remnants, to Babylon, the city mythologized as a place of excess, communicative confusion and catastrophic fall,[15] is indicative of a more general psycho-cultural dislocation – or state of exception – in the wake of the catastrophic history that has intervened between Freud and Grünbein. For the post-catastrophic poet, Freud's system is in itself a form of Babylonian remainder. The hermeneutic discourse of the psychoanalyst is reduced to an emblematic fragment, and a fragment that tends to work under the sign of negation: an iota. It is as such that it is referenced in the poem after the style of Gottfried Benn's urban poetry,[16] 'In Tunneln der U-Bahn' ['In Tunnels of the Underground Railway']. Here, the fragmented poetic subject is scattered '"Deut um Deut"' [iota by iota], yielding the fragmentary, parenthetic association: '(Wie sagt Freud?)' [(What does Freud say?)].[17] The master narrative of the Freudian project, as informed by the principle of hermeneutic interpretation – the *Deutung* of *Die Traumdeutung* [*The Interpretation of Dreams*] – is truncated and recycled in this irreverent act of poetic ventriloquism, so that what Freud says becomes by associative rhyme a sequence of iotas, an accumulation of subliminal fragments registered in the transportation network of the urban

11 Ibid., p. 29.

12 Ibid., pp. 232–33.

13 Ibid., p. 264.

14 See Giorgio Agamben, *Homo Sacer. Sovereign Power and Bare Life* (Stanford: Stanford University Press, 1998).

15 The Babylonish brain incorporates amongst its fragments the corner of a wall in ancient Rome (Grünbein, 'Mein babylonisches Hirn', p. 33).

16 The poem particularly recalls Benn's 'Untergrundbahn' ['Underground Railway'].

17 Durs Grünbein, 'In Tunneln der U-Bahn', in *Schädelbasislektion* (Frankfurt a. M.: Suhrkamp, 1991), pp. 31–35 (p. 31).

underground. Freud is thus one of the voices that is appropriated and questioned in the ongoing process of constitution and interrogation of poetic subjectivity in Grünbein's writing.[18] The post-catastrophic poet is also a postmodern exponent of pastiche, of the ironic manipulation of fragments into new constellations, and his recycling from cultural memory of psychoanalytic models of understanding is accordingly of uncertain reliability.

The master mnemotechnician and manipulator of cultural fragments, Walter Benjamin, can be seen as the mediator between the projects of Freud and Grünbein. The model of a psychoanalytic art and technology of memory underpins the work of Benjamin, albeit in forms that are inflected by his advanced understanding of the mechanics of modern culture. Benjamin's work, and not least his archaeological work on the private and cultural memory structures of cities, takes its cue from the sort of psycho-topographical model found in Freud but opens it up to more complex questioning. The Paris of the *Passagen-Werk* or Berlin of the *Berliner Kindheit um neunzehnhundert* [*Berlin Childhood around 1900*] and *Berliner Chronik* [*Berlin Chronicle*] are newer versions of Freud's Rome, with more recent archaeologies of culture in passage. They are also more sophisticated forms of the *Wunderblock*: magical apparatus for the retrieval of past material and constellations; but at the same time places that record loss and processes of elision. The texts that represent the cities can in their turn be understood as recording machines, but here, too, with an attachment to loss. Benjamin's wonder-filled allegorical work in pursuit of the modern urban unconscious, personal and collective, is also self-consciously subject to the block of the *Wunderblock*, and Grünbein's own version of this project for postmodern times, as it were, recycles the anachronistic apparatus of apprehension and registration.

Benjamin's pre-war Berlin is not yet a place of catastrophic destruction, but its locations are already redolent of Pompeii,[19] that archaeological anti-city, favourite location for a kind of wonderful but also catastrophically blocked urban memory. The volcanic site of what Grünbein calls 'gedächtnisloses Gedächtnis' [memoryless memory],[20] one excavated by the techniques of archaeology and psychoanalysis,[21] is also the other scene or *Schauplatz* of Jensen's *Gradiva*, as read by Freud: an uncanny site where the past may come to life and step forth in

18 For a detailed discussion of this dialogical process and its many interlocutors, see Michael Eskin, *Poetic Affairs. Celan, Grünbein, Brodsky* (Stanford: Stanford University Press, 2008).
19 Webber, *Berlin in the Twentieth Century*, p. 78.
20 Grünbein, 'Kurzer Bericht', p. 12.
21 Grünbein, *Das erste Jahr*, p. 36.

a way that exceeds the routines of archaeological memory-work.[22] It is the ancient city that underlies the modern metropolis for Benjamin's work of cultural archaeology.[23] And it is the place that Grünbein, too, revisits in his writing, where it is depicted as the shadow-city of his post-war Dresden, hailed as 'barockes Pompeji' [baroque Pompeii] in the essay 'Vulkan und Gedicht' ['Volcano and Poem'].[24] As a Pompeian city, Dresden is fashioned as at once catastrophically destroyed and yet recaptured, uncannily, in the wonder of its lost form.

Before we consider the troubled fantasy conurbation of Berlin, Pompeii and Dresden, we should make a brief return to another allegorical scene from the classical world: the primal scene, we might say, of the arts of memory. It is a scene that Grünbein remembers in the essay on his Babylonish brain, or that he – perhaps artfully – misremembers. He remembers, that is, with a kind of memory block, a particular form of writer's block for the memory-writer. The scene is that recounted by Cicero and Quintilian, describing how the poet Simonides of Ceos inaugurated the key technique of the arts of memory.[25] Simonides is called upon to deliver a panegyric at a feast to Skopas, but he angers his patron when he also praises Castor and Pollux. The poet is called away when two strangers (presumably the *dioscuri*, incognito) ask for him at the door, and in his absence the banquet hall collapses, killing all present. Simonides is then able to identify the dead by remembering where they sat. The post-catastrophic scene becomes the template for writing from memory through spatial recall.

Grünbein remembers the scene somewhat otherwise in the 'Babylonish Brain' essay. It finds a prime place in the mind of the writer, cast as an allegorical place of collapsed architecture, as well as discursive convergence and confusion. As Babel joins the conurbation of ancient and modern cities of wonder and catastrophe, the poet finds this scene, itself a function of a palimpsest of accounts, in the Babylonian archaeology of his brain, or perhaps we should say his psyche:

---

22 In his essay on *Das Unheimliche*, Freud cites Schlegel's definition of the *unheimlich* [uncanny] as that which should have remained hidden but has emerged, or 'hervorgetreten ist' [stepped forth]. Freud, *Gesammelte Werke*, XII, p. 235.

23 See Victor Burgin, 'Monument and Melancholia', in *Memory Culture and the Contemporary City. Building Sites*, ed. by Uta Staiger, Henriette Steiner and Andrew Webber (Basingstoke: Palgrave, 2009), pp. 17–31.

24 Durs Grünbein, 'Vulkan und Gedicht', in *Galilei vermißt Dantes Hölle*, pp. 34–39 (p. 38); 'Volcano and Poem' in, *The Bars of Atlantis. Selected Essays*, ed. by Michael Eskin, trans. by John Crutchfield, Michael Hofmann and Andrew Shields (New York: Farrar, Straus and Giroux, 2010), pp. 7–11.

25 For an extended discussion of the role of the Simonides narrative for Grünbein's poetics, see Alexander Müller, *Das Gedicht als Engramm. Memoria und Imaginatio in der Poetik Durs Grünbeins* (Oldenburg: Igel Verlag, 2004), pp. 83–117.

Oder war es ein Zufall, nach dem (einer Legende zufolge, die Cicero in seiner Schrift über die Redner wiedergibt) ausgerechnet ein Dichter als Erfinder der Gedächtniskunst gilt? Sein Name ist Simonides von Keos. Bei einem Festmahl im Haus des thessalischen Fürsten Skopas soll er, nach einem Gedichtvortrag, als das Dach des Festsaals einstürzte, wie durch ein Wunder als einziger mit dem Leben davongekommen sein. Göttliche Fügung oder Notdurft (eine volle Blase vermutlich) hatten ihn vor die Tür geführt. Als er zurückkam, waren sämtliche Teilnehmer des Symposions unter den Trümmern begraben, die Leichen bis zur Unkenntlichkeit entstellt. Niemand konnte die Opfer mehr identifizieren, niemand außer dem einen Dichter. Indem er sich nachher genau an die Sitzordnung erinnerte, half er den Angehörigen, ihre Toten zu finden. Überrascht vom eigenen unbewußten Vermögen, soll er wie nebenbei eine Methode gefunden haben, mit der sich jederzeit die wahllose Erinnerung ordnen ließ. Sein Trick, eine frühe Bewußtseinstechnik, bestand darin, jedem geistigen Bild einen genauen Ort zuzuweisen, die Vielzahl der Eindrücke räumlich zu arrangieren, nach einem Muster, das leicht als Hintergrund aller künftigen Dichtung dienen konnte. Das Gleichnis konnte kaum glücklicher gewählt sein: als überlebender Zeuge hatte er der Trauer der Hinterbliebenen den Weg gewiesen, als Epigrammatiker und Dichter von Totenklagen den Schlüssel zur Erinnerung, Voraussetzung jeden Nachrufs, gefunden. Der Antike blieb er als einer der ersten faßbaren Persönlichkeiten im Gedächtnis, bildgewaltig und suggestiv, ein Wanderer zwischen Innen- und Außenwelt. Seine Mnemonik verdankte sich einem Unfall, sofern die Anekdote stimmt, der Verarbeitung eines Schocks. Dichtung war für ihn, wie Plutarch schrieb, redende Malerei, die Malerei schweigende Dichtung.

Und wieder hört man Horaz heraus, wie er am Ende seines Dichterlebens murmelt ... *ut pictura poesis*.

Doch welches waren die Bilder, die sich am tiefsten einprägten, welche Vorstellungen waren prägnant genug, daß sie sich Zugang verschafften zum Unbewußten? Denn daß dies der Ort ist, von dem sie seit Jahrhunderten nicht mehr vertrieben wurden, ist evident, seit zum Symbolhaushalt der Generationen auch Bruchstücke aus Gedichten gehören. Waren es nicht gerade die ungewöhnlichsten, je nachdem komischen oder grandiosen, häßlichen oder bedrohlichen: Bilder der jähen Schönheit und der Zerstörung, die in ihrer Schroffheit das kollektive Unbewußte am meisten erregten? Drangen nur sie etwa bis dahin vor, wo die Angstlust regierte, wo aus dem Dickicht unklarer Empfindungen die Einsicht hervorbrach, wo Traum und Trost sich auf einer Lichtung trafen? Ich weiß, das es außer verdichteten Bilder anderes gibt ...

[Or was it a coincidence that (according to a legend that Cicero reports in his text on the orators) it is precisely a poetic writer that is taken to be the inventor of the art of memory? His name is Simonides of Ceos. At a feast in the house of the Thessalian King Scopas, it is said that after the presentation of a poem, when the roof of the banquet hall collapsed, as if by a miracle he was the only one to escape with his life. Divine providence or necessity (a full bladder probably) had led him out of the door. When he returned, all the participants in the symposium were buried under the rubble, their corpses disfigured beyond recognition. Nobody could now identify the victims, nobody but this same poet. By remembering precisely the order of seating, he helped the relatives to find their dead. Surprised by his own unconscious ability, he is said as if incidentally to have found a method by which indiscriminate memory could at any time be ordered. His trick, an early technique of consciousness, consisted in attributing to each mental image an exact place, arranging the multiplicity of impressions spatially, according to a model that could easily serve as background to all future

> poetic writing. The choice of analogy could hardly be more felicitous: as surviving witness he showed the way for the mourning of those left behind, as writer of epigrams and threnodies he found the key to memory, the prerequisite for any obituary. He remained one of the first palpable personalities in the memory of the classical world, powerful in his images and evocative, a wanderer between inner and outer worlds. His mnemonics are the product of an accident, in as far as the anecdote is true, the processing of a shock. Poetic writing was for him, as Plutarch wrote, speaking painting, and painting silent literature.
>
> And once more it is Horace one hears, murmuring at the end of his life as poet ... *ut pictura poesis*.
>
> But what were the images that made the deepest impression, what conceptions were pregnant enough to gain access to the unconscious? For it is clear that this is the location from which they have not been driven for centuries, for as long as fragments from poems have belonged to the symbolic household of the generations. Was it not precisely the most unusual, whether comic or grandiose, ugly or threatening, images of sudden beauty and of destruction that aroused the collective unconscious most in their brusqueness? Was it perhaps only they that pressed forward to where pleasure-in-fear ruled, where out of the thicket of unclear sensations insight broke forth, where dream and consolation met in a clearing? I know that there are other things besides condensed images ...][26]

Whether the poet of memory was really saved by a call of nature or by the divine intervention of Castor and Pollux is perhaps secondary. Though, in the context of poetry that is invested in the historical, doing work of testimony, it might prompt ethical concerns as to whether the anecdote in which the memory work of literature is grounded is indeed accurate, so that the scene of origin can be remembered in model fashion. That Grünbein should suggest an involuntary bodily reminder, the full bladder, as the 'Wunder' that is the trigger of the poet's escape and subsequent immortalization is characteristic of his strategies of sublimation and desublimation between the metaphysical and the physical (the orders, one might say, of 'Wunder' and 'Block'). The 'Zufall', or coincidence, that intervenes here is accordingly at once light, capricious and freighted with the sense of catastrophic collapse that it by chance incorporates. 'Zufall' is ready to collapse into 'Unfall', thus aligning Grünbein's account of the original scene of poetic memory work with the version of it that Ingeborg Bachmann performs in her text on post-war Berlin, *Ein Ort für Zufälle* [*A Place for Coincidences*].[27] The accent accordingly falls on the 'Fall' in 'Zufall', much as it does for 'Fallen' in Judith Ryan's reading of *Falten und Fallen* [*Folds and Traps*].[28] In the terms set out in the poem cycle 'Fünf falsche Töne' ['Five Wrong Notes'], 'Zufall', which is allegorized there as Miß

26 Grünbein, 'Mein babylonisches Hirn', pp. 23–24.

27 Webber, *Berlin in the Twentieth Century*, pp. 230–40.

28 Judith Ryan, 'The Skull beneath the Skin', in *A New History of German Literature*, ed. by David E. Wellbery and others (Cambridge, MA: Harvard University Press, 2004), pp. 959–64 (p. 963).

Tyche, is also a 'Mißklang',[29] representative of the wrong notes in question. Miß Tyche becomes associated with the condition of mis-taking or miss-ing, determining that the poetic subject has holes or mistakes in his memory, missing parts. As such, she maintains a reign of terror, and one that is easily mis-represented and mis-apprehended as psychic horror for the subject ('Wenn Tyche's Terror Psyche's Horror wird' [When Tyche's terror becomes Psyche's horror]).[30]

What we have here is a particular kind of charter for the mnemotechnical work of the post-catastrophic poet, in the face of the traumatic effects of 'Zufall'. It is one that conceives of that work in the Freudian-cum-Benjaminian fashion as a transmission of the effects of loss and of shock that mark the psyche, the unconscious both personal and collective, into the work of mourning. The testimonial memory art of mourning involves a processing of material that, following key terms from the Freudian lexicon, is 'verdichtet' and 'entstellt': condensed and distorted or disfigured, in the manner of dream-work in Freud's account.[31] It is a condensed and distorted co-production of pleasure and fear – 'Angstlust', itself a distorted affective condensation – that provides the model for the work of the survivor-poet. For the poet as 'surviving witness' has a special access to the *Wunderblock* of cultural memory and its dense and distorted memory bank. In the dream-language of the unconscious, 'verdichtet' as in the compression of the psyche also, in other words, bears witness to poetic writing as *ver-dichtet*. Out of the distorted pictures and other scenes – also the intertextual pictures and scenes of other poets – with coordinates in the other 'Schauplatz' of the unconscious, the poet names and narrates: *ut pictura poesis* (as is painting so is poetry). It is in this way that Simonides himself, the legendary founder of the technique, also comes to be remembered or artfully misremembered by the latter day poet of memory.

How then does this primal scene of aesthetic memory work act as a model for Grünbein's own poetic writing? We can draw here on his depictions of the latter-day incarnations of Pompeii and Babylon: Dresden and Berlin. Let us start with Dresden, the city allegorized as a place of broken and restored porcelain in the collection of that name devoted to the downfall of what the poet calls 'my city'. We can consider the appearance of this fallen town to which he lays claim in two poems from other collections. The first is 'Kleine Ode zum Dank' ['Little Ode in Thanks'], which evokes the city of personal and collective memory in its opening stanzas thus:

---

29 Durs Grünbein, 'Fünf falsche Töne', in *Schädelbasislektion*, pp. 147–51 (p. 150).
30 Ibid.
31 See Freud, *Die Traumdeutung*, pp. 283–315.

> Auch ich wuchs auf in einer dieser Wunderstädte,
> Die rascher ausradiert sind als gebaut.
> Von allem Prunk, was ließ man mir? Das Himmelsblau.
>
> Und je nach Wind und Witterung den hohen weißen
> Barock der Wolken und ihr sommerliches Rokoko.
> Zumindest dies also: ein familiäres Formgefühl
>
> Für das Zerstörte. Stolpernd über lose Pflastersteine
> Von Kindesbeinen an, war man vertraut
> Mit einer Welt, der Haß galt als Naturkonstante.
>
> [And I too grew up in one of these miracle cities, / That are faster rubbed out than built. / Of all the glory what was left to me? The blue of the heavens. // And depending upon wind and weather the high white / Baroque of the clouds and their summery Rococo. / At least this then: a familiar formal feeling / For what is destroyed. Stumbling over loose paving stones / From an early age, you knew well / A world, for which hate was a natural constant.][32]

This is, in other words, a city recalled in the fashion of the *Wunderblock*. It is an archaeological assemblage of images and inscriptions that may be reconstructed but always as a function of removal or erasure. 'Wunder' thus carries here, as it arguably does for Freud, the traumatic shadow of 'Wunde' – wound, as if its truncation were itself an act of psycho-linguistic wounding. The broken pun is indeed used to frame one of stanzas of the *Porzellan* cycle, where the 'Wunder' of the opening line is echoed in the 'Wunden' of the last.[33] In 'Kleine Ode zum Dank', the 'barockes Pompeji' that is Dresden is conjured up in more or less immaterial projection through the 'Barock der Wolken' which are piled up above it. The clouds that we imagine as painted on a false baroque ceiling cast over Dresden, an architectural fantasy projection, provide a kind of post-catastrophic picturing of the city through *trompe l'oeil* for poetic recall: *ut pictura poesis*. It is also a place where 'von Kindesbeinen an' (literally, from child's legs on – as *Grün-bein* or green-leg, that is) the incipient poet learns to recall by stumbling over dislodged paving stones. He is cast, we might think, between a ruined version of Proust's *mémoire involontaire* in one of its classic forms and the *Stolperstein* or stumbling stone as memorial to the deported such as is found in the pavements of Dresden, Berlin and other German cities. Both *mémoire involontaire* and *Stolperstein* are indeed

32 Durs Grünbein, 'Kleiner Ode zum Dank', in *Strophen für übermorgen* (Frankfurt a. M.: Suhrkamp, 2007), pp. 14–19 (p. 14).

33 Durs Grünbein, *Porzellan. Poem vom Untergang meiner Stadt* (Frankfurt a. M.: Suhrkamp, 2005), poem 35.

invoked as elements in the poetics of breakage and excavation in the *Porzellan* cycle.[34]

The same city of memory is featured in the early post-unification poem that carries its name, 'Gedicht über Dresden' ['Poem about Dresden']. Or perhaps we should say the poem that locates itself above the city – *über* Dresden. It takes up the space of the baroque clouds in 'Kleine Ode zum Dank' in order to view from above the *Trauerspiel* of what the poem depicts as the un-dead 'Barockwrack an der Elbe' [baroque wreck on the Elbe]. It is a point of view that mimics that of air warfare and of reconnaissance after the event. In the manner of Simonides, the memory poet scouts the space of the city in order to recall what was found there. It is a cityscape with a melancholic *genius loci*, where baroque converges with Gothic spectrality, with echoes of Poe's Raven in the '*nevermore*' of the first stanza. For Grünbein, like that other reader of Poe, Walter Benjamin, knows that the *genius loci* of a place that is 'gorged with memories' is the best form of depressant.

Gedicht über Dresden

Scheintote Stadt, Barockwrack an der Elbe
Schwimmend in brauner Lauge, spät fixiert
Taucht sie aus Rotz und Wasser auf, ein Suchbild
Ein Puzzle, königlich, mit dem der Krieg
Die Schrecken der *Zerstörungswelt* entschärfte.
... was diesen Brücken keinen Abbruch tat,
Der Silhouette nicht, den schmalen Türmen
Chiaveris Schwan und dem Balkon Europas, –
Sandstein der alles weichmacht was hier aufwächst.
Das beste Depressivum ist der genius loci
An einem Ort, gemästet mit Erinnerungen,
Schwammfäule, schön getönt als Nostalgie
Narkotisch wie die psychotropen Jamben,
Die anglo-sächsische Version von *nevermore*.

Auch Dresden ist ein Werk des Malerlehrlings
Mit dem in Wien verstümperten Talent
Der halb Europa seinen Stilbruch aufzwang.
In diesem Fall ergab sich wie von selbst
Die Technik flächendeckender Radierung
Durch fremde Bomber, Meister ihres Fachs
In einer Nacht mit schwarzem Schnee im Februar.

34 Grünbein, *Porzellan*, poems 20, 49.

Getreu den Plänen seines Kunstfreunds Speer
    ('Die Zukunft, Albert!') bleibt von *Bausubstanzen*
        Nach Tausend Jahren noch, groß im Verfall
            Die Schönheit der Ruinen, ihr *Ruinenwert*.
                So praktisch kommt Romantik in der Hand
                    Von Ingenieuren. Ein *Gesamtkunstwerk*
                        Singt unter Trümmern noch in höchsten Tönen.

Im Futur II wird alles still geworden sein.

(Für Via Lewandowsky)

[Living-dead city, baroque wreck on the Elbe / Swimming in brown leach, fixed late / It rises up out of snot and water, a picture puzzle, / A jigsaw, right royal, with which the war / Defused the terrors of the *world of destruction*. / ... which did nothing to terminate those bridges, / Nor the silhouette, the slender towers / Chiaveri's Swan and the Balcony of Europe, – / Sandstone that softens everything that grows up here, / The best depressant is the genius loci / In a place, gorged on memories, / Dry-rotting, nicely toned as nostalgia / Narcotic like the psychotropic iambi, / The Ango-Saxon version of *nevermore*. // Dresden too is a work of the apprentice painter / With his talent bungled in Vienna / Who forced his rupture in style on half of Europe. / In this case there arose as if of its own accord / The technique of blanket etching out / By foreign bombers, masters of their metier / In a night with black snow in February. / True to the plans of his art-loving Speer / ('The future, Albert!') there still remains of *building substances* / After a thousand years, great in decay / The beauty of the ruins, their *ruin value*. / Romanticism comes so practically in the hands / Of engineers. A *Gesamtkunstwerk* / Still sings under rubble in the highest tones. // In the future perfect all will have become silent. (For Via Lewandowsky)][35]

Dresden becomes here one dramatic work of city painting amongst many by the apprentice painter from Vienna. Once more, the word 'Fall' proves to be fateful, making 'In diesem Fall' readable less as 'In this case' than 'In this fall'. This case of falling architecture is not a wonderwork, but a product of Hitler's catastrophic rupture of style, whereby 'Stilbruch' [rupture in style] is substituted catachrestically for the obscene 'Zivilisationsbruch' [rupture in civilization] perpetrated according to Hitler's designs.[36] And so the 'Wunderstadt' Dresden is remodelled into a city of ruins, in accordance with the aesthetic vision of Hitler's court architect Speer, with his grotesquely ironic appreciation of the 'Ruinenwert', or ruin value, of monumental constructions. Hitler's work of representation through destruc-

35 Durs Grünbein, 'Gedicht über Dresden', in *Schädelbasislektion*, p. 112.

36 For the resonance of 'Zivilisationsbruch' for Grünbein, see Amir Eshel, 'Diverging Memories? Durs Grünbein's Mnemonic Topographies and the Future of the German Past', *The German Quarterly*, 74.4 (2001), 407–16 (p. 410).

tion of the city of Dresden again involves an anti-aesthetic rubbing out, using as its instrument what might be called the anti-mnemotechnical forces of air war, pressing cities into a condition of virtual cultural amnesia, through blanket erasure or etching out, 'flächendeckender Radierung'.

The image is also etched in the page in shapes that might mimic pictographically a displaced appropriation of the double flash of the SS. It would thus represent a particular conjunction between pictography and typography, a representation in letters of the extra cipher (the double S) that Grünbein highlights amongst the 'giant letters' of Hitler's type-writer, the weapon of mass destruction that figures as a mangled archaeological find from the bunker in a documentary the writer has seen on the last days of the Reich Chancellery.[37] Or we might see it as an angular doubling and overflowing of what Grünbein in *Porzellan* calls the 'slender S' of the Elbe,[38] inviting the bombers. Dresden's topographical monogram also stands emblematically as the frontispiece of *Porzellan* in the photograph of the city taken from the air 'before the destruction' of 1945. Or the poetic shape might represent the driven form in black on white of the Petrarchan, or Celanian, 'black snow' of the second stanza.[39] Or, more generally, it could be seen to display a kind of flattening, a displacement of vertical structures into lateral form. Over-determined in its signification, it is a rebus-like pictogram of destruction, with the stepped regularity of blanket bombing on one side and the broken forms of its effects on the other.

This is a text-image that might recall another set of ekphrastic texts from the memory-bank or the *Wunderblock* of German poetry in times of and after war: the photo-poems from Brecht's *Kriegsfibel* [*War Primer*]. It is a primer that we can assume was one of Grünbein's learning texts. Brecht's text-and-image work on the effects of war provides the basis for imagining a form of representation – *radieren* [etching] – that can also be read as erasure. For Brecht it is focused in the conjunction of technologies of warfare and the technology of photography – etching with light. Writing in 1948, at the time of the airlift, Brecht wryly describes the *Trümmerstadt* or rubble city Berlin as an iconoclastic work of art, artwork we might say in the age of its technical destructibility. It is a collaboration between those antagonists of the *Kriegsfibel*, Hitler and Churchill: 'Berlin, eine Radierung Churchills nach einer Idee Hitlers' [Berlin, a Churchill etching after an idea by Hitler].[40]

37 Grünbein, *Das erste Jahr*, pp. 66–67.
38 Grünbein, *Porzellan*, poem 2.
39 The 'black snow' might well reference the 'black milk' of Celan's 'Todesfuge' ['Death Fugue'], the oxymoron figuring an unnatural sequel in the city to the unnatural world, the 'Ausnahmezustand', of the death camp.
40 Bertolt Brecht, *Werke. Große kommentierte Berliner und Frankfurter Ausgabe*, ed. by Werner Hecht and others, 30 vols (Frankfurt a. M.: Suhrkamp, 1988–1998), XXVII: *Journale 2*, p. 281.

The two artistically disposed war leaders have collaborated in the work of rendering what German would call the Berlin *Stadtbild*, the city's 'image', as 'Radierung' – not so much an etching, as an erasure.

These representations of cities under destruction bear the paradox of the *Wunderblock*. They are as if etched in and erased by the two parts of the mnemotechnical instrument. In the *Kriegsfibel*, that double movement is transferred onto the intermedial configuration of epigrammatic text and photograph, with specific reference to the epigrams of Simonides, and especially the famous verse for the Spartan war-dead at Thermopylae. In Brecht's version, the soldiers returning home 'from inhumanity' and called upon to give witness are French prisoners of war, their own freedom from inhumanity still conditional.[41] The memorial stone to the dead of Thermopylae is here as it were the block that underlies the inscription of the epigram and the photographic image, but the photographic and textual evidence of the *Kriegsfibel*, as indeed of Grünbein's image-writing, is of stone that is subject to destruction, blocks that are no more resistant to ravage than porcelain. The frontispiece image of Dresden 'before the destruction' in *Porzellan* or the photographic evidence of not-yet-destroyed structures and bodies that Brecht's texts call upon are always, in the manner of Benjamin's theory of photography, subject to mortality, to ruination. To follow Roland Barthes's development of Benjamin's theory in his *Camera Lucida*, the memorial representations are caught in a sort of future perfect, representing what will have been.[42] It is the same grammatical mode as closes the 'Gedicht über Dresden'.

Brecht, as war poet in exile from Berlin, traces the *Radierung* of the *Trümmerstadt* that was to have been the World Capital Germania through his recalling of where things are to be found in the etched-out city, or the locations where buildings that are ruins-in-the-making will have been. And Grünbein's work on both Dresden and Berlin can be seen as a continuation of that memory work with somewhat different means, in another tense (the melancholic compound past of what *has been*), and for another generation: anamnesis in the face of massive memory loss.

We conclude therefore with the Berlin of Benjamin, Brecht and latterly of Durs Grünbein, turning to another work of Grünbein's which might have a Brechtian intertext, the calendar text largely written out of Berlin at the millennium, *Das erste Jahr*. In his consideration of the historically fraught topography of the new old capital, Grünbein traces in it the after-images of *Germania*, the would-be 'Weltzentrale' [centre of the world],[43] and like Brecht he fashions his textual re-

41 Brecht, *Werke*, XII: *Gedichte 2*, p. 261.
42 Roland Barthes, *Camera Lucida. Reflections on Photography*, trans. by Richard Howard (London: Vintage, 2000), p. 96.
43 Grünbein, *Das erste Jahr*, p. 26.

construction through intermedial effects. The entry for 18 July is an exemplary case of the text's chrono-topographical representations:

> 18. Juli Topographie Berlin. Die Wilhelmstraße, unscheinbares Zentrum des Schreckens: von hier gingen all die Befehle zur Zerstörung des alten Europa aus. Heute wächst Gras auf dem seltsam hügeligen Gelände rings um den prächtigen Gropius-Bau. Irgendwo zwischen Leipziger Straße, Ebert- und Behrensstraße, am Rande des in Windeseile neu besiedelten Potsdamer Platzes, liegen noch, mehrere Meter tief in der Erde, die Bunkeranlagen, versiegelte Überbleibsel der Reichskanzlei, jener Zentraldienststelle für neuere deutsche Geschichte. Oftmals, wenn ich unterwegs bin im Auto, zu Fuß oder per Fahrrad, versuche ich, ausgehend von diesem nunmehr imaginären Mittelpunkt auf der Landkarte die Stationen zu verbinden wie einen Passionsweg, an dem noch heute die historische Szenenfolge ablesbar ist. Da sind, steinerne Schreibtischkästen, abweisend streng, die Botschaften der ehemaligen Achsenmächte Italien und Japan, in begünstigter Lage entlang der Tiergartenstraße, gefolgt von dem Spukschloß des verbündeten Spanien am Neuen See. Dahinter, am Landwehrkanal, steht noch immer der sogenannte Bendlerblock, das Oberkommando der Wehrmacht, in dem der Militärarzt Gottfried Benn aus- und einging. Dort auf dem Innenhof hat man die Verschwörer des 20. Juli erschossen, den Grafen Stauffenberg etwa, der die verbundene Hand in der Schlinge trug. Einen halben Kilometer weiter ragt im Stadtinnern, am Breitscheidplatz, der abgebrochene Flaschenhals der Gedächtniskirche in den Berliner Himmel, der an dieser Stelle, nicht nur im Hochsommer, jenes gleißende Licht ausstrahlt, eine ausgeglühte, stählerne Helligkeit, wie man sie auf den Photographien der Trümmerstadt von 1945 so oft findet. Vielleicht ist es das Licht, das jene Atmosphäre schafft, die alle die Schauplätze von Verbrechen und Katastrophen entlang der Speerschen Ost-West-Achse bis heute verbindet. Noch immer trifft einen das gleiche schneidende Licht, über der Arena und zwischen den Pylonen des Olympiastadions ebenso wie auf dem Brachfeld hinter dem Portal des einstigen Anhalter Bahnhofs, von dem aus die Züge bis zuletzt an die Ostfront rollten. Es ist ein unbarmherziges Licht, wie von jähen Hausdurchbrüchen und Wäldern, die über Nacht abgeholzt wurden. Überall das gleiche erbitterte Gleißen, wo immer Berlin seine Drohung herausbrüllte gegen den Rest der Welt. Überm Rollfeld des Tempelhofer Flughafens, um das riesige Halbrund des Hangars genauso wie beim Anblick der Straßenflucht, die sich dem Cabriofahrer, nachdem er den Funkturm passiert hat, auf der Avus stadtauswärts bietet. Aus allem leuchtet dieselbe Zuversicht der Reichshauptstadt *Germania* gnadenlos, wie nur die Wochenschau sie den Anbetern auf die gepanzerten Stirnen schrieb.
>
> [18 July Topography Berlin. The Wilhelmstraße, unprepossessing centre of terror: from here all the orders for destruction of the old Europe went out. Today grass grows upon the strangely hilly ground all around the splendid Gropius Building. Somewhere between Leipziger Straße, Ebert- and Behrensstraße, at the edge of the Potsdamer Platz, settled anew like wildfire, there still lies, several metres deep in the ground, the bunker complex, sealed remainder of the Reich Chancellery, that centre of operations for modern German history. Often when I am out and about by car, on foot or by bike, I try, departing from this now imaginary centre-point on the map, to connect the stations like a *via dolorosa*, on which still today the historical sequence of scenes is legible. There are those stone desk cupboards, dismissive and stern, the embassies of the one-time axis powers, Italy and Japan, in a favourable position along the Tiergartenstraße, followed by the haunted castle of allied Spain on the Neuer See. Behind these, on the Landwehrkanal, the Bendler block still stands, the cen-

> tral headquarters of the Wehrmacht, where the military doctor Gottfried Benn came and went. There they shot the conspirators of 20 July, Count Stauffenberg for instance, who carried his bandaged hand in a sling. Half a kilometre further on, in the centre of the city, on the Breitscheidplatz, the broken bottle-neck of the Memorial Church rises into the Berlin sky, which at this place, and not just in the high summer, radiates that stark light, an after-glowing steely brightness such as you so often find on photographs of the city in ruins after 1945. Perhaps it is the light that creates that atmosphere that still today connects all the scenes of crimes and catastrophes along Speer's East-West axis. You still encounter the same cutting light above the arena and between the pylons of the Olympic Stadium as well as on the waste-land behind the portal of the one-time Anhalter Station, from which the trains ran to the last to the Eastern Front. It is a pitiless light, as if from the sudden breaking through of houses or woods cut down over night. Everywhere the same embittered starkness of light, wherever Berlin bellowed out its threat against the rest of the world. Over the runways of Tempelhof airfield, around the giant half-circle of the hangar just as at the view of the flight of roads that offers itself to the driver of a convertible after he has passed the Radio Tower on his way out of town on the Avus motorway. Out of all of this there shines, merciless, the same confidence of the Imperial Capital *Germania*, as was only written by the weekly newsreel on the armoured foreheads of the worshippers.][44]

From the sealed Reich Chancellery bunker as imaginary or phantasmatic central point, the artist of memory as topographer projects an allegorical *via dolorosa* through stations that give evidence of, make legible, the historical *mise-en-scène* of National Socialism. The evidence in question is in the nature of the *Wunderblock*. Beyond the absent presence of the bunker, there are the monumental Nazi era buildings that still remain, un-ruined, from the axis-power embassies to the Olympiastadion and Tempelhof, and there are the ruins of the Memorial Church and the façade of the Anhalter Station, or the wasteland behind it where a great terminus once stood (a terminus that already for Benjamin, before its historical ruination, was an allegorical scene of arrest).[45] There are the hidden hole in the ground, the empty surface, the ruined remains; and there are the uncannily still-present representative structures – Pompeian architectures, resistant building-blocks. For our purposes these can be represented by the Wehrmacht headquarters in the still-standing 'Bendlerblock', a historical block in more senses than one, and one associated with injury (Stauffenberg's arm in the sling), pathology (Gottfried Benn, the doctor-poet, coming and going), and killing. 'Topographie' can be understood here in its literal sense, as the drawing or writing of space (the topography here is repeatedly marked as scene of writing and reading). And the Bendlerblock and other scenic remainders represent the topography of Berlin

---

44 Ibid., pp. 93–94.

45 See Webber, *Berlin in the Twentieth Century*, pp. 82–83.

as *Wunderblock* in its most ambivalent sense (recalling once more the traumatic resonance of 'Wunde'). Blocked out of the representation is the most significant historical trauma of the city and the one most resistant to adequate memorial inscription, the Holocaust, so that the remains of the Anhalter Station are recorded as a façade for a scene of troop movements rather than of deportation.

This chrono-topographical system or *Zeitraum* of blocks, of void space and of fragments is seen and read in a particular historical light. It is the unnatural lighting effect of both the propaganda images of *Germania* in the Nazi-era newsreels and of post-war photographs of the city in ruins: the lighting effects that supported the propaganda apparatus of Nazism, not least in the medium of film, and those returned upon it after the fact to expose its ruin. This bright, steely, cutting, remorseless light is however also dimmed, the light of historical ruin, cast as it is, as if through breaks in buildings. It is, we might say, the characteristic light of allegory, reminiscent of that which falls on spectacles of topographic and architectural glory and ruin in the proto-cinematic dioramas and panoramas as described by Benjamin.[46] It is an uncanny, phantom light that Grünbein then relays, after Benjamin, in the poem on his 'Kindheit im Diorama' ['Childhood in the Diorama'].[47]

In Benjamin's terms, history has allegorically entered the *Schauplatz* here as ruin,[48] an effect of *mise-en-scène* that is co-produced by the historical scene-recording media of photography and newsreel. In the allegorical style, the light – steely and cutting – works between image and text, as the text of Nazi propaganda is inscribed through the pictures on the armoured foreheads of cinema viewers. In the style of the *Wunderblock*, these letters of light are fleeting, self-erasing effects of projection on celluloid, but also etched in. In the dialectical sense developed above, they are *radiert*. The scene enacts this double movement of inscription and erasure through a particular constellation of urban space, historical moment and psychic impact. For the psycho-chrono-topography of Berlin here, as for that other *Wunderstadt* Dresden elsewhere, Grünbein deploys the urban arts of memory to encounter, explore and expose in its evidence, distortions and resistances what we might indeed call a *Wunderblock*.

---

46 Walter Benjamin, *Gesammelte Schriften*, ed. by Rolf Tiedemann and Hermann Schweppenhäuser (Frankfurt a. M.: Suhrkamp, 1991), V: *Das Passagen-Werk*, pp. 654–65; VII: *Nachträge*, pp. 388–89.

47 Durs Grünbein, 'Kindheit im Diorama', in *Strophen für übermorgen*, p. 20. See also the chapter by Klein in this volume.

48 For Benjamin, when history enters the 'Schauplatz' in the *Trauerspiel*, it does so as the pictographic script of transience or ruination, written allegorically on the 'face' of nature. Walter Benjamin, *Gesammelte Schriften*, I: *Ursprung des deutschen Trauerspiels*, pp. 353–54.

Sonja Klein

'Speak, memory!' Durs Grünbein's *Strophen für übermorgen*

> Draußen die Nacht – im Innern ihr Hall.
> So von Geburt an, so wird es sein
>
> In all den Jahren, der Zeit, die dir bleibt.
> Zu atmen, zu sterben im freien Fall ...
>
> [Outside the night – inside its echo. / It will be like this from birth onward // Through all those years, the time you'll have left. / To breathe, to die in free fall].[1]

These lines open Durs Grünbein's collection *Strophen für übermorgen* and foreshadow the poetic essence of the following two hundred pages of highly complex verse. Entitled 'Spruchtäfelchen' ['Votive tablet'], the poem cited above points to a fundamental part of Grünbein's poetological agenda: the word 'Spruchtäfelchen' – which could be understood as either plural or singular – recalls the votives that were offered up to the gods of the dead in antiquity and that were the precursors of the later tradition of sentential tablets. Made either of stone or metal, these tablets communicated texts thanking a god or deity for escape from some dire threat, and they can often be seen hanging on the walls of chapels, churches and other sacred sites. Nowadays, such tablets have assumed a more secular role: made of wood and often painted in bright colours, they offer proverbs and adages for everyday life.

On the face of it, Grünbein's 'Spruchtäfelchen' seems like a fairly traditional articulation of praise to the gods. Yet the poem does not offer placatory sentiments for the 'Dis manibus', nor a plea for mercy or redemption, but, rather, the startling confirmation that death has already triumphed over all. Marking the reciprocity between 'zu atmen' and 'zu sterben', between inspiring and expiring, or breathing your last, death is inscribed in the body from the very inception of life; the 'Zeit, die dir bleibt' is unquestionably the time in which we advance towards death. The laconic 'so wird es sein' leaves the reader in no doubt that the start of this period of 'free fall' coincides with the very beginning of existence. From its very first poem, *Strophen für übermorgen* signals a terminal downward spiral that seems inexorable.

1 Durs Grünbein, *Strophen für übermorgen* (Frankfurt a. M.: Suhrkamp, 2007), p. 9.

This is an unusual way for a poetry collection to open, beginning as it does with its own end and setting out by asserting its own finitude. One is reminded of Novalis's *Hymnen an die Nacht* [*Hymns to the Night*], in which the lyric subject turns his attention from the start to the falling of night and, implicitly, to death: 'Abwärts wend ich mich zu der heiligen, unaussprechlichen, geheimnißvollen Nacht' [Downward I turn to the sacred, unspeakable, mysterious night].[2] Or one might be reminded of Matthias Claudius, whose first volume of *Sämtliche Werke des Wandsbecker Boten* [*Collected Works of the Wandsbeck Messenger*] of 1775 is dedicated to the familiar 'Freund Hain' [Friend Hain], i.e. death, who appears 'als Schutz- und Hausgott vorn an der Haustüre' [as one of the lares or the patron saint at the front door] to his book.[3] Two hundred years later, Samuel Beckett would begin his play *Endgame* with the declaration: 'Fini, c'est fini'. Everything begins with an end, yet this seemingly leads into a poetic vacuum, as the scope of art manifestly fails in the face of death. None of the poets mentioned is silenced by this, however.

In *Strophen für übermorgen* we are presented with a 'Spruchtäfelchen' that could easily be read as a motto for Grünbein's entire oeuvre, as it inextricably unites both the polarizing and central elements of his art in a single verse: mortality and memory. While 'Draußen die Nacht' refers to the transience of all objects and people, 'im Innern ihr Hall' presages memory as the final, poetic echo of what has long since vanished. Grünbein's tone is as unassuming as it is Stoic – 'so wird es sein' – and it is characteristic of his work since the turn of the millennium, most prominently in *Erklärte Nacht* (2002), *Vom Schnee oder Descartes in Deutschland* (2003), *Porzellan. Poem vom Untergang meiner Stadt* (2005) and his collection *Aroma. Ein römisches Zeichenbuch* (2010).

Grünbein's artistic career, however, started on an entirely different track: as a representative of the stylistic avant-garde in the 1980s and 1990s he almost playfully deconstructed traditional lyric forms. Collections such as *Grauzone morgens*, *Schädelbasislektion* and *Falten und Fallen* 'pushed' – as Grünbein stated in his first collection of essays, *Galilei vermißt Dantes Hölle* (1996) – the poetic 'Bruchstücke' [fragments] of 'the unreconciled, the irreconcilable, [...] into [an] abrupt montage' [das Unversöhnte, in schockhafter Montage gefügte].[4] In these

2 Novalis, 'Hymnen an die Nacht', in *Werke, Tagebücher und Briefe Friedrich von Hardenbergs*, ed. by Hans-Joachim Mähl and Richard Samuel (Munich: Hanser, 1988), I, p. 149.

3 Matthias Claudius, *Sämtliche Werke* (Düsseldorf: Artemis & Winkler, 1984), p. 11.

4 Durs Grünbein, 'Mein babylonisches Hirn', in *Galilei vermißt Dantes Hölle und bleibt an den Maßen hängen. Aufsätze 1989–1995* (Frankfurt a. M.: Suhrkamp, 1996), pp. 18–33 (p. 19); 'My Babylonish Brain', in *The Bars of Atlantis. Selected Essays*, ed. by Michael Eskin, trans. by John Crutchfield, Michael Hofmann and Andrew Shields (New York: Farrar, Straus and Giroux, 2010), pp. 59–71 (p. 60).

early poems, the body figured as the main theme and was accurately and mercilessly dissected. Initially, Grünbein held firmly to this idea: 'Zunächst, und daran glaube ich fest, geht alles wirksame Schreiben vom Körper aus' [First and foremost, and this is something I believe absolutely, all effective writing emanates from the body].[5] And indeed, this is how his volume *Schädelbasislektion* begins – with the lines: 'Was du bist steht am Rand / Anatomischer Tafeln' [What you are is defined in the margins / Of anatomical plates].[6]

The poetry of these early years combined the coolly precise vocabulary of the modern sciences with that of the creative arts and in so doing united 'the two cultures' of the sciences and the humanities.[7] The result was a series of highly complex poems in which disparate images, impressions and quotations were joined together in quick succession. In this 'vivisection' of reality, we see the poet's desire to gauge the abundance of worldly phenomena against the mirror of the body and the traces of memory it carries inside:

> Der lyrische Text ist ein Protokoll der inneren Blicke. Der Körper bestimmt, was die Methode ist. Hinter der semantischen Ordnung zeigt sich die anatomische; unter den Schichten, die Hermeneutik wälzt, kommt das lebendige Gewebe zum Vorschein [...]. Denn das Gedicht führt das Denken in einer Folge physiologischer Kurzschlüsse vor.
>
> [The poetic text is the protocol of an inner gazing. Its method is determined by the body. Behind the semantic organization there is always an anatomical one; under the layers that hermeneutics churn, the living cells come to the surface [...]. A poem trots out thought in a sequence of physiological short circuits.][8]

As an excavator who, in line with Walter Benjamin's famous 'thought image',[9] digs up remnants of the past, the poet sets out on a journey through the realm of enigmatic images produced in the brain, through what he terms, referencing Baudelaire, his 'babylonisches Hirn' [Babylonish brain]. Within this self-styled

5 Durs Grünbein, 'Drei Briefe', in *Galilei vermißt Dantes Hölle*, pp. 40–54 (p. 40).
6 Durs Grünbein, 'Was du bist', in *Schädelbasislektion* (Frankfurt a. M.: Suhrkamp, 1991), p. 11.
7 See Charles P. Snow's influential and much debated lecture, 'The Two Cultures', delivered in 1959, in which he argued that the gap between sciences and humanities (the 'two cultures') was a major problem for modern society.
8 Grünbein, 'Mein babylonisches Hirn', p. 33; 'My Babylonish Brain', p. 71.
9 See Benjamin's 'thought image' entitled *Excavation and Memory*: 'He who seeks to approach his own buried past must conduct himself like a man digging'. Walter Benjamin, 'Denkbilder. Ausgraben und Erinnern', in *Gesammelte Schriften*, ed. by Rolf Tiedemann and Hermann Schweppenhäuser, 17 vols (Frankfurt a. M.: Suhrkamp, 1972–1999), IV.1, pp. 400–401; *Selected Writings*, ed. by Michael Jennings (Cambridge, MA: Belknap Press of Harvard University Press, 1996–2003), II, p. 611.

'physiological poetics' or 'Neuro-Poetik', the poet sketches a cerebral cosmos that he fathoms with his poetic sonar. Thus, for Grünbein, at this point, poetry was the result of fragments of memory brought to light from the depths of the body:

> Das Erreichen tiefer Hirnareale, die Markierung in Form einzigartiger Engramme, das ist sein [des Dichters] Ziel, und insofern liegt in der Neurologie die Poetik der Zukunft versteckt. Auf der Jagd nach den Gedächtnisspuren unterwirft er alle anderen Belange seines Lebens der fixen Idee, nur dafür da zu sein, ihn an das Kontinuum verdichteter Bilder anzuschließen, darin liegt das unheilbar Manische seines Tuns. Ein Vers des Kallimachos aus Kyrene bringt ihm genausoviel Gegenwart wie der Zuruf des Postboten vor der Tür.
>
> [Gaining access to the deeper areas of the brain, notation in the form of unique engrams – these are his [the poet's] goals; and this is why the poetics of the future is contained in neurology. In his quest for memory traces, the poet subordinates all other concerns to the obsessive notion that the whole purpose of his existence consists in joining the continuum of condensed images – herein lies the incurable mania of his pursuit. A line of Callimachus of Cyrene is as present to him as the postman's ring at the door.][10]

But this early withdrawal into a physiological world was then, as now, overshadowed by the 'Zerbrechlichkeit des Körpers' [fragility of the body][11] – the inevitability of death. On the one hand, the body acts as a mnemonic medium, an agent of another cosmos far removed from, and far greater than, the manifestations of the external world; on the other hand, it remains subject to the laws of temporality and the immutable fragility imposed by the transience of nature. 'Wohin wollte er bloß' [Where on earth was he headed], was the early query born of resignation, 'mit diesem zerbrechlichen Körper, diesem leicht auszulöschenden Hirn' [with this fragile body, with this brain so easily destroyed].[12] In *Falten und Fallen* we read:

> Grundlos, wie Leben entsteht, ist es bereit
>   zu vergehn in den Kehlen,
> Durch die Finger zu rinnen, die Wand hinab.
>   Was sich nie ausging, war Angst.
>
> [As providentially as life comes into being / It's ready to go again, in your throat, / Between your fingers, dribbling down the walls. / What remained constant was fear.][13]

---

10 'Mein babylonisches Hirn', pp. 20–21; 'My Babylonish Brain', p. 61.

11 See Durs Grünbein, 'Den Körper zerbrechen', in *Galilei vermißt Dantes Hölle*, pp. 75–86; 'Breaking the Body', in *The Bars of Atlantis*, pp. 12–21.

12 Durs Grünbein, *Falten und Fallen* (Frankfurt a. M.: Suhrkamp, 1994), p. 88.

13 Ibid., p. 34; Durs Grünbein, *Ashes for Breakfast*, trans. by Michael Hofmann (New York: Farrar, Straus and Giroux, 2005), p. 143.

Accordingly, the apparent poetic union with the body becomes a dangerous complicity, an unrelenting *memento mori* far removed from the promising youthfulness of an up-and-coming writer. The imminence and constant fear of mortality is inscribed in every line, and it is this premonition that Grünbein attempts to overcome in his first phase as a poet. His youthful consciousness of death engenders the unremitting quality, the sarcasm, the severity and perhaps even the recalcitrance that characterize these poems. At this stage, the poetic phrase 'Draußen die Nacht' was still couched in more caustically specific terms: 'Diese Scheiß Sterblichkeit' [This bloody mortality].[14]

All of this brought Grünbein, at the comparatively young age of 33, the coveted Büchner Prize in 1995 and universal critical praise for a body of work considered to be a forward-looking 'poetry of fragments'.[15] Scholars and reviewers were all the more surprised then, when he went on to publish *Nach den Satiren* in 1999, a collection which seemed to confound the expectations many had of him as an angry young man. To the chagrin of many German critics, the ruptured forms and metres of the early works were replaced in the collections that followed by an increasingly formal harmony, a return to classical metres and subjects and a generally less abrasive aesthetic approach. 'Perhaps', one reviewer lamented, 'this multilingual solidity that has made Durs Grünbein so well-known will one day be called his early work. [...] In terms of form and metre, Grünbein has belied his own programme'.[16] This was not to be the last time the poet would find himself misconstrued as formalistic or as one who had made 'a premature retreat into solemn classicism'.[17] For a long time the decisive transformation in Grünbein's aesthetics remained unexplained, with many German scholars continuing to concentrate on the early works, but recently there has been a shift of focus.

Against this background, the poem 'Ein Kolonist in Octodurus' ['A Colonist in Octodurus'] in *Strophen für übermorgen* can be read as Grünbein's response to the criticism levelled against him since 2000. Donning a poetic mask, the lyric subject gives voice to his alienation and seems to withdraw into internal exile.

14 Grünbein, *Schädelbasislektion*, p. 11.

15 See Michael Braun, 'Vom Rand her verlöschen die Bilder. Zu Durs Grünbeins Lyrik und Poetik des Fragments', *Text + Kritik*, 153.1 (2002), 4–18.

16 Sebastian Kiefer, 'Schock und klassisches Maß', *Neue deutsche Literatur*, July / August 1999, 138–42 (p. 138).

17 See Michael Braun, 'Die vernetzte Zunge des Propheten. Eine kleine Strömungslehre zur Poesie im 21. Jahrhundert', *Neue Zürcher Zeitung*, 1 October 2005, p. 17.

Nun sitz ich hier, ein Exot unter Galliern,
Spiel mit der einen Hand Flöte unterm Gewand,
Dreh mit der anderen einen Jüngling aus Marmor,
Attis sein Name, kalt wie ein Bergsee und schön.

[Now here I sit, an exotic amongst Gauls, / Playing a flute under my robe with one hand, / Turning a youth made of marble in the other, / Attis his name, cold as a mountain lake and beautiful.][18]

The 'Exot', who finds himself alone among barbarians, is forced to pursue his art clandestinely, his song remains unheard. As a kind of talisman he holds the 'Teuren Toten' [dear departed],[19] a marble figure of Attis, a symbol for the dead often depicted on tombstones as a sign of sorrow. This poem portrays someone who maintains close contact with the dead and continues the 'Zwiegespräch mit den Toten' [dialogue with the dead] so vital to Grünbein's writings, and it underscores the importance of tradition by erecting a 'Bridge to Antiquity'.[20] Of course, the marble that Attis is made from promises to outlast the wood in which the 'barbarians' surrounding the lyric subject carve their 'klägliche[n] Götzenbilder, Fratzen und Bestien' [pathetic idols, grimaces and beasts]. The pedestrian and pliable quality of wood, as well as its propensity to decay quickly, is a clear counterpoint to the durability of marble. 'Ein Stoff wie der Stein da' [A material like that stone], Grünbein writes in 'An der Tiberiusbrücke' ['At the Tiberius Bridge'], which 'Geschichte nichts anging, Verfall und Verkehr' [was unaffected by history, dealings and decay].[21] This striking contrast can be construed as a criticism of the fleetingness of contemporary art, which is no longer in a position to remember its cultural roots – something that Grünbein had already pointed out in his literary 'diary' of 2000, *Das erste Jahr*: 'Schon der flüchtigste Blick in eine beliebige Anthologie zeigt: am Ende des zwanzigsten Jahrhunderts ist Lyrik ein Sammelsurium aus Register-Arien für das Banale geworden, ein rhythmisierter Versandhauskatalog' [Even the hastiest glance in any anthology you care to choose demonstrates that lyric poetry at the close of the twentieth century has become a hotchpotch of standardized arias to banality, a rhythmic mail order catalogue].[22]

18 Grünbein, *Strophen für übermorgen*, p. 161.
19 See Durs Grünbein, *Den teuren Toten. 33 Epitaphe* (Frankfurt a. M.: Suhrkamp, 1994).
20 Durs Grünbein, *Das erste Jahr. Berliner Aufzeichnungen* (Frankfurt a. M.: Suhrkamp, 2001), p. 99. See Michael Eskin, '"Bridge to Antiquity". Nostalgia, Exile, and Stoicism in the Poetry of Durs Grünbein', *arcadia*, 39.2 (2004), 356–81.
21 Grünbein, *Strophen für übermorgen*, p. 163.
22 Grünbein, *Das erste Jahr*, p. 246.

The exiled colonist, from whom the 'Siegelring' [signet ring], once a sign of his allegiance to the Emperor, has been confiscated, and whose most treasured relic, the 'kostbares Steingut, der Krug aus Tarent' [precious earthenware, the jug from Tarentum], has apparently been shattered,[23] continues to languish. Tarentum, at once Horace's utopia as well as the idyllic space of the poet and of poetry, seems all the more remote and unattainable in the rocky valley of Octodurus with its 'betrübliche[r] Fluß' [sad river].

This could be one reason for the ostensible escapism expressed in the title *Strophen für übermorgen*, which suggests that a poet who had previously turned his back on the future to fathom the past still in fact hopes that times, and the understanding of poetry, might change. He is not writing stanzas for 'today', but for all those 'die einem dereinst wirklich zuhören können, den unbekannten Lesern von morgen' [who could really one day listen to you, tomorrow's unknown readers].[24] Yet, there are other ways of understanding the title of Grünbein's collection, not least because it is reminiscent of Nietzsche's *Weisheit für übermorgen* [*Wisdom for the Day after Tomorrow*].[25] Assembling aphorisms, thoughts and maxims, Nietzsche's *Weisheit für übermorgen* holds up a mirror to the philosopher's entire intellectual range. *Strophen für übermorgen* is comparable, as we shall see, in that it, too, reflects the broad spectrum of Grünbein's works, from his earliest to his most recent.

Let us consider 'Kindheit im Diorama' ['Childhood in the Diorama'], the fifth poem in the first section of the volume:

> Seltsam, als Kind schon zog ihn Erstarrtes an.
> In den Museen stand er lange vorm Diorama
> Mit den Tieren im Stillstand, natürlich gruppiert
> Vor gemalte Fernen, Urwaldszenen und Himalayas.
> Wie im Märchen, verzaubert, horchten die Rehe auf,
> Trat man im Neonlicht näher mit funkelnden Augen.
> Am Schädel des Höhlenmenschen gleich nebenan

---

23 Indeed, this is an apt metaphor for the 'shattering' response to Grünbein's poetic cycle *Porzellan* in 2005, when reviews compared his poems about the bombing of Dresden in World War II amongst other things to the 'bad jokes of a talkshow-host fooling around'. For a more detailed discussion on this topic, see Sonja Klein, *'Denn alles, alles ist verlorne Zeit'. Fragment und Erinnerung im Werk von Durs Grünbein* (Bielefeld: Aisthesis, 2008), pp. 180–87.

24 Durs Grünbein, 'Warum schriftlos leben', in *Warum schriftlos leben. Aufsätze* (Frankfurt a. M.: Suhrkamp, 2003), pp. 34–65 (p. 62); 'Why Live without Writing', in *The Bars of Atlantis*, pp. 92–115 (p. 113).

25 Friedrich Nietzsche, *Weisheit für übermorgen. Unterstreichungen aus dem Nachlaß* (Munich: DTV, 1994).

Sah er das Loch und vergaß den Keulenhieb
Des Rivalen, den Kampf um die Feuerstelle.
Die ägyptische Mumie hielt Jahrtausenden stand
Mit entferntem Gehirn. Erst beim Schmelzen
Des Ewigen Eises kam dieses Mammut ans Licht.
Die schönsten Schmetterlinge, handtellergroß,
Fand er auf Nadeln gespießt. Einmal schien ihm
Als ob ihre Flügel noch bebten, wie in Erinnerung
An die gefällten Bäume, den tropischen Wind.
Vielleicht daß ein Luftzug durch Schaukästen ging.

[Strange, already as a child he was drawn to the inert.
In museums he would long pause in front of the diorama
With the animals at a standstill, grouped naturally
Against painted scapes, dense forest scenes and Himalaya
Fairy-tale-like, enchanted, the deer would prick up their ears,
As soon as one stepped closer in the neon light, eyes aglow.
Next door, he saw the hole in the caveman's skull
And forgot about the rival's club blow,
Their battle over the fire site.
The Egyptian mummy had withstood millennia
With its brain removed. Only with the melting
Of perpetual ice had this mammoth come to light.
The most beautiful butterflies, palm-size,
He saw skewered with pins. Once, it was
As if their wings were still quivering – in memory
Of all those felled trees and tropical winds.
A draft, perhaps, had blown through the display.][26]

As in 'Spruchtäfelchen', this poetic scene of childhood visits to museums conjures up transience and death. The animals perceived at a standstill are stuffed and hence far removed from their natural habitat. The 'funkelnden Augen' of the child observer are entranced by the *nature morte* of the diorama instead of focusing on the live animals at the zoo. The butterflies – 'Die schönsten Schmetterlinge, handtellergroß' – prove to be dead, 'auf Nadeln gespießt'.

And again the end is also the beginning. The memory of the diorama reconfigured in the poem serves as the scene for an initiation that in retrospect takes on the quality of an epiphany. Here, among the stuffed cadavers of the animals set within the 'verzauberten Schaubildern' [enchanted scenes],[27] the child

26 Grünbein, *Strophen für übermorgen*, p. 20; *The Bars of Atlantis*, p. 22.
27 Durs Grünbein, 'Kindheit im Diorama', in *Galilei vermißt Dantes Hölle*, pp. 116–28 (p. 126); 'Childhood in the Diorama', in *The Bars of Atlantis*, pp. 22–31 (p. 29).

experiences a revelation of his premature demise and a precocious sense of the fragility of time: 'Seltsam', the first line expresses with incredulity, 'als Kind schon zog ihn Erstarrtes an'. The sparkling eyes of the child's gaze observe inanimate material and lifelessness, yet the youthful observer deduces – long before the notion becomes manifest in lyrical form – that lurking behind the stillness of death there is the never-ending promise of another, and more lasting, existence, one comprised of memories of what was once conserved for posterity in the glass cases. Inside the museum, between the 'Bruchstücke [...] d[er] verlorene[n] Paradies[e]' [fragments of paradises lost], – which Proust saw as the only true kinds of paradise, – the poet is confronted with a painful paradox: only those objects that have been lost forever can be rediscovered; only those elements can endure that have been removed from all temporality and no longer exist.[28]

What appears to the child while looking at the dead butterflies is a fragment of memory: 'Als ob ihre Flügel noch bebten, wie in Erinnerung / An die gefällten Bäume, den tropischen Wind'. The butterflies, traditionally symbolizing metamorphosis and rebirth, are products of their poetic stasis, which is their final transformation. They are immortal only because they have died; being conserved under glass is analogous to being remembered in poetic verse. The 'Luftzug', the 'draught' that flows through the cases and causes their wings to quiver, stems from the breath or pneuma of poetry.

Although 'Kindheit im Diorama' was picked up and admired in almost every review of *Strophen für übermorgen*, it actually cites a previous poetological confession. First published some eleven years earlier, it headed an essay (of the same title) in Grünbein's *Galilei vermißt Dantes Hölle*.[29] Despite being written during what is generally seen as *another* phase of Grünbein's artistic development, it could be seamlessly subsumed into the later volume, because it focuses on the motifs of death and memory that have dominated his writing from the start.

Just as in 'Spruchtäfelchen' and 'Kindheit im Diorama', the poetic voice originates in the programmatic poem 'Achillessehne' ['Achilles Tendon'] at the very moment the lyric subject becomes aware of his own mortality:

28 Grünbein, 'Kindheit im Diorama', p. 128; 'Childhood in the Diorama', p. 31. The Proust quotation runs 'car les vrais paradis sont les paradis qu'on a perdus' [since the true paradises are the paradises that we have lost]. Marcel Proust, *À la recherche du temps perdu* (Paris: Éditions Gallimard, 1990), VII: *Le temps retrouvé*, p. 177.
29 See Grünbein, *Galilei vermißt Dantes Hölle*, p. 116.

Und plötzlich war dein Fuß, der linke Fuß
Versunken wie in einer Moosschicht, die gab nach,
Der Knöchel weggesackt, und trat ins Weiche, Leere.
Und unter ihm der Boden tat sich auf, kein Halt mehr.
Gerissen die Achillessehne – wie eine Saite springt.

[And suddenly your foot, the left foot / Sank as if into moss that gave way, / The ankle buckled, and stepped into softness, emptiness. / And under it the ground opened up, no grip anymore. / The Achilles tendon torn – snaps like a string.][30]

The torn tendon, which 'wie eine Saite springt', evokes associations with the string of a lyre, itself a symbol of poetry. However, it also emphasizes the fragility of the body, and is the starting point for an extensive mnemonic process: 'Ein Fallenlassen bis hinab zur Kindheit' [A falling into the depths of childhood]. The narrator's fall, caused by the 'Ausfallschritt beim Federball' [lunge while playing badminton], leads to another, even deeper fall that does not end on the 'Hallenboden' [gymnasium floor], but in the re-evaluation of life long past.

Und noch am selben Abend wird man aufgeschnitten,
Liegt da mit Schlauch im Mund und weiß nicht mehr,
Wo all die Jahre hin sind bis hierher.

[And the very same evening you are sliced open, / Lying there with the tube in your mouth, not knowing, / What happened to all those years gone by.][31]

The involuntary fall gives way to a voluntary 'Fallenlassen' into childhood. Accordingly, everything begins with the end, as the poem itself reaffirms: 'Da fing es an, vielleicht fing es da an' [That's where it all began, perhaps that's where it began].

The injury to the body – which, as already indicated in 'Spruchtäfelchen', is 'Komplize der Nacht' [complicit with the night] that conspires with death – arises from the 'Ausfallschritt', the 'lunge' and, at the same time (in its second meaning) from a 'deviation' from the trodden path. In this guise, it harks back to Proust's stumbling block, which in the final volume of *À la recherche du temps perdu* leads to a complete submersion in the past and eventually to 'finding time again'.

The implicit reference to Proust here is no mere intertextual charade, but rather both a homage and a profession of poetic inspiration. For the influence of Proust's writings on the poet can hardly be overstated: 'Keine Frage, mein liebster

30 Grünbein, *Strophen für übermorgen*, p. 169.
31 Ibid.

Roman [...] ist Marcel Prousts *Suche nach der verlorenen Zeit*' [Without a doubt, my favourite novel is Marcel Proust's *In Search of Lost Time*], Grünbein avows.[32] And this is not simply lip service. Again and again, in his writings and interviews, he returns to *Recherche* and its author, this 'Gedächtnisforscher in schriftstellerischer Verkleidung' [sublime researcher into matters mnemonic].[33] The extent to which many of the motifs and strands of his lyrical poetry are interwoven with Proust has already been shown. In line with this important intertext, the lyric subject in 'Achillessehne' also begins a journey into the past. His 'Humpeln' [limping], which interrupts the continuous and regular course of the present, leads back to times lost. The pain caused by the lame foot is mirrored in the pain that is instigated by the sudden awareness of the losses of the past. Hence, it is no longer the tendon that is painful in the final stanza but the '*Rückreise*' [return journey] as 'ein Wort, / [...] das plötzlich weh tat' [a word / [...] that suddenly hurt]. At this point the poet implicitly cites Nietzsche, who wrote about memory: 'nur was nicht aufhört, *weh zu thun*, bleibt im Gedächtniss' [only something that never ceases *to cause pain* stays in the memory].[34]

In *Strophen für übermorgen*, we follow the author's gaze moving away from the present and into the mnemonic spaces within his inner sanctum of remembrance. Thus 'Der Astronom' ['The Astronomer'] begins with the programmatic admonition:

> Nimm nichts von draußen an, es lohnt sich nicht.
> Denn was da draußen geht, kreist nur um sich
> Wie du, der nur um sich kreist hier im Innern.
> Da ist der Mond, er scheint auf dünnes Eis
> Und bleibt doch Mond wie einer, der schon weiß,
> Es lohnt sich nicht, die Erde zu erinnern.

> [Take nothing from out there, it's not worth it, you'll find. / For what goes on outside, merely spirals in slow decline / Like you, who turns circles here within. / There is the moon: on the thin ice it glows / And yet the moon remains, like one who already knows / That reminding the earth is not worth the trouble.][35]

---

32 Durs Grünbein, 'Abkürzungen durch die Unendlichkeit', *Süddeutsche Zeitung*, 7 April 2006, p. 16.

33 Grünbein, 'Warum schriftlos leben', p. 46; 'Why Live without Writing', p. 101.

34 Friedrich Nietzsche, 'Zur Genealogie der Moral. Eine Streitschrift', in *Sämtliche Werke in 15 Bänden*, ed. by Giorgi Colli and Mazzino Montanari, 2nd edn (Berlin: de Gruyter, 1988), V, p. 295.

35 Grünbein, *Strophen für übermorgen*, p. 139.

The image of the astronomer gazing at the planets and stars is transformed into that of someone who has turned away from the once secure points of orientation in the external world. 'Nimm nichts von draußen an' – an imperative that recalls the famous admonition in Goethe's poem 'Vermächtnis' ['Legacy'] of 1829: 'Sofort nun wende dich nach innen, / Das Zentrum findest du da drinnen / Woran kein Edler zweifeln mag' [Now turn inwards straight away / You will find the centre in there / Which no noble soul can deny].[36] Pondering his inner world, the astronomer clings to the 'Kosmos im Kopf' [cosmos in his head].[37] Just as the stars orbit along their own fixed path, so the astronomer in the poem remains closed off within his own neuronal memory space. 'Wie du, der nur um sich kreist, hier im Innern'. The theme of orbiting, which recurs as the main motif and can even be experienced sensually in the process of reading via repetition and chiastic transposition ('es lohnt sich nicht' in l. 1 and l. 6; 'draußen' in l. 1 and l. 2; 'kreist nur um sich' in l. 3, 'nur um sich kreist' in l. 4; 'Mond' in l. 4 and l. 5), reveals the impracticality of bringing both universes together. External and internal spheres only revolve around one another and remain as separate as 'moon' and 'earth', as 'inside' and 'outside', as 'Draußen die Nacht' and 'im Innern ihr Hall'.

Some sixteen years before this poem, Grünbein had already developed the image of the parallel, yet incompatible worlds of inner and outer reality within an allegorical representation of space. In *Schädelbasislektion*, he portrays the world of the body as sole authority:

Denk von den Wundrändern her, vom Veto
Der Eingeweide, vom Schweigen
Der Schädelnähte. Das Aufgehn der Monde
Über den Nagelbetten führt
Andere Himmel herauf, strenger gestirnt.
Lachhaft die Höhenflüge, getrübt
Aus den engen Knochenhöhlen der Ausblick
Auf Kloaken und Gräberreihen,
Hautflecken, zyklisch, und Sternenbilder, nah.
Weiter ist hier die Umlaufbahn,
Länger dauert es in den kälteren Nächten
Bis die Blutung gestillt ist, Hunger
Den Körper versiegelt, das Schwarze Loch.

36 Johann Wolfgang Goethe, 'Vermächtnis', in *Sämtliche Werke nach Epochen seines Schaffens. Münchner Ausgabe*, ed. by Karl Richter and others, 25 vols (Munich: Hanser, 1985–1998), XVIII.1, pp. 35–36 (p. 35).
37 See *Gehirn und Denken. Kosmos im Kopf*, ed. by Deutsches Hygiene-Museum in cooperation with Via Lewandowsky and Durs Grünbein (Ostfildern-Ruit: Hatje Cantz, 2000).

[Think from the rim of wounds, from the veto
  Of the intestines, the silence
Of the cranial seams. The moonrise
  Of your fingernails adduces
Other heavens more sternly starred.
  Strange the flights, the dim view
From narrow bone arches
  Of cloacas and tombstones,
Scraps of skin, cyclical and constellations at hand.
  The orbit is more generous here,
It takes longer on chillier nights
  For the bleeding to be stanched,
And hunger to tamp the body, the black hole.][38]

The cosmos in the brain is 'weiter' and 'strenger gestirnt' than the heaven of the outer world, which the eye is able to observe on its ludicrous flights through the 'engen Knochenhöhlen'. Looking outward, all that can be seen are 'Kloaken und Gräberreihen'; in other words, the dead and the excreted. The blackness of the pupil, whose perception is so limited, is reflected in the cosmic black hole – here a metaphor and synonym for the body, which, despite its isolation, carries the entire universe within it.[39] However, as we read at the outset of the *Strophen für übermorgen*, the body is the accomplice of death, and 'Diese Scheiß Sterblichkeit' an incontrovertible fact.

Grünbein had already been forced to acknowledge this in 1991, but how much more Stoic is the realization in *Strophen für übermorgen*, when the lyric subject laconically admits that 'Erde, um und umgewühlt, sich jeden nimmt zuletzt' [Earth, turned and turned, takes everyone at the last].[40] Here, the last vestiges of any poetic rebellion against mortality and death have vanished. Grünbein's writing has been underpinned by the same concerns, from its beginnings until today. Their articulation, however, has undergone a major transformation. Grünbein's poetry was, and is, born of the desperation caused by losses suffered; but today this desperation is a 'Verzweiflung in *moderatem* Ton' ['Despair in a *Moderate* Tone'], as the title of one of the poems in the *Strophen für übermorgen* proposes.[41] The same poem ends with a line that further emphasizes the futility of any defiance: 'Ich habs versucht. Nun ja, wer hat es nicht versucht?' [I tried. Well – who hasn't?]. What has brought about this change in tone?

---

38 Grünbein, *Schädelbasislektion*, p. 38; *Ashes for Breakfast*, p. 151.

39 Due to the enormous strength of their gravitational field, nothing can escape from black holes, while their irresistible attractive force sucks in everything in the vicinity.

40 Grünbein, *Strophen für übermorgen*, p. 125.

41 Ibid., pp. 124–25.

The answer is given at the very beginning of the collection, in the last two strophes of 'Spruchtäfelchen', which conclude in elegiac tone:

Überall Nicht-Ich, Welt ohne Rand.
So vieles mißachtet, so wenig bedacht –

Uralter Worte du – flüchtig – Akzent.
Einer von vielen hier, manchem verwandt.

[Everywhere not-I, world without boundary. / So much disregarded, so little considered – / Of the ancient words you – fleeting – accent. / One of many here, related to some.]

Perhaps only when these lines are read aloud are we privy to the sigh that underlies them: 'So vieles miß*ach*tet, so wenig bed*ach*t'. It is the 'Ach' that resonates from the verses, a minute interjection in German, akin to a sigh, which cannot be adequately translated. Yet it might be the most important expression in the volume, 'flüchtig' indeed, but the 'Akzent' of 'Uralter Worte ... manchem verwandt'.

The 'Ach' is 'related' to Alkmene's final word in Kleist's play *Amphytrion*. It also echoes Georg Büchner's Camille Desmoulins, who states in *Dantons Tod* [*Danton's Death*] Act II, scene iii: 'ach, die Kunst!' [Alas, art!][42] – a sentiment that formed a leitmotif in the famous speech 'Der Meridian' ['The Meridian'] delivered by Paul Celan on receipt of the Büchner Prize in 1960.[43] Moreover it is 'related' to possibly the most well-known 'Ach' in German literature, which comes at the beginning of the scene in Faust's study: 'Habe nun, Ach! Philosophie, / Juristerei und Medizin, / Und leider auch Theologie durchaus studiert' / mit heißem Bemühn [Alas, I've studied Philosophy, / The Law and Physic and also, / More's the pity, Divinity, – / With ardent effort, through and through].[44] In the first part of Goethe's tragedy, in the scene in the study at 'Night', we also implicitly find 'Draußen die N*ach*t'. There are many other examples of this 'fleeting' emphasis, which Grünbein explicitly or implicitly introduced into his collection. In 'Die W*ach*tel' ['The Quail'] a whole poem has been dedicated to it: 'Dieses *Ach* aber / eine brüchige Silbe, / Die einen schw*ach* macht, weil sie so vieles enthält' [But this Ach / a fragile syllable / Which makes us weak, as it contains so much].[45]

---

42 Georg Büchner, *Werke und Briefe* (Munich: DTV, 1988), p. 96.

43 Sonja Klein, '"– ach, die Kunst". Celans Meridian oder Poetik aus dem Geiste des Judentums', in *Traditionen jüdischen Denkens in Europa*, ed. by Sybille Schönborn, Karl Solibakke and Bernd Witte (Berlin: Erich Schmidt, 2012), pp. 147–59.

44 Goethe, 'Faust. Eine Tragödie', in *Sämtliche Werke*, VI.1, p. 545; trans. by David Constantine, *Faust. The First Part of the Tragedy* (London: Penguin, 2005), p. 16.

45 Grünbein, *Strophen für übermorgen*, p. 30.

The 'Ach' emphasizes futility by placing the poetic accent on the immutability of mortality. And in its paradoxical emphasizing of its own vainness it is at the same time the 'dennoch', the nevertheless with which the poet counters death by rallying his poetry. This should be understood not only as the successful attempt to stand up to the silent weight of lost time, but also as an effort to recuperate it within poetry. For the poet knows that in the wake of his 'recherche du temps perdu' he can only remember and rediscover those things that have been inveterately lost to life. He knows that only the torn tendon can initiate 'ein Fallenlassen bis hinab zur Kindheit', and that only the butterflies pinned to the board survive in their poetic stasis. 'Speak, memory!', or, as Grünbein states in 'Hippocampus': 'Wort für Wort ging es fort, / Seither, wenn Erinnerung rief' [Word for word it went on, / Since then, when memory called].[46]

In this poetic return to memory, the losses are mourned but their irrevocability is inevitably accepted. 'Wozu klagen, Spätgeborner?' [Why complain, you late-born son?] is the question posed in the opening line of Grünbein's *Porzellan* cycle published in 2005. The lyric subject knows that the destruction of Dresden during the Second World War, the 'Untergang meiner Stadt' ['Downfall of my city'] is irreversible, thus making any lament seem futile: 'Lang verschwunden war / Die Geburtsstadt, Freund, als deine Wenigkeit erschien' [It was long gone / The city of your birth, friend, as your poor existence came to light].[47] And yet, by the end of this volume of forty-nine elegies, he has regained a portion of this lost past, both within and through poetry. In harkening to 'Was die Töchter Mnemosynes ihm diktieren' [What the daughters of Mnemosyne dictate to him], he finds 'eine Welt im kleinen' [a world in miniature], hidden 'tief im Erdreich, wo der Staub noch flüstert' [deep within the Earth, where the dust still whispers].[48]

And even in *Vom Schnee oder Descartes in Deutschland*, the omnipotence of death – which must ultimately carry every philosophical system and the 'cogito ergo sum' to the point of absurdity – is stopped in its tracks, at least for a while, by memory: 'Der Tod – undenkbar ... unvorstellbar ... unerkannt, / Sprang über Logik und Kalkül hinweg' [Death – unthinkable ... inconceivable ... unrealized / Ignored all logic and calculus].[49] Thus the central poem of the poetic cycle, 'Ars

46 Ibid., p. 25.

47 Durs Grünbein, *Porzellan. Poem vom Untergang meiner Stadt* (Frankfurt a. M.: Suhrkamp, 2005), poem 1.

48 The phrase is a further reference to Benjamin's *Excavation and Memory*; Grünbein, *Porzellan*, poem 49.

49 Durs Grünbein, *Vom Schnee oder Descartes in Deutschland* (Frankfurt a. M.: Suhrkamp, 2003), p. 137.

memoriae', turns away from reality and to the inner world of remembrance: 'Der Kopf ein Saal, darin Gemälde, streng nach Plan sortiert, *Imago* für *imago* von der Schöpferwelt dort draußen' [The head a hall, therein paintings, sorted strictly according to plan, *imago* for *imago* from the creative world out there].[50]

The Stoical tone and formal mastery with which Grünbein has formulated the realization of human mortality since the turn of the millennium, does not, however, signify any kind of resignation, less so 'a premature retreat into solemn classicism'. Rather these mark perhaps one of the hardest steps an artist can take: not merely to accept death, but to make what is inevitable fruitful. For it is this transience of people and things – one of the key elements of Marcel Proust's writings – that is reinterpreted as an indispensable starting point for the process of literary and poetic reclamation. Just as legend tells how Simonides' invention of the 'Ars memoriae' could only come about through the catastrophe and death that resulted from the collapse of Scopas's house, so, too, the poet can only resurrect events of the past that are forever beyond his grasp.[51]

Accordingly, *Strophen für übermorgen* could only begin with 'Night Thoughts', with the gesture of a 'Hymne an die Nacht' such as Novalis wrote at the end of the eighteenth century. The stone 'Spruchtäfelchen' is an offering and votive to the gods of the dead – proffered in mourning but also in sad recognition of the fact that only they enable true poetry. This is the painful paradox of the poetic art: without 'Draußen die Nacht' there is no 'Hall im Innern'. Only in the finitude of things, only in their demise, can there be a start to a new and lasting form of existence. 'Viva la muerte' [Long live death] as Grünbein avers in 'Von den Flughäfen' ['About Airports'].[52]

It is this awareness of life in death which forms the basic condition for the aesthetic and formal transformation of Grünbein's writing. And *Strophen für übermorgen* provides a synthesis of the many threads of the last twenty years, weaving them into a unified texture and making the poet's development after 1999 both consistent and essential. In his Stoic 'Ach' we find embedded the symbol of poetic language sui generis; and it is a language that no longer stands in opposition to finitude and mortality, as was the case in Grünbein's early collections. Rather, he now accentuates these aspects of life, imparting to his words a deeply creative momentum for what is to come. Thus, the language of poetry is transformed into the apotropaic facet that all great art contains: it breaks the spell out of which it arises.

50 Ibid., p. 104.
51 See Andrew Webber's contribution in this volume.
52 Grünbein, *Strophen für übermorgen*, p. 63.

In this sense poems are, as Grünbein put it in 2003, 'Pausen im Sterben' [pauses in dying].[53] But they can only be that because they affirm death as an essential prerequisite. Nearly two hundred years earlier, Johann Wolfgang Goethe had formulated the same idea in his enigmatic poem 'Selige Sehnsucht' ['Blessed Longing'] in *West-östlicher Divan* [*West-Eastern Divan*]:

> Und so lang du das nicht hast,
> Dieses: Stirb und Werde
> Bist du nur ein trüber Gast
> auf der dunklen Erde.
>
> [And until you have possessed / dying and rebirth / you are but a sullen guest / On the gloomy earth.][54]

It is only in the acceptance of the metamorphosis of a constant 'dying and rebirth' that poetry becomes a 'Memento [...] überm Abgrund der Existenz. Einige Atemlängen lang trotzt das Gehirn seiner eignen Vergänglichkeit' [a memento suspended over the abyss of existence. For the duration of a few breaths, the brain defies its own transience].[55] The end is indeed only the beginning.

---

53 Durs Grünbein, 'Betonte Zeit', in *Warum schriftlos leben*, pp. 74–93 (p. 87); 'Accented Time', in *The Bars of Atlantis*, pp. 116–31 (p. 126).
54 Goethe, 'Selige Sehnsucht', in *Sämtliche Werke*, XI.1.2, p. 21.
55 Grünbein, 'Betonte Zeit', p. 87; 'Accented Time', p. 127.

Ruth J. Owen

A Poetics of Presence. Travel Cycles in *Aroma* and *Lob des Taifuns*

This chapter makes a case for regarding Durs Grünbein as a travel writer. It examines five cycles of his poems as sustained encounters with foreign places, using as a framework for analysis the concept of presence.[1] By exposing three key manifestations of Grünbein's poetics of presence – the here-and-now, bodily presence and the presence of the poem – it theorizes aspects of poetry and travel that distinguish these cycles within Grünbein's oeuvre and within contemporary poetry. Presence is understood as the opposite of absence, as the condition of being present, especially physically present. Attendance in a particular place might be said to extend from embodied human appearance to textual presence. As the focus of a poetics, it works counter to post-unification German writing obsessed with absence. On the contrary, the performance of the present moment, the signature of Grünbein's travel writing, precludes nostalgia. In departing from the national sphere, this poetry leaves behind German endings and coming-to-terms, the project of recasting the GDR past and registering what has been lost. Instead disembarking somewhere else entirely, it discovers the impact of foreign places on body, voice and language: out of context, all three become highly mutable, in the process enlarging lyric possibilities through the textual exchange with foreign places.

Since time immemorial, travel abroad has made poets into journeymen, pursuing mastery of their craft through journeying. By supplementing the known, such travel brings a different sensibility and renews their search for language. Their tried techniques are tested under new circumstances and combined with the trying-on of new forms and lexis found abroad. In Grünbein's cycles, foreign places are written viscerally, deploying a poetics of presence that takes poetry skating along the surface of the here-and-now, propelled by the human body's sensory perceptions. While this applies to Grünbein's writing of both Italy and Japan, ultimately the two destinations prompt poetries as distinct in their material presence as their visual impact on the page suggests from the off. The language of travel poetry is revealed to be no simple channel; German itself moves, travels if you will, in the encounter.

---

1 While employed here to very different ends, the concept is in part indebted to Hans Ulrich Gumbrecht, *Production of Presence. What Meaning Cannot Convey* (Stanford: Stanford University Press, 2004).

Poetry as Travel

Grünbein's cycle 'Aroma' and the four cycles in *Lob des Taifuns* are twenty-first-century travelogues evoking stays in Italy and in Japan, respectively.[2] They combine a tourist's with a poet's perspective, dwelling on the weather and the sights, as well as reflecting on poetics and language. In 'Aroma', the poems are sited in 'Rom, das von Formen, Farben, Aromen pulsiert' [Rome, pulsing with shapes, colours, aromas].[3] Besides being embedded in the cycle's title, the city's name recurs many times through the poems, as do the names of its districts and edifices. In *Lob des Taifuns*, a place name is inserted into the middle of each poem: Tokyo, Kyoto, Shizuoka, Hiroshima, Miyajima or Kamakura. Readers thus keep being reminded that these are travel cycles: German poems from a non-German setting. In his Frankfurt Poetics Lecture of 2009, Grünbein himself encapsulated the significance of place for poetics: 'Der Ortsname sei hier erwähnt, weil es wie immer nicht ganz unwichtig ist, von wo aus einer spricht' [I mention the place name because it is always of some significance where someone is speaking from].[4] In the 'Aroma' cycle and the cycles in *Lob des Taifuns*, place names foreground and sustain a similar sense that the poems' places of origin matter. They convey what Grünbein has elsewhere termed 'das Gefühl von einem Draußen' [the sense of an outside],[5] an outside beyond the poem, any self it conjures up, and its language-specific culture: an outside, that is, beyond what is written.

Nonetheless, this outside is evoked precisely within elaborate poetry that draws attention as much to its internal means as to encounters with foreign places. After all, travel poetry is a relatively rare phenomenon as opposed to travel prose, especially beyond the nineteenth century. Grünbein's travel cycle is a substantial sequence of lyric poems highly homogeneous in form and tending to function as a whole. Whilst there is a narrative element, the dynamics are finally lyric, emotive and associative, resulting from the effective juxtaposition of poems and an accumulation of small scenes and motifs. On the one hand, the cycle displays shifts in focus and tone; on the other, it has a unifying sense of source and of psychological response to the location, as well as a degree of thematic continuity and an overarching appropriative energy, that render the cycle a coherent unit.

---

2 Durs Grünbein, 'Aroma', in *Aroma. Ein römisches Zeichenbuch* (Berlin: Suhrkamp, 2010), pp. 11–67; *Lob des Taifuns. Reisetagebücher in Haikus* (Frankfurt a. M.: Insel, 2008).

3 *Aroma*, p. 36.

4 Durs Grünbein, *Vom Stellenwert der Worte. Frankfurter Poetikvorlesung 2009* (Berlin: Suhrkamp, 2010), p. 7.

5 Durs Grünbein, 'Moderne Höllen' ('Modern Hells'), in *Die Bars von Atlantis. Eine Erkundung in vierzehn Tauchgängen* (Frankfurt a. M.: Suhrkamp, 2009), pp. 45–46 (p. 46).

Titling the cycle and not the individual poems further underscores the cycle as the dominant segment. Poems in *Lob des Taifuns* are arranged into four titled cycles: 'Zerrüttungen nach einer Tasse Tee oder Reisetage mit Issa' ['Irreconcilable Differences after a Cup of Tea, or Days Travelling with Issa'], 'Regentropfen auf einem Brillenglas' ['Raindrops on a Glasses' Lens'], 'Lob des Taifuns' ['In Praise of the Typhoon'], and 'Stunden im Schneidersitz' ['Hours Sitting Cross-legged']. They constitute lyric diaries of trips to Japan in 1999 (thirty-eight poems), 2002 (thirty-six poems), 2003 (twenty-one poems) and 2005 (thirty-seven poems). 'Aroma: Opus incertum' is an even longer cycle, comprised of fifty-three travel poems numbered with Roman numerals from I to LIII. (Sixteen have an italicized motto to the right of the title space; two have a title in brackets beneath the Roman numeral but, overall, poem titling has been replaced by numeration.) To an extent, such 'untitling' is a refusal to grant the interpretive authority that potentially simplifies the reader's approach to a titled poem. It also gestures towards immediacy and a conception of the cycle's constitutive poems as successive moments in an unfolding 'now'. The dating of the 'moment poems' in *Lob des Taifuns* is another marker of each cycle's overall cohesion.[6] Like the Roman numerals in the 'Aroma' cycle, these dates – in the middle of each poem – signal that the cycles are not miscellanies, but collections with chronologies. The dates, like the numerals, are continuous, a progression with a direction, indicative of the movement in travel itself.

Title spaces in Grünbein's travel cycles reflect self-conscious choices, as Anne Ferry's analysis of the general importance of modern poem titling highlights:

> Since the end of the eighteenth century the very process of expanding and eventually evading or escaping earlier conventions of titling has made the act of choosing how to use the title space still more self-conscious, the effect of the choice more loaded.[7]

Made prominent by the use of Latin, the subtitle of the cycle 'Aroma', 'Opus incertum', means building using irregularly shaped tuff stones. A line drawing of this Roman architectural feature, made by Winckelmann in 1808, is reproduced at the head of the 'Aroma' cycle with the necessary explanation, to reinforce the loaded choice. Winckelmann's name not only signals a German predecessor in

6 On pre-Grünbein 'moment poems' see Susanne Ledanff, *Die Augenblicksmetapher. Über Bildlichkeit und Spontaneität in der Lyrik* (Munich: Hanser, 1981), especially on West German poetry of the 1960s and 1970s, pp. 215–65.

7 Anne Ferry, *The Title of the Poem* (Stanford: Stanford University Press, 1996), p. 246.

Rome, but the importance of emulating the ancients.[8] A variant on the more familiar 'Opus magnum' ('magnum opus' in English), the subtitle phrase also refers to an artwork which, rather than one's greatest, has uncertain or doubtful status. As a poetological metaphor, the building technique,[9] reinforced by the drawing, suggests that the Rome poems can be regarded as stones assembled and constructed into the structure of this uncertain opus. The layout of one sixteen-line poem per page, forming a heavy block of left-justified, long-lined text, further hints at this architectural conception of the poems as stones (especially by comparison with the jagged fringed Japan poems awkwardly strung across page breaks).

To subtitle the *Lob des Taifuns* cycles 'Reisetagebücher in Haikus' [Travel Diaries in Haikus] is also to suggest certain poetological ideas. These poems are not in fact haikus after all and this part of the title is a misdirection. To label them travel diaries is to make a claim about the origin of the writing; it supposes that we read travelogues differently than poetry from home and that they extend, if only by a little, the German encounter with Japan. They supplement existing cultural memory of travels written in German, seeking to trigger in readers a vibration corresponding to what the implied writer felt abroad. As we read more by the same tourist-poet, a character emerges through the sum of the various inferred views and reactions. This applies equally to the embodied tourist-poet of the 'Aroma' cycle. However, the sense of someone recording impressions is undermined by indications that the poems have only an ambiguous and indeterminate relation to lived experience. For one thing, 'I'-utterances are relatively few, and untitling means that any self referred to is open or at least ambiguous: there is no prefatory indication as to who is saying a poem or who is to hear it; and there are many allusions to the cultural imaginary, especially to reading material. In order to take measure of how such elements combine, this enquiry into the cycle 'Aroma' and the four cycles in *Lob des Taifuns* examines presence in three aspects: first, its temporal dimension in the poems, their concern with the here-and-now; second, presence produced by evoking the body and the visceral, prioritizing sensory experience and overtly embodying the

---

8 See Winckelmann's bon mot from *Gedanken über die Nachahmung der griechischen Werke in der Malerei und Bildhauerkunst* (Nendeln: Kraus, 1968 [1755]), p. 8: 'Der einzige Weg für uns, groß, ja wenn es möglich ist, unnachahmlich zu werden, ist die Nachahmung der Alten' [The only way for us to become great, inimitable, if that is possible at all, is by emulating the ancients.]

9 See also the comparison between poetry and architecture in the essay 'Der verschwundene Platz', in Durs Grünbein, *Antike Dispositionen. Aufsätze* (Frankfurt a. M.: Suhrkamp, 2005), pp. 279–91, especially p. 279.

voice; and finally, the significance of poetry's materiality and concreteness for a poetics of presence. This focus allows an exploration of distinctive features of the works as travel cycles as well as of their relation to some of Grünbein's earlier collections.

This focus is also invited by the poem 'Forma urbis Romae', which opens *Aroma* and stands as a preface to the 'Aroma' cycle. The three lines closing that first poem culminate in a frontal assertion of presence:

> Wann sind wir? fragt sich im stillen,
> Der auf schwankendem Boden steht.
> Wir sind hier. Jetzt sind wir.

> [When are we? wonders, in the quiet, / Someone on shaky ground. / We are here. Now we are.][10]

Whilst the 'shaky ground' on which the questioner stands is an image of uncertain and changeful circumstances, the answer to his question is a resounding declaration that what can be articulated is existence in the here-and-now: 'Wir sind hier. Jetzt sind wir'. This type of tone in Grünbein's work has been called 'frontality' by Michael Hofmann and a sense of 'something being blurted'.[11] It recurs across Grünbein's oeuvre, although it is not as much commented upon as the cynical, sarcastic tone. The chiasmus of Grünbein's final line puts the emphasis on 'now', pushing it up against the caesura such that 'here' and 'now' are together at the peak of the line. This line also uses a collective 'we' voice far from prolific in Grünbein's poetry. Here, at the culmination of the entry poem to the whole collection, as well as to the collection's eponymous cycle, the first person plural stands out. In part, it is a pun drawn from the 'you are here' arrow affixed to tourist maps. It is also a response to Rome in particular, to disappearance and dust, to the writerly tourists who have gone before. The 'we' that speaks the poem emerges as a presence hyper-aware of its spatial-temporal location.

---

10 *Aroma*, p. 9.

11 Michael Hofmann, 'Translator's Preface', in Durs Grünbein, *Ashes for Breakfast: Selected Poems* (London: Faber and Faber, 2005), pp. vii-xv, (pp. viii, x).

The Here-and-Now

Grünbein's writing of Rome 'in Rome' (a Roma) demonstrates absorption of the ancient past that leaves it ever-present – often by means of single words, referring to ancient figures. Eras are interlaced in poem XIV where the gladiators in helmets are two motorcyclists in a city-centre crash or in a phrase like 'Da kommt eine Nymphe in Jeans' [There's a nymph wearing jeans] from poem XLII.[12] In poem XVII, a simile draws the past into the Roman present: 'Ostia, die kleine Pforte, erwartet die Jumbos, Touristentransporter, / Wie Octavians Flotten nach der siegreichen Heimkehr von Actium' [Ostia, the small gateway, is expecting the jumbo jets, tourist transporters, / like Octavian's fleets after victoriously returning home from Actium].[13] For all the newness of the present, contemporary travel echoes a remnant of the past. A related technique of using names from ancient Rome to intervene in the present occurs in poem XXII, which raises the question 'Was hätte Catullus dazu gesagt?' [What would Catullus have said to that?].[14] The reappearance of Octavian or Catullus exemplifies how in this particular place particles from the ancient past occupy the here-and-now. As in the earlier collection *Nach den Satiren*, Grünbein's poems work to restore ancient remnants to the Roman present. Indeed, in a compelling summing-up of historical connection in Grünbein's work preceding *Aroma*, Michael Eskin has declared:

> [I]n Grünbein's texts past and present are mutually engaged and interlaced in such a way as to produce and open up a qualitatively novel dimension of significance in which neither past nor present are left where they presumably are and in which poetic subjectivity emerges as the very focus and conduit of their enmeshment.[15]

The 'Aroma' cycle goes about such interlacing too, leaving nothing quite where it was thought to be, the now expanding backwards, the poetic subject moving between 'man', 'du', even 'Sie', occasionally 'ich', such that revelation comes about in the process. Subjects and visited sites seem to exist in an unstable equilibrium.

In Rome, the time frame in which events are judged to be currently relevant is represented as a spacious present. In the fifth poem of 'Aroma' we find the contention that it has floors: 'Die Frage: in welchem Stockwerk Gegenwart befinden Sie sich?' [The question is which floor of the present are you on?].[16] Towards the

---

12 *Aroma*, pp. 26, 56.
13 Ibid., p. 29.
14 Ibid., p. 35.
15 Michael Eskin, *Poetic Affairs. Celan, Grünbein, Brodsky* (Stanford: Stanford University Press, 2008), p. 68.
16 *Aroma*, p. 17.

end of the cycle, poem LII suggests that the usual irrevocability of time past has been suspended here:

> Das Jahr ist zu Ende, aufgebraucht. *Fine dell'anno* ... Und es gibt
> Keine Wiederkehr all der herrlichen Augenblicke.
>   Hier aber stürzt
> In breitem Schwall aus fünf steinernen Luken die Acqua Paola
>
> [The year is over, used up. *Fine dell'anno* ... And / All the glorious moments will never return. // Here, however, / In the broad swell from five stone holes tumbles the Acqua Paola][17]

Apparent passing is contradicted by the prominent assertion of presence, 'hier aber' [here, however], at the Roman water monument. All the recurrences of 'here' and 'now' in the cycle have this 'but' implied, if not explicit. Here is where what was thought past is found to remain. It means Rome, the place that the poem is spoken from, as well as the Rome poem itself in its absorptive work. Thus, on seeing the Pons Fabricius, an apostrophe in poem XVIII to the ancient who commissioned the bridge exhibits familiarity of tone:

> He, Fabricius, alter Wegverwalter: heute hab ich sie überquert,
> Las unterm Bogen silbern in Sprayer-Schrift das 'Ti amo Giulia'
> Und sah am Pfeiler aus Tuffstein die Wasser sich seelenruhig teilen.
>
> [Hey, Fabricius, old road-administrator: today I crossed it, / Read under the arch in silver spray paint the 'Ti amo Giulia' / And saw the waters part, peaceful of soul, either side of the tuff-stone pillar.][18]

The levity of this address, with the timeless themes of love and parting, conveys Fabricius's proximity to the tourist-poet. Their moment of direct communication makes the ancient of one unit with the present, the latest graffiti just a new inscription beside the old, the bridge a symbolic location running between past and present. The words 'hier' and 'heute' [here, today] in this poem are indicative of its reiteration of the here-and-now as filled with glimpses of the past.

Repetition of 'hier' throughout the 'Aroma' cycle renders it a watchword.[19] In some cases, it is connected with epiphany. For poem XLI, culminating in a dating like a diary entry, here means the Via Appia and specifically the mausoleum of Metella. Its epiphany, time playing tricks, depends on the travertine (like tuff, a rock Rome is made of) and the equally Rome-specific sculptures of bulls and

17 Ibid., p. 66.
18 Ibid., p. 31.
19 For example, ibid., pp. 37, 39 (twice), 54, 58.

Hercules. An off-kilter panorama unfolds, eliding the modern and the ancient, the near and the distant, amid which a Japanese couple is observed looking for a photo opportunity where once Goethe sought a place to draw. The absurdity of the ever-broadening Roman here-and-now is explicit in poem XL:

> Wie absurd das ist, hier zu sein – in der berühmten urbanen Senke
> Zwischen allen Extremen historisch erfüllter Zeit.
>
> [How absurd it is to be here – in the famous urban dip / Between the greatest extremes of time steeped in history.][20]

Rome has been famous, its sights heard about before, at least since the era of the Grand Tour. Combining travel poetry with Rome, traces of classical civilization, and the cultivating of historical and architectural awareness links Grünbein's cycle to the Grand Tour of the seventeenth to nineteenth centuries. The link attests to the presence of tradition in contemporary writing and the importance of emulation and revisiting.

In 'Aroma', German poetry is revisiting Rome. The numerals and hexameter emulate Goethe's *Römische Elegien* [*Roman Elegies*], and the quotations in the title spaces of the poems, rather than just a pretentious posture, prompt the reflection that Grünbein's Rome is as much a response to texts as to travel. Thus poems are not only expressions of reactions and experiences, but of these as mediated by reading. In *Vom Stellenwert der Worte*, Grünbein referred to 'die Kontinuität der dichterischen Überlieferung' [the continuity of transmission from poet to poet].[21] Italy, especially Rome, is a passed-down place. Unlike Japan, it is pre-written by German poets, especially given Goethe's *Italienische Reise* [*Italian Journey*] (although prose), Ludwig Tieck's *Reisegedichte eines Kranken* [*Travel Poems by an Ill Man*] (written in Italy in 1805–6, although little known now) and Heinrich Heine's tripartite *Reisebilder* [*Travel Pictures*] (which include Italy but not exclusively). Rolf Dieter Brinkmann's Italian poems may be dwarfed by his *Rom, Blicke* [*Rome, Views*] volume of 'materials', but in *Westwärts 1&2* [*Westwards 1&2*] nonetheless 'Hymne auf einen italienischen Platz' ['Hymn to an Italian Plaza'], the ironic cod-Italian 'Roma die Notte' ['Roma by Nighta'] and 'Canneloni in Olevano' are Italian travel poetry.[22] The effect of such precursors is to place Grünbein in a canonical tradition where every poet needs to write Rome, like every actor needs to play Hamlet.

20 Ibid., p. 54.
21 Grünbein, *Vom Stellenwert der Worte*, p. 55.
22 Rolf Dieter Brinkmann, *Westwärts 1&2. Gedichte* (Reinbek bei Hamburg: Rowohlt, 1975), pp. 85–94; Brinkmann, *Rom, Blicke* (Reinbek bei Hamburg: Rowohlt, 1979). See also Jan Röhnert, '"Canneloni in Olevano". Auch Brinkmann in Arkadien? Anmerkungen zu Rolf Dieter Brinkmanns

In *Lob des Taifuns* precursors come from the same era as the Grand Tour, if a different tradition, and function as writing companions. In this collection, the past is made present not only through the ancientness of some sights but also through reading famous Japanese poets of the haiku. Certain spots facilitate the presence of Matsuo Bashō (1644–94), Yosa Buson (1716–83) and Kobayashi Issa (1763–1827). Bashō, whose poetry includes travel diaries, makes one spot significant: 'Hier setzte Bashô den ersten Schritt ins Dichterleben' [Here Bashō took his first step into life as a poet].[23] The location 'here' forges a link that is sustained in the two following poems, too. Buson, who attempted to revive the haiku tradition of Bashō, is evoked in a poem prompted by the house dedicated to Buson's memory, where he in turn had erected a pavilion to commemorate Bashō's visit to the same spot a hundred years earlier.[24] Issa, another great of the haiku tradition, is named in one cycle title as a travelling companion and comes to the fore in the poem about re-reading his haikus on suffering as a stepchild and orphan.[25] Being in Japan is thus staged as bringing into reach in an intense way these long-dead poets, whose presence is recuperated through both being in the places they lived and reading their poetry there.

A poetics of the 'here-and-now' is expounded in the afterword to *Lob des Taifuns* where Grünbein compares his haikus to polaroids – snap shots made in the moment, the work of a snatched instant.[26] He suggests that the briefest impression is turned into poetry on the spot, capturing something fleeting in the tiniest quantum of language.[27] His haiku, the first part of each poem in the collection, indeed resembles a notebook jotting, made in response to the here-and-now. Within the German tradition, it is reminiscent of Rolf Dieter Brinkmann's lyric concept of the 'snapshot'.[28] Keeping alive wonder whilst also espying the quotidian, the polaroid corresponds to the poems evoking the kanji in the sea or the

---

Italienbild in seinen Gedichten', in *Rolf Dieter Brinkmann: Blicke ostwärts – westwärts* (Vechta: Eiswasser, 2001), pp. 90–99.

23 *Lob des Taifuns*, p. 38.

24 Ibid., p. 25.

25 Ibid., p. 13.

26 Grünbein, 'Siebzehn Silben des Augenblicks' ('Seventeen Syllables of the Moment'), *Lob des Taifuns*, pp. 101–111 (p. 107).

27 Ibid., p. 108.

28 As encapsulated in 'Notiz', *Standphotos. Gedichte 1962–1970* (Reinbek bei Hamburg: Rowohlt, 1980), p. 185: 'Ich denke, daß das Gedicht die geeignetste Form ist, spontan erfaßte Vorgänge und Bewegungen, eine nur in einem Augenblick sich deutlich zeigende Empfindlichkeit konkret als snapshot festzuhalten' [I think that the poem is the form most suited to capturing tangibly, as a snapshot, a spontaneous grasp of what is happening or in motion, a sensibility that reveals itself clearly only for a moment].

plastic bottle on the platform.[29] The reader is invited to notice such objects as artefacts, implicitly in many instances, and sometimes explicitly:

> Im Rinnstein schwimmt, schau:
> Eine einzelne Nudel.
> Der Regen kocht Suppe.
>
> [In the gutter is swimming, look: / A single noodle. / The rain is making soup.][30]

Besides the appealing levity of these lines, the familiar imperative 'schau', interrupting the flow from the main verb to its subject, installs the reader as a companion accompanying the tourist-poet and simply asked to look. The same effect is achieved by 'sieh nur zu' [just watch] in another poem.[31] The reader's attention is drawn to what is only fleeting: a noodle, the weather, a witty remark. The tourist-poet offers the reader a place to stand for a moment amid the flux and observe them.

Constructed as diary entries, the poems in *Lob des Taifuns* tend generally to evoke moments of the present, with some having no verb at all. The first three lines of a poem from 'Regentropfen auf einem Brillenglas' exemplify the absence of any tense:

> Das hölzerne Tor
> In der Bucht von Miyajima –
> Ein rotes *kanji* im Meer.
>
> [The wooden gate / In the bay of Miyajima – / A red *kanji* in the sea.][32]

The effect of there being no verb is to re-create the moment of revelation, when architecture and script are equated, not as a memory, but as a present moment. Deploying the dash is a provocation to readers to make the leap. Whilst such a poem as a whole reveals itself as highly retouched, the opening three lines are premised on the immediacy of the snap shot. To the extent that the shapes of gates, shrines and other architectural features are prominent in the cycles, this instance is also typical, keeping in view the look of 'here'.

In its isolation of single figures and single objects, however, especially noticing rubbish for example, *Lob des Taifuns* recalls some of the poems in *Grauzone morgens* and subsequent 'diorama' poems. Monumentalizing the moment, cap-

---

29 *Lob des Taifuns*, pp. 44, 79.
30 Ibid., p. 67.
31 Ibid., p. 16.
32 Ibid., p. 44.

turing glimpses of what is seen and the passion of the observer thus resembles the technique Grünbein earlier applied to Germany, specifically to GDR Dresden and Berlin.[33] Its purpose now is also part of the reception of his Japanese reading, however. In his afterword to *Lob des Taifuns*, Grünbein comments on what inspired him about Issa's poetry: 'In der Konzentration auf den intensiv erlebten Augenblick schmolz alle Fremdheit hin' [By concentrating on the intensively experienced moment, all the foreignness melted away].[34] Back with the temporal dimension of presence, Grünbein's comment highlights a capacity to endure disorientation abroad by means of focusing on the moment.

Rather than any mastery, a sense of foreignness accumulates in *Lob des Taifuns*, many poems turning away from contact with people and attending instead to surfaces, artefacts and natural features. The distance due to an alien language manifests itself where people are observed from afar whilst the poems scarcely mention speaking to anyone. Language, found in shapes and signs, is visual rather than verbal for this alien tourist-poet, in this location. The experience of an anonymizing environment is imaged in the final poem of the fourth cycle, where glasses and a mask obscure a face.[35] Where the tourist-poet does speak with Japanese people, he seems obscured in turn, either by the equation of German culture with Romantic music or the English-speaking West: thus, in the first cycle, a waitress has learnt German because of Schubert and in the third, a female translator who plays Brahms speaks to him;[36] in the fourth, a seamstress speaks to him in broken English.[37] These slightest contacts, amid many hotels, trains and streets, constitute reflections on cultural translation. Transliterated Japanese words, such as '*Shitsurei*' and '*Hazure*',[38] indicate the limits of linguistic translation and make it the focus of poems, further thematizing a lack of acquaintance. Often the tourist-poet is alone reading seventeenth- and eighteenth-century haiku writers or about ritual suicide in ancient Japan,[39] communing with dead male poets (Baudelaire even) or breaking into self-talk that is also indicative of the tourist-poet's detached status:

---

33 Ruth J. Owen, 'The Beginning of a Role. Durs Grünbein's post-*Wende* poetry', in Ruth J. Owen, *The Poet's Role. Lyric Responses to German Unification by Poets from the GDR* (Amsterdam: Rodopi, 2001), pp. 233–72, especially p. 267 on the diorama, pp. 268–71 on glimpses, pp. 271–72 on monumentalizing the moment, and p. 280 on the passion of the observer.
34 *Lob des Taifuns*, p. 106.
35 Ibid., p. 98.
36 Ibid., p. 64.
37 Ibid., p. 81.
38 Ibid., pp. 43, 47.
39 Ibid., p. 70.

Nun, wie weit bist du
Gekommen, Oktoberkind,
Auf dem Weg fort von dir?
1. November 2005
Nara

[So how far have you / Got, child of October, / Along the path away from yourself?][40]

Whilst positing travel as a moving away from the self and from German identity, this rhetorical question invites the conclusion that there is, in the end, no escape at all, even faraway in Nara. It is among a small number of the poems about the traveller (rather than the destination) that together expose an inner self, who is otherwise as out of range as the other people encountered.

A cluster of poems where the here-and-now is pre-loaded with one known association originate in Hiroshima. A biographical context for this visit and a spontaneous connection with Dresden were mentioned in Grünbein's interview with Renatus Deckert, before the Japan book was realized, and suggest a distinctive perspective on Hiroshima:

> Dieser Untergang hat alles getränkt, was mir je einfiel und worüber ich schreibe. Daraus folgt dann auch die spontane Verbundenheit mit einem Ort wie Hiroshima. Ich bin eines Tages ganz bewußt dorthin gepilgert. [...] Die zwei Tage dort in Hiroshima, ich habe sie bis heute nicht wirklich verarbeitet. Es gibt darüber bisher nur ein paar lose Notizen. Ein Haiku, zum Beispiel, ziemlich banal, hält die Abwehrhaltung des Nachgeborenen fest. 'In Hiroshima / Die schwerste Zen-Übung ist: / Nicht *daran* denken.'
>
> [The destruction of Dresden has saturated everything I have ever thought or written about. This is where the spontaneous connection with a place like Hiroshima comes from too. One day I consciously made my pilgrimage. [...] The two days I spent there in Hiroshima I haven't really processed yet. Until now I've just made a few loose notes about them. For example, there's a haiku, fairly banal really, which captures the defensiveness of someone born after. 'In Hiroshima / The trickiest Zen meditation is / Not to think about *it*.'][41]

The lines quoted in the interview reappear as the opening of the first of seven Hiroshima poems in *Lob des Taifuns*.[42] They use a form of praeteritio, announcing the omission, saying by not saying; for when here means Hiroshima, the '*daran*'

---

40 Ibid., p. 86.
41 'Gespräch mit Durs Grünbein', in *Die wüste Stadt. Sieben Dichter über Dresden*, ed. by Renatus Deckert (Frankfurt a. M.: Insel, 2005), pp. 189–212 (p. 196).
42 Five dated 30 June 2002, *Lob des Taifuns*, pp. 42–44, with two further dated 2 July 2002, pp. 47–48.

must refer to the atom bomb. The following poem echoes Rilke, re-using the blue hydrangea as an image of regeneration now applied to Japan. It thus comes to the bombing not just from the perspective of someone born after, but from a German-literary vantage-point. In the third Hiroshima poem, the little word 'jetzt' [now] carries the whole contrast between 1945 and 2002. If these poems thus amplify one historical fact by oblique references to the absence of impact on the horticultural and the meteorological present, the next two jolt by sketching a bar that could be almost anywhere. One uses broken, international English and the figure of a Ukrainian topless dancer, the other a beer-mat slogan and a grinning barman, to emphasize the ordinariness that the place makes extraordinary. Predecessor poems in German, such as Volker Braun's 'Hiroshima, 57 N.D.B.' or, the most famous, Marie Luise Kaschnitz's 'Hiroshima', might also be said to show the ordinary offset by the extraordinariness of the bombing.[43] The last two Hiroshima poems by Grünbein in *Lob des Taifuns* add to the collection's brief encounters with anonymous female spectres: 'Ausgerechnet in Hiroshima schenkte eine freundliche ältere Japanerin dem Reisenden ein sogenanntes Rubbel-Los' [In Hiroshima of all places, a friendly elderly woman gave the traveller a so-called scratchcard].[44] The next poem registers the shock of sameness, when a woman at a street food stall resembles the tourist-poet's mother. Thus the encounter with Hiroshima is refracted through a lens that renders everything extraordinary; the pre-loaded place name, the pre-knowledge of the bombing, is the measure of every impression in these poems.

The emotion of presence in the same place, in a different now, is used repeatedly in both the Japan and the Italy cycles. A succinct version of this nostalgia is the technique of re-encounter in the second cycle in *Lob des Taifuns*: one poem in the cycle 'Regentropfen auf einem Brillenglas' traces hearing waves on the same coastal spot as three years before; another re-encounters a 'hier' in the rush of rickshaws, whilst the subsequent poem on the same page, timed at fifteen minutes later, retracts the nostalgia of the déjà-vu; a third example is the poem on sighting a dusty German book in a second-hand shop still there just as three years earlier.[45] Sentiment is invested in these re-encounters, the German book even personified, as the poems celebrate little moments of familiarity. These re-encounters within the collection point up the wider significance attached to effects of presence. In Japan, as in time-warped Rome, the tourist-poet's travels in the

43 Volker Braun, 'Hiroshima, 57 N.D.B.', *Neue Beiträge zur Germanistik*, 111 (2003), 31; Marie Luise Kaschnitz, 'Hiroshima', *Neue Gedichte* (Hamburg: Claasen, 1957), p. 25.
44 *Lob des Taifuns*, p. 47.
45 Ibid., pp. 38, 49, 53.

here-and-now have the status of many, tiny re-encounters. In the term Jeffrey Gray used of post-war American travel poetry, they register 'mastery's end'.[46] What Grünbein's travel cycles offer instead of mastery is a poetry commemorating renewed presence.

Bodily Presence

When colonial-style mastery of the foreign is long gone, travel poetry turns to what is present, in reach, tangible for human bodies. In the 'Aroma' cycle, an extended sense of the here-and-now is sustained through attention to physiological details and sensory perception. Perception of bodies proliferates too: Rome is defined as a city under the dictatorship of beautiful bodies, where people come 'zur Fleischbeschau' [to inspect the flesh];[47] there are bodies on the roof terraces and on the billboards. Allusions to 'müde Knochen' [tired bones] and 'das Husten der Grubenleute' [the coughing of the mine folk] are typical of the way bodily presences behind the scenes also recur throughout the cycle.[48] Organs function here as active subjects: 'Wir sind in Trastevere, weiß die Nase. Das Auge sichtet befriedigt' [We are in Travestere, my nose tells me. My eye sifts the sights contentedly].[49] The Roman ground is itself conceived as flesh that yields further body parts:

> Irgendwo gräbt wer in diesem Haufen, sticht den Spaten ins weiche
> Fleisch der gesättigten Erde, zieht einen Frauentorso ans Licht
>
> [Somewhere someone is digging in this pile, sticking a spade into the soft / Flesh of the satiated earth, pulling to the surface a female torso][50]

The traveller is forever finding bodies in Rome, whether the statues of gods, 'die bärtigen Riesen' [the bearded giants], or excavating 'ein Musentorso, Maecenas-Kopf' [a muse's torso, a bust of Maecenas].[51] The close of poem XXXVI reveals that the sense of here-and-now might be at risk, were it not for recognition of the human body:

---

46 'Mastery's end' refers to postcolonial-era poets receiving impressions but no longer assuming mastery of the alien world before them, in Jeffrey Gray, *Mastery's End. Travel and Postwar American Poetry* (Athens: University of Georgia Press, 2005).
47 *Aroma*, p. 29.
48 Ibid., pp. 34, 35, 48.
49 Ibid., p. 32.
50 Ibid., p. 33.
51 Ibid., pp. 42, 43.

> Nicht nur der Schatten kann hier, auch der Sinn für die Gegenwart
> Leicht abhanden kommen – tauchte nicht plötzlich der eigene Fuß
> Im Museum auf, als Fragment eines Mannes in Marmorsandalen.[52]
>
> [Here it would be easy to lose not only your shadow but also your sense of the present / – Were it not for your own foot appearing suddenly / In the museum, as a fragment of a man in marble sandals.]

A sense of co-presence is explicitly derived from a foot that is both the tourist's own and the Roman marble sculpture. Poem XXXII presents body parts – the feet, especially the heel – as perceiving subjects, which draw the past into the present. Hard skin makes every tourist who walks round Rome into a legionnaire: 'Anatomie ist es, der lateinische Name für jedes zerbrechliche Glied, / Was sie all verbindet zuletzt, die Körper' [It is anatomy, the Latin name for every fragile part, / Which connects them all in the end, the bodies].[53] Anatomy makes connections 'hier', the poem alluding explicitly to pores, forehead, ankle and calf muscle, as the measure of Rome.

The very opening poem of the 'Aroma' cycle evokes the alien dust of Rome as the taste of history, registered on the body by a furry tongue. At its central turn, where the line splits, sensory perception encompasses taste, scent and sight:

> Der Staub des Forums, ein Mondstaub andrer Art, aufgewirbelt
> Von den Pilgermassen, die zähneknirschend in Rom erst begreifen:
> So schmeckt Geschichte.
>   Dies ist ihr bittres, mehlstumpfiges Aroma,
> Das die Schleimhäute reizt, auf die Retina einen Schleier legt.
>
> [The dust of the forum, an alternative kind of moondust, thrown up / By the amassed pilgrims who discover in Rome that / This is what history tastes like. // This is its bitter, floury aroma / That irritates the mucous membranes, laying a veil across the retina.][54]

Either side of the poem's sole split line – a visually emphasized part of the page – the words 'Aroma' and 'Rom' draw attention to the embedding of the city's name in the title that designates olfactory perception. After the first poem's teeth, mucous membranes and retina, the second opens with further body parts: rosy fingernails, finer beard stubble, silky hair, which register the physical effect of being in the sunny South. The third poem closes by contrasting the torso of a statue and the bodies of tourists, the first porous and scarred, the second exhausted and cor-

52 Ibid., p. 50.
53 Ibid., p. 45.
54 Ibid., p. 13.

pulent. But the two are in fact akin: transitoriness is marked on both.[55] Grünbein's travel cycle thus evokes a body that recognizes its likeness to numerous foreign bodies: the living, the sculpted, the pictured, as well as the body of the city. The city itself is personified using body metaphors: 'So zeigt dir Rom die kalte Schulter' [This is how Rome shows you the cold shoulder]; 'Die Stadt atmet aus' [The city exhales]; 'Einen Nabel zeigt man dir am Forum, Opfergrube oder Ofenloch' [You are shown a navel at the forum, a sacrificial pit or a stove hole].[56] And the cycle repeatedly asserts that in this bodied city the human body determines perception: thus in poem IV, 'Adrenalin putzt die Linsen, stellt den Blick scharf' [Adrenaline cleans your lenses, sharpens your vision].[57] The tourist's body is often the literal starting-point for poetry, as in the opening of poem X:

> April, und schon erwacht man mit Schweiß im Angesicht.
> Ein Ventilator schneidet die dicke Luft, den Levkoienduft
> In feine Streifen, die dann am Körper kleben, ein Tesafilm
> Für Moskitoflügel, Akazienpollen, italienische Schlager.

> [April and already you wake up with sweat on your face. / A fan is cutting the thick air, the scent of gillyflowers, / Into thin strips, which then cling to your body, a sticky tape / For mosquito wings, acacia pollen, Italian pop hits.][58]

The voice of this poem is an embodied voice recording sense impressions, of the sweat that is both palpable and metaphorical for the way the city sticks. To encounter Italy is thus to come into physical contact with it, appropriating this world through sticky skin. Voice is embodied explicitly like this in many of the 'Aroma' poems: 'Man biegt aus der Gasse und reibt sich die Augen' [You turn out of the alley and rub your eyes],[59] for example, is an opening line, launching the poem as the expression of an embodied subject. Writing Rome, so Grünbein's 'Aroma' demonstrates, entails the tourist-poet's optical and epidermal sensitivity.

Sounds play a part in the presence effects of the 'Aroma' cycle and expose the tourist's aural sensitivity too. For instance, the rainstorm of poem XXVIII is evoked as the sound of shooting, a rattling iron curtain descending, a rushing in the ear canal and hail hitting the tops of the cars, setting off the car alarms. In an earlier essay, Grünbein drew attention to Rome as a city of sounds that makes it easy for writers:

---

55 Ibid., p. 15.
56 Ibid., pp. 40, 54, 59.
57 Ibid., p. 16.
58 Ibid., p. 22.
59 Ibid., p. 52.

> Was Rom betrifft, bedarf es wahrlich keines feinen Gehörs, um dieses Brodeln und Zischen unter den Sohlen zu spüren. [...] [Dichter haben] ein Organ für die Stimmen und Laute, die sich seit Menschengedenken an einem Ort akkumulieren. Vergangenheit oder Zukunft, in puncto Lärm ist der Unterschied unerheblich; im Labyrinth des Gehörgangs wird immer nur Gegenwart draus.
>
> [As for Rome, you don't even need sensitive hearing to perceive its burbling and hissing underfoot. [...] [But writers have] an organ for detecting the voices and sounds which have been accumulating in a place since time immemorial. Whether past or future makes little difference as regards noise; in the labyrinth of the ear canal both always turn into present.][60]

The essay contends that sensory perception is always an effect of the present, however much it is a matter of cultural memory of the past and cultural imagination of the future. This is born out in the 'Aroma' cycle where, being in contact with things, the body is the dominant reference for the here-and-now.

Though the Japan cycles are less littered with bodies than 'Aroma', bodily presence is indicated through the priority of sensory perception, especially of ephemeral sights and sounds seized upon to characterize the place as both familiar and strange in some measure. Irmela Hijiya-Kirschneit, in an early review of *Lob des Taifuns*, referred to the sensory experience conveyed in the poems: 'We see, hear, taste the Japanese surroundings, along with Grünbein'. Her remarks on the collection's 'surface-skimming yet sharply drawn images' highlight the use of sensory first impressions.[61] Sights are the dominant sources for representing moments of now, but the poems also evoke sounds memorably: whether the seventeen pharyngeal clicks overheard in the second poem of the collection, the ping pong sound of shoes, or Tokyo's power-station-like roar.[62] In the middle of the first cycle of *Lob des Taifuns*, the dramatized speaker's bodily presence is more overt, however:

> Wohin willst du denn, Kopf?
> He, was treibt ihr da, Füße?
> Wir baden, du Arsch.
>
> [Where are you going, head? / Hey, what are you doing, feet? / We're having a bath, you arse.][63]

60 Durs Grünbein, 'Schlaflos in Rom. Versuch über den Satirendichter Juvenal' ('Sleepless in Rome. Essay on the Satirical Poet Juvenal'), in *Antike Dispositionen*, pp. 328–68 (p. 329).
61 Irmela Hijiya-Kirschneit, 'Die Nudel im Rinnstein', *Frankfurter Allgemeine Zeitung*, 12 February 2009, p. 32.
62 *Lob des Taifuns*, pp. 11, 18, 37.
63 Ibid., p. 20.

Such body apostrophe generates humour and reveals a playfulness that frequently surfaces in the collection. Humour generally, which tends to lie in wry recognitions and the perception of incongruities, may indeed alone attest to a poetics of presence, the more where humour combines with body imagery.

The prevalence of body imagery in Grünbein's poetry before the travel cycles has been remarked upon.[64] His was amongst the contemporary poetry in German exemplifying 'the lyric perspective's proximity to the body': 'with his collection *Schädelbasislektion*, [he] became the best-known exponent of the 1980s' urban-anatomical'.[65] Since then, travelling the human body's interior has been superseded by the tourist body venturing into various outsides. In an aside, Michael Eskin has referred to the last lines of 'Julia Livilla' from *Nach den Satiren*, where Grünbein's Seneca is coughing and in pain as 'rendering the poem viscerally palpable and immediate by underlaying it with the dramatized speaker's bodily presence'.[66] This is what happens in the travel cycles, too, the tourist-poet's voice being explicitly embodied. Analyzing *Vom Schnee oder Descartes in Deutschland*, Sonja Klein summarized the importance of the body for Descartes's manservant: 'To understand the outside world, he relies on the body and his sensory abilities'.[67] This summary of the body as a sensitive instrument applies equally to the tourist-poet encountering the outside in the travel cycles.

If this section of the enquiry into presence in the Rome and Japan cycles emphasizes links with the writing of the body throughout Grünbein's oeuvre, there is nonetheless a difference, too. Continuing to write the body jars with the generic conventions of travel writing. Florian Berg, reflecting on Grünbein's earlier poetics, draws the crucial distinction:

> His poetics then examines the constructive moment of perception, which is determined by human physiology. It entails a shift in the concept of perception, replacing an observed reality (of surfaces) with an observer-created reality (of mental constructions). Perception and language thus remain inextricable from the body behind them.[68]

---

64 For example, Michael Eskin, 'Body Language. Durs Grünbein's Aesthetics', *arcadia*, 37.1 (2002), 42–66.

65 Ruth J. Owen, 'Bodies in Contemporary Poetry', in *Schaltstelle. Neue deutsche Lyrik im Dialog*, ed. by Karen Leeder (Amsterdam: Rodopi, 2007), pp. 269–91 (pp. 269, 270).

66 Eskin, *Poetic Affairs*, p. 76.

67 Sonja Klein, *'Denn alles, alles ist verlorne Zeit'. Fragment und Erinnerung im Werk Durs Grünbeins* (Bielefeld: Aisthesis, 2008), p. 118.

68 Florian Berg, *Das Gedicht und das Nichts. Über Anthropologie und Geschichte im Werk Durs Grünbeins* (Würzburg: Königshausen & Neumann, 2007), p. 35.

In the travel cycles, the observed 'here' – primarily of the architectural surfaces – is not ousted by the 'here' created by the observer; rather, both remain in tension, for the use of language is changed by travel, the very material presence of the poem bending to its place of origin.

The Presence of the Poem

Grünbein's travel cycles put value on recognizing the poetic and linguistic forms used to mediate realities. Roman numerals, long hexameter lines and the regularly sixteen-line blocks in the 'Aroma' cycle indicate the place leaving concrete marks on the poems written there. Grünbein's Rome is defined not only architecturally but linguistically: Italian words, usually italicized, pepper the 'Aroma' cycle. Whilst their meanings are mostly accessible in context, primarily they reflect the language of the place penetrating into the German poem: 'Frizzante o naturale', 'mezzogiorno', 'Benvenuto', 'bravo', 'morituri' and 'stronzo', 'motorini', 'Carabiniere' and 'Aiuto', 'velina', 'il diluviale', 'ferragosto', 'Lavazza', 'Averna'.[69] Such use of Italian vocabulary proliferates the variables within the German text, but is transparent and sparse enough not to suggest a wholesale departure from its monolingual status. Whilst an absorption of the place's language, it is not as radical an encounter as with the Japanese language in *Lob des Taifuns*.

In the Japan cycles, each diary entry is made up of small text blocks at odds with the norms of lyric text presentation. It combines a three-line haiku or five-line tanka in large font, below this a precise date in small font, below that a location in small font, plus in many of the texts a prose commentary of sorts. All this is in German, reading from left to right and down the page. Then the poem continues in the vertical characters of the Japanese translation, with a gap between what in German is marked by the differing font sizes – the haiku or tanka proper and its accompanying text blocks. The whole poem is a hybrid form: not just a haiku-style German poem (as the cycle subtitle misdirects) or poem with translation (as the volume's title page misdirects), but a unique form in two scripts. The two scripts correspond to a doubling, the semantic replication of the German in Japanese, but not in the conventional way a translation is presented with parallel texts: rather, the doubling is re-enacted in a single text space and in each poem of the cycle, the two languages making in each instance a single poem. *Lob des Taifuns* is thus Grünbein's first collection of 'post-monolingual' poems.

69 *Aroma*, pp. 13, 16, 17, 18, 24, 26, 35, 42, 44, 61, 62.

Most Grünbein readers will not in general know Japanese, so, for them, the Japanese script is impenetrable, mute: a visual presentation without sounds. Whatever the perils of asking a German readership to contend with this, it emphasizes the glyphic nature of visual signs, drawing attention to the concrete look of the whole printed poem on the page: the German running horizontally from left to right, the Japanese running vertically with the columns ordered from right to left. This poetry is concrete because its conspicuous feature is its visual appearance. It is shaped poetry, in a repeated pattern, calling attention to the space of the page, through the different sized fonts, the different vectors of its scripts, and each entry's rigid but simple structure. The presence of the Japanese in the German poem is unlike anything else in contemporary German poetry or in travel writing. Although it may recall Pound's use of Chinese characters inserted into *The Cantos*, these are finally just single logograms, whereas the Japanese in *Lob des Taifuns* is a rewriting of Grünbein's German, which in turn is a writing of Japan. It manifests the idea of travel as an encounter with unknown language and, in this case, lettering. Although the title page and paratexts announce that the Japanese is a reiteration of the meaning already read in German, the more striking effect is that most readers cannot look straight through the whole poem to meaning. Whilst it risks alienating some readers, the Japanese thus emphasizes the materiality of the whole poem, its spatial organization as an individual text and as part of a cycle of spatially similar texts. It renders the poem a complicated presence: offering Japanese reception of the reception of Japanese culture in German, it foregrounds the irreducible incongruity between two languages.

It also renders the poetry collaborative: Grünbein and Yûji Nawata have collaborated to produce each poem for Grünbein's diary (rather contradicting the 'snap shot' poetics asserted in the afterword). The synthesis of two languages in one text allows a strange lyric form to emerge, previously unseen, entertaining differing degrees of opacity in its different parts and for different readers. The Japanese that might be assumed completely opaque yields Tokyo and dates which can be deduced visually, albeit not sounded, because of their frequent recurrence over the cycles; the opening German lines, assumed completely transparent, turn out to be mystifying in many instances, needing to be propped up on dates and place names and, more often than not, a prose crib that contextualizes the verse. The collaborative nature of the writing is thus part of a hybridity that combines haiku or tanka, diary entry, travel record in prose and translation. By literally exchanging words, Grünbein explores the possibility of the reciprocal, transcultural poem.

The explanatory prose notes below the date and place lines, and before the Japanese, are often longer than the haiku-like or tanka-like openings. Some function as a kind of commentary, mostly from the perspective of a tourist new to

Japan; many expose the creative moment. They tend to explain the haiku or tanka part in terms of where and when it was written or reveal something otherwise mysterious about the juxtaposition of elements mentioned in the larger-font lines. Often accounting for how the poem came into being, they are unpretentious, semantically and formally contrasting with the more demanding haiku or tanka part of the poem: a prosaic cousin, prosaic since in prose, prosaic as in less imaginative.

The haiku idea of seventeen syllables 5–7–5 has been adopted by Grünbein for his haiku-like openings, although German-language prosody never cares about syllables and anyway only the Western reception equates syllables with the sound units counted in Japanese-language poetry.[70] Further, Japanese haikus have traditionally been printed in a single vertical line and tend to take aspects of the natural world as their subject matter, while haikus in Western languages often appear in three lines to ape the three phrases of Japanese haikus and may deal with any subject matter. Within German poetry, Erich Fried, for example, claimed ancient Japanese lyric forms, especially the tanka, as an influence.[71] Grünbein is therefore drawing on the reception of the haiku and tanka forms, in particular the post-1960 reception following the Japanese-American scholar and translator Kenneth Yasuda.[72] Yasuda's translations apply a 5–7–5 syllable count in English and his theory includes the concept of a 'haiku moment' based in personal experience. This concept has resonated with poets in North America and Europe, and seems to be congruent with Grünbein's 'Reisetagebücher in Haikus'. It was implicit in Roland Barthes's wry remark about Western haiku adoption: 'You are entitled, says the haiku, to be trivial, short, ordinary; enclose what you see, what you feel, in a slender horizon of words, and you will be interesting'.[73]

Grünbein's poetics of presence in *Lob des Taifuns* tallies with aspects of Barthes's conception of haiku. Barthes makes the haiku's arrest of meaning indicative of Japan in *Empire of Signs* and its purposes opposite to those of Western literature. Likewise, the hybrid-haiku form is a form for Grünbein's Japan, created

70 Those units are known as moras (or morae) to English-speaking linguists, the tanka consisting of 31 moras with the pattern 5–7–5–7–7; the haiku consisting of 17 moras, in three phrases of 5–7–5 moras.

71 Dirk van Stekelenburg, 'Man kann sich wehren. Gespräch mit Erich Fried', in *Einer singt aus der Zeit gegen die Zeit. Erich Fried 1921–1988. Materialien und Texte zu Leben und Werk*, ed. by Volker Kaukoreit and Heidemarie Vahl (Darmstadt: Häusser, 1991), pp. 43–58 (p. 49).

72 Kenneth Yasuda, *The Japanese Haiku. Its Essential Nature, History, and Possibilities in English, with Selected Examples* (Rutland: Tuttle, 1957).

73 Roland Barthes, *Empire of Signs*, trans. by Richard Howard (New York: Hill and Wang, 1983), p. 70.

in Japan, for a creating of Japan in German poetry. The one poem in his collection not in this combination form evokes being in a plane over Denmark and Sweden on the way back.[74] The lyric form changes on re-entering Europe. Having this formally exceptional poem in the collection emphasizes the status of the dominant form as a form for Japan. It indicates travel as an encounter with language that marks formally the poetry produced there. To similar ends, the only rhyme, something unknown to Japanese haikus, comes in the penultimate poem of the first cycle when over Siberia, flying home.[75] Besides the haiku as a form epitomizing Japan, Barthes's *Empire of Signs* posits further ideas about presence that might be said to be made manifest in Grünbein's *Lob des Taifuns*: first, Barthes's dream of knowing a foreign language without understanding it, so as 'to perceive the difference in it without that difference ever being recuperated';[76] this corresponds to the incompleteness of perception, the lighter, more ludic Grünbein poems, and their incorporation of the Japanese text. And second, Barthes's Tokyo where 'every discovery is intense and fragile, it can be repeated or recovered only by memory of the trace it has left in you: to visit a place for the first time is thereby to begin to write it';[77] this corresponds to the intensity and fragility evoked by the memory traces of Grünbein's visits. Thus within its connections to haiku reception, *Lob des Taifuns* attests to a particular resonance with Barthes, recasting a connection that goes back within Grünbein's oeuvre as far as the *Wende* cycle title 'Die Leeren Zeichen' ['The Empty Signs'].[78]

It was also Barthes who declared, in *Camera Lucida*, that '[e]very photograph is a certificate of presence'.[79] The use of photographs in Grünbein's Japan collection emphasizes presence in terms of the place the poems originated and in terms of their materiality. Each cycle in *Lob des Taifuns* has a picture at its opening, three tourist postcards: a child kabuki actor in sepia, a Shinto shrine in sepia, a Buddhist statue from the national museum, plus a contemporary card advertising prostitutes with a cartoon image of two schoolgirls. Serving as visual supplements to the texts, as the Winckelmann 'Opus incertum' sketch does to 'Aroma', they suggest visual clichés of Japan accumulated by the tourist-poet. In part, they render the poems akin to the ephemeral written messages expected on the reverse

74 *Lob des Taifuns*, p. 56.
75 Ibid., p. 32.
76 Barthes, *Empire of Signs*, p. 6.
77 Ibid., p. 36.
78 Durs Grünbein, 'Die Leeren Zeichen', in Durs Grünbein, *Schädelbasislektion* (Frankfurt a. M.: Suhrkamp, 1991), p. 67.
79 Roland Barthes, *Camera Lucida. Reflections on Photography*, trans. by Richard Howard (London: Vintage, 2000), p. 87.

of postcards. Images within the 'Aroma' and *Lob des Taifuns* cycles are captioned only at the back of the books and thus tend to function generically like this. In 'Aroma', there are two monochrome architectural drawings, both early maps of sorts.[80] The first shows the ship-shaped island in the River Tiber mentioned in the following poem and the second shows a plan of catacombs mentioned in the following poem.[81] So, unlike the Japan postcards, they are partly illustrative. Since early maps are obsolete in the present, as postcards increasingly are too, both prompt one to consider the poetry to be just as partial and time-bound a representation of the respective cultures encountered.

Looking back across Grünbein's oeuvre for work formally akin to the travel cycles discussed, the two book-length lyric cycles *Vom Schnee oder Descartes in Deutschland* and *Porzellan. Vom Untergang meiner Stadt* stand out, as does *Das erste Jahr* in its use of diary form. The difference in 2008 and 2010 is how these forms work in conjunction with travel and the transcultural: the long lyric cycle as a travel diary is a kind of translation, the portage home of the foreign. The tourist-poet is forever hovering between surprise and familiarity. Evoking the here-and-now and bodily presence creates an affinity for the foreign place, making there as here. In this one might even detect a trace of the ex-GDR poet: *Vom Stellenwert der Worte* mentions Eastern European socialism's measures against every kind of 'Auslandsliebe' [love for the foreign].[82] Where the 'Aroma' cycle displays the tourist-poet's sensibility amid the long-loved foreign, the more innovative *Lob des Taifuns* cycles inscribe a new love. In the Japan cycles, an innovation in German poetry, language is refracted through a place and cannot return intact to home ground. The tourist-poet seeks on the other side of the world the material necessary for absorption before a new advance in lyric language can be made. Here, the poem is where two cultures come into contact. In the co-presence of German and Japanese lie the possibilities, stemming from reciprocity, but also the perils, of the transcultural poem.

80 *Aroma*, p. 182.
81 Ibid., pp. 30, 47.
82 Grünbein, *Vom Stellenwert der Worte*, p. 32.

Helen Vendler

Europe after the Last Rains. On *Ashes for Breakfast*

The appearance of some poems in British and U.S. journals notwithstanding, it was not until the 2005 publication of *Ashes for Breakfast: Selected Poems* – crisply and colloquially translated by the English poet Michael Hofmann – that an English-speaking reader could approach Durs Grünbein's coruscating writing. 'I was happy in a sandy no-man's land', the poet says in his devastatingly ironic 1991 sonnet sequence, 'Portrait of the Artist as a Young Border Dog', evoking his student life in the East by casting himself as a patrol dog 'in the suicide strip, equidistant from East and West'.[1] 'I was half zombie, half *enfant perdu*' (p. 85), he says (alluding to Heine's poem by that name about a broken-hearted young sentry), 'Myself just a cipher in a simultaneous equation' (p. 87). With the demolition of the Wall in 1989, with even the 'two or three names for the place of separation' vanishing into oblivion, 'nothing is left to recall the trick / By which a strip of land became a hole in time' (p. 87). 'Being a dog', says a defining poem early in 'Portrait of the Artist', 'is having to when you don't want to, wanting to / When you can't, and always somebody watching':

> Hundsein ist Müssen, wenn du nicht willst, Wollen
> Wenn du nicht kannst und immer schaut jemand zu. (p. 68)

The rigidity of being fettered in will and placed under surveillance emerges in the iron grip of Grünbein's epigram. The young poet left the East as soon as possible, only to discover, with many others, the vices and disappointments of the West. Although he became permanently ill at ease with respect to place, he is supremely at home in language, a writer of notable essays (as discussed elsewhere in this volume) as well as of these masterful poems. He has won prize after prize in Germany for his poetry (see Preface).

Even I, with no formal knowledge of German (but after years of lieder and opera, able to follow it haltingly *en face*), couldn't help but stay awake all night reading (with the translator's aid) Grünbein's severe work. In the fourteen years covered by *Ashes for Breakfast*, from the 1988 *Mornings in the Grayzone* through the 2002 *Configured Night* (*Erklärte Nacht*, echoing Schönberg's *Verklärte Nacht*

1 Durs Grünbein, *Ashes for Breakfast. Selected Poems*, trans. by Michael Hofmann (New York: Farrar, Straus and Giroux, 2005), p. 83. Further references to this work are given in parenthesis in the main text.

[*Transfigured Night*]), as well as the other works discussed in this volume, Grünbein has produced an absolutely unignorable body of poetry. With Grünbein, as with other poets whose language I did not know – Miłosz, Syzmborska, Tranströmer – I have been compelled to write on the principle that those poets were so striking, even in translation, that some proportion of their poetic qualities could be described and investigated. Many things from foreign poems can be imported into consciousness – montages of images, epigrams, historical panoramas, allegorical emblems, passages of personal distress – and English-speaking poets have often owed significant developments in their own writing to works they cannot read in the original (see Seamus Heaney's *The Haw Lantern*, visibly influenced by Eastern European poetry).

Ashes for Breakfast contains only what Michael Hofmann found himself able and willing to translate from a very large mass of work. Hofmann, who is capable of extraordinary stylistic invention, says of the 'tracing' required in translation, 'I have the ability, I think, to go over lines, and make it seem like freehand':

> The worst thing in a translation, it seems to me, is the appearance of being remote-controlled, *ferngesteuert*. You have to look comfortable, voluntary. The Grünbein translations will look like – I hope to God they do look like – not the product of steel rulers and midnight oil, but like poems that want to be poems [...]. What I'm anxious *not* to do is offer something exotic, wooden, pointless, and dead. (pp. xi, xiii)

Hofmann can be proud: his language is springy on the page. And even if it must, from time to time, depart rather far from the actual word-for-word brilliance of a Grünbein line, it usually keeps the poet's import and tone. And tone in Grünbein – dry, sarcastic, impassioned, aggressive – is as crucial as the electric metaphors invigorating his poetry. There is hardly a page here that doesn't contain a real poem, out of Grünbein by Hofmann, a poem 'real' enough – in emotion, in cadence, in imagination – to make a reader's hair stand on end.

What was it in Grünbein that so seized my attention that I couldn't put down *Ashes for Breakfast*? In part it was the sardonic humour, in part the savagery, in part a violent candour – all expressed in lines of cool formal elegance. In Grünbein's pages, uncontrollable feeling encounters the at-first-invisible control of an expert technique, creating that exciting 'deadlock' of equally strong matter and manner that Robert Frost in his *Notebooks* found essential to poetry. Grünbein's earlier poems are allowed more sprawl than the later ones (which are hard, tight, classical, even when they are most slangy or scandalous in indignation). Grünbein's successive volumes are linked by a submerged autobiography (usually impersonally expressed), which in its unfolding draws the reader on from poem to poem. One of the earliest autobiographical poems in this collection ('Trilce, César', on Grünbein's discovery of Vallejo) shows the poet as one of East Germany's young generation of writers longing to escape a boring stasis, a deadening isolation:

> There were days it was all we could manage
> to say, 'It may never happen' or
> 'Something will turn up ...' bored in
>
> overheated libraries where, in moments
> before they completely glazed over
> our glances found themselves drifting
> like smoke rings
> under the lofty coffered ceilings
> of Alexandrian reading rooms.
> Most of us
>
> wanted to get away (to New York
> or someplace): we were students
>
> with funny cracked voices
> enthusiastically turning
> failed projects in our heads [...]. (p. 5)

The early poems are pervaded by the deterioration of East Germany, where the poet's aesthetic sense is stifled; he groans as his gaze passes from place to place. In a 'bubbling stream' with 'old auto tires, broken glass, household junk' and 'polystyrene and crap', there bobs a child's toy, a 'yellow plastic duck' (in German, 'ein grüner Badefisch'), and at the sight of this filth-covered souvenir of infancy the poem resists its own disgust, imploring: 'Kommt / Wellen klaren Wassers, kommt' ['Come, / waves of crystal waters, come', p. 39]. The ghost of Schubert's flowing water and the 'Come' of 'Veni Creator' hover behind the repellent polluted brook, one of many cases in which the shades of lost ideals form the implicit background to Grünbein's jeremiads.

Mornings in the Grayzone tightens up considerably with a series of 'monological poems'. These are manifestos exploring the poet's aesthetic: like Yeats, he aims at poems at once cold and passionate. As Grünbein wittily puts it in 'Monological Poem #1':

> There are hot forms and
> cold forms and poems
>
> no matter how you break them and
> what you print them on
>
> are always cold (no matter how
> hot they were at the manufacturing stage). (p. 43)

But in spite of his ambition to remain in cold charge of his hot material, Grünbein, like many another poet, discovers that poems have a will of their own, often the contrary mirror-image of his own conscious aims. As he writes in the equally witty 'Monological Poem #4':

> You pursue your own
> eccentric designs you re-
>
> fine the images you order
> the moments but you don't
>
> listen to them
> as quite differently in their own ways
>
> they pursue their eccentric
> designs refine
>
> images show chance movements
> move differently
>
> in the same spaces and damned
> if they're going to listen to you. That
>
> is the nub. (p. 51)

'Das // ist der springende Punkt', says the German, 'That is the crucial point' of poetry: it has to awaken itself under the poet's hand, and sketch out its own desires. It was inevitable that Grünbein, with his elegant architectural sense, should see, and wryly rue, the way in which the poem of the linguistic unconscious runs in competition with the one pursued by the poet's will.

The result of the opening of the West to Grünbein's scrutiny was the extraordinarily unsettled 1994 sequence called 'Variations on No Theme', with its thirty-nine untitled and unrhymed thirteen-line quasi-sonnets (deriving, says Hofmann, from Brodsky's 'A Part of Speech'). Grünbein's 'Variations' seem the exacerbated utterances of a mind in terminal distress, imagining, even when taking a shower, surreal threats linked to the German past:

> And in the morning, you turn on the shower
>   And out comes ... water, what did you think?
> Red and blue stand for hot and cold.
>   The skin wasn't peeled off in strips like wallpaper.
> That's just a nightmare, silly.
>   There's no thorn in the towel, no blood
> On the tiles – the plug hole's gurgle

Signifies cleanliness, not death.
As to whether they still make soap
Out of bones, the foam drying
On the lines of your palms takes the fifth.
Dragged along by the hair, briefly, fear-
Fully animated, a short-lived suspicion dies. (p. 103)

Possessing neither the formal perfection of the fourteen-line sonnet, nor the twelve-line balance of the douzain, these thirteen-line poems are models of disequilibrium. Avoiding the first-person 'I', as he often does, and resorting here to brief second-person self-address, Grünbein adopts, as a sign of precariously-maintained instability, the pretext of a tone of absolute objectivity: 'Rot und Blau / Steht auf den Hähnen für Heiß und Kalt'. In another poem, the speaker finds his external surroundings unreal, and only books remain as sustenance:

Unreal, the room you live in by yourself,
The fly-spotted mirror, dust
In the corners clustering round a long hair
That's been lying there for weeks.
No bowl of fruit, no vase,
The only cornucopias, stacked tight,
Are the books [...]. (p. 109)

In German, the 'long hair' is a 'Frauenhaar,' a woman's hair: the forlorn room has lost its other inhabitant.

The mode of this member of the sequence, one of disenchanted inventory, governs many of the chilling 'Variations', which embark, after the first thirteen poems, on an autobiographical journey. Grünbein begins with birth, when the cutting of the umbilical cord is the first sundering by the Fates (p. 123); now, the 'trusting smile' (p. 125) of the earliest photographs dissolves and rejects the present gaze of the speaker. Childhood brings 'the conspiracy / Among the growns to feed and stifle you', provoking 'Great clouds of hysteria / Where you learned to walk, and to fight back' (p. 129). In time, a form of unbearable response begins to stain everything – from a fishmonger's shop to a cat's cry – with horror:

[...] With a shudder
You see the crab with rubber bands
Round its claws, the trout and eel nuzzling
The slimy belly of the vast carp.
A cat cries in the car trunk for air. (p. 143)

As 'Variations' continues, the green of spring and the song of the blackbird induce a temporary relenting of the malice of time, but even then, the speaker is conscious of graves under his feet:

> Nothing is lost, not while grass sprouts
>   From every crack [...]
>   [...] How your heart leaps
>   To hear the scolding blackbird
> Defend her patch of lawn by the side of the road,
>   And green everywhere. Your walk takes you
> Over graves, knocked down to pathway. (p. 155)

Nature's rebirth, however welcome in itself, cannot cure the intensity of exposure present in the most shocking, if still impersonally phrased, self-portrait in 'Variations', the poem beginning 'Shivering under masks of knowledge'. 'So wird man Sarkast', 'This is how one becomes sarcastic', Grünbein explains (although Hofmann translates the impersonal 'man' into the second-person 'you'). The poem anatomizes the human being produced by life in East Germany, confined to the oratory of its 'cheerful killers' on the TV monitor:

> Shivering under masks of knowledge,
>   Freaked out by the extraordinary,
> Dreamless by day under cynical clocks,
>   Timetables, scales, counseled by
> Cheerful killers, in front of the monitor –
>   It made you sarcastic. (p. 159)

By the end of the poem, the self has had its sight immedicably corrupted: 'The backs of your eyes peopled by monsters' in Hofmann; in German, 'Der Augengrund, von Insekten bewohnt'. The insects (as actual forms) seem to me more frightening than monsters (out of legend). The despair in the ironist's retrospect is felt in the shadow-presence in the poem of the child he was, whose 'sweet songs' antedated the sarcasm of the present.

The darkness of Grünbein's vision has disturbed readers and reviewers. The poems, with their grim gaze, rarely offer relief from their short, knifing sentences. They challenge the reader to a contest in truth-telling: can you really, O reader, deny this unsparing account? For readers who find a confirming darkness in themselves, in society, or in the powers that be, Grünbein appears as a voice in the wilderness, an astringent corrective to the mandatory blandness of those cheerful murderers talking at us from the TV.

Grünbein's principled refusal of all transcendence did not falter after 'Variationen'. In the 1999 *After the Satires*, his sight trains itself on society. In the original edition, Grünbein comments on the reference in his title to the satyr-plays following the tragedies: 'After the satires: that meant once everything had been said and chewed over, the way home, the hangover, the time for intellectual play and digestion'. Judith Ryan, as she quotes this note, remarks:

> The poems attempt to register a bitter awakening on the part of East Germans after the first excitement of German reunification has worn off. Expecting to enjoy the economic prosperity or 'full plate' of the Federal Republic, former East Germans are disappointed to find that their lives are still difficult and that they are not always fully accepted by their new fellow citizens. Traces of the East German past remain engraved, as it were, on the faces and in the minds of those who experienced it.[2]

The frequent critique, by others, of his bleakness is embedded in Grünbein's 'Memorandum':

> Poets, so they tell us, are awkward customers
>
> Not up to much. Even laughter has a keener, full-throated edge
> When they're not around. They're not very amusing. (p. 203)

No, poets are not very amusing. Even college students, confronting Emily Dickinson, ask, 'Does she *always* have to be so *depressing*?' The peculiar exhilaration that attends every reading of a stunning poem is felt, perhaps, by only a minority: those reading solely for content are put off by 'depressing' observations. The discontented demand that poetry should be 'healing' or 'uplifting' or 'optimistic' or 'humane' (or 'accessible') reaffirms the truth expressed by Eliot that 'human kind cannot bear very much reality'. Perhaps poets of innately optimistic temperament are found more appealing than poets of the steely-eyed sort, just as poems of simple vocabulary tend to be preferred to poems of knotty intellectuality. Yet it is, in fact, an optimistic act to write any poem at all: the act implies the trust that another mind will meet the poem half way, and an even deeper trust that language can become adequate to a human predicament.

The 'thirteen fantasies' that Grünbein clustered (in the volume *After the Satires*) under the hellish title 'Ashes for Breakfast' seem to abandon the faith in both the classics and in the sciences that had been a bulwark in his writing. Although the individual poems in 'Ashes for Breakfast' are intricately formal and for the most part rhymed, their content is often brutal. Human beings, members of the animal kingdom, seem hardly distant from those primates whose busy louse-

2 Judith Ryan, 'The Skull beneath the Skin', in *A New History of German Literature*, ed. by David E. Wellbery and others (Cambridge, MA: Harvard University Press, 2004), pp. 959–64 (pp. 961–62).

hunting has evolved into our ceaseless 'Unrast', restlessness, 'the ruin of our species'. Behold man in Grünbein's pitiless portrait:

> Between snack bar and coitus, how often, miles from the Olduvai Gorge,
> The hairy geezer puts in an appearance, hobbling along on the backs of
> his hands,
> Failing abjectly as he reaches for the stars, because of a crooked ladder or
> a jammed elevator.
> (So much for *The Origin of Species* or *Civilization and Its Discontents*.) (p. 207)

The veneer of education, *ad astra per aspera*, seems miserably thin before such an apparition. There are even, for Grünbein, disheartening moments 'When the books close ranks and it transpires they don't speak' – 'sie bleiben stumm' (p. 209). Nor is the accumulation of money any answer to life's griefs: 'Isn't all money the property / In any case of the bank? Oh to be a child again, grubbing in real feces' (p. 215). Goings-on in the outer world are only a momentary distraction: after reading the newspaper, the poet announces, 'I have breakfasted on ashes. My daily bread'. Here the poet, speaking in the lyric first person, is the man of letters who looks for a sustaining word in the daily paper, and finds none. The muse of history, Clio, will not reveal any significance in current events:

> I have breakfasted on ashes, the black
> Dust that comes off newspapers, from the freshly printed columns.
> When a coup makes no stain, and a tornado sticks to half a page.
> And it seemed to me as though the Fates licked their lips
>
> When war broke out in the sports section, reflected in the falling Dow.
> I have breakfasted on ashes. My daily bread.
> And Clio, as ever, keeps mum ... There, just as I folded them up,
> The rustling pages sent a shiver down my spine. (p. 221)

And yet Clio, for all her intermittent silence, is Grünbein's principal muse. He came to consciousness within the disastrous history of twentieth-century Germany and has had to re-imagine that history for himself: he has had to meditate on the fire-bombed Dresden where he was born and on the invisibly-divided Berlin where he now lives. Besides 'Ashes for Breakfast', there are three other distinctive rhymed sequences in *After the Satires*: 'Berlin Rounds' and 'Greetings from Oblivion City' (both about Berlin) and 'Europe after the Last Rains' (about Dresden). It must give a shiver to citizens of Berlin to see their contemporary city-sites given sharp definition by Grünbein, with his perpetually simmering sense of an imperfectly-buried past. The poem in 'Berlin Rounds' about Friedrichshain (the area in which the poet has his study) ends with the half-forgotten evils of the

Russian occupation: ‘That pleas went unheeded in the cellars / Is something you can sense, in Friedrichshain’ (p. 237). But not everybody wants to sense such things. As the new Potsdamer Platz is being constructed, human scale vanishes, and the Russian-occupied past vanishes along with it:

> What’s going on here, you ask, nothing looks familiar
> As you hunch under cranes. Didn’t you use to be a giant
> And have the place at your feet? Squares shrank to Lilliputian scale
> When you surfaced. One ‘Atchoo!’ brought down whole apartment blocks.
>
> This used to be waste ground, sand, and a bit of scorched grass,
> Not marked on the map. Now no one believes you when you say
> Goya’s colossus used to sit here, waiting for it to revert to steppe. (p. 241)

Grünbein’s sudden surges into another plane – from Potsdamer Platz to Goya’s grossly over-sized man-eating monster – are one of the features of his agile imagination, which can swoop in a single line, with the celerity of incensed intelligence, from the banal present to the anguished past.

The tone taken about Berlin lightens somewhat in Grünbein’s postcard-sequence, ‘Greetings from Oblivion City’. My favourite moment of lightness is the one in which the poet thinks up new constellations appropriate to industrialized post-modernity:

> [...] Among the new
> Constellations, glittering alongside the Lyre, the Swan, and Sagittarius,
> Is a sports car at full tilt, hounded by a Dinosaur.
> Over the Revolver hangs the back-to-front Baseball Cap [...].
>
> Seen from the air, the city looks like a scrambled text anyway
> That only beings with polyhedron eyes could ever crack. (p. 245)

And it was time (one thinks, reading Grünbein) that the modern fetish of working-out got its comeuppance:

> A studio at night. A picture window. Running on the spot,
> Earplugs in, you see women strapped to metal equipment
> That resembles torture bench and garrote.
> *Fitness* is the magic word here [...]. (p. 249)

Other social fetishes are anatomized: tooth veneers, cryo-coffins, TV dinners, political correctness, movies as the new opiate of the people, hormones. In Orwellian fashion, ‘happiness is the first duty of every citizen. / Whoever is happy, is unstoppable’. Suicide is forbidden: ‘You can vote for anything, it seems, but not for death’ (p. 251).

But it is in the formidable 1994 eleven-poem Dresden sequence, 'Europe after the Last Rains', that we see the most melancholy (and angry) Grünbein. He returns to the place of his youth, but it has disappeared. 'Memory has no real estate ... no city / where you come home and you know where you are' (p. 267). Remembering the 1945 firebombing of the city, Grünbein asks, '[I]s it the same city in the valley / as the pilot saw in its phosphorescent glory?' (p. 269):

> It was at one and the same time
> long doomed, still inhabited, and already forgotten
> by the last of its fly-by-night tenants, the Furies flitting
> from civilization to ashes. (p. 269)

In post-war Dresden, fragments of baroque architecture could still be seen along the Elbe; and Grünbein's analogizing mind juxtaposes those fragments with looming architectural shapes unearthed from the remote past:

> Along the scuffed banks, worn brown in parts,
> you still encountered massy baroque. Some souls might find
> their personal Angkor Wat there in the chilly moonlight. (p. 275)

The eleven poems of 'Europe after the Last Rains' (unlike the uniform thirteen-line ones of the 'Variations on No Theme') differ so greatly in poem-length, rhyme scheme and line-length that they exert a formal fascination. Several poems play with various species of quatrain-rhyme; there is a dizain here, a douzain there. And Poem IV is a sonnet, rhyming oddly, as it brackets the octave with its *a* rhyme, and the sestet with its *e* rhyme: *abcd bcda efg fge* (I separate the rhyme-units for convenience, but there are no spaces between the lines in the poem). Strange though it seems in its rhyme, this sonnet depends on one of the perennial sonnet-conventions, the 'running over' (from sheer emotion) of the octave into the ninth line. After the ninth line, Dresden goes aflame, the water of its river useless to its burning inhabitants.

Only at the sixth poem of the eleven-poem 'Europe' does one recognize the strict structure of the whole arc: 5 + 1 + 5. Poem VI, the central one, reveals the death of Grünbein's grandmother in the successive bombings of Dresden in February 1945 by the Royal Air Force and the American Army Air Force. The incendiary firestorm that engulfed the city killed thousands. (The late Allied decision to take Dresden as an objective for bombing has been heatedly disputed since the War.) I will quote the whole of this extraordinary poem of Apocalypse (which includes the Angels of the Last Trump), first in English and then in its formally rhymed pentameter quatrains (one of the stateliest of measures). The first and last stanzas, connecting the beginning and the end, are composed in embraced quatrains, *abba*; the three middle stanzas have alternately-rhymed quatrains, *abab*. The poem as a whole, punctuated by three successive waves of bombers, is dedicated 'to my grandmother, Dora W.':

> When the first wave of bombers came, she was
> In hospital with scarlet fever. The air-raid alarm
> Tore many from their dreams. The winter air grew warm,
> And the night was bright as day.
>
> Like ghosts in their white nightshirts,
> They ran barefoot to the Elbe meadows ...
> Panic, a surge of air from the bomb bays,
> Before the angels trumpeted from on high.
>
> And when the second wave of bombers came,
> The city vanished into a silent film, and no shadow fell
> As it burned through the wall of flame,
> That was objective to some, and a trap to others.
>
> On one twentieth-century night, planes
> Delivered a second stone age.
> The odd bomb shelter, like the tomb behind the stone,
> Housed man, wife, and child, all done to a crisp.
>
> And when the third wave came, she was walking
> Calmly in the line of refugees, on tottering legs
> To the afterlife. There were no tears,
> Nothing left to cry with in whatever was left. (p. 277)

Even in translation, the poem is arresting (although 'done to a crisp' seems to me a false note). But the original – with its elegiac subject, its harrowing images, its basis in family history, its dryness of statement, and its solidity of technique – seems to me a work destined to last. It should be noticed that the central stanza, representing the firestorm, is the only one composed of a single sentence, and that the last line of the poem, truncated from the usual five beats to four, opens a final vacancy into which Grünbein's grandmother vanishes:

> *Meiner Großmutter Dora W.*
>
> Und als der erste Angriff kam, sie lag
> Im Krankenhaus mit Scharlach. Der Alarm
> Riß viele aus dem Schlaf. Vom Glutwind warm
> War draußen Winter, und die Nacht war Tag.

> Gespenster, die im weißen Nachthemd spuken,
> Rannten sie barfuß an die Elbewiesen.
> ... – Panik, ein Luftstrom aus den Feuerluken,
> Bevor aus allen Wolken die Posaunen bliesen.
>
> Und als der zweite Angriff kam, verschwand
> Die Stadt im Stummfilm, und kein Schatten fiel
> Als sie verbrannte durch die Flammenwand,
> Den einen Falle und den andern Ziel.
>
> Aus einer Nacht im Zwanzigsten Jahrhundert
> Flogen Maschinen eine zweite Steinzeit an.
> In manchem Kellergrab, ein Höhlenwunder,
> Fand man verbacken Kind und Frau und Mann.
>
> Und als der dritte Angriff kam, sie ging
> Gefaßt im Flüchtlingszug, auf schwachen Beinen
> In eine Nachwelt ein. Da war kein Weinen,
> Das auf den Trümmern noch verfing. (p. 276)

Grünbein is not unaware of what went on in Dresden before the bombing. In Poem VIII, recalling the destruction by bombs of masterpieces of painting and music, he acquiesces in that loss 'in the name of what happened there' the death transports bringing innocent people to concentration camps. Then he asks the forbidden question: 'Was it worth it?':

> [...] in the name of what happened there
> One gives up the Vermeer (burned)
>
> And the Bach (disappeared).
> Was it worth it? That whole cities,
> From which the death transports rolled
> Became wastelands on Lethe's banks. (p. 281)

Before the final subsidence of his Dresden sequence into blank erasure, Grünbein allows himself a surreal report of the city's chaos during the bombing, as circus animals flee into the fire, watched with dismay by the damaged statues of Apostles surveying the destruction from the roofs of churches. With understandable and unreasonable bitterness towards the young bombers, the poet remarks of the circus animals that none of them was a monster:

Compared to the smart boys, the pilots,

Who went after man and beast on diving raids.
They did their stunts without a net or trapeze
Above the arena. The charred
Apostles on the roofs stand there in dismay. (p. 283)

The dismay of the charred Apostles as they gaze on the firestorm is a view from outside the world of bomber and bombed alike – a view unattainable, perhaps, to anyone but these appalled statues.

Germany's earlier twentieth century, led by a Führer and his followers, and populated by combatants, resisters, refugees, camp victims, children, 'righteous Gentiles' and a host of subsidiary figures, has had its chronicles written and re-written, just as the later twentieth century, with the Russian and American occupation, the Wall, the airlift and the fall of East Germany, has had its own distinct forms of retrospection. One candid and chilling version of this history has been, and is being, told by Germany's poets. Grünbein's account stands as an illumination and corrective to the more impersonal accounts of scholars.[3]

3 This chapter first appeared as a review of Grünbein's *Ashes for Breakfast* in *The New Republic*, 5 November 2008, pp. 44–47.

‘Cadences in the Gaps of Time’. The Poet, the Past and *Porzellan*

Durs Grünbein in Conversation with Michael Eskin and Christopher Young

‘Returning to the present, let me close quickly and simply with a final scene. When I woke up after the initial euphoria on the evening of 7 October 1989 in Berlin, the first day of a wave of demonstrations that swept the other Germany away, I was astounded to find myself in front of an enormous machine.’ These lines come from your Büchner Prize acceptance speech, and the machine you were talking about was a tank. At the end of the passage, you write something fascinating: ‘It was my body, in a pre-verbal state, that wanted to give into exhaustion like a little child: it had held out for longer and had been constrained more forcibly than thoughts, which are always ready for flight. It was as if, with the tank behind me, I had wanted to sleep through history just for once, just for a minute, forgetting my body in a dreamless sleep, before everything began to move again.’ What was an extraordinary series of events for German history clearly became an extraordinary moment for a German poet. But a little puzzling.

The important phrase here is ‘*dreamless* sleep’, the sudden desire, in the middle of history, to take some time out. Sleep comes to us all and besieges us with dreams, which as a rule only prolong what has been besieging us in our waking life – sometimes even deepening and intensifying it. The passage you cite, in fact, was the most important conclusion I drew from the whole experience at the time. I had had enough of all the ideologies of the twentieth century. All of them claimed to explain humanity and improve it via collective measures. But in essence, both of the twentieth century’s great totalitarianisms – the Marxist and the National Socialist models of socialism – brought about, in Germany at least, the complete oppression of humanity. As a child of the post-war period, born in the 1960s, I was a victim of these historical developments, and the moment described in the passage was the first time I realized I would be free of it all. I know how childish this seems, but in that particular situation it was my deepest wish, and I realized immediately there was probably nowhere in the world I would find any peace in the midst of what was happening. If possible, I didn’t even want to be haunted by it in my dreams. This passage has something of the character of a prayer. When I saw this tank during the demonstrations in the middle of the street with its gun turned inwards, unsettlingly, it was a picture of great immediacy. I'd seen military pictures of vehicles like this that drive in one direction with the gun pointing forwards, but this one was parked with its gun turned in. And for me, it was a symbol of civil war: the tank was there because we, the civilians, were the problem. As we know now, everything turned out fine. It's up to historians to work out the whys and wherefores, but at that moment, for me, it meant either the final chapter of this state or the first chapter of the apocalypse. And my first reaction was: I'll stop here and lean against the tank, because – and this is a problem I have – I never seem to stand up to superior strength. All I knew was that everything was senseless, that lives might be lost, that one day people might try to explain it – like Tiananmen Square – and that perhaps it might never be made better again. I feared more bloodshed in German history, a history whose chapters were already full of it and also full of the fact that we never work through it or try to verify it, but instead just let the misery accumulate further.

So what happened next?

I went back to Prenzlauer Berg into the streets where it was darker, and went out with friends. But perhaps a part of me remained sitting there. There are scenes like that in films, a sort of shadow play, where one part of a character clambers out of himself and goes off somewhere else. That was me.

It's an interesting moment. You speak elsewhere of 'sudden illuminations'. In fact, again and again in your work, experience and history are described as illuminating. Is it not contradictory that, faced with the 'sudden illumination' of a tank, the poet wanted to go to sleep?

No. That moment was probably, unconsciously, influenced by a much larger conception of time. Over the years I've become aware of how writing deals with time. Poems and writing poetry are both like cadences in the gaps of time. Remembering very precise details, or how we experienced things, always makes us return to these moments, and this is what constitutes poetry. Poetry is not just about composing a text about this or that; rather, it's retarding the remembrance of something hidden deep inside the body as a terrible, shocking experience. Good experiences have this shocking quality as well. The whole process of writing is always somehow about this and tries to break the continuum of time with these experiences – that's a paradox, certainly, but it's the impression I get. Gaps appear in time, and, I believe, memory itself is something paradoxical, in as much as we create gaps in time and time is always running away from us. These gaps could be stretched again and again, until we find ourselves living in a paradise of memory. But until that point we can only slip into the crevice and back out again. That's the basic idea, and maybe that's what I mean by 'sudden illumination'.

Chronological time flows away from us; we are aware of it, we pursue it every day in the media or by looking at the calendar, but we know the much greater and more interesting terrain is where we thwart this chronology. This possibility is usually ignited by details of great clarity, by remembering the specificities of what we have experienced. Theories of psychological disease will have something to say about this: some diseases manifest themselves when certain memories are forced to return over and over. The writer has a similar disease, but he's aware of it and tries to work with it.

What happened to the part of you that remained there? Did it stay in the gap of time? Or is it here with us?

I kept on going – into this new age, very actively and very keenly. I had finally overcome the part of me that conformed to the advance of history. For me, the meaninglessness of history is very much part of the present day. What I do now, for example, is more meaningful: my life with family and friends – all these things are much more important than a historical existence.

Is this a pragmatic or emotional position, or do you have a broader philosophical view of history?

I'm quite Hegelian. I believe that history in a classical sense has completely come to an end. The fundamental ideas of Western culture – religious, ethical, economic, philosophical, perhaps even artistic – have all reached the same point, and there is essentially nothing new to add. With globalization it's now about spreading these ideas as far as possible. Things do, of course, change a little – that's the idea of cultural interaction, after all – but these days the Hegelian notion of intellectual processes following each other across the spectrum of humanity only happens when pre-existing ideas mix together. Nothing is absolutely new. That's not a bad thing, distances are shortening and certain processes are speeding up, but the project of intellectual development has become rather closed off.

History is much more exciting anyway when it doesn't have a specific meaning. There are a lot of exciting innovations in technology and the sciences, but humanity no longer has a shared historical project. It's been absolved, as it were, of the burden. To say history is 'meaningless' isn't actually negative, it just means that the problem no longer exists. In the same way, at some point the problem of religion became individualized, so that we don't have to fight about it anymore. It's now down to everyone to decide for themselves whether to accept 'God' or not. Likewise, the improvement of the human race through social utopias is now a matter of personal choice. Collective pressures are, thank God, a thing of the past. It was this kind of 'meaning' I wanted to say was over. It's no longer possible to give history a meaning, no single meaning is capable of gaining a consensus. It's quite simple: at the moment, we're experiencing the politics of different legislatures, whether you think that's a good thing or not – and it's going to grind everything down into nothing but a series of mini-episodes, which won't bring about anything new. But as I said, that's not a bad thing.

It does sound pessimistic, though.

No, not at all! (laughs). The words 'But that's not a bad thing' are really important.

You mentioned disintegration. In one of your essays you wrote that disintegration also brings about a certain kind of productivity. You use the word 'fruitfulness'. In the context of East Germany you said that the fall of the Berlin Wall was a 'healing shock' for you. You saw how a society, 'a whole cosmos with all its honest ways of living, disappeared overnight like a phantom'. And subsequently you described the fall of the Wall as a kind of disintegration, which only became fruitful a few years later. Disintegration, loss, fruitfulness ...

What I said was that there was a complete disintegration of hierarchy. The GDR had the most efficient security service in the whole of Eastern Europe. I witnessed how it and the state it supported all collapsed in on themselves. I would have thought they would have had some sort of firewall, but everything just collapsed so silently. This collapse of hierarchy was the greatest thing I'll ever experience. I know today that I'll never experience anything like it again for the rest of my life. The social structures we have today are completely different. The administrative and bureaucratic relations in our Western states, our party democracy, corporate bodies, etc., institutions of all kinds, 'systems', as Luhmann would say – these are all, thank God, horizontally rather than vertically hierarchical, if you'll excuse the paradox. They are very fixed and clear. And everybody knows that, despite reforms and little bits of elasticity built in here and there, they form the 'iron cage' (to pick up a term from Weber) of our existence. It's all much less repressive than the one I lived through in the East, and I'll never experience its disintegration like I did in the East.

How did this disintegration become fruitful for you?

It was the moment of freedom. I was lucky enough to be set free, unexpectedly, in a very concrete sense: I felt released from an absolute, hierarchical, state pressure. The disintegration of the East was a great luxury for those who experienced it young enough; for the older ones, it was nothing more than a heap of broken glass. I walked on happily, out of that heap.

How did this affect your poetry?

Well, that's one of those huge questions. There is definitely a before and after. It's something I'm still having to work out gradually. Here and there I've begun carefully to separate the before and after, but I've still a long way to go. In the East, everything seemed relatively linear and circular. It was like going round and round in a small, sealed-off, geographically isolated space. In the West, my behaviour changed radically. Life in a free society seems, more than anything, to be full of opportunities, but I also realized it would be incredibly difficult to develop any form of epic framework because everything is possible simultaneously. I could split myself into five different biographical personae. It was also obvious that I was in urgent need of remedial lessons in civilization and humanity. For the first time, I saw architecture afresh and was enchanted to encounter all kinds of art in the original. Suddenly I had a whole number of new things to read that had never occurred to me before. Yet at the same time there was the new pressure of having to choose between options, of having to position myself. In the closed society of the East, interestingly, there seemed to be endless amounts of time. But now, paradoxically, I believe that East Germany never existed.

You'll need to explain that.

For historians, naturally, the GDR existed, but actually it never really did. We have this idea of the 'other Germany' precisely because it never managed to register in any substantial way. The GDR was experienced by one or two generations, but it certainly won't have any lasting effect, I'm quite sure of that. These forty years will pass away, because they were nothing essential. For a short while in the Middle Ages there were two popes: East Germany was little more than Avignon, and understandably as soon as Rome re-established itself, nobody was interested in Avignon. It was just an historical detour, a dubious project that very quickly foundered. Very early on, I expressed the opinion that East Germany could only have existed in the large-scale geo-strategic calculations of the superpowers, in this case as a result of Yalta, which brought about the Sovietisation of one part of

Germany and the Americanization of the other under the control of the Western powers. The beautiful paradox is that all of this could be roughly predicted during the war, one or two years before it actually happened. Again, I cannot think of the GDR as an historical necessity, only as a proviso that didn't bring about any far-reaching mental changes. In fact, these regions are trying to get back to how they were the last time there was a unified Germany, that is, before the war. This brings me to my research on Dresden and Saxony. It's become very clear to me that I come from a particular part of Germany. I'm not from Bavaria or Schleswig-Holstein: I'm a Saxon. As soon as I realized this, I became much more interested in the history of the region. My starting point was that at the beginning of the twentieth century, Dresden was a relatively prosperous industrial and cultural region – which it will become again, by the way. Regional character is important all over the world. Saxony will return to what it once was, so this exception of the GDR, this proviso, will soon be forgotten.

Is it not too simple to write off East Germany as just an episode? For many it was more than that. Many people's lives were shaped very strongly by it, for better or worse.

I'm already on record as saying that it was different for those who spent a large part of their lives in East Germany. It's a matter of perspective. On the one hand, we shouldn't underestimate those who made the GDR thier project. A certain percentage of the population was active, and these people were the architects of socialism on many levels. There was also the great passive majority who were slotted in on all levels via the relatively efficient collective machinery of politics. If they say today, in retrospect, that was our life, then that's completely understandable. What I'm saying is that, when considered in a long-term historical perspective, the GDR will be nothing more than an episode. Unfortunately, I'm not a proper historian, otherwise I would come up with a few other examples of strange detours over the last 800 years. There are islands in time when something different happens for a while but is later reversed. The main current of history is much calmer and smoother and flows right over it. It's as simple as that.

When you say 'I'm a Saxon' you introduce two important concepts: 'I' and 'Saxon', the subject and the collective. We should explore these with you in more detail. What does it mean when you write the word 'I' in your poems?

There are quite different 'I's. There are very immediate 'I's and very distanced 'I's; some 'I's are pure historical personae; and sometimes there's a rather intimate, an almost diary-like 'I'. As a rule, they are all somehow monumentalized 'I's.

Where are the exceptions? Are there poems in which the autobiographical 'I' is Durs Grünbein?

Well, the closer you think you're getting to authenticity, the further you're moving away from it. Maybe that's not entirely right – perhaps some kind of notation for it, or a nimble way of writing, could catch the faintest breath of the movements of the 'I'. But my texts tend to re-establish distance. For me, the voice is the main impulse, even now as I'm speaking, whenever I say 'I'. Speaking is what's important. I can't define how close to or far from reality, experience or the particular moment the 'I' is in any given sentence. What I'm formulating is an attempt to get hold of something anthropological. I think that's the case for everyone.

For every poet, at least ...

For every person, I think. But your question is perfectly justified, because in many of my poems I want to come up with something disruptive and suddenly bring the 'I' right up close. In fact, I long to come closer to the 'you', the reader, through short emphases on the 'I'. That would be my absolute dream. But I have a great longing to speak directly, to a new, young audience, for example. I don't want to hide myself away completely. The distanced 'I' only predominates when I'm processing something bad or something general.

Could we think of this as the dissolution of the first person?

I'm not keen on clearly defined concepts of the poetic 'I' that neatly formulate it like a basic motif or category you can apply. Rather, I think the potential meaning of 'I' in a poem covers a massive spectrum. I believe this so strongly that one day, I think, I'll dissolve the 'I' completely in a long work. But the only way I can dissolve it is to use it continuously. None of the other strategies – surrealism or techniques of ecstasy – convince me. Hildegard of Bingen and Teresa of Avila didn't get any further than Emily Dickinson. Her 'I' is as clear as glass, and amongst other things it's constantly present and at the same time allegorical. You feel straight away she's also saying something general. Think of the famous line 'I heard a fly buzz when I died'. Who's speaking here? It's a curious 'I', expressed in the past tense. Is the speaker dead or alive? Then we're told the banal fact that flies were buzzing at the decisive moment. And at the same time, there's the attempt to lodge the 'I' into the gaps of time. This 'I' tries to speak in the gaps of time in which we all sometimes find ourselves – for example, when we read intensively. That's my thesis anyway.

Do you read in a particular way?

To read correctly is to escape briefly from the continuum of time, to escape, primarily, from your own historical moment and your own self-imposed need to be doing this or that, and perhaps even from the great draining-away of time that affects all humanity. Reading is a discontinuous act to which you can always return. It doesn't matter to me whether I'm reading something by someone who was alive five hundred years ago – as long as it's of a certain quality – or something written ten years ago. I believe in the universal concatenation of such moments. We read across time and across the history of mankind, and in that sense we're always somehow leaping out of time. When we read, we're probably trying to get closer to our real selves. That was Proust's great realization in the last volume of the *Recherche*. The reader reads into himself. We're getting quicker at deciding 'That's not me' or 'I don't find myself here', and that text is immediately discarded. Other texts stay with us and come infinitely close to us. That's how I read.

Does the same thing apply to poets when they observe?

Observation is one thing, and writing another. I find it very distressing when I'm unable to convey what I see. It's a difficult thing to do: writing is a relatively abstract way of notating what you perceive. But the more experience you have of reading, the easier it can be to comprehend someone else's perception. Prose, naturally, has certain advantages – it's all to do with the technique of constructing sentences or the intensity of description at a certain moment. Poetry, by contrast, is based more on evocation. In fact, poetry is always just 'O, my rose'. Even if there are ten more lines, it's still only 'O, my rose'. Prose is the description of the rose. Practised readers can engage with this 'O my rose' very quickly, because they only need a few more hints to immerse themselves intensively in the image. Then they begin to develop the picture themselves, which means they're reading within themselves.

What role does the visual play here? Paintings, silent films and Buster Keaton crop up time and again in your poetry?

Absolutely. There's even something of a secret desire about it, a desire to appear to others like a podcast and to be able, in a few words, to conjure up a short film clip for others, something that goes beyond abstract communication and reaches, if possible, toward a very concrete form of communication. For me, the allusion to pictures and films brings about the podcast-effect. Maybe the recipients even see more details in it than I do because they've watched it more carefully.

In contrast to this, Borges thought it was completely sufficient to say, simply, 'the jug' or 'the sword'. Borges's theory of the imagination is one of the most interesting I've come across, because he believed that we communicate perfectly adequately with nouns like these, which are resistant to time and to some extent work in all cultures. I've always found the simple 'jug', 'sword' or 'rose' insufficient. I'd rather have something more exact. You begin to add colours or the shades of the day, or to be more exact with botanical names. It's actually this kind of rose, and so on. When you go to the next level, you communicate your feelings, too, about this particular rose. That, for me, sums up the whole history of poetics over the last 2000 years: becoming more specific.

Let's turn now to Porzellan, *a poem whose last line seems to touch on many of the topics we've covered so far: 'er tauscht die Zeiten, Räume, Maße, tauscht und tauscht' [he exchanges times, spaces, measures, exchanges and exchanges].*

It's just a short poetic line, but I think it describes generally what happens in poetry, which is, after all, a constant process of exchange between reader and poet. It's a multiple exchange of timelines or entire ages – the immediate now of the reader is exchanged for a past in which whatever is being read was written. I don't write historical novels – if I write about Descartes, then it's because I want to recall the immediacy of the past, not to produce a costume drama. My work is about actualizing the past, which is another exchange of time – I go and fetch it quickly. I've been really pleased to receive some very personal letters from readers who hadn't imagined how great it could be to find a long-lost ghost, as if by magic, suddenly standing by their side. That's what I meant when I said 'tauscht und tauscht' [exchanges and exchanges]. Reading produces the greatest happiness in me, even more so than writing. Reading is my greatest pleasure because it always allows me to reverse the implacable biological film of time draining away. Goethe says somewhere that it's the spirit that ages early and age that rejuvenates, and this captures exactly what I experience all the time. As a young man I could read something by someone very much older and be affected by it. Now that I'm older, I revive whenever I read something fresh and youthful. That's the pleasure of reading. Only reading can do this; reading creates a constant alternative to chronological time.

Not all chronological time is easy to reverse. Why did you write poems about Dresden? It's a rather delicate subject in England, not to mention in Germany.

Well, it's my home town, it's where I was born, where I spent the first twenty years of my life, where my mother was born, and where my maternal ancestors lived for a very long time. My father's family came from Thuringia. My paternal grandfather, who was declared unfit for military service, was eventually called up right at the end of the war and, after a stint in Gotha, was transferred to Dresden. He saw the bombing from the barracks to the north of the city. It's a coincidence how these biographical paths crossed.

The destruction of this cultural centre – this baroque pearl, this wonderful synthesis of Italian and German Europe – was so traumatic that many people couldn't get over the loss. At some point, I realized there's a particularly vehement culture of memory in Dresden. Other German cities were completely destroyed, too, but only in Dresden do you have this topos of inconsolability, of absolute annihilation. In the course of many conversations over my lifetime I realized that people automatically talk about how they saw the city before it was destroyed. I've spoken a few times to the critic Joachim Kaiser, who passed through the city at the age of seventeen on the eve of the bombing. He told me that in his experience the only place to match Dresden was Venice. It was a breathtaking, magnificent ensemble.

All of this was gone by the time I was born and stepped, quite literally, onto an empty stage. It was like the set of a Beckett play: cleared out, excavated, swept away. But the foundations told you what it once had been. And one day, as a writer, you take on the responsibility of remembering. I went to study in Berlin and have been travelling the world since 1989, but the memory of my hometown is still very strong. Take the rebuilding of the Frauenkirche [Church of Our Lady]. It doesn't matter what you think of it – hundreds of people, including Nobel-Prize winners who had long since moved to New York, devoted their skill and time to it. This wasn't politically motivated. Uniquely, it was all down to the people. It's a symbol of this work of mourning, and I see it as an interesting, elegiac model for the protection of history. When I was younger, I spoke about Dresden in a relatively raw, distanced tone: most of my rather sarcastic views on the history of the twentieth century come from this period. The older I've become, the more consciously I've acknowledged Dresden as a personal loss. An early poem of mine, with the rather objective, even *neusachlich*, title 'Gedicht über Dresden' ['Poem about Dresden'], was an attempt to deal with it once and for all, in a distanced manner. Later, I said I didn't want to write on the subject again. One phrase in particular – 'Barockwrack an der Elbe' [Baroque wreck on the Elbe] – was widely quoted and appeared all over the press. Some Dresdeners took against me because of it – understandably – but you have to live with such things. One of the adventures of writing poetry is that you sometimes come up with lines that you have to carry with you and explain for the rest of your life. I completely understand what the Dresdeners objected to, but I'm proud when people react against what I've written, because it means it has affected them, even if it is to cause them pain.

But isn't there a certain fascination hidden in that particular poem?

It's an attempt to arrive at a historical position on this event. We were entirely to blame for the downfall ourselves, no ifs or buts. But the poem explores the fact that, as a failed artist, Hitler was first active in pursuing the politics of destruction, but then became passive and was only jointly responsible for the destruction that befell Europe and Germany. I can see the technical mastery in the bombers' work of destruction. New research has shown just how advanced the methods they used were. The bombing of Dresden was *the* major performance – everything before it was a mere rehearsal. I've learnt from Alexander Kluge in particular that, objectively speaking, even this darkest hour in the history of the twentieth century has to be understood as an expression of the absolute achievement of our civilization. The greatest brains, on both sides, worked on this destructive master plan. The bombing of Dresden marks a change of era: in contrast to a baroque city and its courtly culture, which was largely created by craftsmen, artists and well-meaning individuals, in the twentieth century we enter the age of engineering. Certain things only happen now through the division of labour, they are anonymous and objectified: we're living in the world of Max Weber. All these things play a role in the poem, through the old matrix of pure elegy, albeit a paradoxical elegy in which even the self-thematization of the speaker's role is opposed to pure sentimentality. This picture – a mental, internal depiction of the city that came to me gradually, like a film developing slowly, as I considered the destruction over the years – is a very rich one now, and it informs my opinions on what should happen to the city today; for instance, the infamous proposal for a new bridge across the Elbe. I believe we're now entering an age when it's important to preserve certain things, didactically valuable places, where young people can see how different life used to be. We should protect these things, in the same way we protect nature. But the rows about the bridge are all connected to the idea of a picture-postcard Dresden, which came under severe attack in the twentieth century. In one of the darkest lines in *Porzellan*, I argue with the citizens of Dresden in the 1930s, telling them: 'you've gambled it all away'. Those who thought they could get along politically with Hitler gambled away part of my heritage. And today I'm saying, it wasn't your place to do that, it didn't belong to you. All you had to do was pass it on, to bring it undamaged and healthy into the future. Today's generations are doing that, they're fighting for it. In my poetry, I'm making restitution for what has been lost – in a very imperfect way, but I see it as my task, at least.

And how does that work together with the elegiac?

I know it's unusual to consider these things diachronically, but the modern elegy is different from its old romantic predecessor, which only mourned the passing of certain great ages. Those were concrete elegies, expressed from the perspective of an individual speaker. The modern elegy is a constant battle between knowledge and emotion; it has to give itself up to knowledge; and at its core, it contains a contradiction between insight into the inevitable processes of modernization on the one hand and an increasing awareness of loss on the other, a contradiction that irrevocably rips it apart.

Would you say that Porzellan is a long sequence of modern elegies?

Above all, it's a declaration of love. I said once it was my troubadour song and that the city was my beloved. That's a rather idiosyncratic view, and the collection certainly wasn't received that way. People wondered whether someone born in the 1960s had a right to talk about 'the downfall of my city'. But I'm an exile of time. Because of where I was born, I entered into a particular posthumous relationship with the past. I'm the survivor who has to pick up the pieces. But what's good about all this is the strong emotional connection. It's like in Minnesang, just that the object is the city rather than the lady.

I think most scholars read Minnesang differently from you. They see it as art: in Minnesang, the unobtainable is simply a rule of the genre. But in the case of Dresden it's something different, not just something artistic, and the feelings you have are real, aren't they?

I think we can look at these things from different angles. For me, Minnesang was based, first and foremost, on real, genuine adoration. At some point it became established, and gradually it turned into a game, a language-game. But its root remained hidden within it, like the root of Attic love poetry: there was a real emotional relationship between Sappho and Alkaios; later it became a game, renewing itself whenever something real became involved. That's why the Roman love poets were so good, because they were really poor guys when it came to relationships. Studies have shown that Propertius's Cynthia and Catullus's Clodia were real women who made the poets suffer. So, the game renews itself, but at the same time it's a game with pure form. Why did I fall in love with the Baroque, which is a simple calculation of form or mannerism? Because I saw it as an expression of a historical way of feeling. I can't separate the two. I could say: *Porzellan* is just a game. The rule was that every year on 13 February I would write a ten-line poem. Over the course of time a few poems came to be written, and at some point it became a little ritual. I sat down and wrote, and it had the simple character of a game. A further dimension to the game was the fact that different voices began to appear. The speaker interrupts himself, or a really contradictory voice makes itself heard: 'Don't do it like that!' or 'What's your problem here?'. Or there's the voice of a historian, even the voice of a completely distanced observer, who had nothing to do with it at all. All these things get played out. The overriding rule was that in my formal engagement with the poem, at least, I had to remember that it was still a game, albeit one on the edge of real emotions. For me, that's the basic premise of writing.

Did you know each year where you had got to, what you had already written?

I had a folder I put the poems in, and at some point I had a look and thought I could make a cycle out of them. When we came to publishing them, the order and layout became very important. Some poems appear opposite each other, just the way they were lying in the folder. But on the whole, it was not an option to print them one after another. I wanted to stage big pauses. We had to show there was a pause between certain poems before things start up again. Sometimes you can see how dialogues come about. There's a circular structure, too, you can start from the beginning again, motifs are played out.

After it was published, I realized that the porcelain motif would become the basic key to it or metaphor for it all. There's no other single word that would have allowed me to describe what happened in Dresden. Even today, porcelain is the great positive myth about that baroque culture.

The Meißen palace has a room dedicated to alchemists and to Johann Friedrich Böttger, the man who invented porcelain. It was Saxony's primary export, although recent studies have shown that it was an economic disaster for merchants, who invested more than they got in return. But that's typical of baroque culture in general. The Baroque was always celebratory and representative in character, and can't be explained by the rules of capitalism. The baroque economy went through a cycle of crisis points. Under Chancellor Brühl it was so bleak that they basically had to sell everything. The idea we have of the Baroque is that this golden age of debt somehow facilitated an unprecedented concentration of cultural powers: collections of paintings came together, enormous architectonic ensembles were produced, and there was celebration: fireworks, water music, endless tables, hunting, love affairs. This, for me, is the essence of the Baroque. The only things that remained after the festivities were mussel shells in the form of buildings and artefacts. This, I realized, was what it was all about. So for me, *Porzellan* is more than just a title, or even a metaphor. It's a powerful key to the whole thing and stands at the very centre of memory culture. Porcelain is also one of the few things handed down in all families. Even when there was nothing left, there was still one small plate to pass down. I knew lots of Dresden families of all classes – even poor ones – who saw the collection of small plates in their side-board as the heart of cultural transmission. Excavators are forever finding porcelain. There's a really magical poem by Czesław Miłosz from the 1940s, called 'Porzellan', which helped me. When Miłosz went to America, he had a vision that all that was left of Europe was a few shards of porcelain and that that was what archaeologists would uncover from our era.

The word 'porcelain' is incredibly interesting. We mustn't forget that it became a very erotic cultural model, and there's secret eroticism hidden in my cycle of poems, too. There are allusions to courtly eroticism, to August the Strong, who imprisoned Böttger, and his mistresses. This is then transferred to other things: the city was a mistress.

A mistress for whom or for what?

The bombs. It's a very brutal, typical twentieth-century image. They're rape fantasies.

Whose rape fantasy? The city's or Durs Grünbein's?

It was reality.

No it wasn't, this is just your transferral.

It was fit young men who fired the bombs into this womb. You should look at the heroic logic of the Second World War, the sporting side to those who led the war. It's enormous.

We can understand that the bombers might feel like men letting something drop into a womb. But surely it's important that the town didn't see itself as a woman with her legs spread. A rape always involves two people: the victim and the perpetrator. But the question is: to what extent was it actually rape?

This city attracted the bombs for a very particular reason. We can talk about military camps being attacked and say that some production sites had to be bombed. But really – and this is the greatest taboo in any discussion of this particular episode in the air war – there is only one thing we should, and must, talk about. In Dresden, beauty was attacked. Dresden was attacked precisely because it was beautiful and defenceless. And because it was an attack on the defenceless part of European culture, it was essentially an attack on the bombers' own culture. It was the pure desire for destruction: you destroyed our artistic treasures, so we'll destroy yours. There's a poem in my early cycle 'Europa nach dem letzten Regen' ['Europe after the Last Rains'], in which I describe this from the perspective of a young bomber – 'Las Vegas an der Elbe' ('Las Vegas on the Elbe'). Today we get pictures from the Iraq war and you can see that it's a lot of fun to fire away at something, to shoot massive fireworks over great distances. That's the essence of bombing: you don't feel it at all. Bombers turn round after they've dropped their load. It's powerful!

In fact, it's pure baroque splendour. The dialectic is exciting, at least for a structural thinker like me. In Dresden, a baroque work of art was staged for the last time, the last great celebratory act, the destruction of a baroque city in baroque proportions. No-one has gauged the contradictions of the twentieth century, in which a visual feast for one person can mean instant conflagration for thousands of others below.

What do you mean when you say 'no-one has gauged it'?

It can't be reined in by any theory. Military historians have no language for it, cultural historians have no suitable means of verifying it. Maybe the arts offer the only way of getting at it, but they lack the means too. Let me give you an example. I studied the different phases of Picasso's work on *Guernica* intensively, looking at how the painter struggled pictorially with that particular bombing, until he came up with a solution of enormous expressive power. But even then, he still faced the problem that there is no suitable way for an artist to express such a thing. Is he revelling in it? Is he overly fascinated by it? Or has he at least managed to generate some sympathy symbolically? But in reality, this can't be produced. I know the bombing of Dresden opened the scissors so wide that one blade was a totally sexual lecherousness, the other an absolute, dark pain we can no longer fathom. It's completely different from other forms of warfare. One person presses a button and three thousand people go up in flames like human torches and die in great physical suffering. It's such a huge contradiction that just thinking about it won't bring us any closer to it. You can declare a veto on pictures or even on thinking. It's as if certain metaphors were inadmissible or ill-considered. I measured my metaphors too, but not quite as strongly.

You've been very clear on where you stand morally in relation to the National Socialist and indeed the East German regime. But even so, is it permissible for a German poet to talk about the attack on Dresden as rape or rape fantasy?

It's permissible to talk about every attack like that, Coventry and Hiroshima too. But I'm not primarily a German poet. I'm always assuming the UNESCO perspective. I'm like the conscience of mankind, worrying about all its treasures. I'm not reproaching anyone. Or maybe I am! My one clear reproach is: your own people destroyed it! They gambled it away. It's not a reproach against the English, not in the slightest. I can understand the English position very well. But I mourn the fact that all of that was taken away from us by young British servicemen. Nazism didn't lose any of its substance when the German cities were bombed. These people – and here I take the same line as Thomas Mann – cannot be equated with German culture. I'm always at pains to make this distinction. I'm sorry, I have to. They are not one and the same thing. Those few years aren't enough to say: that was the essence of German culture. Some point to a long history of German irrationality. Lukács famously traced a path from Schelling to Hitler. It's madness to take this line, madness. Only someone on the Left could come up with that. I'm vehemently against it. I can see no continuity from Schelling to Goebbels or Hitler.

(Translated by Sarah Bowden[4])

4 With thanks to Lukas Werner for his sterling work on transcribing the original interview.

Collated by Lukas Werner

Durs Grünbein. A Bibliography

Primary Works

Poetry

Grünbein, Durs, *Grauzone morgens. Gedichte* (Frankfurt a. M.: Suhrkamp, 1988).
Grünbein, Durs, *Schädelbasislektion. Gedichte* (Frankfurt a. M.: Suhrkamp, 1991).
Grünbein, Durs, *Von der üblen Seite. Gedichte 1985–1991* (Frankfurt a. M.: Suhrkamp, 1994).
Grünbein, Durs, *Falten und Fallen. Gedichte* (Frankfurt a. M.: Suhrkamp, 1994).
Grünbein, Durs, *Den teuren Toten. 33 Epitaphe* (Frankfurt a. M.: Suhrkamp, 1994).
Grünbein, Durs, *Nach den Satiren. Gedichte* (Frankfurt a. M.: Suhrkamp, 1999).
Grünbein, Durs, *Una Storia Vera. Ein Kinderalbum in Versen* (Frankfurt a. M.: Insel, 2002).
Grünbein, Durs, *Erklärte Nacht. Gedichte* (Frankfurt a. M.: Suhrkamp, 2002).
Grünbein, Durs, *Vom Schnee oder Descartes in Deutschland* (Frankfurt a. M.: Suhrkamp, 2003).
Grünbein, Durs and Lucius Annaeus Seneca, *An Seneca. Postskriptum. Die Kürze des Lebens* (Frankfurt a. M.: Suhrkamp, 2004).
Grünbein, Durs, *Porzellan. Poem vom Untergang meiner Stadt* (Frankfurt a. M.: Suhrkamp, 2005).
Grünbein, Durs, *Der Misanthrop auf Capri. Historien / Gedichte* (Frankfurt a. M.: Suhrkamp, 2005).
Grünbein, Durs, *Gedichte. Bücher I–III (Grauzone morgens, Schädelbasislektion, Falten und Fallen)* (Frankfurt a. M.: Suhrkamp, 2006).
Grünbein, Durs, *Strophen für übermorgen. Gedichte* (Frankfurt a. M.: Suhrkamp, 2007).
Grünbein, Durs, *Liebesgedichte* (Frankfurt a. M.: Insel, 2008).
Grünbein, Durs, *Lob des Taifuns. Reisetagebücher in Haikus* (Frankfurt a. M.: Insel, 2008).
Grünbein, Durs, *Germanischer Komplex* (Detmold: Literaturbüro Ostwestfalen-Lippe, 2009).
Grünbein, Durs, *Aroma. Ein römisches Zeichenbuch* (Berlin: Suhrkamp, 2010).
Grünbein, Durs, *Libellen in Liberia. Gedichte und Berichte*, ed. by Brigitte Labs-Ehlert (Detmold: Literaturbüro Ostwestfalen-Lippe, 2010).
Grünbein, Durs, *Limbische Akte. Gedichte*, ed. by Norbert Hummelt (Leipzig: Reclam, 2011).
Grünbein, Durs, *Koloss im Nebel. Gedichte* (Berlin: Suhrkamp, 2012).

Prose

Grünbein, Durs, *Den Körper zerbrechen. Rede zur Entgegennahme des Georg-Büchner-Preises 1995. Mit der Laudatio 'Portrait des Künstlers als junger Grenzhund' von Heiner Müller* (Frankfurt a. M.: Suhrkamp, 1995).
Grünbein, Durs, *Galilei vermißt Dantes Hölle und bleibt an den Maßen hängen. Aufsätze 1989–1995* (Frankfurt a. M.: Suhrkamp, 1996).
Grünbein, Durs, Brigitte Oleschinski and Peter Waterhouse, *Die Schweizer Korrektur*, ed. by Urs Engeler (Basel: Engeler, 1995).
Grünbein, Durs, *Das erste Jahr. Berliner Aufzeichnungen* (Frankfurt a. M.: Suhrkamp, 2001).

Grünbein, Durs, *Warum schriftlos leben? Aufsätze* (Frankfurt a. M.: Suhrkamp, 2003).
Grünbein, Durs, *Antike Dispositionen. Aufsätze* (Frankfurt a. M.: Suhrkamp, 2005).
Grünbein, Durs, *Gedicht und Geheimnis. Aufsätze 1990–2006* (Frankfurt a. M.: Suhrkamp, 2007).
Grünbein, Durs, *Ein kleines blaues Mädchen. Zu Rainer Maria Rilke 'Das Karussell'* (Detmold: Literaturbüro Ostwestfalen-Lippe, 2007).
Grünbein, Durs, *Der cartesische Taucher. Drei Meditationen* (Frankfurt a. M.: Suhrkamp, 2008).
Grünbein, Durs, *Die Bars von Atlantis. Eine Erkundung in vierzehn Tauchgängen* (Frankfurt a. M.: Surhkamp, 2009).
Grünbein, Durs, *Vom Stellenwert der Worte. Frankfurter Poetikvorlesung 2009* (Berlin: Suhrkamp, 2010).
Grünbein, Durs, *Dream Index / Aus der Traum (Kartei)* (Ostfildern: Hatje Cantz, 2012).

Translations

Aischylos, *Die Perser. Stück und Materialien*, aus dem Griechischen von Durs Grünbein (Frankfurt a. M.: Suhrkamp, 2001).
Seneca, *Thyestes*, Lateinisch und deutsch, aus dem Lateinischen von Durs Grünbein, mit Materialien zur Übersetzung und zu Leben und Werk Senecas, ed. by Bernd Seidensticker (Frankfurt a. M.: Insel, 2002).
Kane, Sarah, *4.48 Psychose*, in Sarah Kane, *Sämtliche Stücke. Zerbombt. Phaidras Liebe. Gesäubert. Gier. 4.48 Psychose*, ed. by Corinna Brocher and Nils Tabert, with an introduction by David Greig (Reinbek bei Hamburg: Rowohlt Taschenbuchverlag, 2002).
Aischylos, *Sieben gegen Theben*, aus dem Griechischen von Durs Grünbein (Frankfurt a. M.: Suhrkamp, 2003).

Other

Grünbein, Durs, and others, *Der letzte Limes* (Cologne: König, 2000).
Grünbein, Durs, *Gehirn und Denken. Kosmos im Kopf*, ed. by Deutsches Hygiene-Museum in cooperation with Via Lewandowsky and Durs Grünbein (Ostfildern-Ruit: Hatje Cantz, 2000).
Grünbein, Durs, 'Bogen und Leier. Nachwort', in Heiner Müller, *Ende der Handschrift. Gedichte von Heiner Müller* (Frankfurt a. M.: Suhrkamp, 2006), pp. 99–116.
Grünbein, Durs, and Peter Cornelius, *Die Götter Griechenlands*, ed. by León Krempel and Peter-Klaus Schuster (Berlin: DuMont, 2004).
Grünbein, Durs, *Berenice. Ein Libretto nach Edgar Allan Poe für eine Oper von Johannes Maria Staud* (Frankfurt a. M.: Suhrkamp, 2004).
Grünbein, Durs, and Markus Lüpertz, *Daphne – Metamorphose einer Figur* (Bad Homburg: Altana Kulturforum, 2005).
Grünbein, Durs, and Markus Lüpertz, *Mercurius – Der Koloss im Nebel* (n.p: Deutsche Post DHL, 2009).
Grünbein, Durs, 'Vergeblichkeit denken. Nachwort', in George Steiner, *Warum Denken traurig macht. Zehn (mögliche) Gründe* (Frankfurt a. M.: Suhrkamp, 2006), pp. 79–90.
Grünbein, Durs, and Thomas Florschuetz, *Museumsinsel* (Cologne: König, 2006).
Grünbein, Durs, 'Eine Träne für Petronius. Nachwort', in Petronius, *Das Gastmahl des Trimalchio* (Frankfurt a. M.: Insel, 2006), pp. 89–105.

Grünbein, Durs, 'Versiegelte Zeit. Nachwort', in Thomas Venclova, *Gespräch im Winter. Gedichte* (Frankfurt a. M.: Suhrkamp, 2007), pp. 107–17.
Grünbein, Durs, 'Libretto', in *Oktoberfilm. Dresden 1989*, by Ralf Kukula (Dresden: Balance Film GmbH, 2009).
Grünbein, Durs, and Markus Lüpertz, *Daphne – Versionen eines Mythos. Zeichnungen und Gedichte* (Frankfurt a. M.: Insel, 2009).
Grünbein, Durs, 'Palette für Mohn. Nachwort', in Gottfried Benn and Thomas Florschuetz, *Blumen* (Berlin: Insel, 2011), pp. 79–90.
Grünbein, Durs, 'Elegien für einen Irrtum. Vorwort', in Gottfried Benn, *Statische Gedichte (Gedichte 1937–1947)* (Berlin: Insel, 2011), pp. 7–34.
Grünbein, Durs, 'Der Verschollene. Nachwort', in Felix Hartlaub, *Kriegsaufzeichnungen aus Paris. Kommentierte Ausgabe* (Berlin: Suhrkamp, 2011), pp. 147–63.

Recordings

Grünbein, Durs, *Das Ohr in der Uhr. Gedichte aus 13 Jahren* (Munich: Hörverlag, 2001).
Grünbein, Durs, and others, *Reise. Toter* (Bonn: Sans Soleil, 2001).
Grünbein, Durs, and others, *Vom Schnee oder Descartes in Deutschland* (Munich: Hörverlag, 2005).
Grünbein, Durs, *Durs Grünbein liest in der Augusteerhalle der Herzog August Bibliothek. Gudrun Boch im Gespräch mit dem Autor* (Wiesbaden: Harrassowitz, 2005).
Grünbein, Durs, *Durs Grünbein liest Strophen für übermorgen* (Munich: Hörverlag, 2008).
Grünbein, Durs and others, *Dresden. Eine literarische Einladung* (Berlin: DAV, 2008).

English Translations

Grünbein, Durs, *Ashes for Breakfast. Selected Poems*, trans. by Michael Hofmann (New York: Farrar, Straus and Giroux, 2005; London: Faber and Faber, 2006).
Grünbein, Durs, *Descartes' Devil. Three Meditations*, trans. by Anthea Bell (New York: Upper West Side Philosophers, 2010).
Grünbein, Durs, *The Bars of Atlantis. Selected Essays*, ed. by Michael Eskin, trans. by John Crutchfield, Michael Hofmann and Andrew Shields (New York: Farrar, Straus and Giroux, 2010).
Grünbein, Durs, *The Vocation of Poetry*, trans. by Michael Eskin (New York: Upper West Side Philosophers, 2011).
Grünbein, Durs, *Mortal Diamond. Poems*, trans. by Michael Eskin (New York: Upper West Side Philosophers, 2013).

Interviews

Bednarz, Klaus, and Durs Grünbein, 'Durs Grünbein. Den Teuren Toten', in *Von Autoren und Büchern. Gespräche mit Schriftstellern*, ed. by Klaus Bednarz and Gisela Marx (Hamburg: Hoffmann und Campe, 1997), pp. 204–10.
Bienderra, Anke, Sabine Wilke and Durs Grünbein, '"Wie kann man zwei auseinanderbrechende Jahrhunderte verbinden?" Interview mit Durs Grünbein', in Sabine Wilke, *Ist alles so geblie-*

ben, wie es früher war? Essays zu Literatur und Frauenpolitik im vereinten Deutschland (Würzburg: Königshausen & Neumann, 2000), pp. 113–21.

Böttiger, Helmut, and Durs Grünbein, 'Benn schmort in der Hölle. Ein Gespräch über dialogische und monologische Lyrik', *Text + Kritik*, 153.1 (2002), 72–84.

Böttiger, Helmut, and Durs Grünbein, 'Die Hölderlin-Linie. Gespräch mit Durs Grünbein', *Sinn und Form*, 56.5 (2004), 606–20.

Breidbach, Olaf, and Durs Grünbein, 'Die Wissenschaft denkt nicht', in http://www.kunst-als-wissenschaft.de/bibliothek/ergebnis.asp?DownloadID=33.

Deckert, Renatus, and Durs Grünbein, 'Auch Dresden ist ein Werk des Malerlehrlings', in http://www.lose-blaetter.de/S3_dres.html.

Dittberner, Hugo, Hartmut Kasper and Durs Grünbein, 'Ein Nachtrag. Durs Grünbein im Gespräch mit Hartmut Kasper und Hugo Dittberner über heutiges Essay-Schreiben und die Tradition des Essays', in Martin Ahrends, *Der erste Satz des Philosophen*, ed. by Hugo Dittberner (Göttingen: Wallstein, 1996), pp. 143–64.

Doerry, Martin, Volker Hage and Durs Grünbein, 'Tausendfacher Tod im Hirn. Büchner-Preisträger Durs Grünbein über Utopien, das Ende der DDR und die Zukunft der Lyrik', *Der Spiegel*, 41 (1995), 221–30.

Eskin, Michael, and Durs Grünbein, 'Descartes' Devil. Durs Grünbein im Gespräch mit Michael Eskin', *Trans-Lit2*, 16.1 (2010), 5–9.

Eskin, Michael, and Durs Grünbein, 'Tauchen mit Descartes. Gespräch mit Durs Grünbein', *Sinn und Form*, 63.3 (2011), 389–402.

Fioretos, Aris, and Durs Grünbein, 'Gespräch über die Zone, den Hund und die Knochen', *Akzente*, 43.6 (1996), 486–501.

Fioretos, Aris, and Durs Grünbein, 'Gespräch in der Wüste', *Akzente*, 47.5 (2000), 393–408.

Fioretos, Aris, and Durs Grünbein, 'Die Eroberung Berlins', *Akzente*, 51.1 (2004), 12–29.

Fischer, Ernst Peter, and Durs Grünbein, 'Vermessen. Wissenschaft zwischen Ratio und Spiritualität', in http://www.gartenheim.de/aktuelles-neu/veranstaltungsarchiv/vermessen.html.

Frühwald, Wolfgang, and Durs Grünbein, 'Die Lust, sich im Universum zu bewegen. Ein Gespräch mit dem Dichter Durs Grünbein über Poesie, Neurobiologie und die Bilder vom Menschen', in *Das Design des Menschen. Vom Wandel des Menschenbildes unter dem Einfluss der modernen Naturwissenschaften*, ed. by Wolfgang Frühwald (Cologne: DuMont, 2004), pp. 294–309.

Heinrichs, Hans-Jürgen, and Durs Grünbein, 'Gespräch mit Durs Grünbein. Hinweise auf ein Stück Gedankenmusik', *Sinn und Form*, 60.1 (2008), 47–59.

Hofmann, Frank, and Durs Grünbein, 'Vom Sinn des Erbrechens. Ein Gespräch mit Durs Grünbein', *Schwarzes Quadrat. Für Einblicke und Ausfälle*, 2 (1993), 45–48.

Irmer, Thomas, and Durs Grünbein, 'Der Mensch ist in die Jahre gekommen. Durs Grünbein im Gespräch mit Thomas Irmer', in *TheaterKulturVision. Arbeitsbuch*, ed. by Therese Hörnigk, Bettina Masuch and Frank M. Raddatz (Berlin: Theater der Zeit, 1998), pp. 11–13.

Irmer, Thomas, and Durs Grünbein, 'Durs Grünbein im Gespräch mit Thomas Irmer', in Lucius Annaeus Seneca, *Thyestes* (Frankfurt a. M.: Insel, 2002), pp. 111–14.

Jocks, Heinz-Norbert, and Durs Grünbein, *Durs Grünbein im Gespräch mit Heinz-Norbert Jocks* (Cologne: DuMont, 2001).

Kasaty, Olga Olivia, and Durs Grünbein, 'Ein Gespräch mit Durs Grünbein. Berlin, 26. August 2005', in Olga Olivia Kasaty, *Entgrenzungen. Vierzehn Autorengespräche über Liebe, Leben und Literatur* (Munich: Text + Kritik, 2007), pp. 73–99.

Koelbl, Herlinde, and Durs Grünbein, 'Durs Grünbein', in Herlinde Koelbl, *Im Schreiben zu Haus.*

Wie Schriftsteller zu Werke gehen. Fotografien und Gespräche (Munich: Knesebeck, 1998), pp. 212–17.

Lewandowsky, Via, and Durs Grünbein, '"Schnell gesagt ist halb zerfallen". Ein Gespräch', in Micha Brendel, Liane Burkhardt and André Meier, *'Bemerke den Unterschied'* (Nürnberg: Verlag für Moderne Kunst, 1991), pp. 30–33, 51–52.

Naumann, Thomas, and Durs Grünbein, 'Durs Grünbein. "Poetry from the Bad Side". Ein Gespräch', *Sprache im technischen Zeitalter*, 30.124 (1990), 442–49.

Neubauer, Michael, and Durs Grünbein, 'Sezierer, Sprachspieler, Satiriker. Interview mit Durs Grünbein', *GrauZone*, 3 (1995), 9–11.

Pöppel, Ernst, and Durs Grünbein, 'Schauder des Schaffens. Durs Grünbein im Gespräch mit dem Neurowissenschaftler Ernst Pöppel', *Der Spiegel*, 51 (2003), 214–20.

Ruzzenenti, Silvia, and Durs Grünbein, 'Poesie und Essay. Ein Interview mit Durs Grünbein', *Euphorion*, 102.4 (2008), 503–13.

Stoehr, Ingo R., and Durs Grünbein, '"Erneuerung in jeder Hinsicht". Ein Gespräch mit Durs Grünbein' / '"Renewal in Every Respect". A Conversation with Durs Grünbein', *Dimension2. Contemporary German-Language Literature*, 4.3 (1997), 366–75.

Secondary Literature

Adam, Meike, '"Das Fremdeste paarend und das nächste treffend". Hofmannsthal, Kafka, Grünbein und der Mehrwert literarischen Sprechens', *KulturPoetik*, 6.1 (2006), 78–95.

Ahrend, Hinrich, 'Essayistische Lyrik. Grünbeins Grenzgänge zwischen Poesie und Poetik', in *Schreiben am Schnittpunkt*, ed. by Bremer, Lampart and Wesche, pp. 135–68.

Ahrend, Hinrich, *'Tanz zwischen sämtlichen Stühlen'. Poetik und Dichtung im lyrischen und essayistischen Werk Durs Grünbeins* (Würzburg: Königshausen & Neumann, 2010).

Albrecht, Michael von, 'Nach den Satiren. Durs Grünbein und die Antike', in *Mythen in nachmythischer Zeit. Die Antike in der deutschsprachigen Literatur der Gegenwart*, ed. by Bernd Seidensticker and Martin Vöhler (Berlin: de Gruyter, 2002), pp. 101–16.

Arnold, Heinz Ludwig, ed., *Durs Grünbein* (*Text + Kritik*, 153.1 [2002]).

Batram, Debora, 'Das problematische Fundament von Grünbeins "Berenice"', in *Schreiben am Schnittpunkt*, ed. by Bremer, Lampart and Wesche, pp. 121–34.

Berg, Florian, *Das Gedicht und das Nichts. Über Anthropologie und Geschichte im Werk Durs Grünbeins* (Würzburg: Königshausen & Neumann, 2007).

Berg, Florian, 'Die Kunst im Zeitalter der Wissenschaft. Über René Descartes bei Durs Grünbein', *Sprache im technischen Zeitalter*, 45.183 (2007), 314–24.

Birtsch, Nicole, 'Orientierungsversuche im Niemandsland zwischen Medizin und Poetik. Das Verhältnis zwischen Körpergedächtnis und Poesie in Texten von Durs Grünbein', in *Einschnitte. Identität in der Moderne*, ed. by Oliver Kohns and Martin Roussel (Würzburg: Königshausen & Neumann, 2007), pp. 103–15.

Bormann, Alexander von, 'Im Dickicht des Nicht-Ich. Durs Grünbeins Anapäste', in *Signaturen der Gegenwartsliteratur. Festschrift für Walter Hinderer*, ed. by Dieter Borchmeyer (Würzburg: Königshausen & Neumann, 1999), pp. 171–84.

Böthig, Peter, *Grammatik einer Landschaft. Literatur aus der DDR in den 80er Jahren* (Berlin: Lukas, 1997).

Böttiger, Helmut, 'Durs Grünbein. Die sibirischen Abenteuerspielplätze', in Helmut Böttiger,

Rausch im Niemandsland. Es gibt ein Leben nach der DDR (Berlin: Fannei und Walz, 1994), pp. 86–95.

Böttiger, Helmut, '"Manches Wort war ein Altersfleck". Durs Grünbein oder die Verarbeitung dessen, allzu früh auf dem Olymp angelangt zu sein', in *Aufgerissen. Zur Literatur der 90er*, ed. by Thomas Kraft (Munich: Piper, 2000), pp. 53–66.

Böttiger, Helmut, 'Durs Grünbein. Auf dem Olymp', in Helmut Böttiger, *Nach den Utopien. Eine Geschichte der deutschsprachigen Gegenwartsliteratur* (Vienna: Zsolnay, 2004), pp. 112–25.

Braun, Michael, *'Hörreste, Sehreste'. Das literarische Fragment bei Büchner, Kafka, Benn und Celan* (Cologne: Böhlau, 2002).

Braun, Michael, '"Vom Rand her verlöschen die Bilder". Zu Durs Grünbeins Lyrik und Poetik des Fragments', *Text + Kritik*, 153.1 (2002), 4–18.

Braun, Michael, '"Barockwrack an der Elbe". Gedächtnisorte in Durs Grünbeins Dresden-Gedichten', *Der Deutschunterricht*, 58.2 (2006), 79–86.

Bremer, Kai, Fabian Lampart and Jörg Wesche, eds, *Schreiben am Schnittpunkt. Poesie und Wissen bei Durs Grünbein* (Freiburg i. Br.: Rombach, 2007).

Bremer, Kai, 'Vom Monolog der Toten zum Drama des Bewußtseins. Grünbein und das zeitgenössische Theater', in *Schreiben am Schnittpunkt*, ed. by Bremer, Lampart and Wesche, pp. 103–20.

Bremer, Kai, Fabian Lampart and Jörg Wesche, 'Poesie und Wissen bei Durs Grünbein. Einführende Überlegungen', in *Schreiben am Schnittpunkt*, ed. by Bremer, Lampart and Wesche, pp. 7–16.

Burdorf, Dieter, ed., *Die eigene und die fremde Kultur. Exotismus und Tradition bei Durs Grünbein und Raoul Schrott* (Iserlohn: Institut für Kirche und Gesellschaft, 2004).

Camartin, Iso, 'Der hohe Stil und das makabre Spiel oder: Warum schreibt Durs Grünbein Epitaphe?', *Jahrbuch der Deutschen Akademie für Sprache und Dichtung* (1996), 99–108.

Camartin, Iso, 'Die Anatomie und das Lebensgefühl', in *Peter-Huchel-Preis 1995. Durs Grünbein, Texte, Dokumente, Materialen*, ed. by Wolfgang Heidenreich (Baden-Baden: Elster, Rio, 1998), pp. 25–32.

Cappellotto, Anna, '"Sotto la scrittura agisce il nervo". La poesia cerebrale di Durs Grünbein', in *Verso una neuroestetica della letteratura*, ed. by Massimo Salgano (Rome: Aracne, 2009), pp. 107–36.

Cappellotto, Anna, 'Vom pawlowschen Hund zum Grenzhund Durs Grünbeins. Berührungspunkte zwischen sozialen und ästhetischen Experimenten', in *'Ein in der Phantasie durchgeführtes Experiment'. Literatur und Wissenschaft nach Neunzehnhundert*, ed. by Raul Calzoni and Massimo Salgaro (Göttingen: V & R unipress, 2010), pp. 337–57

Chŏn, Yŏng-ae, 'Scripto ergo sum. Zu Durs Grünbeins "Vom Schnee oder Descartes in Deutschland"', *Zeitschrift für deutschsprachige Kultur und Literaturen*, 15 (2006), 97–114.

Chŏn, Yŏng-ae, 'Die poetische Bewältigung der (Nach-)Wende. Zu Durs Grünbeins "Vom Schnee oder Descartes in Deutschland"', in *Germanistik im Konflikt der Kulturen*, ed. by Jean-Marie Valetin, X: *Geschlechterdifferenzen als Kulturkonflikte; Regiekunst und Development-Theatre; Streiten im Lichte der linguistischen und literaturwissenschaftlichen Dialogforschung; Deutsche Sprache und Literatur nach der Wende* (Bern: Lang, 2008), pp. 437–45.

Concetti, Riccardo, 'M(a)us(ol)ei delle scienze. Riflessioni sulla lirica di Hans Magnus Enzensberger e Durs Grünbein', in *Tra Frankenstein e Prometeo. Miti della scienza nell'immaginario del '900*, ed. by Francesca Montesperelli (Naples: Liguori, 2006), pp. 203–17.

Cooper, Ian, 'Direction, Disruption, Voice. Durs Grünbein's "Historien" and "Neue Historien"', *Germanic Review*, 84.2 (2009), 99–121.

Cordibella, Giovanna, '"Il sarcastico di Dresda". Zur Durs Grünbein-Rezeption in Italien', in *Schreiben am Schnittpunkt*, ed. by Bremer, Lampart and Wesche, pp. 57–76.

Cramer, Sibylle, 'Laudatio auf Durs Grünbein', in *Verleihung der Bremer Literaturpreise 1992 an Ror Wolf und Durs Grünbein*, ed. by Rudolf-Alexander-Schröder-Stiftung (Bremen: Rudolf-Alexander-Schröder-Stiftung, 1992), pp. 26–29.

Czernin, Franz Josef, 'Falten und Fallen. Zu Durs Grünbeins Gedichtband' [1995], in Franz Josef Czernin, *Der Himmel ist blau. Aufsätze zur Dichtung* (Weil am Rhein: Engeler, 2007), pp. 29–56.

Dąbrowska, Anna, 'Die Polyphonie in Gedichten von Durs Grünbein', *Studia niemcoznawcze*, 34 (2007), 385–96.

Dąbrowska, Anna, 'Die Dichtung von Durs Grünbein und die Musik', in *Authentizität und Polyphonie. Beiträge zur deutschen und polnischen Lyrik seit 1945. Für Gerhard R. Kaiser zum fünfundsechzigsten Geburtstag*, ed. by Jan Volker Röhnert (Heidelberg: Winter 2008), pp. 225–36.

Daiber, Jürgen, *Der Mittagsdämon. Zur literarischen Phänomenologie der Krise der Lebensmitte* (Paderborn: Mentis, 2006).

De Boever, Arne, 'Innerhalb / Außerhalb der textlichen Falte / Falle. Durs Grünbein anno 2003', *Germanistische Mitteilungen*, 57.1 (2003), 41–58.

De Boever, Arne, 'Durs Grünbein', in *Duitstalige literatuur na 1945*, II: *Duitsland na 1989, Oostenrijk en Zwitserland*, ed. by A. Gilleir and B. Philipsen (Louvain: Peeters, 2006), pp. 19–35.

Deckert, Renatus, 'Der Nachgeborene auf dem Barockwrack. Durs Grünbein über Dresden', *Sinn und Form*, 56.2 (2004), 240–50.

Deckert, Renatus, *Die wüste Stadt. Sieben Dichter über Dresden* (Frankfurt a. M.: Insel, 2005).

Deckert, Renatus, *Ruine und Gedicht. Das zerstörte Dresden im Werk von Volker Braun, Heinz Czechowski und Durs Grünbein* (Dresden: Thelem, 2010).

Döring, Jörg, 'Von den Nachgeborenen. Brechts "Ballade von den Seeräubern" und Durs Grünbeins "O Heimat, zynischer Euphon"', in *Bertolt Brecht (1898–1956)*, ed. by Jörg Döning and Walter Delabar (Berlin: Weidler, 1998), pp. 355–77.

Döring, Jörg, 'Großstadtlyrik nach 1989. Durs Grünbeins "In den Tunneln der U-Bahn" und Bert Papenfuß' "hunger, durst und such"', in *Text der Stadt – Reden von Berlin. Literatur und Metropole seit 1989*, ed. by Jörg Döring and Erhard Schütz (Berlin: Weidler, 1999), pp. 95–118.

Drynda, Maciej, 'Durs Grünbeins "Die Schädelbasislektion" auf Polnisch, oder: Wie sich das allmähliche Schriftwerden einer Postwendeidentität hat zweifach in eine andere Sprache übertragen lassen', in *Identitätskonstruktionen in fiktionalen und nicht-fiktionalen Texten. Übersetzung und Rezeption*, ed. by Beate Sommerfeld and Karolina Kęsicka (Bern: Lang, 2010), pp. 89–103.

Dürbeck, Gabriele, '"Wenn es stimmt, dass wir schwierige Tiere sind". Anatomie und Anthropologie in Durs Grünbeins "Mensch ohne Großhirn"', *Zeitschrift für Germanistik*, 19.1 (2009), 133–45.

Ehinger, Claudia, 'Durs Grünbein – "Ein Kind seiner Zeit"? oder: Wie politisch ist Grünbeins Lyrik? Eine exemplarische Untersuchung anhand des Gedichtes "Eine hagere Frau"', in *Verbalträume. Beiträge zur deutschsprachigen Gegenwartsliteratur*, ed. by Andrea Bartl (Augsburg: Wißner, 2005), pp. 83–94.

Erhart, Walter, 'Literaturwissenschaft und Physik. Aus Anlass von Durs Grünbeins "Vom Schnee oder Descartes in Deutschland" (2003)', in *Literaturwissenschaft – interdisziplinär*, ed. by Lothar van Laak and Katja Malsch (Heidelberg: Synchron, 2010), pp. 115–26.

Ertel, Anna Alissa, *Körper, Gehirne, Gene. Lyrik und Naturwissenschaft bei Ulrike Draesner und Durs Grünbein* (Berlin: de Gruyter, 2011).

Eshel, Amir, 'Diverging Memories? Durs Grünbein's Mnemonic Topographies and the Future of the German Past', *German Quarterly*, 74.4 (2001), 407–16.

Eskin, Michael, '"Stimmengewirr vieler Zeiten". Grünbein's Dialogue with Dante, Baudelaire, and Mandel'shtam', *Germanic Review*, 77.1 (2002), 34–50.

Eskin, Michael, 'Body Language. Durs Grünbein's Aesthetics', *arcadia*, 37.1 (2002), 42–66.

Eskin, Michael, '"Bridge to Antiquity". Nostalgia, Exile, and Stoicism in the Poetry of Durs Grünbein', *arcadia*, 39.2 (2004), 356–81.

Eskin, Michael, 'Risse, die durch die Zeit führen. Zu Durs Grünbeins Historien', in Durs Grünbein, *Der Misanthrop auf Capri* (Frankfurt a. M.: Suhrkamp, 2005), pp. 107–21.

Eskin, Michael, 'Descartes of Metaphor. On Durs Grünbein's "Vom Schnee"', in *Schaltstelle. Neue deutsche Lyrik im Dialog*, ed. by Karen Leeder (Amsterdam: Rodopi, 2007), pp. 163–79.

Eskin, Michael, '"Ich bin ... mir selbst begegnet". Zu einer Denkfigur bei Benn, Celan und Grünbein', in *Gottfried Benn – Wechselspiele zwischen Biographie und Werk*, ed. by Matías Martínez (Göttingen: Wallstein, 2007), pp. 133–47.

Eskin, Michael, 'Of Sailors and Poets. On Celan, Grünbein, and Brodsky', *German Life and Letters*, 60.3 (2007), 315–28.

Eskin, Michael, *Poetic Affairs. Celan, Grünbein, Brodsky* (Stanford: Stanford University Press, 2008).

Eskin, Michael, 'Wake-Up Call. Durs Grünbein with Rilke, Descartes, and Pushkin', *Poetica*, 41.1–2 (2009), 189–217.

Essen, Gesa von, '"So viele Zeiten zur selben Zeit". Geschichte und Gedächtnis in Grünbeins "Das erste Jahr"', in *Schreiben am Schnittpunkt*, ed. by Bremer, Lampart and Wesche, pp. 79–102.

Fischer, Markus, '"Blieb nur der Städtehimmel, dieser kolossale Rachen". Zur Großstadtthematik im Werk Durs Grünbeins', in *'Historische Gedächtnisse sind Palimpseste'. Hermeneutik – Historismus – New Historicism – Cultural Studies. Festschrift zum 70. Geburtstag von Gotthart Wunberg*, ed. by Roland S. Kamzelak (Paderborn: Mentis, 2001), pp. 21–41.

Fischer, Roman, 'Die Zersplitterung des Ich. Zur Physiologie des Dichters Durs Grünbein', *Die Drei*, 2 (1997), 107–13.

Fromm, Waldemar, 'Die Literatur und das Gehirn. Zur Rezeption der Naturwissenschaften bei Botho Strauß und Durs Grünbein. Ein Vergleich', *KulturPoetik*, 9.2 (2009), 235–51.

Fuchs, Anne, 'The Bombing of Dresden and the Idea of Cultural Impact', in *Cultural Impact in the German Context. Studies in Transmission, Reception, and Influence*, ed. by Rebecca Braun and Lyn Marven (Rochester, NY: Camden House, 2010), pp. 36–57.

Fuhrmann, Manfred, 'Zeitdiagnose am Widerpart Roms', *Sprache im technischen Zeitalter*, 37.151 (1999), 276–85.

Fuhrmann, Manfred, 'Juvenal – Barbier – Grünbein. Über den römischen Satiriker und zwei seiner tätigen Bewunderer', *Text + Kritik*, 153.1 (2002), 60–67.

Fujii, Kenji, 'Anatomie und Gedächtnis. Über Durs Grünbeins Gedichtzyklus "Niemands Land Stimmen"', *Doitsu bungaku*, 106 (2001), 93–100.

Gabriel, Nicole, 'Le poète en "jeune chien garde-frontière". Durs Grünbein et la "Wende"', *Études germaniques*, 35.1 (2000), 73–97.

Ganseuer, Christian, 'Das Meister-Schüler-Prinzip. Eine Durchquerung von Durs Grünbeins Essay "Das Lächeln des Glückgotts"', in *Durchquerungen. Für Ralf Schnell zum 65. Geburtstag*, ed. by Iris Hermann and Anne Maximiliane Jäger-Gogoll (Heidelberg: Winter, 2008), pp. 89–94.

Ganseuer, Christian, *Poesie und Poetologie. Untersuchungen zum Verhältnis von literarischer Theorie und poetischer Praxis bei Durs Grünbein* (dissertation), in http://dokumentix.ub.uni-siegen.de/opus/volltexte/2009/400/index.html.

Garrard, Malcolm, 'Durs Grünbein. French Kiss', in *Poetry Project. Irish Germanists Interpret German Verse*, ed. by Florian Krobb and Jeff Morrison Florian (Bern: Lang, 2003), pp. 269–73.

Geisenhanslüke, Achim, '"Mensch ohne Grosshirn". Durs Grünbein und das Ende der Utopien?', in *Die eigene und die fremde Kultur. Exotismus und Tradition bei Durs Grünbein und Raoul Schrott*, ed. by Burdorf, pp. 63–78.

Gerhardt, Volker, 'Ein Arzt der Kultur. Laudatio auf Durs Grünbein anlässlich der Verleihung des Nietzsche-Preises des Landes Sachsen-Anhalt am 27. August 2004', *Nietzscheforschung*, 12 (2005), 13–21.

Goebel, Rolf J., '"Ein Hollywood aus Versatzstücken heißester europäischer Geschichte". Durs Grünbein's Berlin as Cinematic Spectacle', *Gegenwartsliteratur. A German Studies Yearbook*, 4.1 (2005), 1–20.

Goebel, Rolf J., 'Gesamtkunstwerk Dresden. Official Urban Discourse and Durs Grünbein's Poetic Critique', *The German Quarterly*, 80.4 (2007), 492–510.

Grage, Joachim, 'Stockholm gris. Gehirn, Stadt und Text bei Aris Fioretos und Durs Grünbein', *Skandinavistik. Zeitschrift für Sprache, Literatur und Kultur der Nordischen Länder*, 34.1 (2004), 133–49.

Grimm, Erk, 'Das Gedicht nach dem Gedicht. Über die Lesbarkeit der jüngsten Lyrik', in *Deutschsprachige Gegenwartsliteratur. Wider ihre Verächter*, ed. by Christian Döring (Frankfurt a.M.: Suhrkamp, 1995), pp. 287–311.

Grimm, Erk, 'Mediamania? Contemporary German Poetry in the Age of New Information Technologies. Thomas Kling and Durs Grünbein', *Studies in Twentieth Century Literature*, 21.1 (1997), 275–301.

Grimm, Erk, 'Divided Legacies. East German Writers in the Middle East', in *The Cultural After-Life of East Germany. New Transnational Perspectives*, ed. by Leslie Adelson (Baltimore: Johns Hopkins University Press, 2002), pp. 60–92.

Gross, Marek, *Bruch und Erinnerung Durs Grünbeins Poetik. In den Straßen Roms. Ein Gespräch mit Durs Grünbein* (Berlin: LIT, 2011).

Große, Wilhelm, 'Descartes / Grünbein oder Das Dreieck aus Philosophie, naturwissenschaftlichem Denken und Literaturpoesie. Anmerkungen zu Durs Grünbeins "Vom Schnee oder Descartes in Deutschland"', *Literatur im Unterricht*, 6.3 (2005), 219–27.

Hamm, Peter, 'Vorerst – oder: Der Dichter als streunender Hund. Lobrede auf Durs Grünbein', *manuskripte*, 33.122 (1993), 103–6.

Heidenreich, Wolfgang, ed., *Ernst-Huchel-Preis 1995. Durs Grünbein. Texte, Dokumente, Materialien* (Baden-Baden: Elster, Rio, 1998).

Helbig, Holger, '[untitled]', *Literatur in Wissenschaft und Unterricht*, 30.1 (1997), 73–74.

Hennemann, Alexa, *Die Zerbrechlichkeit der Körper. Zu den Georg-Büchner-Preisreden von Heiner Müller und Durs Grünbein* (Bern: Lang, 2000).

Heske, Henning, 'Geschmeidige Gepardin und fliegender Fisch. Tiermotive in der Lyrik von Durs Grünbein', *Literatur im Unterricht*, 4.3 (2003), 191–96.

Heske, Henning, *Goethe und Grünbein. Aufsätze zur Literatur* (Bonn: Bernstein-Verlag, 2004).

Heudecker, Sylvia, 'Durs Grünbein in der Kritik', in *Schreiben am Schnittpunkt*, ed. by Bremer, Lampart and Wesche, pp. 37–56.

Hoffmann, Paul, 'Einführung in die Lesung von Durs Grünbein im Hölderlinturm in Tübingen am 26. Januar 1996', in Paul Hoffmann, *Das erneute Gedicht* (Frankfurt a. M.: Suhrkamp, 2001), pp. 107–12.

Hoffmann, Torsten, 'Poetologisierte Naturwissenschaften. Zur Legitimation von Dichtung bei Durs Grünbein, Raoul Schrott und Botho Strauß', in *Schreiben am Schnittpunkt*, ed. by Bremer, Lampart and Wesche, pp. 171–90.

Hohl, Cosima, 'Endstation Weltflucht? Durs Grünbeins Gedicht "Vita brevis"', in *Verbalträume. Beiträge zur deutschsprachigen Gegenwartsliteratur*, ed. by Andrea Bartl (Augsburg: Wißner, 2005), pp. 63–82.

Huch, Hans-Günther, *Phantasie und Wirklichkeit. Phänomene dichterischer Imagination in der Poesie der Moderne. Gespräche mit Gedichten von Ezra Pound bis Durs Grünbein* (Würzburg: Königshausen & Neumann, 2002).

Huch, Hans-Günther, '"Ich schätzte die Beredsamkeit sehr, und ich war in die Poesie verliebt ...". Durs Grünbeins Epos "Vom Schnee" – ein historischer Roman?', in *Literatur im Spiel der Zeichen. Festschrift für Hans Vilmar Geppert*, ed. by Werner Frick, Fabian Lampart and Bernadette Malinowski (Tübingen: Francke, 2006), pp. 314–28.

Huch, Hans-Günther, 'Der Blick auf die griechischen und römischen Gründerväter westlicher Kultur. Durs Grünbeins Beziehung zur Kultur der Antike', *Akzente*, 53.1 (2006), 12–27.

Irmer, Thomas, 'Durs Grünbein', in *Deutschsprachige Lyriker des 20. Jahrhunderts*, ed. by Ursula Heukenkamp and Peter Geist (Berlin: Erich Schmidt, 2007), pp. 711–21.

Joist, Alexander, *Auf der Suche nach dem Sinn des Todes. Todesdeutungen in der Lyrik der Gegenwart* (Mainz: Matthias Grünewald, 2002).

Klein, Sonja, *'Denn alles, alles ist verlorne Zeit'. Fragment und Erinnerung im Werk von Durs Grünbein* (Bielefeld: Aisthesis, 2008).

Klein, Sonja, '"Ach, daß es für Gedichte einen Louvre gäbe!" Durs Grünbein und das Museum im Kopf', in *'... das hohe Geistergespräch'. Über Literatur im musealen und digitalen Raum*, ed. by Sabine Brenner-Wilczek and Sikander Singh (Bielefeld: Aisthesis, 2008), pp. 169–74.

Klein, Sonja, '"Imago für Imago von der Schöpferwelt dort draußen". Durs Grünbeins "Vom Schnee" oder die Melancholie der Sprache', *Symposium*, 63.3 (2009), 207–19.

Knoblich, Aniela, '"Luftstrom aus alten Städten". Geschichte und Erfahrung des Dichters bei Durs Grünbein', in *Erfahrung und Geschichte. Historische Sinnbildung im Pränarrativen*, ed. by Thiemo Breyer and Daniel Creutz (Berlin: de Gruyter, 2010), pp. 317–31.

Kocziszky, Éva, 'Schiller und das Klassische in der Lyrik der Spätmoderne. Durs Grünbein: "Auf der Akropolis"', in *Im Schatten eines anderen? Schiller heute*, ed. by András F. Balogh (Bern: Lang, 2010), pp. 161–67.

Köhn, Lothar, 'Den teuren Toten. Lyrische Historiographie bei Enzensberger und Grünbein', *Germanica*, 21 (1997), 133–56.

Kopacki, Andrzej, 'Schneelandschaften. "Nacht" von Rolf Dieter Brinkmann und "Yeti" von Durs Grünbein in einer vergleichenden Lektüre', in *Wege der Lyrik in die Moderne*, ed. by Gunter Martens (Würzburg: Königshausen & Neumann, 2003), pp. 175–84.

Köppe, Tilmann, 'Grünbeins Idee von der Erkenntnis des Dichters', in *Schreiben am Schnittpunkt*, ed. by Bremer, Lampart and Wesche, pp. 259–70.

Korte, Hermann, '"Tag X"', in Hermann Korte, *Lyrik von 1945 bis zur Gegenwart*, 2nd rev. edn (Munich: Oldenburg, 2000), pp. 125–28.

Korte, Hermann, 'Habemus poetam. Zum Konnex von Poesie und Wissen in Durs Grünbeins Gedichtsammlung "Nach den Satiren"', *Text + Kritik*, 153.1 (2002), 19–33.

Korte, Hermann, 'Durs Grünbein', in *Kritisches Lexikon zur deutschsprachigen Gegenwartsliteratur*, 72. Nachlieferung (Munich: Text + Kritik, 2002), pp. C-H.

Korte, Hermann, 'Zivilisationsepisteln. Poetik und Rhetorik in Grünbeins Gedichten', in *Die eigene und die fremde Kultur. Exotismus und Tradition bei Durs Grünbein und Raoul Schrott*, ed. by Burdorf, pp. 79–95.

Krämer, Olav, 'Ich und Welt. Durs Grünbeins Zyklus "Niemands Land Stimmen" und sein Gedicht "Nach den Satiren I"', *Jahrbuch der deutschen Schillergesellschaft*, 48 (2004), 348–74.

Krämer, Olav, 'Bildliches Denken als Erkenntnismodus zwischen Poesie und Wissenschaft. Grünbein über Dante, Darwin, Hopkins und Goethe', in *Schreiben am Schnittpunkt*, ed. by Bremer, Lampart and Wesche, pp. 241–57.

Krellner, Ulrich, '"Zwischen Antike und X". Zur Poetologie Durs Grünbeins', in *Zwischen Globalisierungen und Regionalisierungen. Zur Darstellung von Zeitgeschichte in deutschsprachiger Gegenwartsliteratur*, ed. by Martin Hellström and Edgar Plate (Munich: Iudicum, 2008), pp. 41–52.

Krellner, Ulrich, 'So wenig Anfang war selten. Durs Grünbeins Berliner Aufzeichnungen "Das erste Jahr"', in *Autobiographisches Schreiben in der deutschsprachigen Gegenwartsliteratur*, ed. by Ulrich Breuer, 3 vols (Munich: Iudicium, 2006–2009), III (2009), pp. 198–207.

Laak, Lothar van, 'Die Bilder der Wissenschaft – die Bilder der Literatur. Das interdisziplinäre Potenzial der Einbildungskraft im Blick auf Eichendorff und Grünbein', in *Literaturwissenschaft – interdisziplinär*, ed. by Lothar van Laak and Katja Malsch (Heidelberg: Synchron, 2010), pp. 131–42.

Lampart, Fabian, '"Jeder in seiner Welt, so viele Welten ...". Durs Grünbeins Dante', *Text + Kritik*, 153.1 (2002), 49–59.

Lampart, Fabian, '"Tropismen an den Rändern alter Formen". Annäherungen an Durs Grünbeins Lyrik aus den Jahren der Wende', in *Engagierte Literatur in Wendezeiten*, ed. by Willi Huntemann and others (Würzburg: Königshausen & Neumann, 2003), pp. 133–47.

Lampart, Fabian, '"Der junge Dichter als Sphinx". Durs Grünbein und die deutsche Lyrik nach 1989', in *Schreiben am Schnittpunkt*, ed. by Bremer, Lampart and Wesche, pp. 19–36.

Laufhütte, Hartmut, 'Gedicht in Grauzonen. Zu Durs Grünbeins "Olé"', in *Liebensgedichte der Gegenwart*, ed. by Hiltrud Gnüg (Stuttgart: Reclam, 2003), pp. 70–78.

Laufhütte, Hartmut, 'Totgesagte leben länger. Von der Unzulänglichkeit einer anachronistischen Theorie und der Lebendigkeit einer modernen Textart. Balladendichtung in der zweiten Hälfte des 20. Jahrhunderts', in *Die deutsche Ballade im 20. Jahrhundert*, ed. by Srdan Bogosavljević and Winfried Woesler (Bern: Lang, 2009), pp. 11–28.

Leeder, Karen, '"ich fühle mich in grenzen wohl". The Metaphors of Boundary and Boundaries of Metaphor in "Prenzlauer Berg"', in *Prenzlauer Berg. Bohemia in East Berlin?*, ed. by Philip Brady and Ian Wallace (Amsterdam: Rodopi, 1995), pp. 19–44.

Leeder, Karen, *Breaking Boundaries. A New Generation of Poets in the GDR* (Oxford: Clarendon Press, 1996).

Leeder, Karen, 'The "poeta doctus" and the New German Poetry', *The Germanic Review*, 77.1 (2002), 51–76.

Leeder, Karen, "Cold Media: The Science of Poetry and the Poetry of Science", *Interdisciplinary Science Reviews*, 30.4 (2005), 301–311.

Leeder, Karen, 'The Poetry of Science and the Science of Poetry. German Poetry in the Laboratory of the Twentieth Century', *German Life and Letters*, 60.3 (2007), 412–29.

Leeder, Karen, 'Die Poesie der Wissenschaft und die Wissenschaft der Poesie. Das Gedicht im Labor des 20. Jahrhunderts', in *Germanistik im Konflikt der Kulturen*, ed. by Jean-Marie Valetin, VII: *Bild, Rede, Schrift; Kleriker, Adel, Stadt und außerchristliche Kulturen der Vormoderne; Wissenschaften und Literatur seit der Renaissance* (Bern: Lang, 2008), pp. 437–45.

Lehmkuhl, Tobias, 'Die Bombardierung Dresdens in Durs Grünbeins Gedicht "Europa nach dem letzten Regen"', *Ostragehege*, 27 (2002), 18–21.

Lehmkuhl, Tobias, 'Grünbein ohne Gegenwart', *Ästhetik und Kommunikation*, 34.122/123 (2003), 147–49.

Magenau, Jörg, 'Durs Grünbeins anatomisches Theater', *Der Deutschunterricht*, 48.3 (1996), 66–71.

Magenau, Jörg, 'Der Körper als Schnittfläche. Bemerkungen zur Literatur der "Neuen Innerlichkeit". Texte von Reto Hänny, Ulrike Kolb, Ulrike Draesner, Durs Grünbein, Thomas Hettche, Marcel Beyer und Michael Kleeberg', in *Baustelle Gegenwartsliteratur. Die neunziger Jahre*, ed. by Andreas Erb (Opladen: Westdeutscher Verlag, 1998), pp. 107–21.

Malinowski, Bernadette, and Gert-Ludwig Ingold, '"... im andern dupliziert". Zur Rezeption cartesischer Erkenntnistheorie und Naturwissenschaft in Durs Grünbeins "Vom Schnee oder Descartes in Deutschland"', in *Schreiben am Schnittpunkt*, ed. by Bremer, Lampart and Wesche, pp. 271–306.

Martus, Steffen, and Claudia Benthien, 'Schnee von gestern – Schnee von heute. Die "Wiederkehr der Frühen Neuzeit" bei Durs Grünbein', *Zeitschrift für Germanistik*, 21.2 (2011), 241–55.

Matuschek, Stefan, 'Moralist und Flaneur, oder: Hätte Baudelaire Grünbein für Barbier gehalten? Zu Durs Grünbein, "Nach den Satiren"', *Germanisch-Romanische Monatsschrift*, 54.1 (2004), 109–16.

Matuschek, Stefan, 'Assoziativ, konsekutiv, parasitär. Formen und Funktionen der Intertextualität bei Durs Grünbein', in *Authentizität und Polyphonie. Beiträge zur deutschen und polnischen Lyrik seit 1945. Für Gerhard R. Kaiser zum fünfundsechzigsten Geburtstag*, ed. by Jan Volker Röhnert (Heidelberg: Winter, 2008), pp. 237–44.

Mergenthaler, Volker, 'Coventry und Dresden, Ninive und Sodom. Durs Grünbeins Koordinaten mythologischer Sinnstiftung nach dem 11. September 2001', in *In the Embrace of the Swan. Anglo-German Mythologies in Literature, the Visual Arts and Cultural Theory*, ed. by Rüdiger Görner and Angus Nicholls (Berlin: de Gruyter 2010), pp. 168–86.

Meyer, Anne-Rose, 'Physiologie und Poesie. Zu Körperdarstellungen in der Lyrik von Ulrike Draesner, Durs Grünbein und Thomas Kling', *Gegenwartsliteratur. A German Studies Yearbook*, 1 (2002), 107–33.

Meyer, Anne-Rose, 'Metropolenpoesie. Durs Grünbeins Berlin-Gedichte', *Gegenwartsliteratur. A German Studies Yearbook*, 4 (2005), 21–47.

Millot, Cécile, '"Porcelaine" de Durs Grünbein. Un enfant de l'après-guerre face à la destruction de Dresde ou les difficultés du devoir de mémoire', *Allemagne d'aujourd'hui*, 178 (2006), 143–58.

Monroe, Jonathan, 'Avant-Garde Poetries after the Wall', *Poetics Today*, 21.1 (2000), 95–128.

Müller, Alexander, *Das Gedicht als Engramm. Memoria und Imagination in der Poetik Durs Grünbeins* (Oldenburg: Igel, 2004).

Müller, Heiner, 'Portrait des Künstlers als junger Grenzhund', in Durs Grünbein, *Den Körper zerbrechen. Rede zur Entgegennahme des Georg-Büchner-Preises* (Frankfurt a. M.: Suhrkamp, 1995), pp. 25–29.

Naumann, Barbara, 'Gewalt der Sprache. Nietzsches Descartes-Kritik, Grünbeins Descartes', in *Die Literatur der Literaturtheorie*, ed. by Boris Previšić (Bern: Lang 2010), pp. 133–44.
Naumann, Barbara, 'Der (un-)treue Librettist und der Wahn im Detail. Durs Grünbeins Operntext "Berenice" nach Edgar Allan Poe', in *Texttreue*, ed. by Jürg Berthold and Boris Previšić (Bern: Lang, 2008), pp. 183–95.
Neubauer, Michael, 'Erfrischendes aus Ostdeutschland. Neue Lyrik hat das Land. Anmerkungen zum Werk Durs Grünbeins', *GrauZone*, 2 (1995), 17–19.
Opitz, Michael, 'Durs Grünbein', in *Metzler Lexikon Weltliteratur. 1000 Autoren von der Antike bis zur Gegenwart*, ed. by Axel Ruckaberle (Stuttgart: Metzler, 2006), II, pp. 74–76.
Opitz-Wiemers, Carola, 'Lagebeschreibung – vom letzten Lyrikjahrzehnt des 20. Jahrhunderts', in *Perspektivensuche. Zur Darstellung von Zeitgeschichte in deutschsprachiger Gegenwartsliteratur*, ed. by Edgar Platen (Munich: Iudicum, 2002), pp. 177–96.
Osterkamp, Ernst, 'Durs Grünbeins Memorandum zur Lage der Poesie nach den Utopien', in *Poetologische Lyrik von Klopstock bis Grünbein. Gedichte und Interpretationen*, ed. by Olaf Hildebrand (Cologne: Böhlau, 2003), pp. 324–34.
Owen, Ruth J., *The Poet's Role. Lyric Responses to German Unification by Poets from the GDR* (Amsterdam: Rodopi, 2001).
Owen, Ruth J., 'Science in Contemporary Poetry. A Point of Comparison between Raoul Schrott and Durs Grünbein', *German Life and Letters*, 54.1 (2001), 82–96.
Owen, Ruth J., '"Eine im Feuer versunkene Stadt". Dresden in Poetry', *Gegenwartsliteratur. A German Studies Yearbook*, 1 (2002), 87–96.
Owen, Ruth J., 'Bodies in Contemporary Poetry', in *Schaltstelle. Neue deutsche Lyrik im Dialog*, ed. by Karen Leeder (Amsterdam: Rodopi, 2007), pp. 269–91.
Payk-Heitmann, Andrea, 'Der 11. September 2001 im (fiktionalen) Tagebuch. Überlegungen zu Durs Grünbein und Max Goldt', in *Nine Eleven. Ästhetische Verarbeitungen des 11. September 2001*, ed. by Ingo Irsigler and Christoph Jürgensen (Heidelberg: Winter, 2008), pp. 49–66.
Pickerodt, Gerhart, 'Durs Grünbein und der Aschermittwoch der DDR', in *Verrat an der Kunst? Rückblicke auf die DDR-Literatur*, ed. by Karl Deiritz and Hannes Krauss (Berlin: Aufbau, 1993), pp. 99–103.
Quadrelli, Paola, 'Durs Grünbein. La condizione umana', in *'Le storie sono finite e io sono libero'. Sviluppi recenti nella poesia di lingua tedesca*, ed. by Maurizio Pirro, Marcella Costa and Stefania Sbarra (Naples: Liguori, 2003), pp. 201–13.
Ravetto, Miriam, '"Falten und Fallen" di Durs Grünbein. Il messaggio poetico attraverso la lingua e le morfie foniche', in *Poesia civile. Contributi per un dibattito*, ed. by Giusi Baldissone (Novara: Interlinea, 2010), pp. 65–69.
Rauch, Marja, 'Topographie de la mémoire. Berlin dans la poésie de la seconde moitié du XXe siècle', *Allemange d'aujourd'hui*, 148 (1999), 134–47.
Reitani, Luigi, 'Durs Grünbein. "Berlin, ein toter saß an dreizehn Wochen ...". La morte in diretta', in *Poesia tedesca contemporanea. Interpretazioni*, ed. by Anna Chiarloni (Alessandria: dell'Orso, 1996), pp. 269–73.
Riedel, Wolfgang, 'Poetik der Präsenz. Idee der Dichtung bei Durs Grünbein', *Internationales Archiv für Sozialgeschichte der deutschen Literatur*, 24.1 (1999), 82–105.
Renner, Ursula, 'Schädel-Meditationen. Zur Kulturgeschichte eines Denkmodells', in *Biologie, Psychologie, Poetologie*, ed. by Ursula Renner and Walburga Hülk (Würzburg: Königshausen & Neumann, 2005), pp. 171–200.
Reißer, Johann, '"Langsam kommen die Uhren auf Touren, jede geht anders". Das Auseinanderfallen der Zeitordnungen in Durs Grünbeins Nach-Wende-Lyrik vor dem Hintergrund

der Zeitkonzeption Gilles Deleuzes', in *Nach-Wende-Narrationen. Das wiedervereinigte Deutschland im Spiegel von Literatur und Film*, ed. by Gerhard Jens Lüdeker and Dominik Orth (Göttingen: V & R unipress, 2010), pp. 175–90.

Reumkens, Noël, *Kunst, Künstler, Kontext und Konzept. Intermediale und andersartige Bezugnahmen auf Visuell-Künstlerisches in der Lyrik Mayröckers, Klings, Grünbeins und Draesners* (Würzburg: Königshausen & Neumann, 2012).

Röhnert, Jan Volker, 'Zur Freude der Marmeladenindustrie. Amerikanische Filme – deutsche Gedichte. Brecht, Brinkmann, Grünbein', *Neue deutsche Literatur*, 52.9 (2004), 34–42.

Ruzzenenti, Silvia, 'Durs Grünbein e il saggio. Invito alla lettura', *Comunicare*, 7 (2007), 231–39.

Ruzzenenti, Silvia, 'Durs Grünbein. Poesia e saggio. Un'intervista', in *Il saggio. Forme e funzioni di un genere letterario*, ed. by Giulia Cantarutti, Luisa Avellini and Silvia Albertazzi (Bologna: Mulino, 2007), pp. 235–47.

Ryan, Judith, 'Das Motiv der Schädelnähte bei Durs Grünbein', in *Schreiben nach der Wende. Ein Jahrzehnt deutscher Literatur 1989–1999*, ed. by Gerhard Fischer and David Roberts (Tübingen: Stauffenburg, 2001), pp. 301–15.

Ryan, Judith, 'The Skull beneath the Skin' in *A New History of German Literature*, ed. by David E. Wellbery and others (Cambridge, MA: Harvard University Press, 2004), pp. 959–64.

Ryan, Judith, '"Spurlose Frühe". Durs Grünbeins "Vom Schnee" und das Problem der Wende', in *Weiterschreiben. Zur DDR-Literatur nach dem Ende der DDR*, ed. by Holger Helbig and Kristin Felsner (Berlin: Akademie, 2007), pp. 163–81.

Schuhmann, Klaus, 'Restbestände. Heiner Müller, Volker Braun, Durs Grünbein. Echos und Nekrologe', *Neue deutsche Literatur*, 50.6 (2002), 156–60.

Seibt, Gustav, 'In den Albtraum erwachen. Durs Grünbeins Gedicht "Alba"', in Gustav Seibt, *Das Komma in der Erdnußbutter. Essays zur Literatur und literarischen Kritik* (Frankfurt a. M.: Suhrkamp, 1997), pp. 66–71.

Sinisi, Barbara, 'Durs Grünbein tra afasia e poesia. Critica sociale e disincanto ideologico di un poeta del dopo-guerra fredda', *Il confronto letterario*, 25.2 (2009), 435–55.

Spoerhase, Carlos, 'Durs Grünbein', in *Killy Literaturlexikon. Autoren und Werke des deutschsprachigen Kulturraumes*, ed. by Wilhelm Kühlmann and others (Berlin: de Gruyter, 2009), IV, pp. 470–471.

Spoerhase, Carlos, 'Über die Grenzen der Geschichtslyrik. Historischer Anachronismus und ästhetische Anachronie in Durs Grünbeins Werk, am Beispiel seiner Arbeiten über Descartes', *Zeitschrift für Germanistik*, 21.2 (2011), 263–83.

Stockhorst, Stefanie, 'Ästhetisierung der Anatomie. Medizinische und literarische Referenzräume in Durs Grünbeins "Schädelbasislektion"', in *Schreiben am Schnittpunkt*, ed. by Bremer, Lampart and Wesche, pp. 191–212.

Sturm-Trigonakis, Elke, 'Formen der Alterität in der neuen deutschen Dichtung. José F. A. Oliver und Durs Grünbein', *Wirkendes Wort. Deutsche Sprache und Literatur in Forschung und Lehre*, 48.3 (1998), 376–407.

Térmens Samsó, Josep, 'Durs Grünbein. Poèmes', *Marges*, 57.12 (1996), 37–51.

Tholen, Toni, 'Vaterschaft und Autorschaft. Zur Bestimmung eines prekären Verhältnisses in der Gegenwartsliteratur am Beispiel von Durs Grünbeins "Das erste Jahr. Berliner Aufzeichnungen"', *Weimarer Beiträge. Zeitschrift für Literaturwissenschaft, Ästhetik und Kulturwissenschaften*, 55.2 (2009), 180–195.

Trapp, Erin, 'Unfulfillable Wishing. Depression in the Gray Zone', *Modern Language Notes*, 124.3 (2009), 708–27.

Vecchiato, Daniele, '"Enttäuscht buchstabiert man Ve-ne-dig, und es klingt wie erledigt". Kritische Annäherung an Durs Grünbeins Venedig-Gedichte', *Annali di Ca' Foscari*, 48.1–2 (2010), 289–330.

Völker, Klaus, 'Die Schrecken der Auflösung. Zu Durs Grünbeins Arbeiten für das Theater', *Text + Kritik*, 153.1 (2002), 44–48.

Wallmann, Hermann, 'Handlinien. Datumsgrenzen. Über zwei Gedichte von Durs Grünbein', *Germanica*, 21 (1997), 157–62.

Wesche, Jörg, 'Biotopoi. Tiergarten, Müllberg und Tiefsee als Orte literarischer Regression', in *Schreiben am Schnittpunkt*, ed. by Bremer, Lampart and Wesche, pp. 213–39.

Wilczek, Reinhard, 'Randnotizen zum Tod in der Mediengesellschaft. Durs Grünbeins Epitaphe von "Den Teuren Toten" im Deutschunterricht', *Literatur im Unterricht*, 4.3 (2003), 197–209.

Wilke, Sabine, 'Vorm Telephon und auf Sendersuche. Die Poetik zeitgenössischer Autoren am Beispiel von Durs Grünbein', in Sabine Wilke, *Ist alles so geblieben, wie es früher war? Essays zur Literatur und Frauenpolitik im vereinten Deutschland* (Würzburg: Königshausen & Neumann, 2000), pp. 105–11.

Winkler, Ron, *Dichtung zwischen Großstadt und Großhirn. Annäherungen an das lyrische Werk Durs Grünbeins* (Hamburg: Kovač, 2000).

Zanucchi, Mario, 'Das Diorama und der sarkastische Blick. Kritische Betrachtungen zur Poetik Durs Grünbeins', *Weimarer Beiträge. Zeitschrift für Literaturwissenschaft, Ästhetik und Kulturwissenschaften*, 51.2 (2005), 219–35.

Zimmer, Ilonka, 'Durs Grünbein – Auswahlbibliographie 1988–2001', *Text + Kritik*, 153.1 (2002), 85–91.

Ziolkowski, Theodore, 'Two Juvenal Delinquents. Robert Lowell and Durs Grünbein', *Classical and Modern Literature*, 26.1 (2006), 12–32.

Contributors

Ian Cooper was Fellow of the Alexander von Humboldt Foundation, Göttingen University, Germany, and is now Lecturer in German at the University fo Kent at Canterbury, UK.

Michael Eskin is the Cofounder and Vice President of Upper West Side Philosophers, Inc., New York, USA.

Sonja Klein is Research Fellow, University of Düsseldorf, Germany.

Karen Leeder is Professor of Modern German Literature, University of Oxford, and Fellow and Tutor in German, New College, Oxford, UK.

Ruth J. Owen is Senior Lecturer in German, Cardiff University, UK.

Alexander Regier is Associate Professor of English, Rice University, USA.

Noël Reumkens is Research Associate at the Vrije Universiteit Brussel, Belgium.

Helen Vendler is Arthur Kingsley Porter University Professor, Harvard University, USA.

Andrew Webber is Professor of Modern German and Comparative Literature, University of Cambridge, UK.

Christopher Young is Professor of Modern and Medieval German Studies, University of Cambridge, UK.

Index

References in *italics* see footnotes